HAWKMAN

ALLIES & ENEMIES

Dan DiDio
VP-Editorial

Peter Tomasi
Ivan Cohen
Editors-original series

Stephen Wacker
Associate Editor-original series

Bob Greenberger
Senior Editor-collected edition

Robbin Brosterman
Senior Art Director

Paul Levitz
President & Publisher

Georg Brewer
VP-Design & Retail Product Development

Richard Bruning
Senior VP-Creative Director

Patrick Caldon
Senior VP-Finance & Operations

Chris Caramalis
VP-Finance

Terri Cunningham
VP-Managing Editor

Alison Gill
VP-Manufacturing

Lillian Laserson
Senior VP & General Counsel

Jim Lee
Editorial Director-WildStorm

David McKillips
VP-Advertising & Custom Publishing

John Nee
VP-Business Development

Gregory Noveck
Senior VP-Creative Affairs

Cheryl Rubin
VP-Brand Management

Bob Wayne
VP-Sales & Marketing

DC Comics, 1700 Broadway, New York, NY 1001[redacted]
A Warner Bros. Entertainment Company
Printed in Canada. First Printing.
ISBN: 1-4012-0196-2
Cover illustration by John Watson.

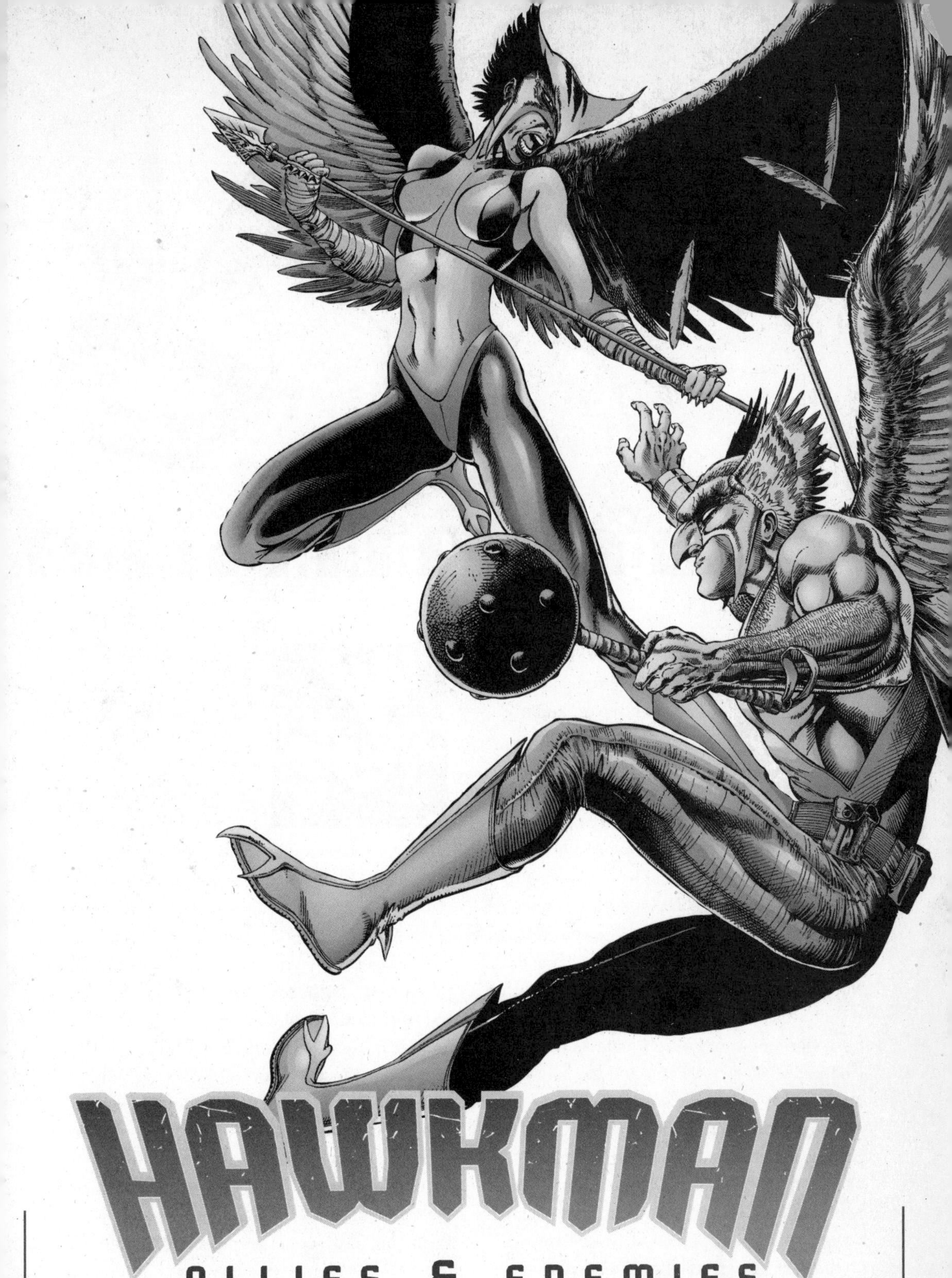

HAWKMAN

ALLIES & ENEMIES

Geoff Johns James Robinson WRITERS

Rags Morales Don Kramer Ethan Van Sciver PENCILLERS

Michael Bair Prentis Rollins Dennis Janke Tim Truman Mick Gray INKERS

John Kalisz COLORIST Bill Oakley Ken Lopez Kurt Hathaway LETTERERS

HAWKMAN

Prince Khufu has lived a thousand lives, and in each one has waged a battle against evil. His journey began during the 15th Dynasty of Ancient Egypt. Hath-Set murdered Khufu, and his lover, Chay-Ara, but since both had been exposed to the alien Thanagarian Nth metal their souls were altered. Time and again, the lovers were reborn and fought against evil until death reclaimed them. The cycle has repeated over the centuries and each time, Khufu has emerged as a champion. A generation ago, Khufu fought as the first Hawkman, legendary warrior and member of the Justice Society of America. A temporal anomaly swallowed Khufu until his soul answered a higher calling and returned to earth, this time with the memories of all his previous lives intact. Once more he is Carter Hall, a.k.a. Hawkman, striving to balance his innate warrior's anger with the princely wisdom of his ancient beginnings. He is blinded by his love for Kendra Saunders, the latest reincarnation of Chay-Ara.

HAWKGIRL

Kendra Saunders experienced a frightening event in Austin, Texas, leading her to attempt suicide. This resulted in her body's becoming the home for the soul of an Egyptian princess (who was one of Kendra's ancestors). Midlife reincarnation is a rare occurrence, and little of Princess Chay-Ara's life and memories have surfaced since the event. Plagued by nightmares from her parents' mysterious and untimely deaths, Kendra left Austin and lived with her grandfather, Speed Saunders. He began training her for her destiny, to become the new Hawkgirl. Once she took flight, she grew to love the freedom it provided and she has since joined the Justice Society of America. Chay-Ara's eternal lover, Prince Khufu, recently returned to mortal form as Hawkman. He has struggled to accept that Kendra is just beginning to process the memories of her past lives and that their eternal love must, for now, wait.

THE ATOM

Ray Palmer is a scientist who harnessed the properties of a white dwarf star. This led to the creation of unique size and weight controls that enable him to reduce his physical form to that of an atom, or even smaller. One of the first heroes to join after the Justice League of America's founding, he is in the forefront of this generation's heroes. Eschewing heroics for research and teaching, the Atom remains available as a reserve member.

DR. FATE

Hector Hall was born to Carter Hall and Shiera Sanders, the Hawkman and Hawkgirl of generations past. Putting himself under great pressure to prove his worth to his father, Hector adopted his own costumed identity as the Silver Scarab. He fought valiantly until he was cursed by a reincarnation of Hath-Set and his body died. Yet, his soul has endured and he has assumed other personas, most recently being reborn as the latest champion for the Lords of Order. Many others have assumed the mantle of Fate, wearing the enchanted Helmet and amulet of Nabu, an ancient Lord of Order, and Hector is once again striving to live up to the great expectations of others.

NIGHTHAWK

A 19th-century reincarnation of Khufu, Hannibal Hawkes adopted the costumed guise of Nighthawk to continue his warrior ways. Hawkes was a traveling fix-it man, using his innate experience to handle most any kind of repair while donning an ebony mask and using six-shooters to mete out rough frontier justice. Riding his jet-black stallion Nightwind, he rode the plains, eventually meeting up, in St. Roch, with the woman known as Cinnamon, a reincarnation of his beloved Chay-Ara. Together they loved and battled side by side until Hath-Set's eternal curse caught up to them, bringing death and eventual rebirth.

CINNAMON

A woman known only as Kate was orphaned early in life when her widower father, a Wyoming sheriff, was gunned down by bank robbers. She grew up in an orphanage until, at age 18, she set out on her own, desiring nothing more than to find the robbers who stole her father's life and her own childhood. This quest for vengeance brought her to the town of St. Roch and Emile Graydon, the last of the bank robbers. As she shot him in a showdown, Nighthawk took out Graydon's associate. When they met, sparks flew as the reincarnated Khufu and Chay-Ara were reunited once more. They became lovers and fought together until the cycle was completed and death claimed them. Details of Cinnamon's exploits have been preserved and became fodder for a popular late 20th-century musical.

THE GENTLEMAN GHOST

Everything known about Gentleman Jim Craddock comes entirely from his own claims. The Ghost has announced that he is a notorious highwayman who terrorized the English countryside two hundred years ago and was hanged for his crimes, but not before swearing he would live forever. This may indeed be true since the Ghost has appeared time and again, usually in combat against Hawkman in what appears to be a personal vendetta. The exact connection between the Ghost and the many reincarnations of Khufu remains a mystery.

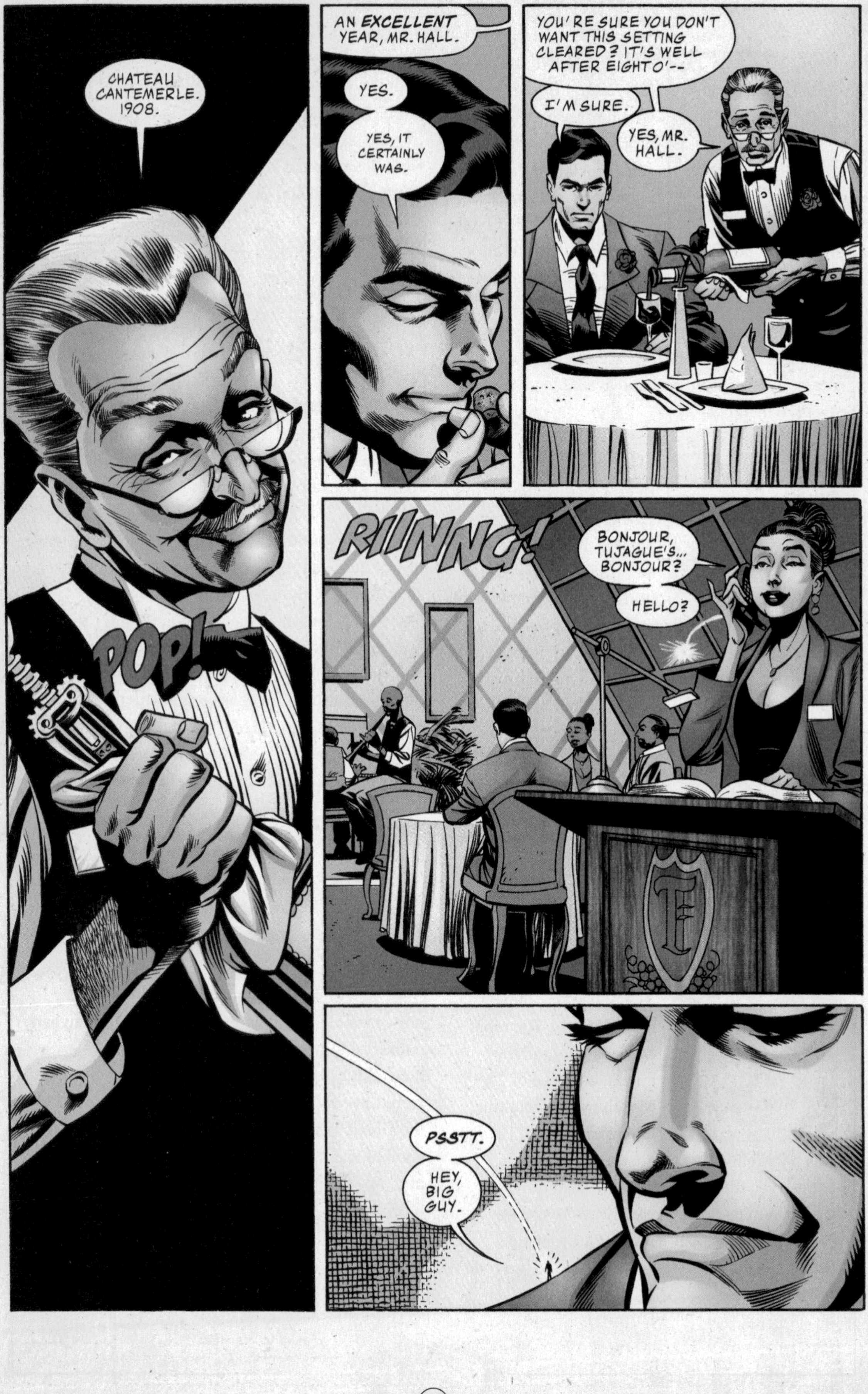

CHATEAU CANTEMERLE. 1908.
POP!
AN EXCELLENT YEAR, MR. HALL.
YES.
YES, IT CERTAINLY WAS.
YOU'RE SURE YOU DON'T WANT THIS SETTING CLEARED? IT'S WELL AFTER EIGHT O'--
I'M SURE.
YES, MR. HALL.
RIINNG!
BONJOUR, TUJAGUE'S... BONJOUR?
HELLO?
PSSTT.
HEY, BIG GUY.

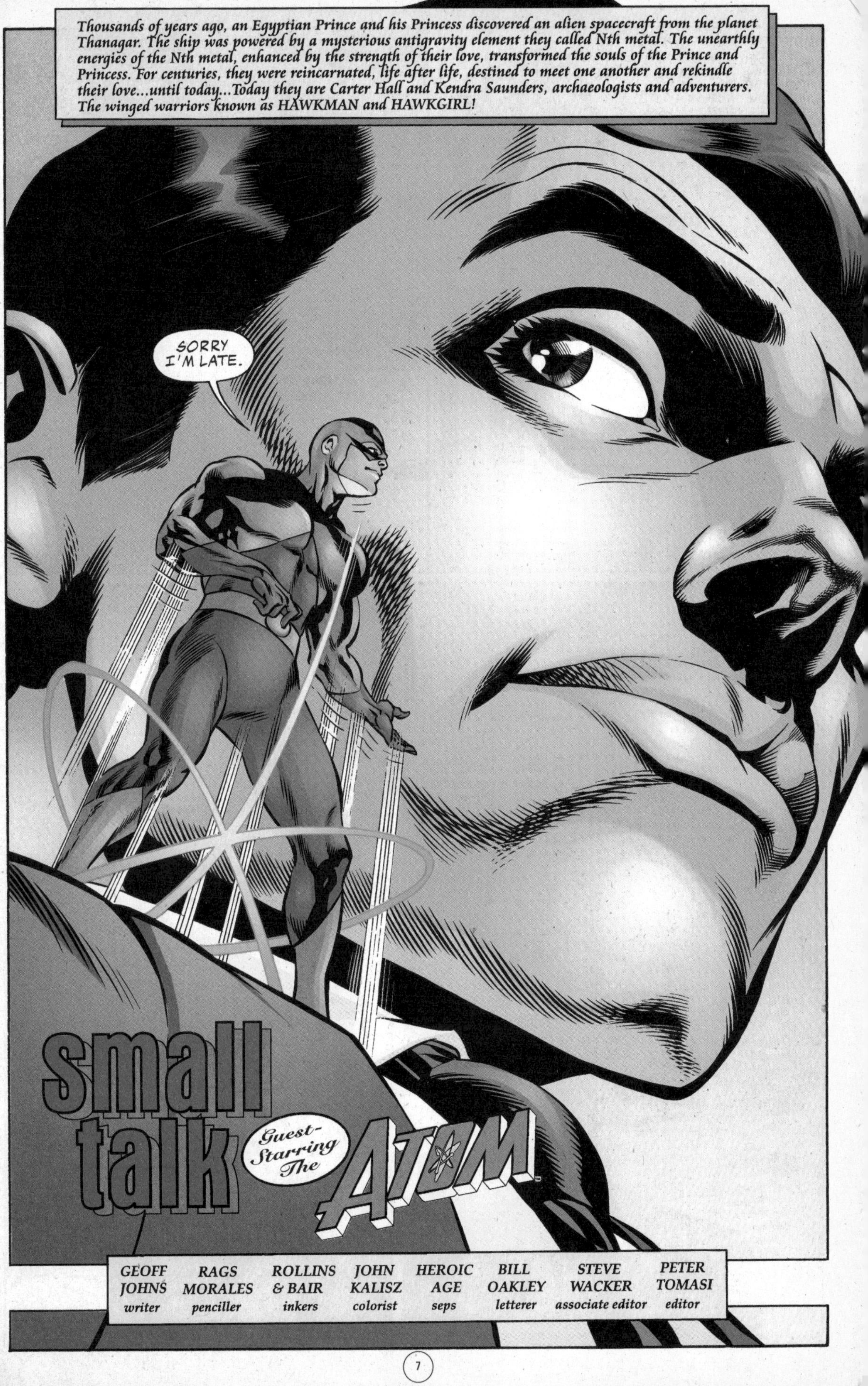
Thousands of years ago, an Egyptian Prince and his Princess discovered an alien spacecraft from the planet Thanagar. The ship was powered by a mysterious antigravity element they called Nth metal. The unearthly energies of the Nth metal, enhanced by the strength of their love, transformed the souls of the Prince and Princess. For centuries, they were reincarnated, life after life, destined to meet one another and rekindle their love...until today...Today they are Carter Hall and Kendra Saunders, archaeologists and adventurers. The winged warriors known as HAWKMAN and HAWKGIRL!
SORRY I'M LATE.
small talk
Guest-Starring The ATOM
GEOFF JOHNS writer
RAGS MORALES penciller
ROLLINS & BAIR inkers
JOHN KALISZ colorist
HEROIC AGE seps
BILL OAKLEY letterer
STEVE WACKER associate editor
PETER TOMASI editor

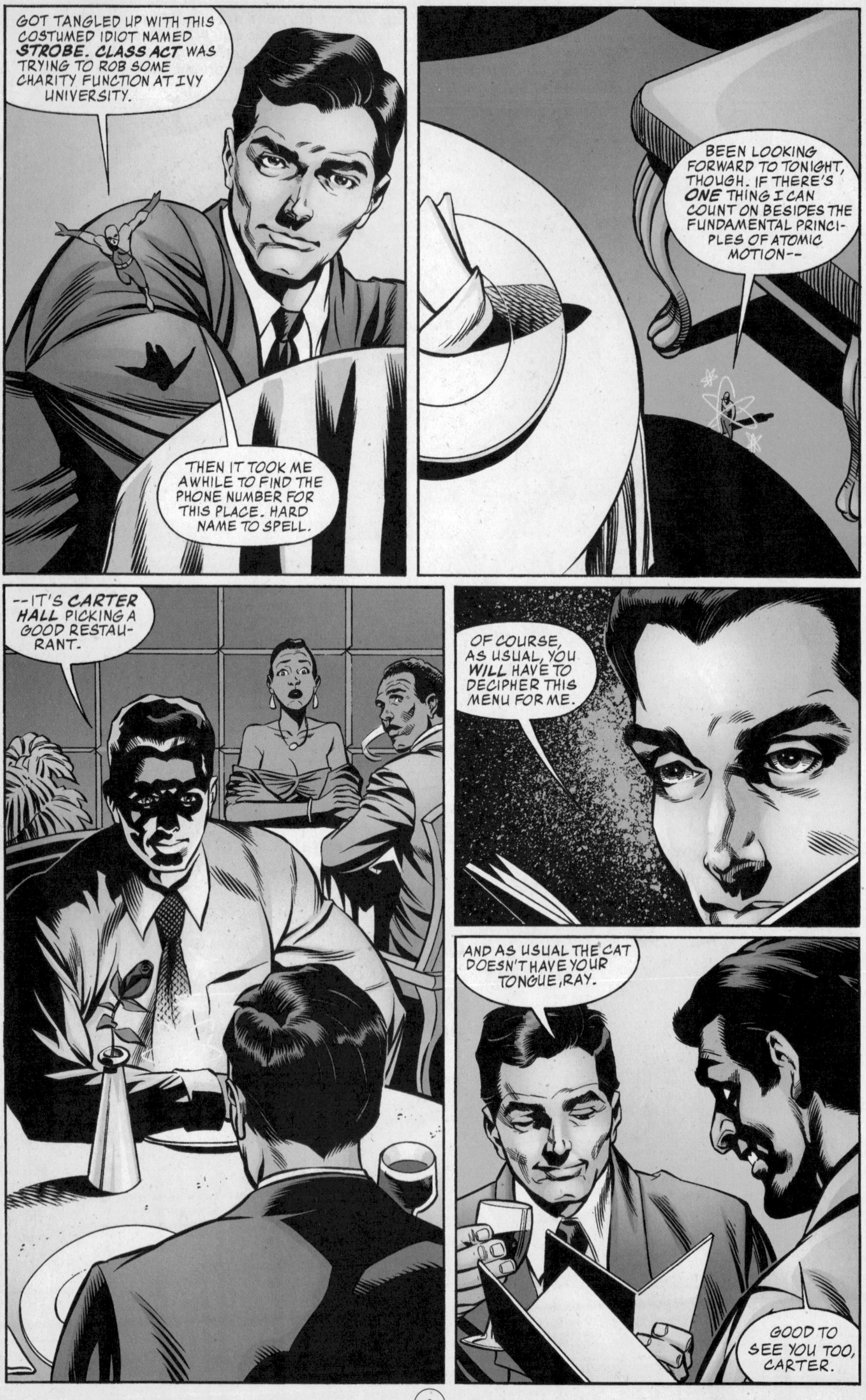
GOT TANGLED UP WITH THIS COSTUMED IDIOT NAMED STROBE. CLASS ACT WAS TRYING TO ROB SOME CHARITY FUNCTION AT IVY UNIVERSITY.
THEN IT TOOK ME AWHILE TO FIND THE PHONE NUMBER FOR THIS PLACE. HARD NAME TO SPELL.
BEEN LOOKING FORWARD TO TONIGHT, THOUGH. IF THERE'S ONE THING I CAN COUNT ON BESIDES THE FUNDAMENTAL PRINCIPLES OF ATOMIC MOTION--
--IT'S CARTER HALL PICKING A GOOD RESTAURANT.
OF COURSE, AS USUAL, YOU WILL HAVE TO DECIPHER THIS MENU FOR ME.
AND AS USUAL THE CAT DOESN'T HAVE YOUR TONGUE, RAY.
GOOD TO SEE YOU TOO, CARTER.

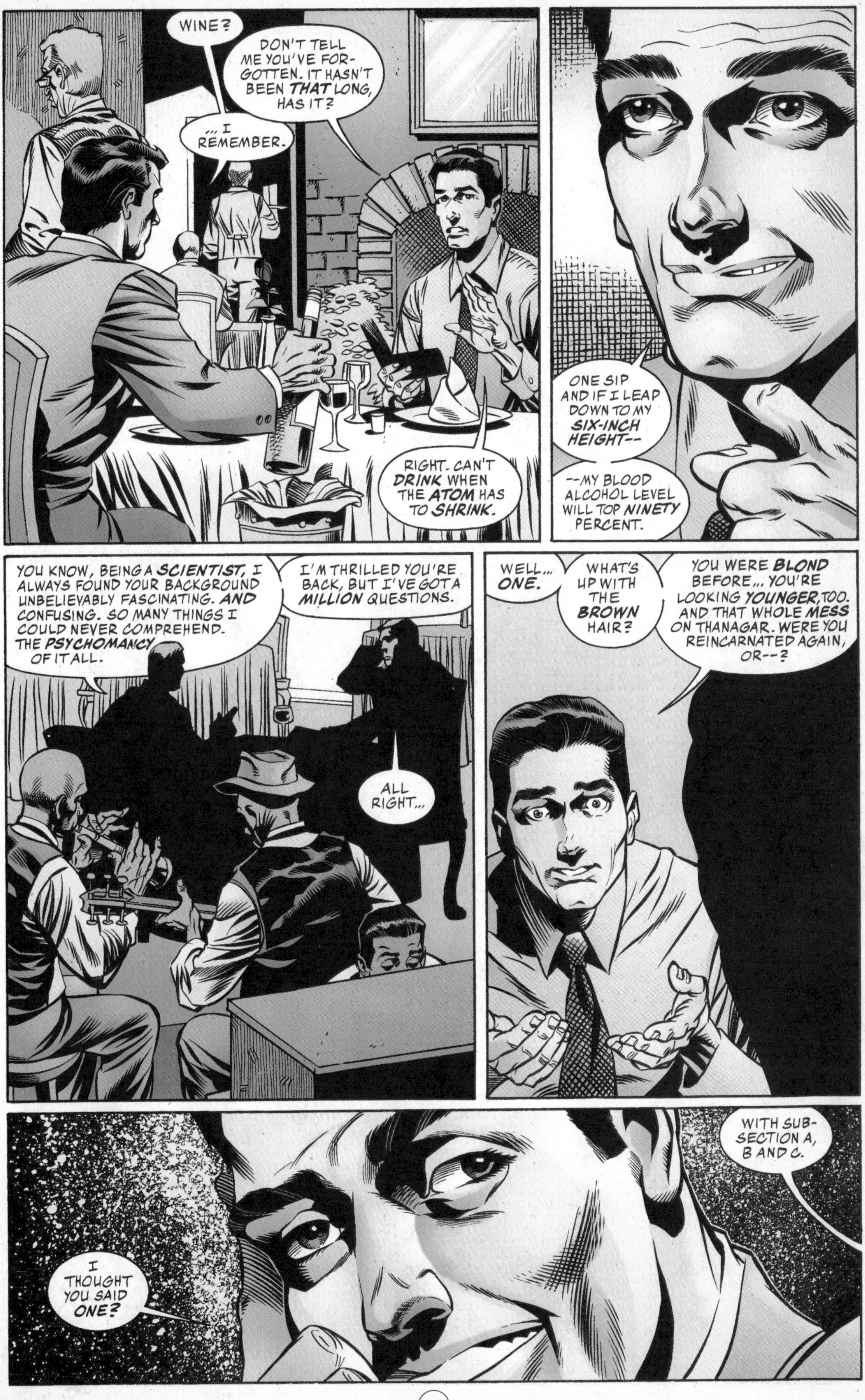

WINE?
DON'T TELL ME YOU'VE FOR-GOTTEN. IT HASN'T BEEN THAT LONG, HAS IT?
... I REMEMBER.
RIGHT. CAN'T DRINK WHEN THE ATOM HAS TO SHRINK.
ONE SIP AND IF I LEAP DOWN TO MY SIX-INCH HEIGHT--
--MY BLOOD ALCOHOL LEVEL WILL TOP NINETY PERCENT.
YOU KNOW, BEING A SCIENTIST, I ALWAYS FOUND YOUR BACKGROUND UNBELIEVABLY FASCINATING. AND CONFUSING. SO MANY THINGS I COULD NEVER COMPREHEND. THE PSYCHOMANCY OF IT ALL.
I'M THRILLED YOU'RE BACK, BUT I'VE GOT A MILLION QUESTIONS.
ALL RIGHT...
WELL... ONE.
WHAT'S UP WITH THE BROWN HAIR?
YOU WERE BLOND BEFORE... YOU'RE LOOKING YOUNGER, TOO. AND THAT WHOLE MESS ON THANAGAR. WERE YOU REINCARNATED AGAIN, OR--?
WITH SUB-SECTION A, B AND C.
I THOUGHT YOU SAID ONE?

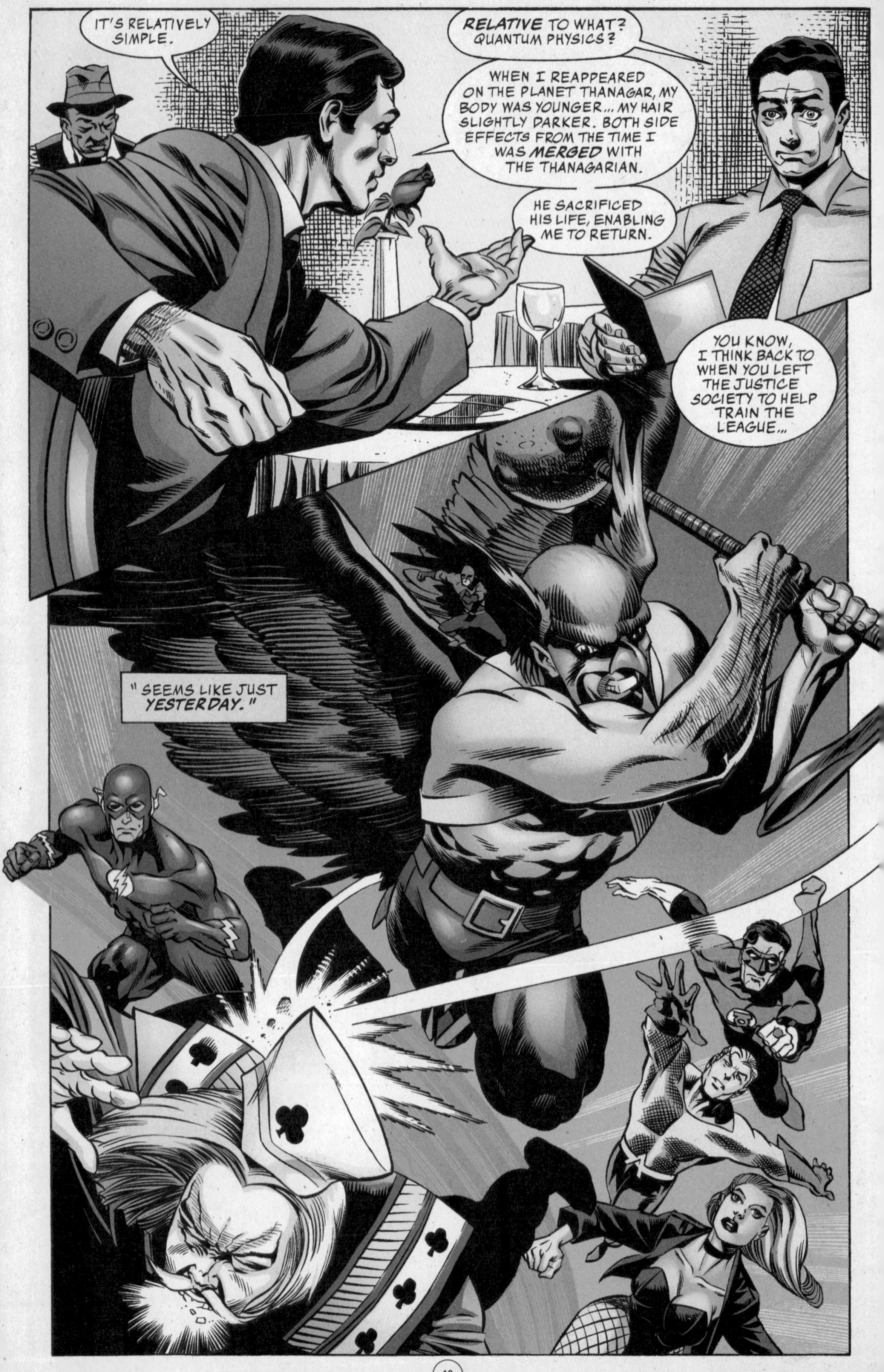
IT'S RELATIVELY SIMPLE.
RELATIVE TO WHAT? QUANTUM PHYSICS?
WHEN I REAPPEARED ON THE PLANET THANAGAR, MY BODY WAS YOUNGER... MY HAIR SLIGHTLY DARKER. BOTH SIDE EFFECTS FROM THE TIME I WAS MERGED WITH THE THANAGARIAN.
HE SACRIFICED HIS LIFE, ENABLING ME TO RETURN.
YOU KNOW, I THINK BACK TO WHEN YOU LEFT THE JUSTICE SOCIETY TO HELP TRAIN THE LEAGUE...
"SEEMS LIKE JUST YESTERDAY."

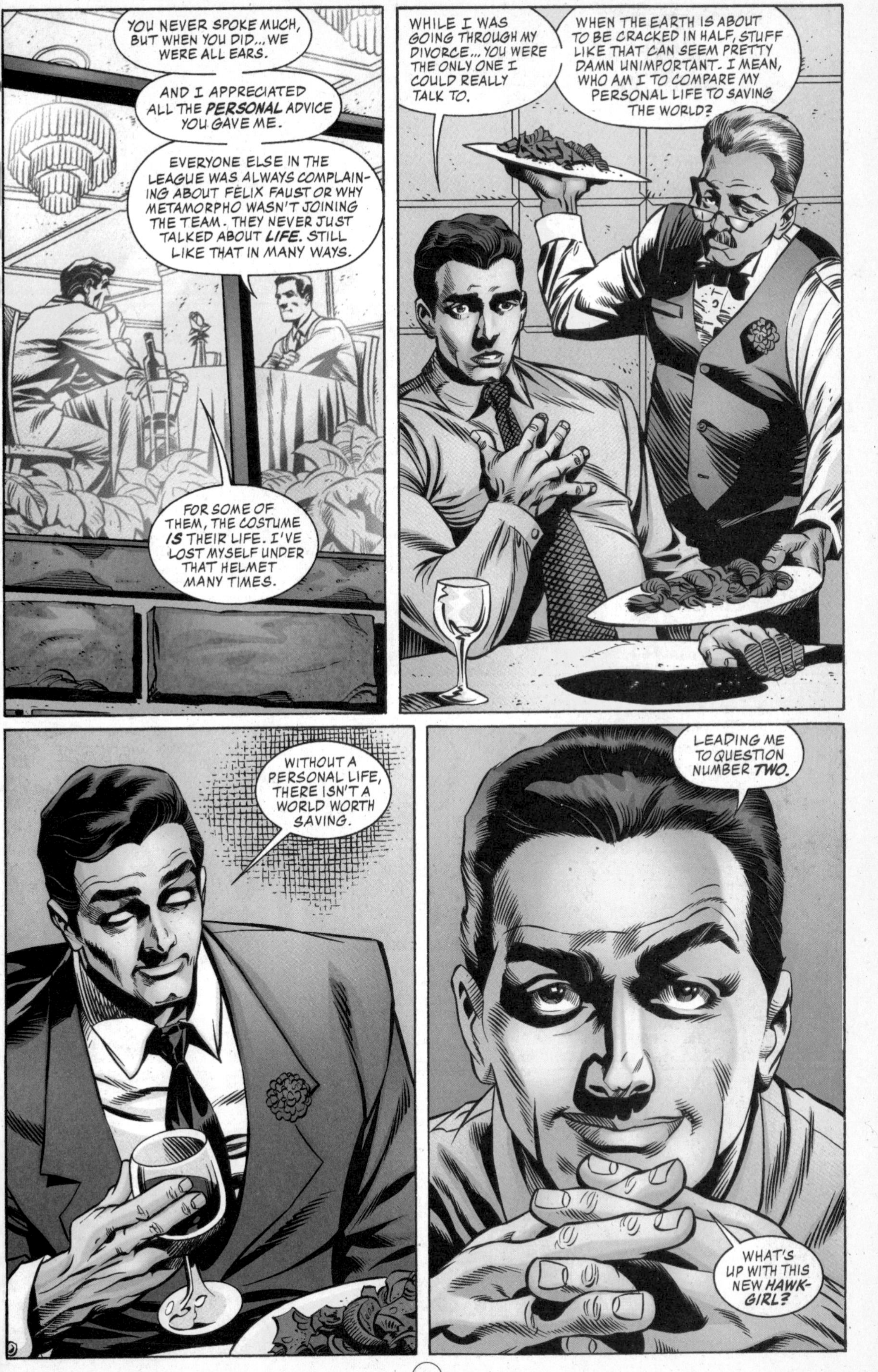
YOU NEVER SPOKE MUCH, BUT WHEN YOU DID... WE WERE ALL EARS.
AND I APPRECIATED ALL THE PERSONAL ADVICE YOU GAVE ME.
EVERYONE ELSE IN THE LEAGUE WAS ALWAYS COMPLAINING ABOUT FELIX FAUST OR WHY METAMORPHO WASN'T JOINING THE TEAM. THEY NEVER JUST TALKED ABOUT LIFE. STILL LIKE THAT IN MANY WAYS.
FOR SOME OF THEM, THE COSTUME IS THEIR LIFE. I'VE LOST MYSELF UNDER THAT HELMET MANY TIMES.
WHILE I WAS GOING THROUGH MY DIVORCE... YOU WERE THE ONLY ONE I COULD REALLY TALK TO.
WHEN THE EARTH IS ABOUT TO BE CRACKED IN HALF, STUFF LIKE THAT CAN SEEM PRETTY DAMN UNIMPORTANT. I MEAN, WHO AM I TO COMPARE MY PERSONAL LIFE TO SAVING THE WORLD?
WITHOUT A PERSONAL LIFE, THERE ISN'T A WORLD WORTH SAVING.
LEADING ME TO QUESTION NUMBER TWO.
WHAT'S UP WITH THIS NEW HAWK-GIRL?

THE SCENE OF THE CRIME.

YOU REALLY THINK FORENSICS'LL FIND *ANY-THING*, CHIEF? I MEAN, IT HAPPENED A *LONG* TIME AGO. HUNDREDS, HECK, MAYBE *THOUSANDS'A* PEOPLE HAVE COME IN AN' OUTTA THIS ROOM.

WHY IN THE *WORLD* ARE WE SETTIN' UP *BASE CAMP* IN HERE, ANYWAY? AND WHY HAS *HAWKGIRL* REFUSED TO SET FOOT INSIDE THE PRECINCT?

THAT'S *HER* BUSINESS, *NOT OURS*, ROOKIE. HAWKGIRL WANTS TO GO OVER THE CASE HERE, WE DO IT HERE. SHE'S A *VALUABLE* ASSET TO THIS CITY, HER AND HAWKMAN BOTH. WE'RE GONNA BEND OVER BACKWARDS, SIDEWAYS, WHATEVER WE NEED TA DO.

YOU READ THE *ORIGINAL* REPORT ON THE SAUNDERS MURDER CASE?

NO.

I HAVE, AND IT'S *LAUGHABLE*. OPEN AND SHUT. *NO* INVESTIGATION. NOW *QUIT* COMPLAININ' AN' MAKE YOURSELF USEFUL. LEMONADE. NO SUGAR.

YESSIR.

HEY, CHIEF!

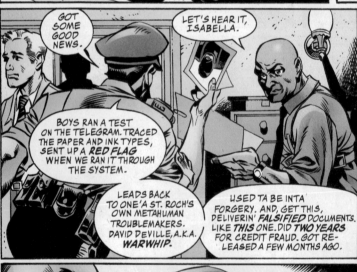

GOT SOME GOOD NEWS.

LET'S HEAR IT, ISABELLA.

BOYS RAN A TEST ON THE TELEGRAM. TRACED THE PAPER AND INK TYPES, SENT UP A *RED FLAG* WHEN WE RAN IT THROUGH THE SYSTEM.

LEADS BACK TO ONE'A ST. ROCH'S OWN METAHUMAN TROUBLEMAKERS. DAVID DEVILLE, A.K.A. *WARWHIP*.

USED TA BE INTA' FORGERY. AND, GET THIS, DELIVERIN' *FALSIFIED* DOCUMENTS. LIKE *THIS* ONE. DID *TWO YEARS* FOR CREDIT FRAUD. GOT RELEASED A FEW MONTHS AGO.

WE DID SOME *HUNTIN'*. GOT AN ADDRESS.

1344 Desire Apt. #57

FWTCH!

GOOD WORK.

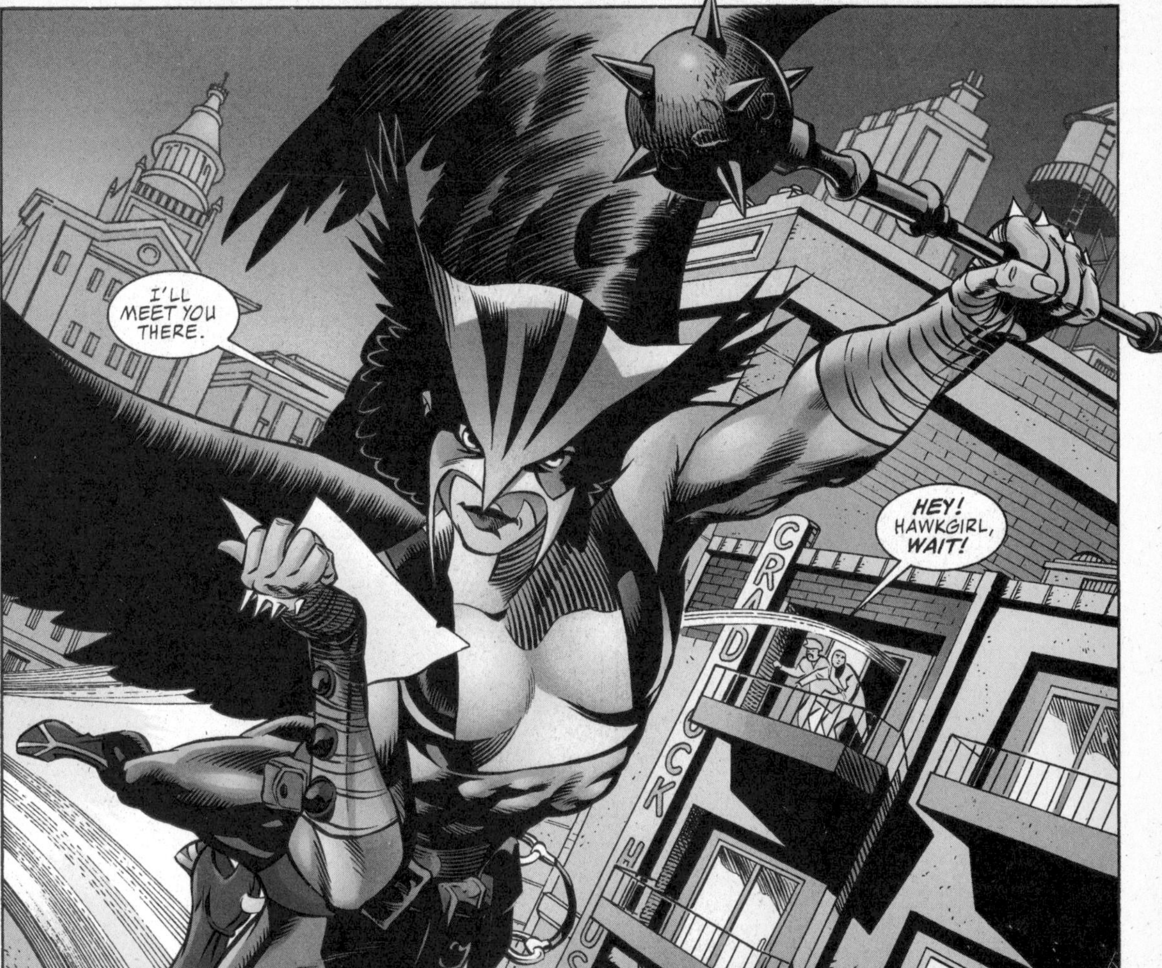
I'LL MEET YOU THERE.
HEY! HAWKGIRL, WAIT!

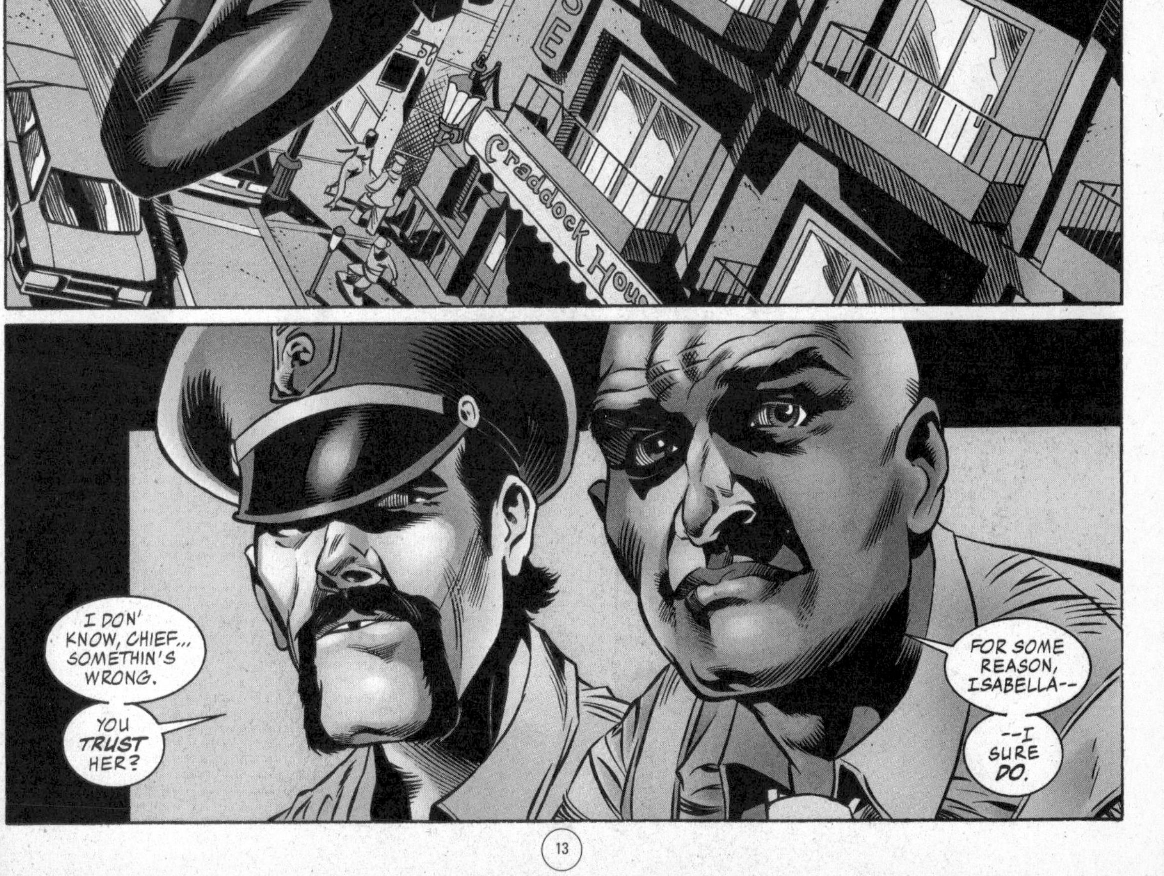
I DON' KNOW, CHIEF... SOMETHIN'S WRONG.
YOU TRUST HER?
FOR SOME REASON, ISABELLA--
--I SURE DO.

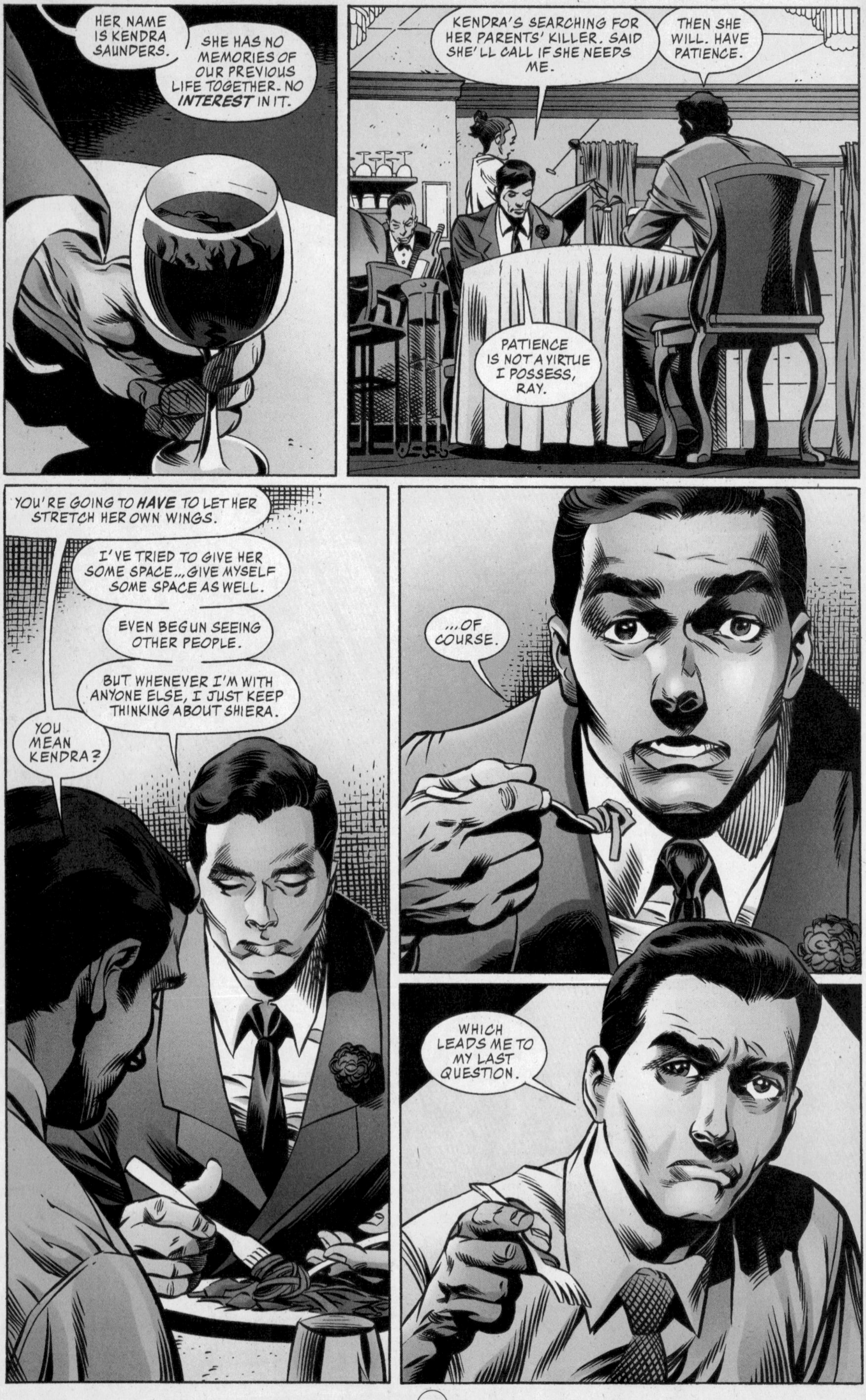
HER NAME IS KENDRA SAUNDERS.
SHE HAS NO MEMORIES OF OUR PREVIOUS LIFE TOGETHER. NO INTEREST IN IT.
KENDRA'S SEARCHING FOR HER PARENTS' KILLER. SAID SHE'LL CALL IF SHE NEEDS ME.
THEN SHE WILL. HAVE PATIENCE.
PATIENCE IS NOT A VIRTUE I POSSESS, RAY.
YOU'RE GOING TO HAVE TO LET HER STRETCH HER OWN WINGS.
I'VE TRIED TO GIVE HER SOME SPACE... GIVE MYSELF SOME SPACE AS WELL.
EVEN BEGUN SEEING OTHER PEOPLE.
BUT WHENEVER I'M WITH ANYONE ELSE, I JUST KEEP THINKING ABOUT SHIERA.
YOU MEAN KENDRA?
...OF COURSE.
WHICH LEADS ME TO MY LAST QUESTION.

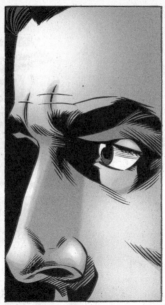
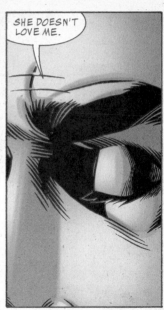

DO YOU LOVE HER?

SHE DOESN'T LOVE ME.

THAT'S **NOT** WHAT I ASKED.

LOOK. YOU HELPED ME ONCE WHEN I HAD **PROBLEMS.** I'M GOING TO TRY TO RETURN THE FAVOR... SO THIS MAY BE **PAINFULLY** BLUNT. BUT IT'S **HONEST.**

YOU SHOULDN'T FORCE ANYTHING. I MEAN... I DON'T KNOW. MAYBE THE PLANETS DIDN'T ALIGN RIGHT THIS TIME. MAYBE CUPID'S ARROWS MISSED.

TAKE IT FROM ME. I GOT MARRIED ON A WHIM. IT WAS NEVER **TRUE** LOVE. I JUST **THOUGHT** IT **MADE SENSE.**

LOVE ISN'T A WORD ANYONE SHOULD **THROW** AROUND LIGHTLY.

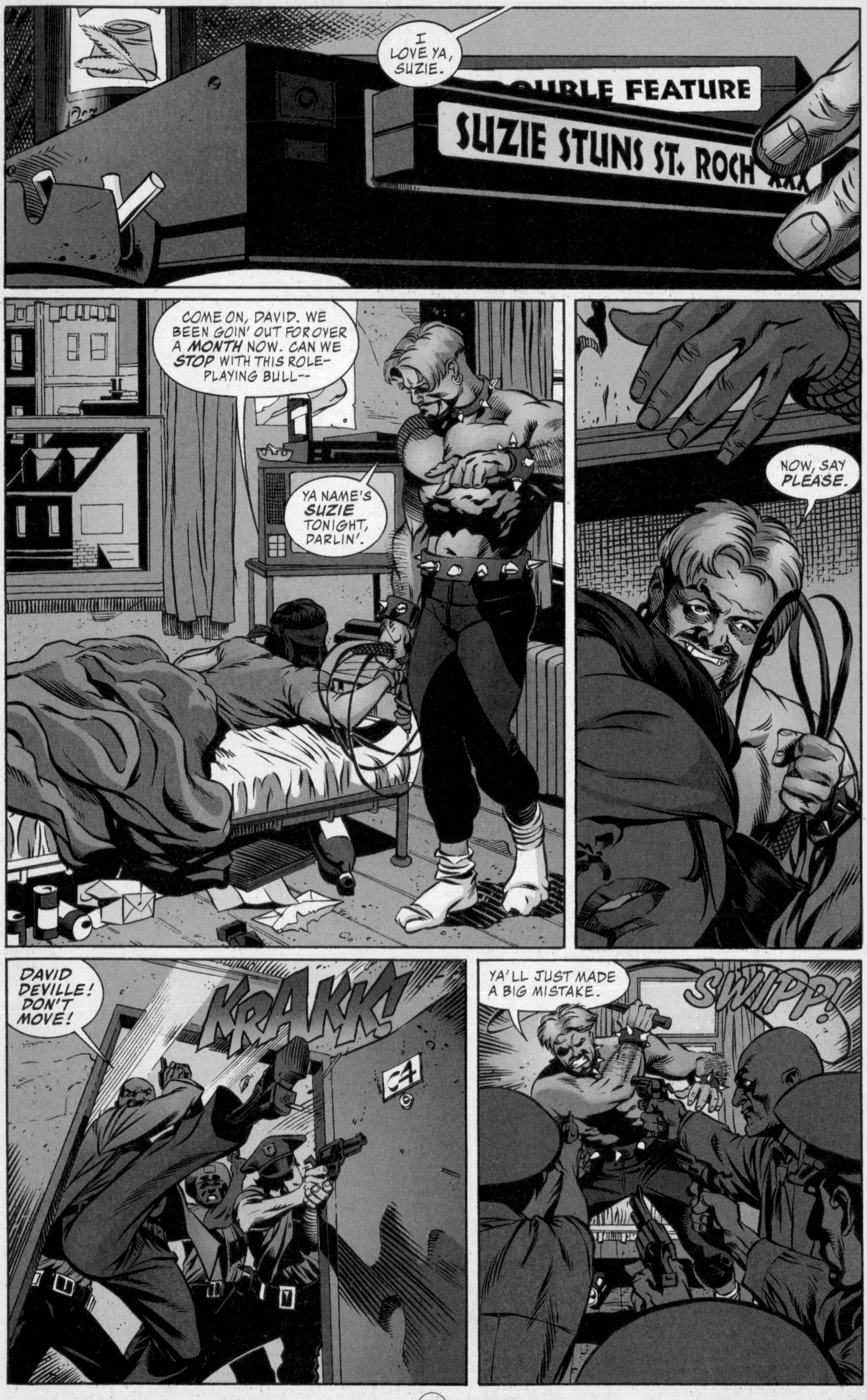
I LOVE YA, SUZIE.
DOUBLE FEATURE
SUZIE STUNS ST. ROCH XXX
COME ON, DAVID. WE BEEN GOIN' OUT FOR OVER A MONTH NOW. CAN WE STOP WITH THIS ROLE-PLAYING BULL--
YA NAME'S SUZIE TONIGHT, DARLIN'.
NOW, SAY PLEASE.
DAVID DEVILLE! DON'T MOVE!
KRAKK!
C4
YA'LL JUST MADE A BIG MISTAKE.
SWIPP!

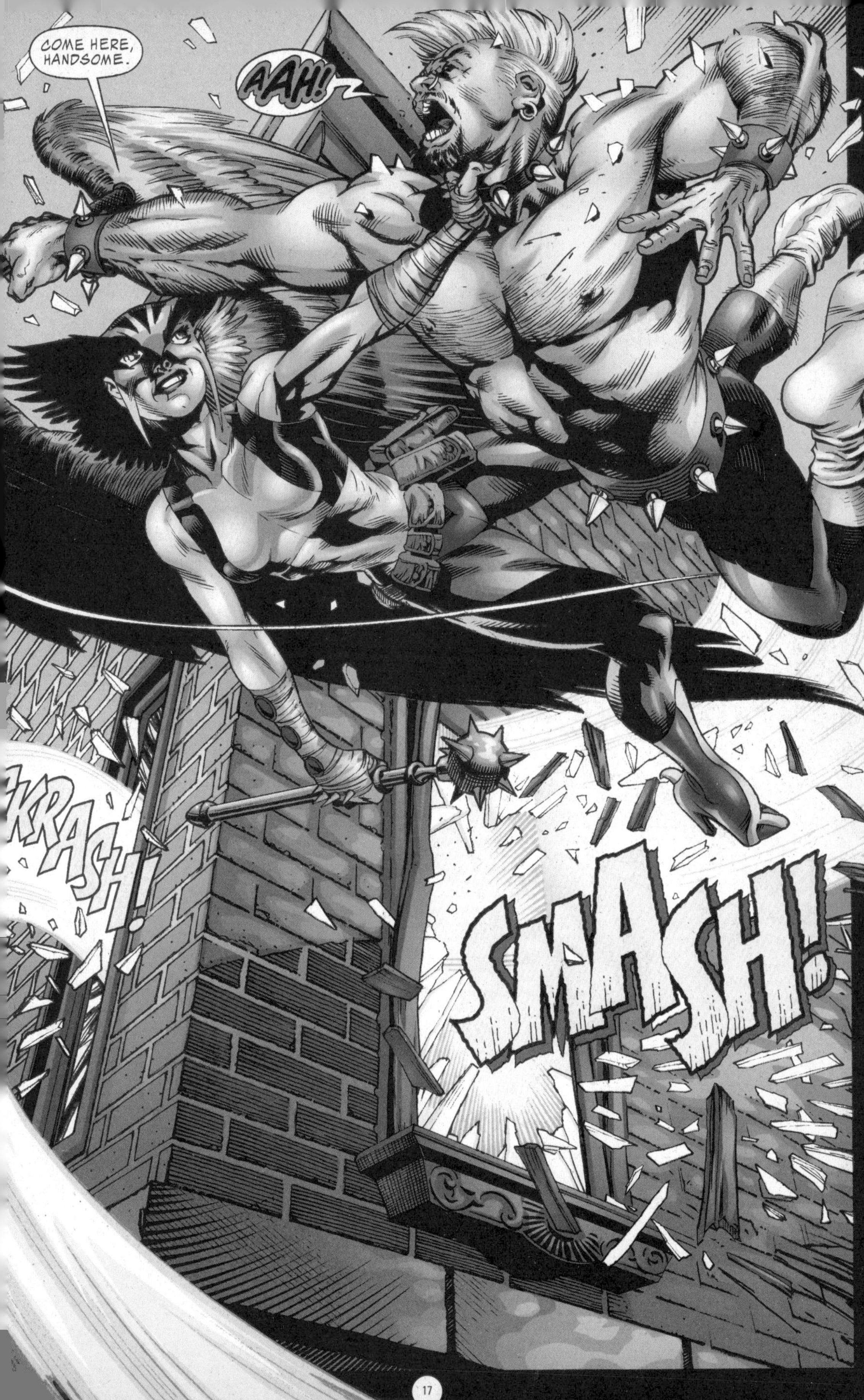
COME HERE, HANDSOME.
AAH!
KRASH!
SMASH!

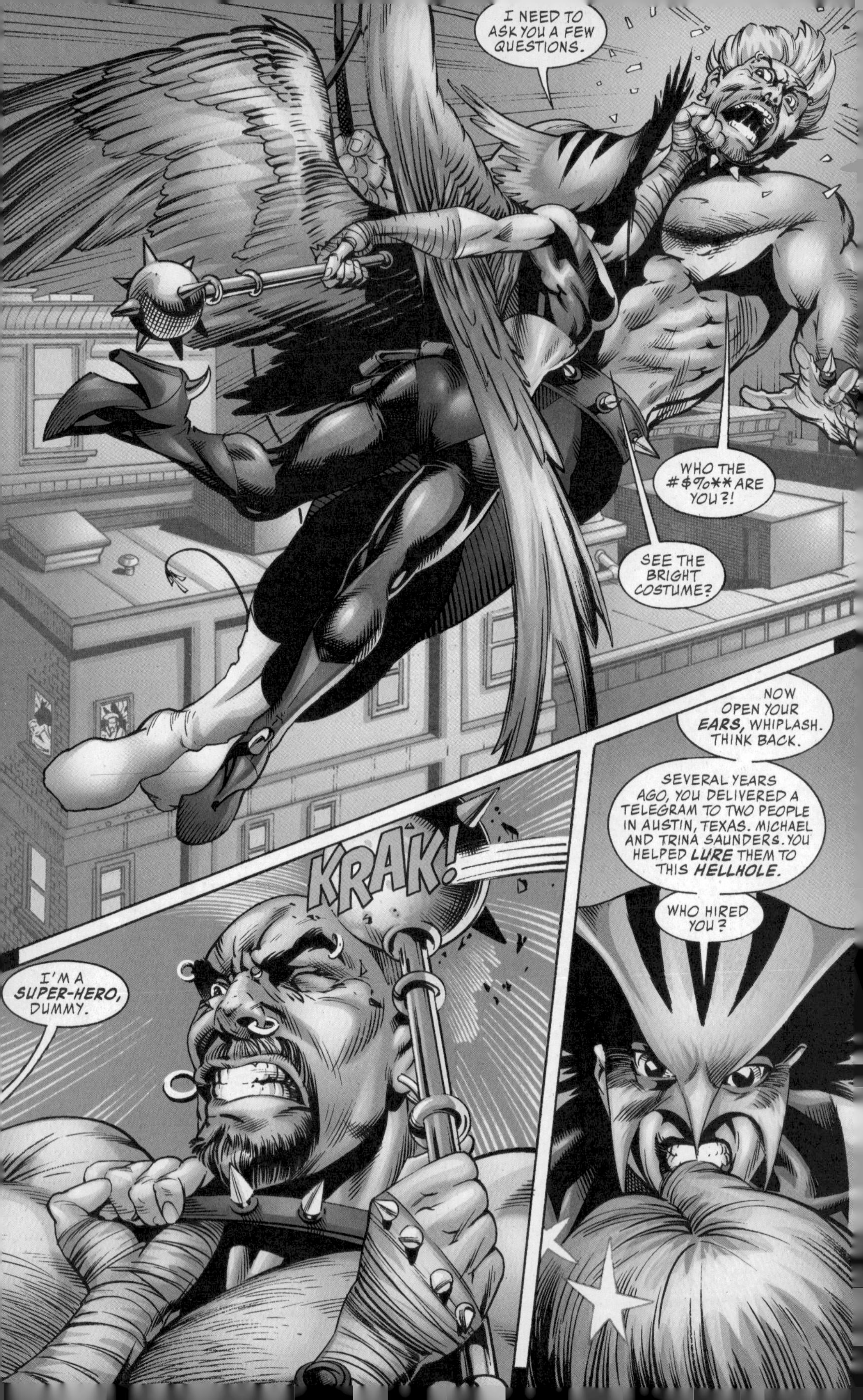
I NEED TO ASK YOU A FEW QUESTIONS.
WHO THE #$%**ARE YOU?!
SEE THE BRIGHT COSTUME?
I'M A SUPER-HERO, DUMMY.
KRAK!
NOW OPEN YOUR EARS, WHIPLASH. THINK BACK.
SEVERAL YEARS AGO, YOU DELIVERED A TELEGRAM TO TWO PEOPLE IN AUSTIN, TEXAS. MICHAEL AND TRINA SAUNDERS. YOU HELPED LURE THEM TO THIS HELLHOLE.
WHO HIRED YOU?

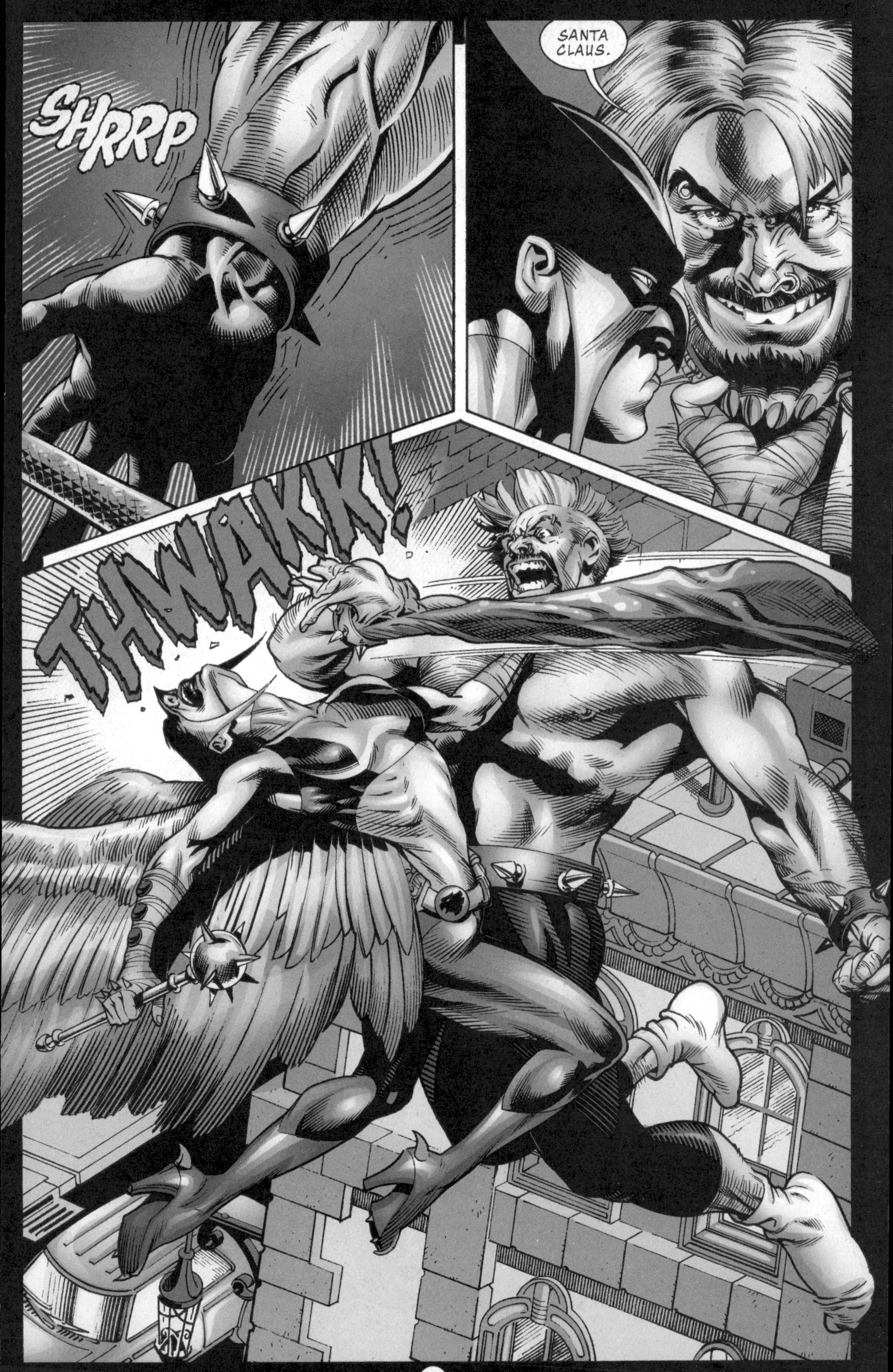
SHRRP
SANTA CLAUS.
THWAKK!

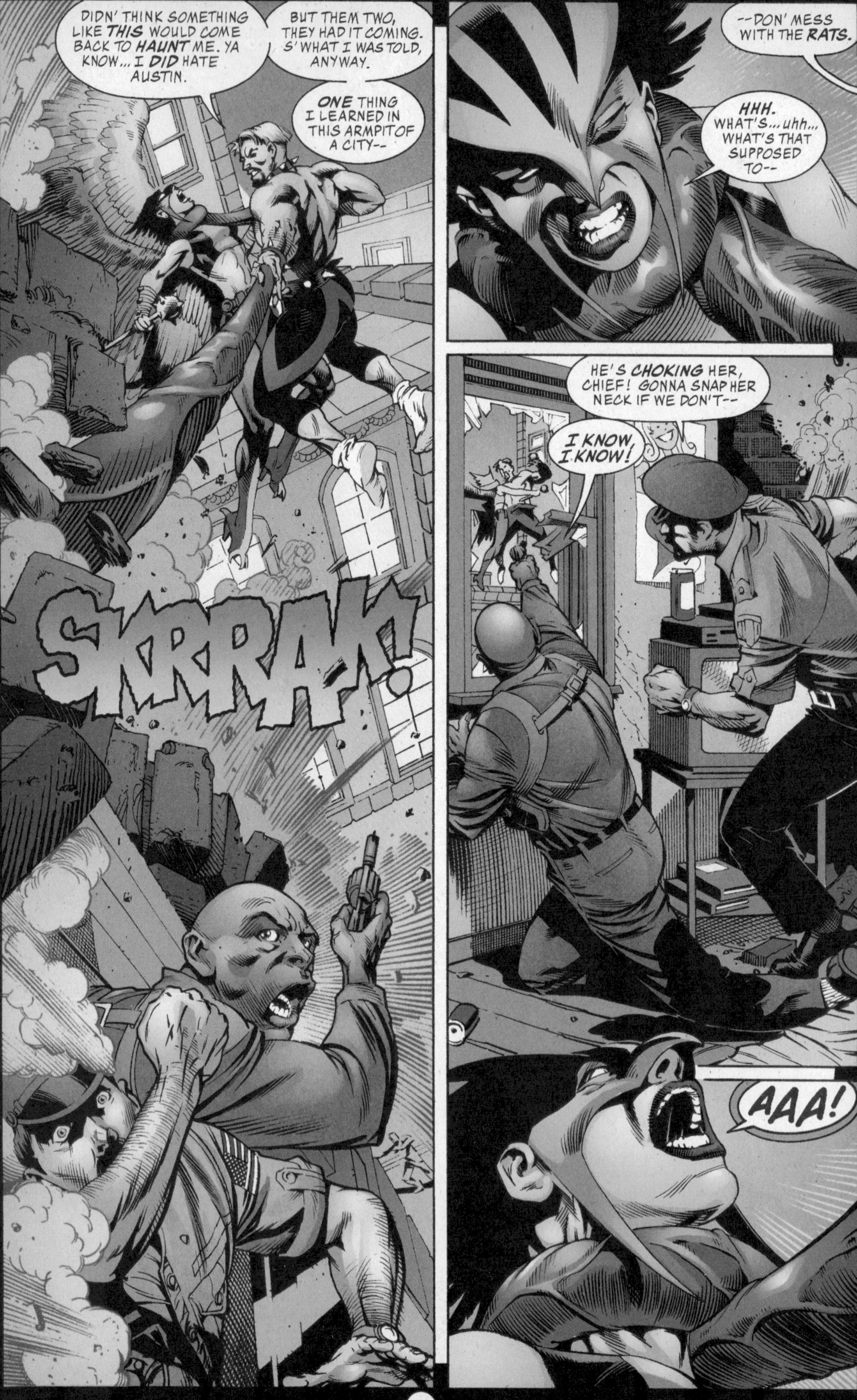

DIDN' THINK SOMETHING LIKE THIS WOULD COME BACK TO HAUNT ME. YA KNOW... I DID HATE AUSTIN.
BUT THEM TWO, THEY HAD IT COMING. S' WHAT I WAS TOLD, ANYWAY.
ONE THING I LEARNED IN THIS ARMPIT OF A CITY--
--DON' MESS WITH THE RATS.
HHH. WHAT'S...uhh... WHAT'S THAT SUPPOSED TO--
SKRRAK!
HE'S CHOKING HER, CHIEF! GONNA SNAP HER NECK IF WE DON'T--
I KNOW, I KNOW!
AAA!

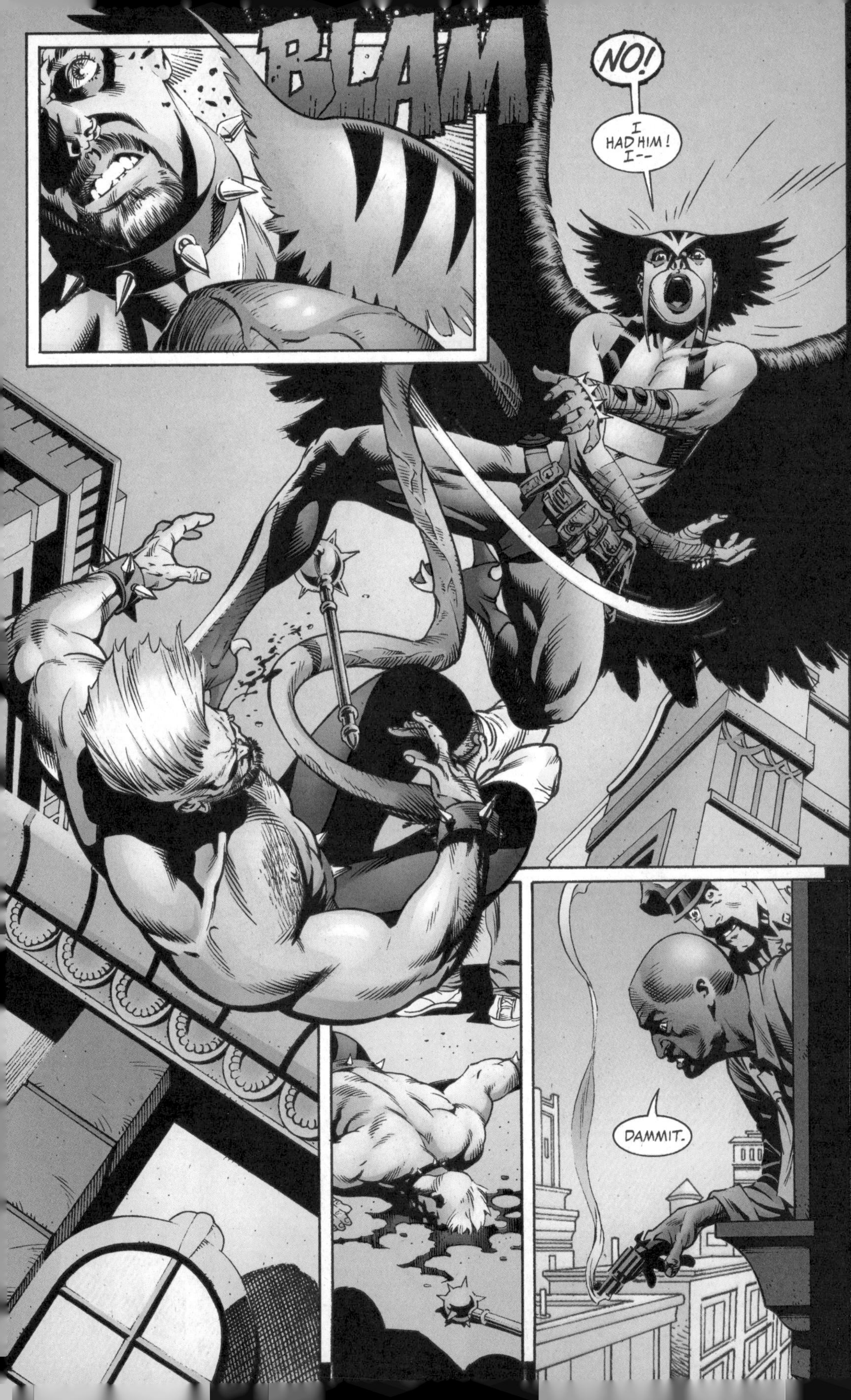
BLAM
NO!
I HAD HIM! I--
DAMMIT.

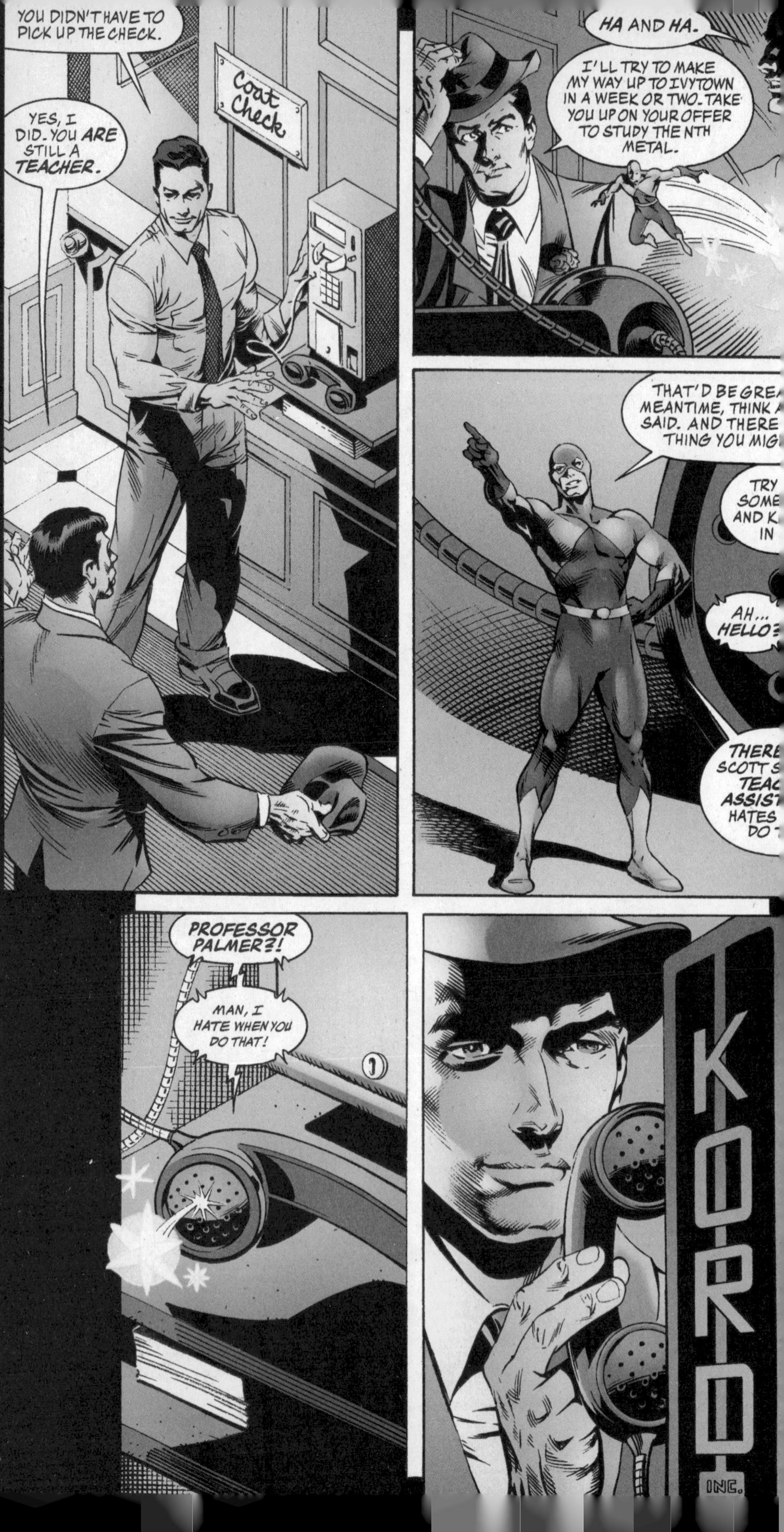
YOU DIDN'T HAVE TO PICK UP THE CHECK.
YES, I DID. YOU ARE STILL A TEACHER.
Coat Check
HA AND HA.
I'LL TRY TO MAKE MY WAY UP TO IVYTOWN IN A WEEK OR TWO. TAKE YOU UP ON YOUR OFFER TO STUDY THE NTH METAL.
THAT'D BE GREA MEANTIME, THINK A SAID. AND THERE THING YOU MIG
TRY SOME AND K IN
AH... HELLO?
THERE SCOTT S TEAC ASSIST HATES DO
PROFESSOR PALMER?!
MAN, I HATE WHEN YOU DO THAT!
KORD INC.

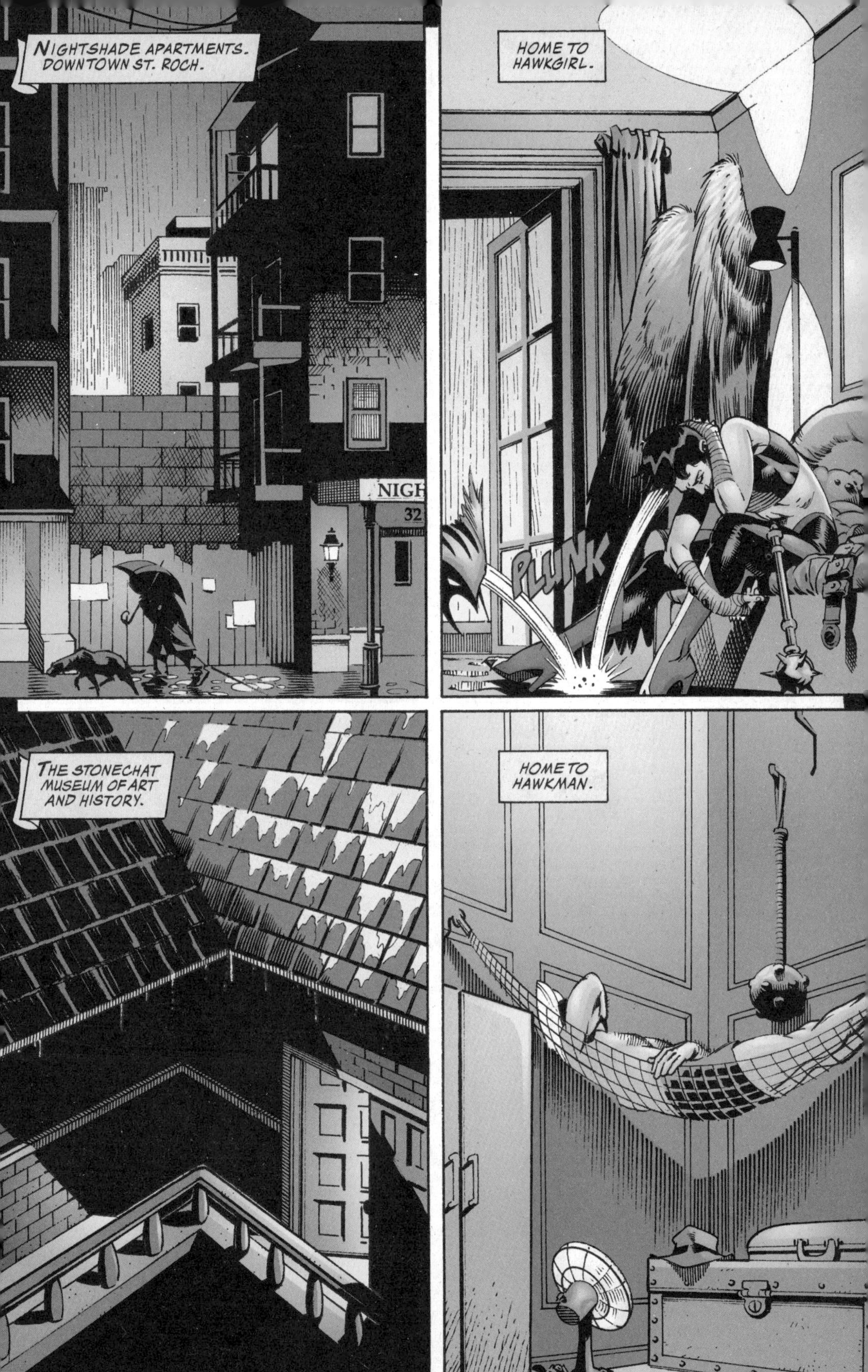
NIGHTSHADE APARTMENTS. DOWNTOWN ST. ROCH.
NIGH
32
HOME TO HAWKGIRL.
PLUNK
THE STONECHAT MUSEUM OF ART AND HISTORY.
HOME TO HAWKMAN.

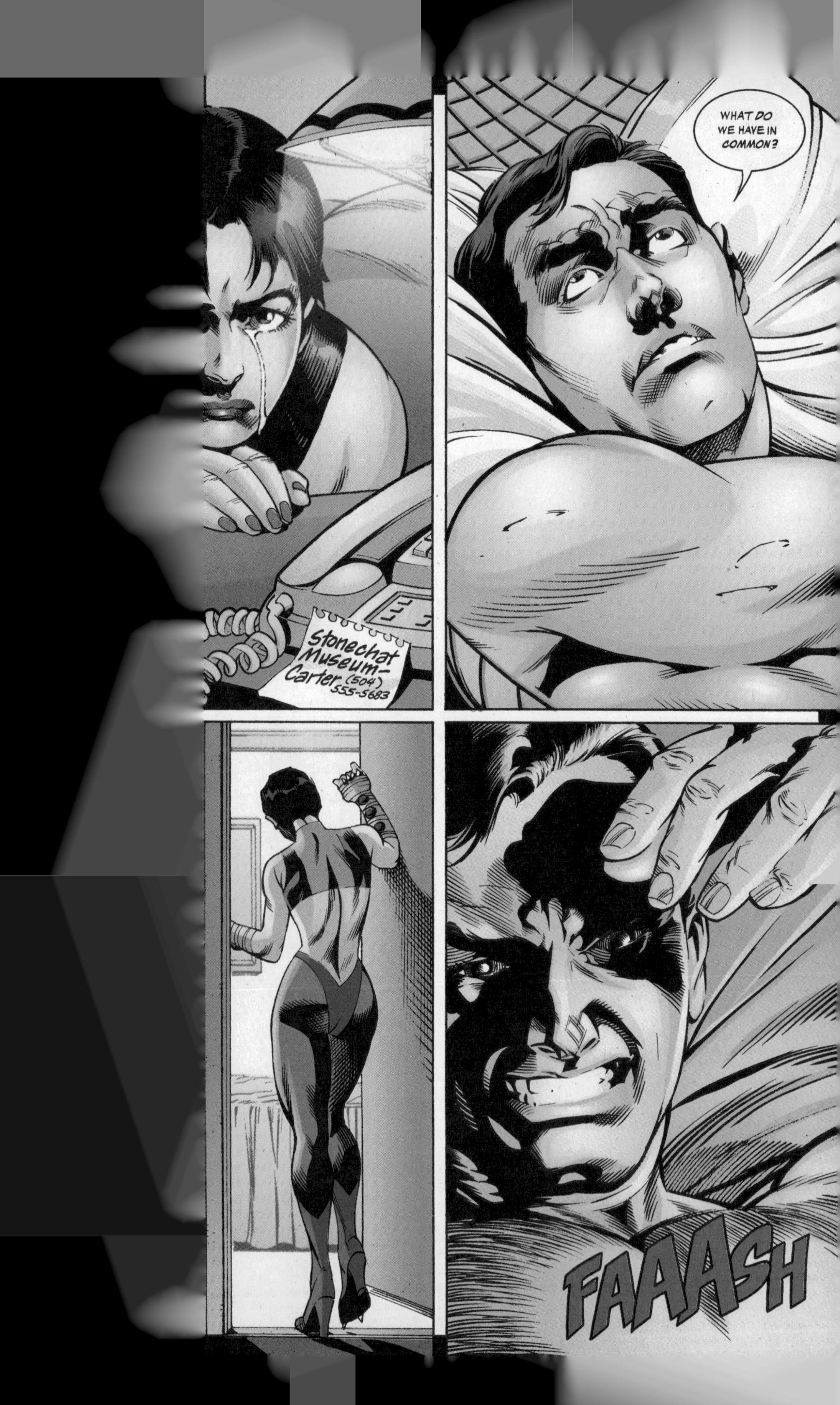
Stonechat Museum- Carter (504) 555-5683
WHAT DO WE HAVE IN COMMON?
FAAASH

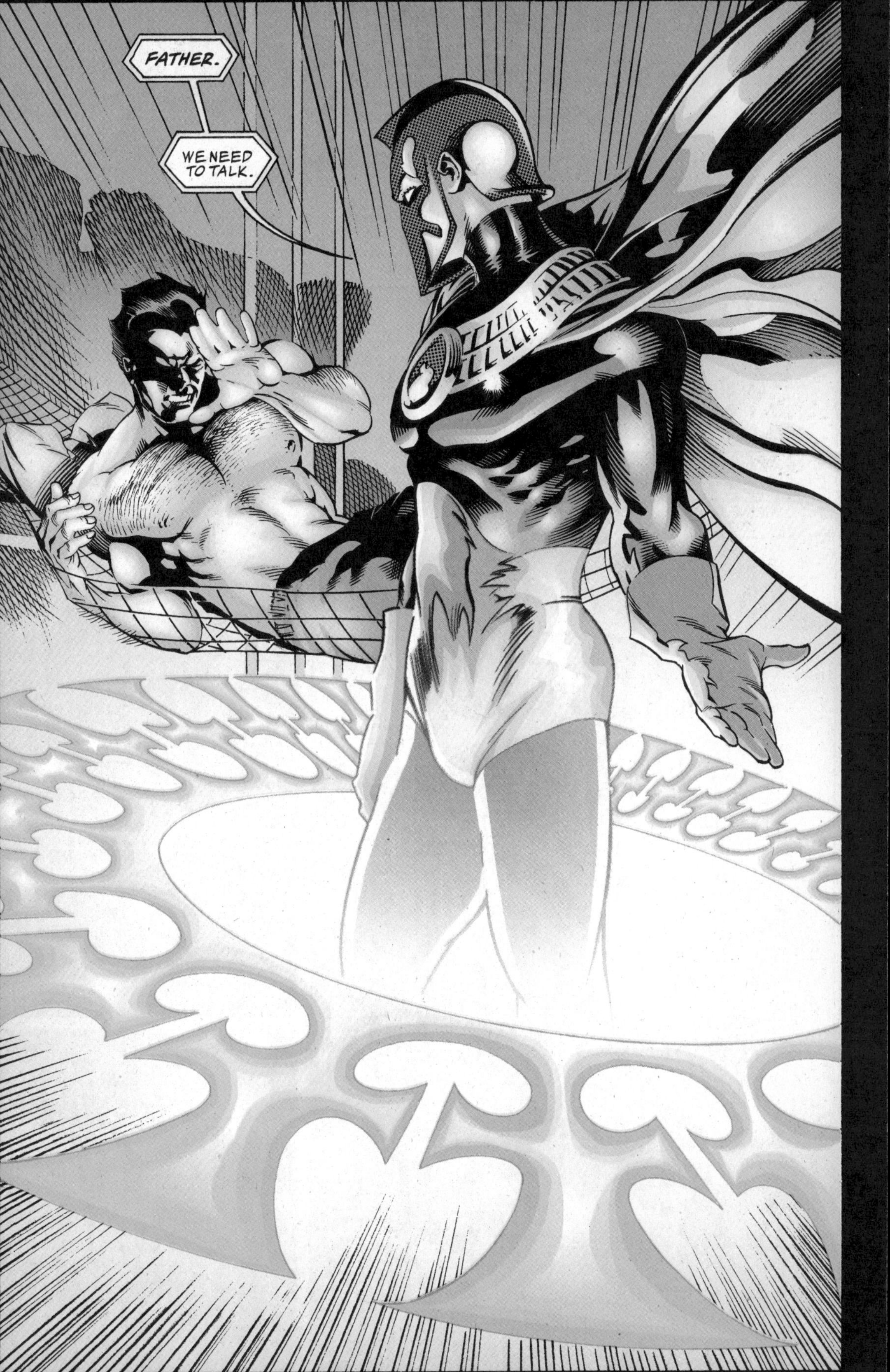
FATHER.
WE NEED TO TALK.

EPILOGUE: SPEED SAUNDERS

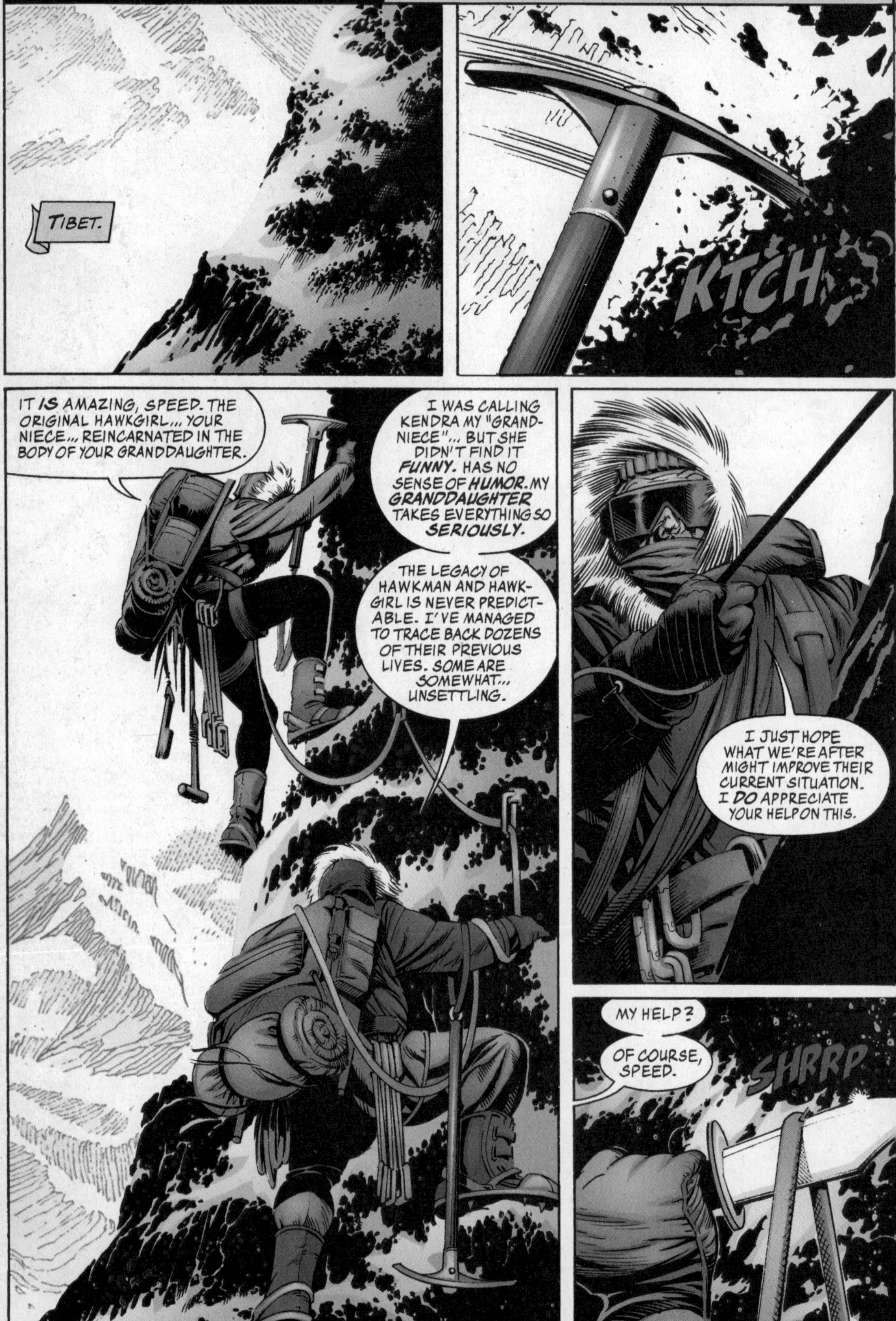

TIBET.
KTCH
IT IS AMAZING, SPEED. THE ORIGINAL HAWKGIRL... YOUR NIECE... REINCARNATED IN THE BODY OF YOUR GRANDDAUGHTER.
I WAS CALLING KENDRA MY "GRAND-NIECE"... BUT SHE DIDN'T FIND IT FUNNY. HAS NO SENSE OF HUMOR. MY GRANDDAUGHTER TAKES EVERYTHING SO SERIOUSLY.
THE LEGACY OF HAWKMAN AND HAWK-GIRL IS NEVER PREDICT-ABLE. I'VE MANAGED TO TRACE BACK DOZENS OF THEIR PREVIOUS LIVES. SOME ARE SOMEWHAT... UNSETTLING.
I JUST HOPE WHAT WE'RE AFTER MIGHT IMPROVE THEIR CURRENT SITUATION. I DO APPRECIATE YOUR HELP ON THIS.
MY HELP?
OF COURSE, SPEED.
SHRRP

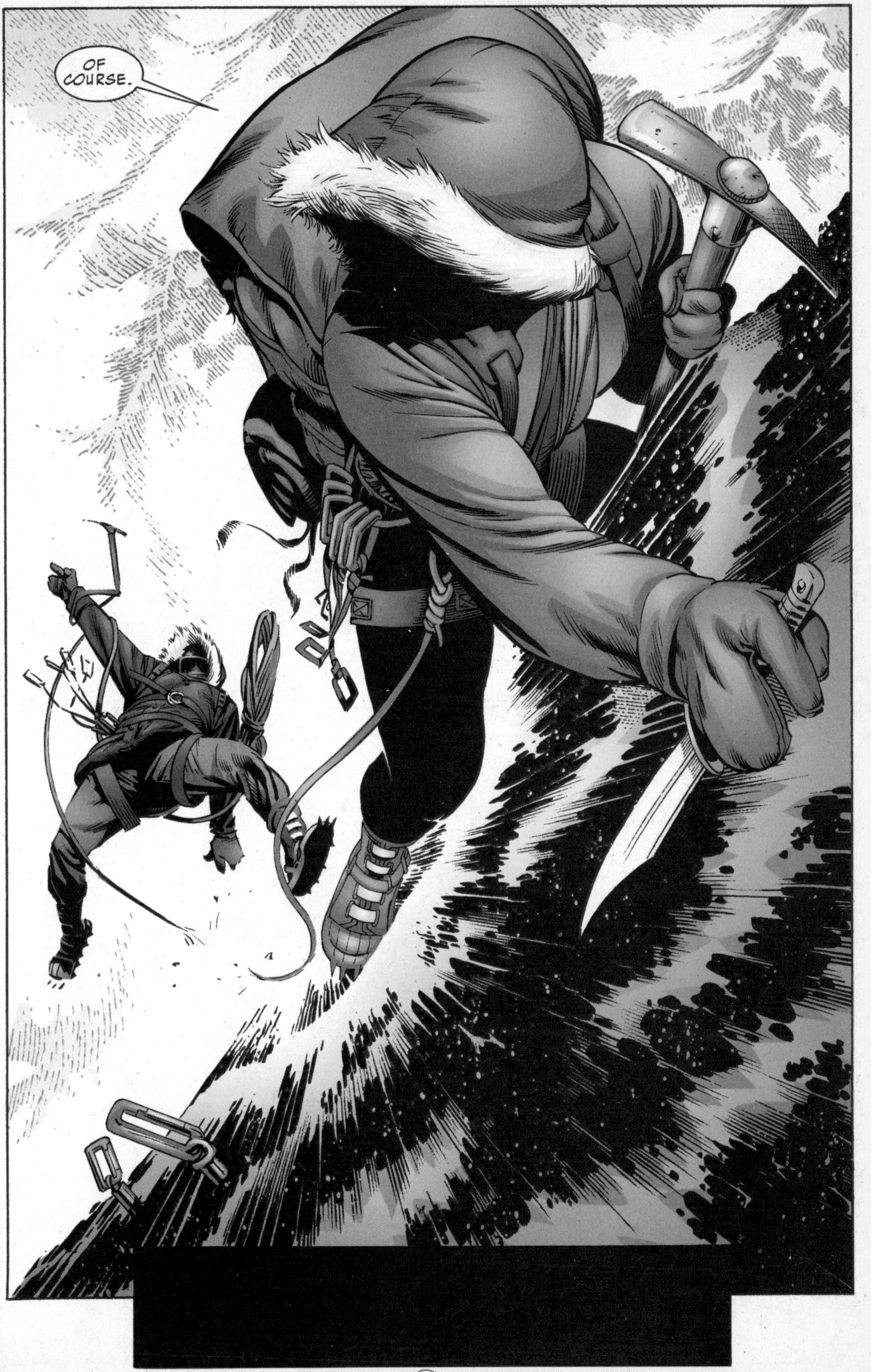
OF COURSE.

[redacted]

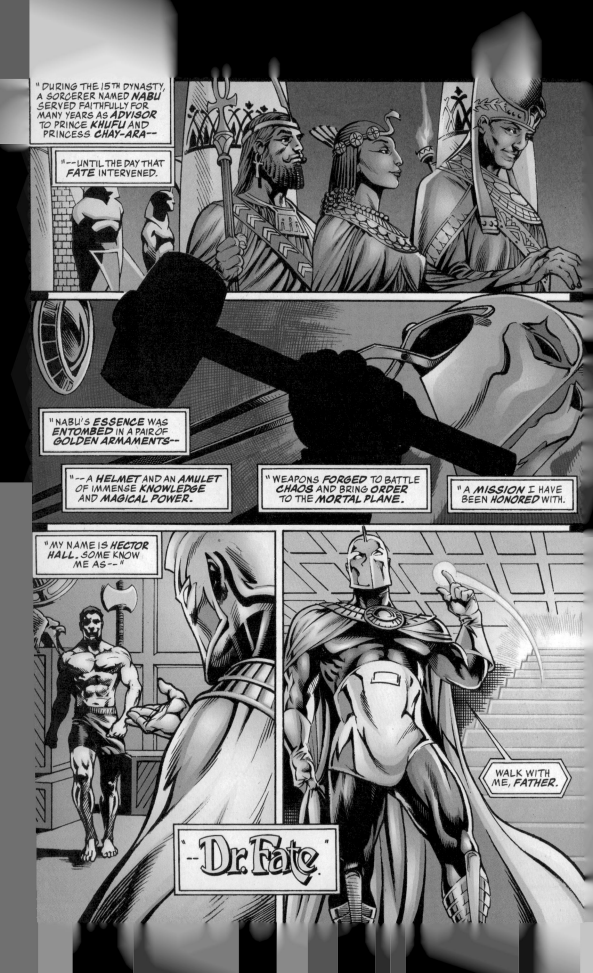

"DURING THE 15TH DYNASTY, A SORCERER NAMED *NABU* SERVED FAITHFULLY FOR MANY YEARS AS *ADVISOR* TO PRINCE *KHUFU* AND PRINCESS *CHAY-ARA*--"

"--UNTIL THE DAY THAT *FATE* INTERVENED."

"NABU'S *ESSENCE* WAS *ENTOMBED* IN A PAIR OF *GOLDEN ARMAMENTS*--"

"--A *HELMET* AND AN *AMULET* OF IMMENSE *KNOWLEDGE* AND *MAGICAL POWER.*"

" WEAPONS *FORGED* TO BATTLE *CHAOS* AND BRING *ORDER* TO THE *MORTAL PLANE.*"

" A *MISSION* I HAVE BEEN *HONORED* WITH."

"MY NAME IS *HECTOR HALL.* SOME KNOW ME AS--"

WALK WITH ME, *FATHER.*

"--Dr. Fate."

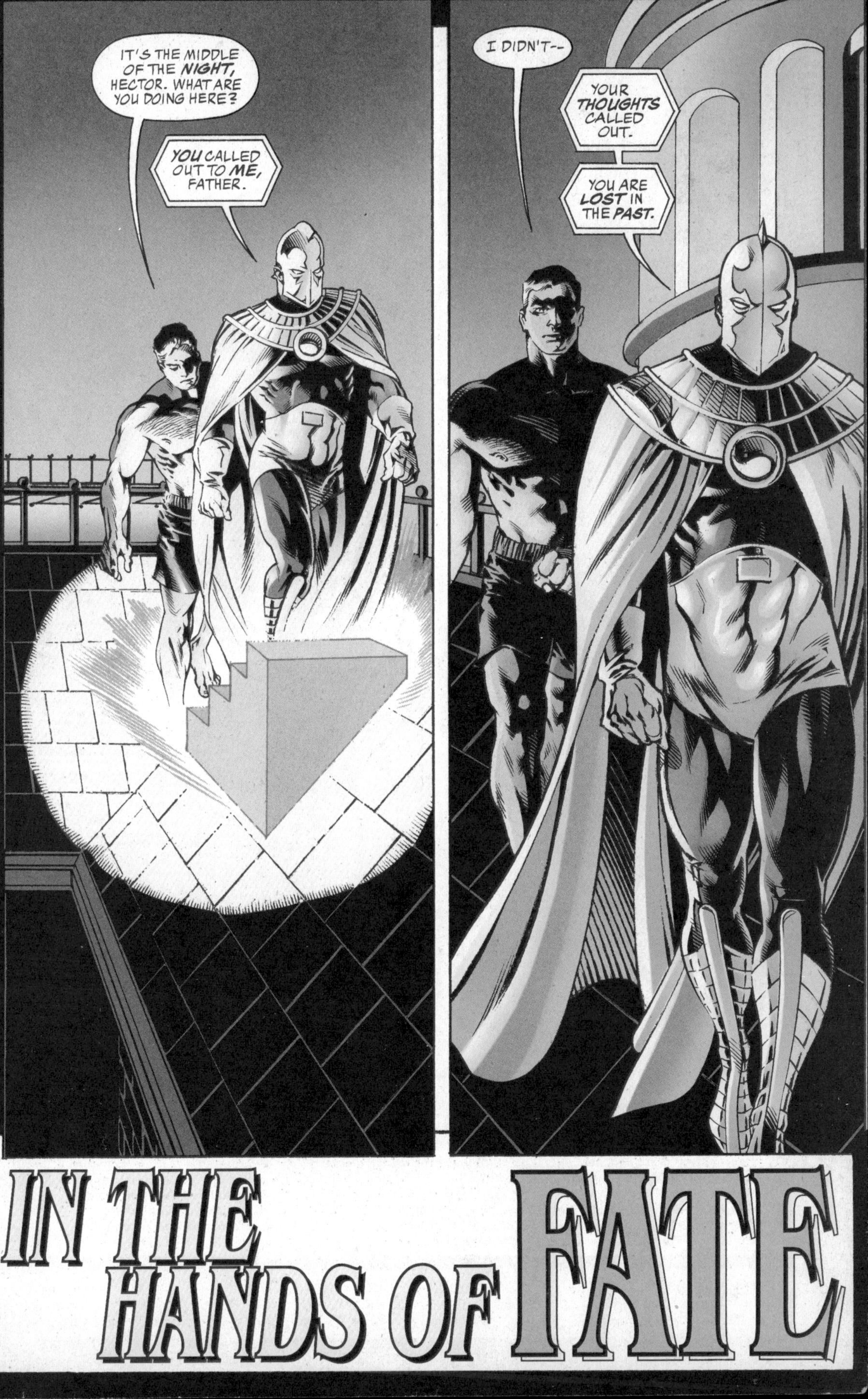
IT'S THE MIDDLE OF THE NIGHT, HECTOR. WHAT ARE YOU DOING HERE?
YOU CALLED OUT TO ME, FATHER.
I DIDN'T--
YOUR THOUGHTS CALLED OUT.
YOU ARE LOST IN THE PAST.
IN THE HANDS OF FATE

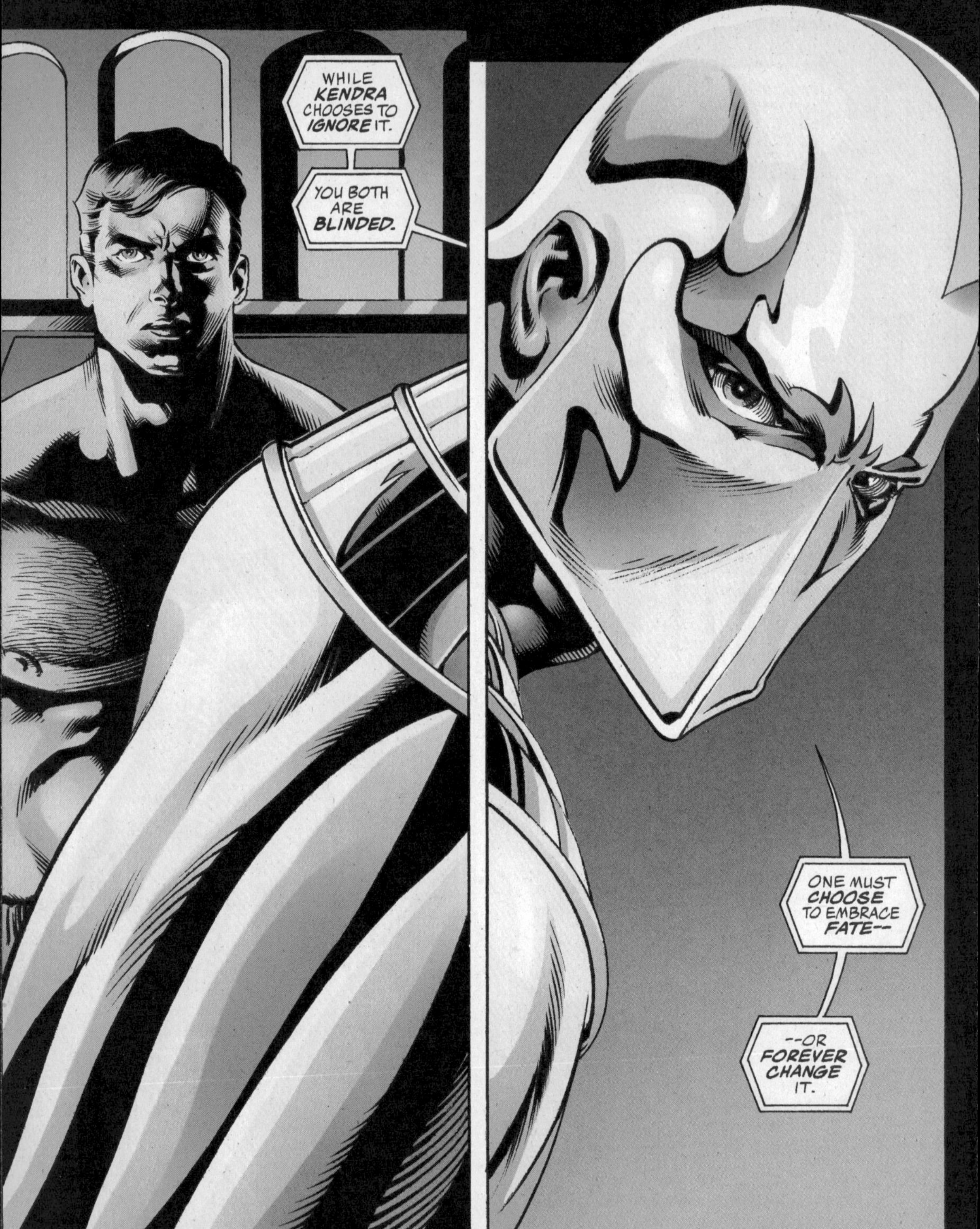
WHILE KENDRA CHOOSES TO IGNORE IT.
YOU BOTH ARE BLINDED.
ONE MUST CHOOSE TO EMBRACE FATE--
--OR FOREVER CHANGE IT.

Thousands of years ago, an Egyptian Prince and his Princess discovered an alien spacecraft from the planet Thanagar. The ship was powered by a mysterious antigravity element they called Nth metal. The unearthly energies of the Nth metal, enhanced by the strength of their love, transformed the souls of the Prince and Princess. For centuries, they were reincarnated, life after life, destined to meet one another and rekindle their love...until today...Today they are Carter Hall and Kendra Saunders, archaeologists and adventurers. The winged warriors known as HAWKMAN and HAWKGIRL!

GEOFF JOHNS & JAMES ROBINSON *story* · GEOFF JOHNS *words* · RAGS MORALES *penciller* · MICHAEL BAIR *inker* · JOHN KALISZ *colorist* · HEROIC AGE *seps* · BILL OAKLEY *letterer* · STEVE WACKER *associate editor* · PETER TOMASI *editor*

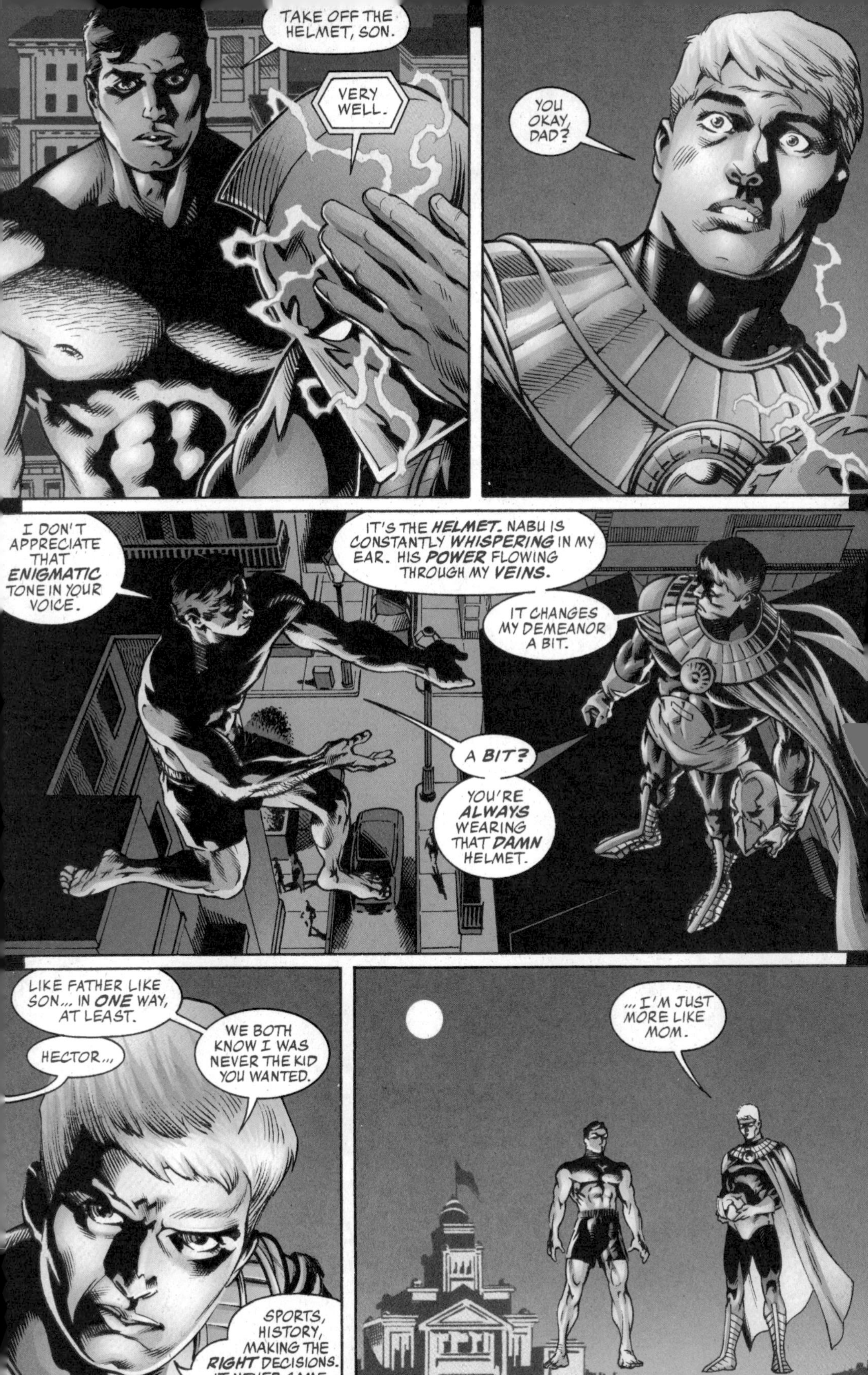

TAKE OFF THE HELMET, SON.
VERY WELL.
YOU OKAY, DAD?
I DON'T APPRECIATE THAT ENIGMATIC TONE IN YOUR VOICE.
IT'S THE HELMET. NABU IS CONSTANTLY WHISPERING IN MY EAR. HIS POWER FLOWING THROUGH MY VEINS.
IT CHANGES MY DEMEANOR A BIT.
A BIT?
YOU'RE ALWAYS WEARING THAT DAMN HELMET.
LIKE FATHER LIKE SON... IN ONE WAY, AT LEAST.
HECTOR...
WE BOTH KNOW I WAS NEVER THE KID YOU WANTED.
SPORTS, HISTORY, MAKING THE RIGHT DECISIONS. IT NEVER CAME NATURALLY. I'M MORE LIKE...
...I'M JUST MORE LIKE MOM.

I DON'T THINK YOU'RE ANY LESS OF A MAN THAN--
WE CAN TALK ABOUT PERSONAL LIVES LATER, DAD.
THERE'S ANOTHER REASON I CAME HERE.
TO DELIVER A MESSAGE.
A WARNING IN TRUTH--
--OF YOUR INESCAPABLE FATE!!
FWAASH!!

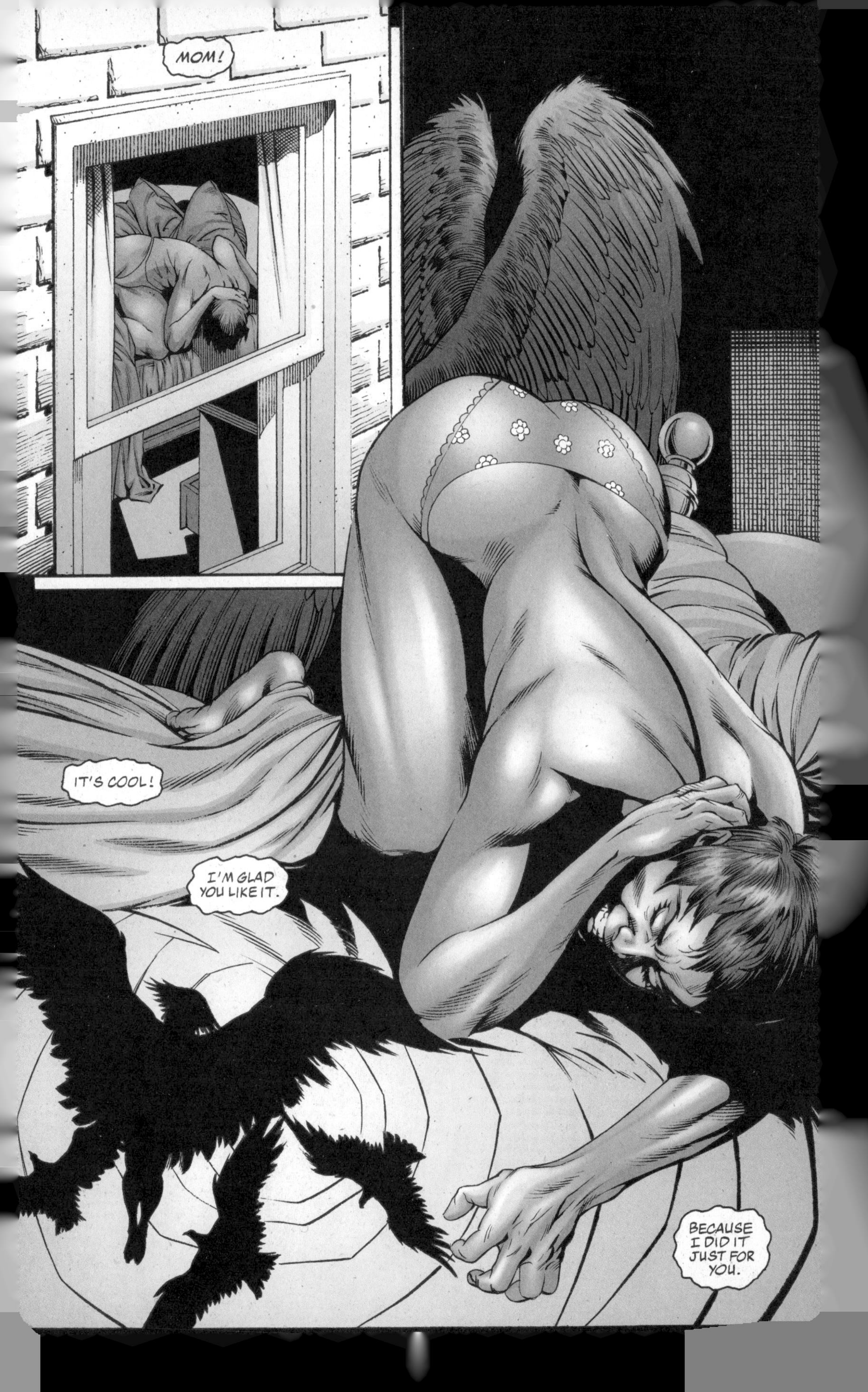
MOM!
IT'S COOL!
I'M GLAD YOU LIKE IT.
BECAUSE I DID IT JUST FOR YOU.

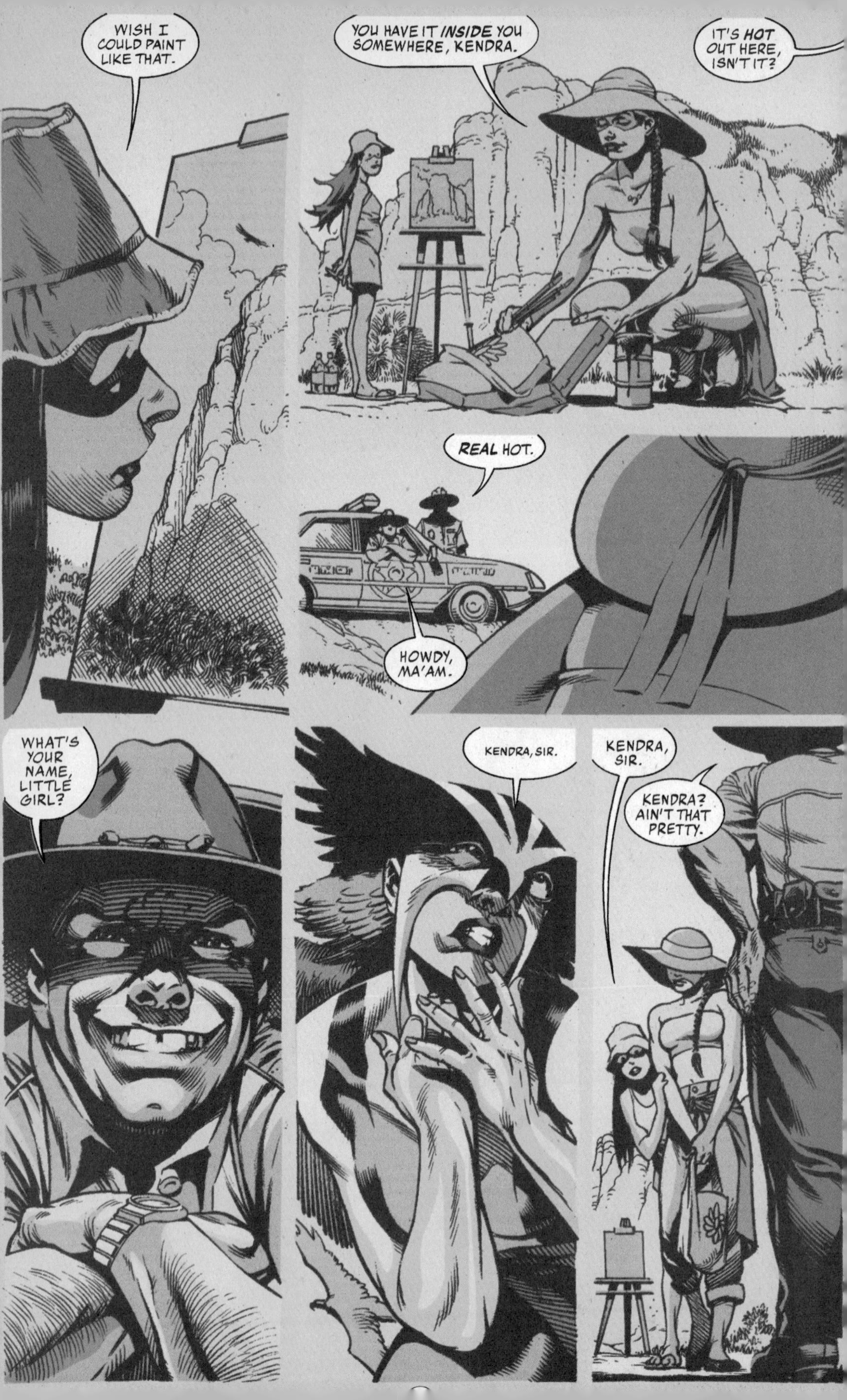

WISH I COULD PAINT LIKE THAT.
YOU HAVE IT INSIDE YOU SOMEWHERE, KENDRA.
IT'S HOT OUT HERE, ISN'T IT?
REAL HOT.
HOWDY, MA'AM.
WHAT'S YOUR NAME, LITTLE GIRL?
KENDRA, SIR.
KENDRA, SIR.
KENDRA? AIN'T THAT PRETTY.

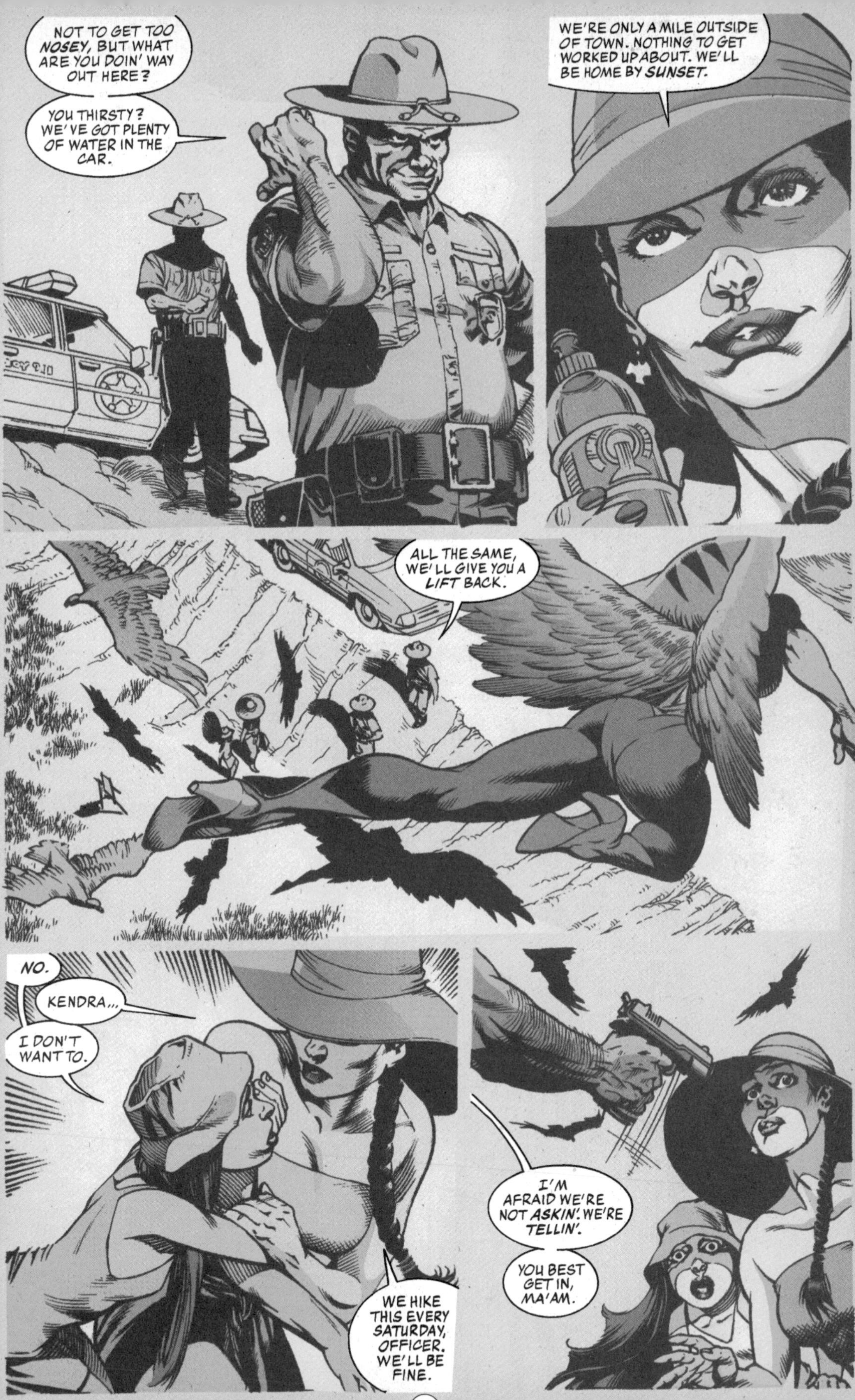
NOT TO GET TOO NOSEY, BUT WHAT ARE YOU DOIN' WAY OUT HERE?
YOU THIRSTY? WE'VE GOT PLENTY OF WATER IN THE CAR.
WE'RE ONLY A MILE OUTSIDE OF TOWN. NOTHING TO GET WORKED UP ABOUT. WE'LL BE HOME BY SUNSET.
ALL THE SAME, WE'LL GIVE YOU A LIFT BACK.
NO.
KENDRA...
I DON'T WANT TO.
WE HIKE THIS EVERY SATURDAY, OFFICER. WE'LL BE FINE.
I'M AFRAID WE'RE NOT ASKIN'. WE'RE TELLIN'.
YOU BEST GET IN, MA'AM.

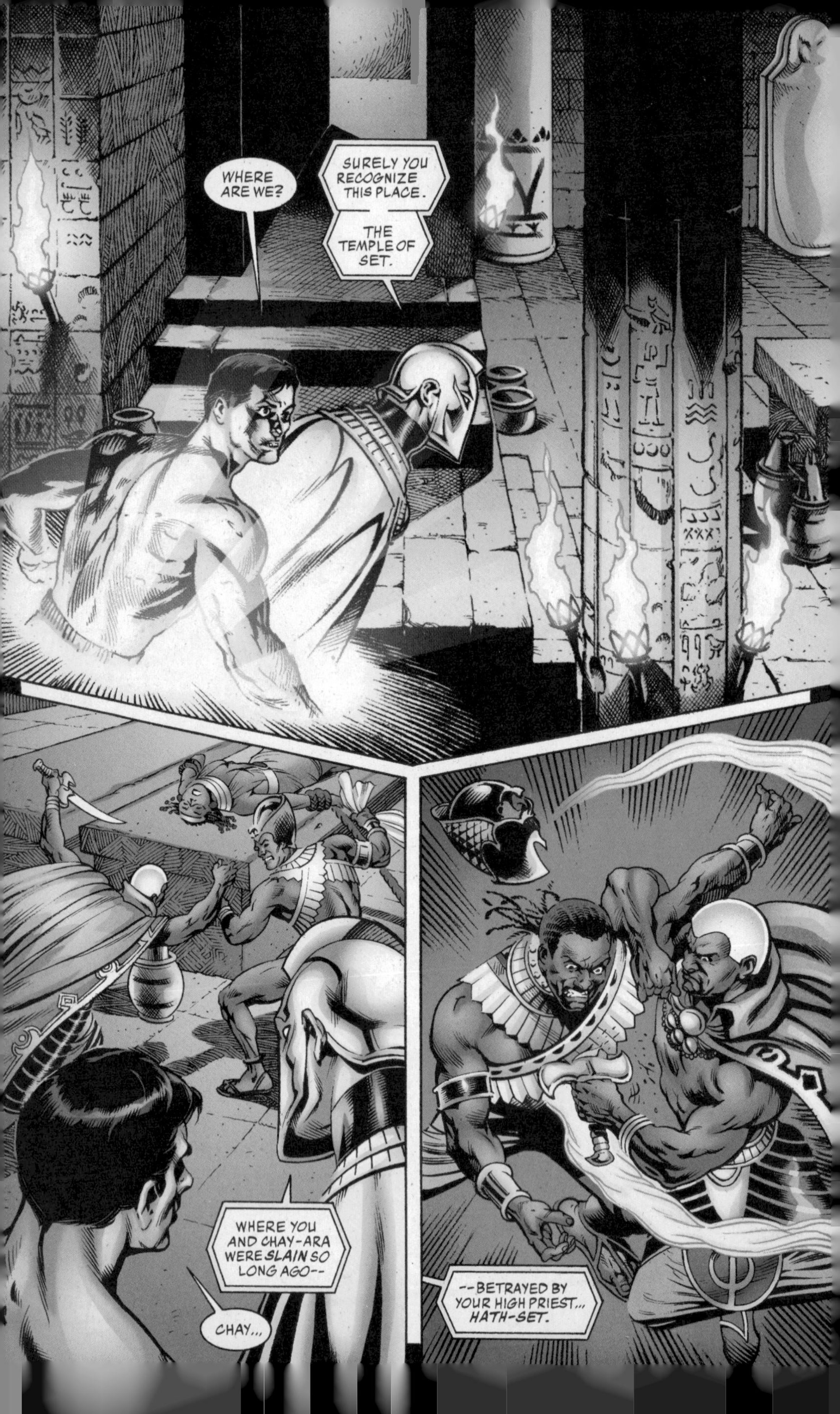
WHERE ARE WE?
SURELY YOU RECOGNIZE THIS PLACE.
THE TEMPLE OF SET.
WHERE YOU AND CHAY-ARA WERE SLAIN SO LONG AGO--
CHAY...
--BETRAYED BY YOUR HIGH PRIEST... HATH-SET.

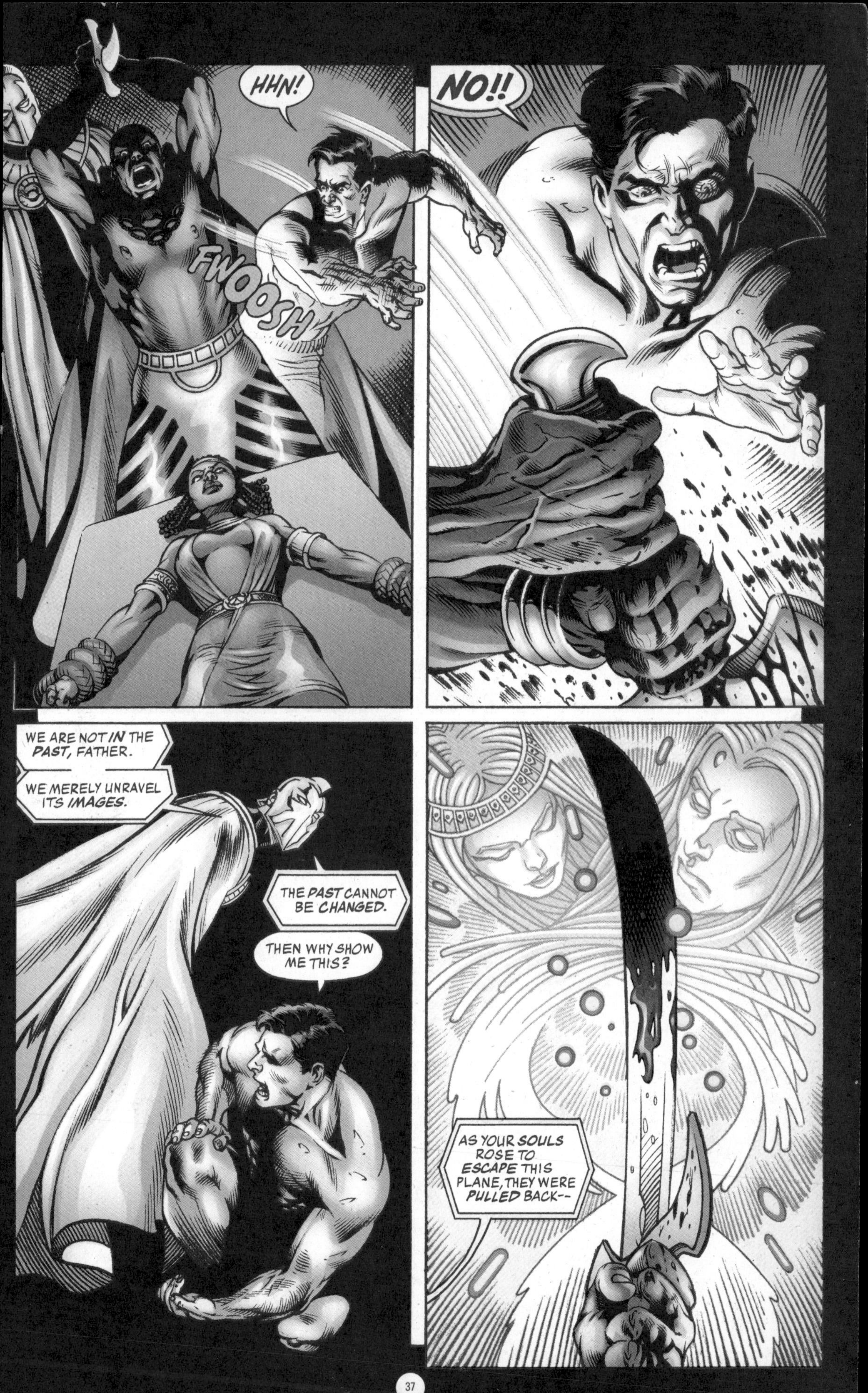
HHN!
FWOOSH
NO!!
WE ARE NOT IN THE PAST, FATHER.
WE MERELY UNRAVEL ITS IMAGES.
THE PAST CANNOT BE CHANGED.
THEN WHY SHOW ME THIS?
AS YOUR SOULS ROSE TO ESCAPE THIS PLANE, THEY WERE PULLED BACK--

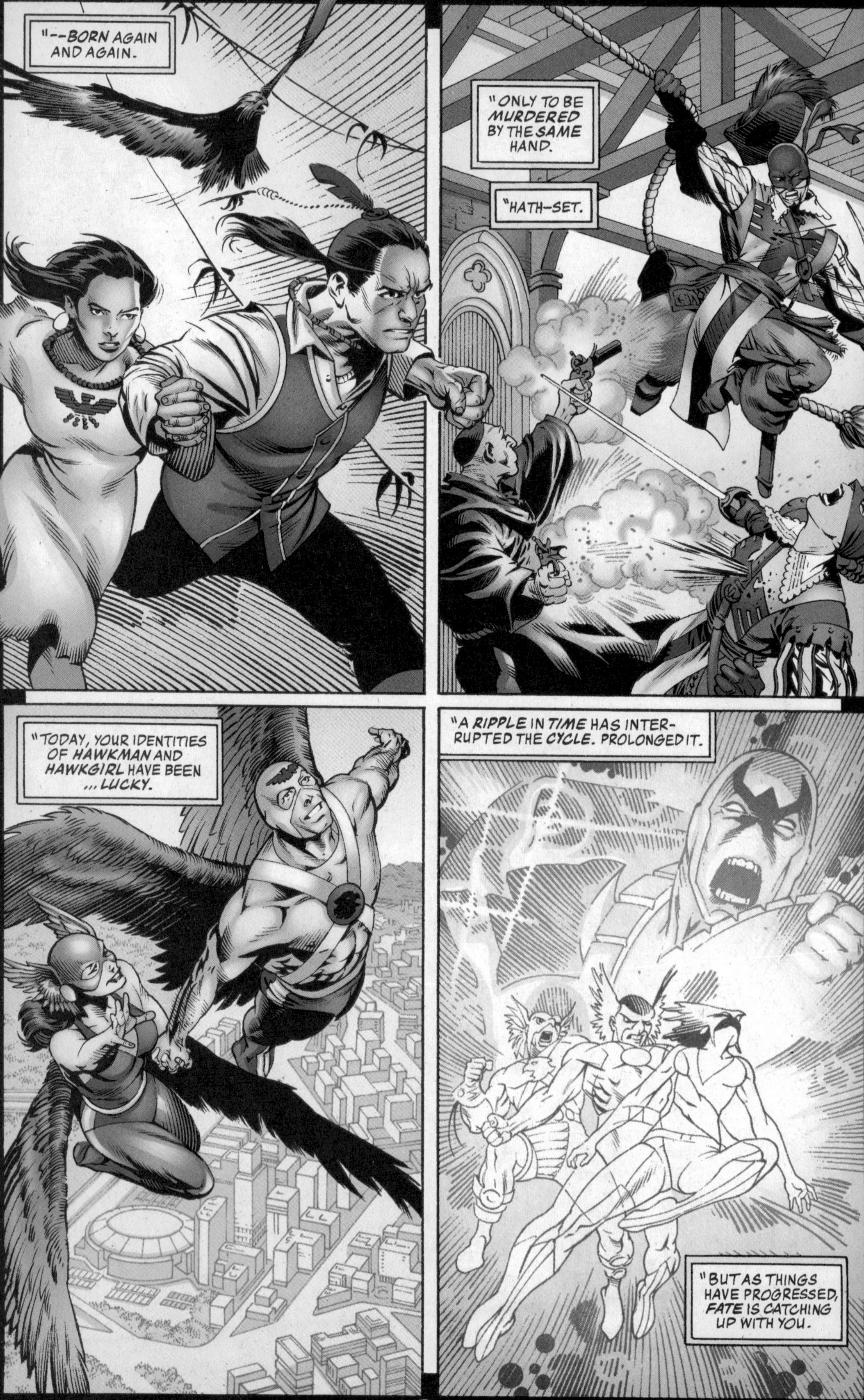
"--BORN AGAIN AND AGAIN.
"ONLY TO BE MURDERED BY THE SAME HAND.
"HATH-SET.
"TODAY, YOUR IDENTITIES OF HAWKMAN AND HAWKGIRL HAVE BEEN ...LUCKY.
"A RIPPLE IN TIME HAS INTERRUPTED THE CYCLE. PROLONGED IT.
"BUT AS THINGS HAVE PROGRESSED, FATE IS CATCHING UP WITH YOU.

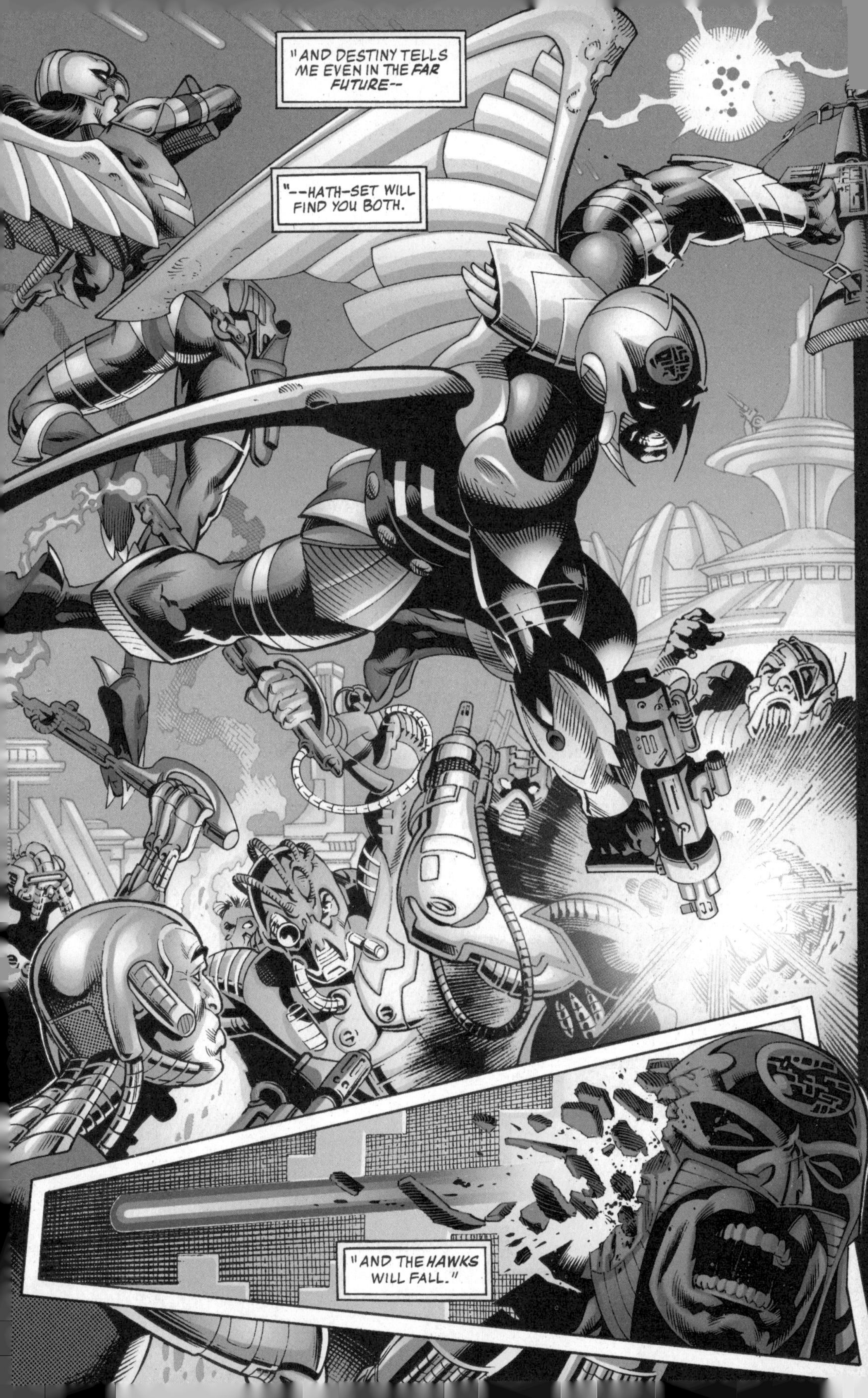
"AND DESTINY TELLS ME EVEN IN THE FAR FUTURE--
"--HATH-SET WILL FIND YOU BOTH.
"AND THE HAWKS WILL FALL."

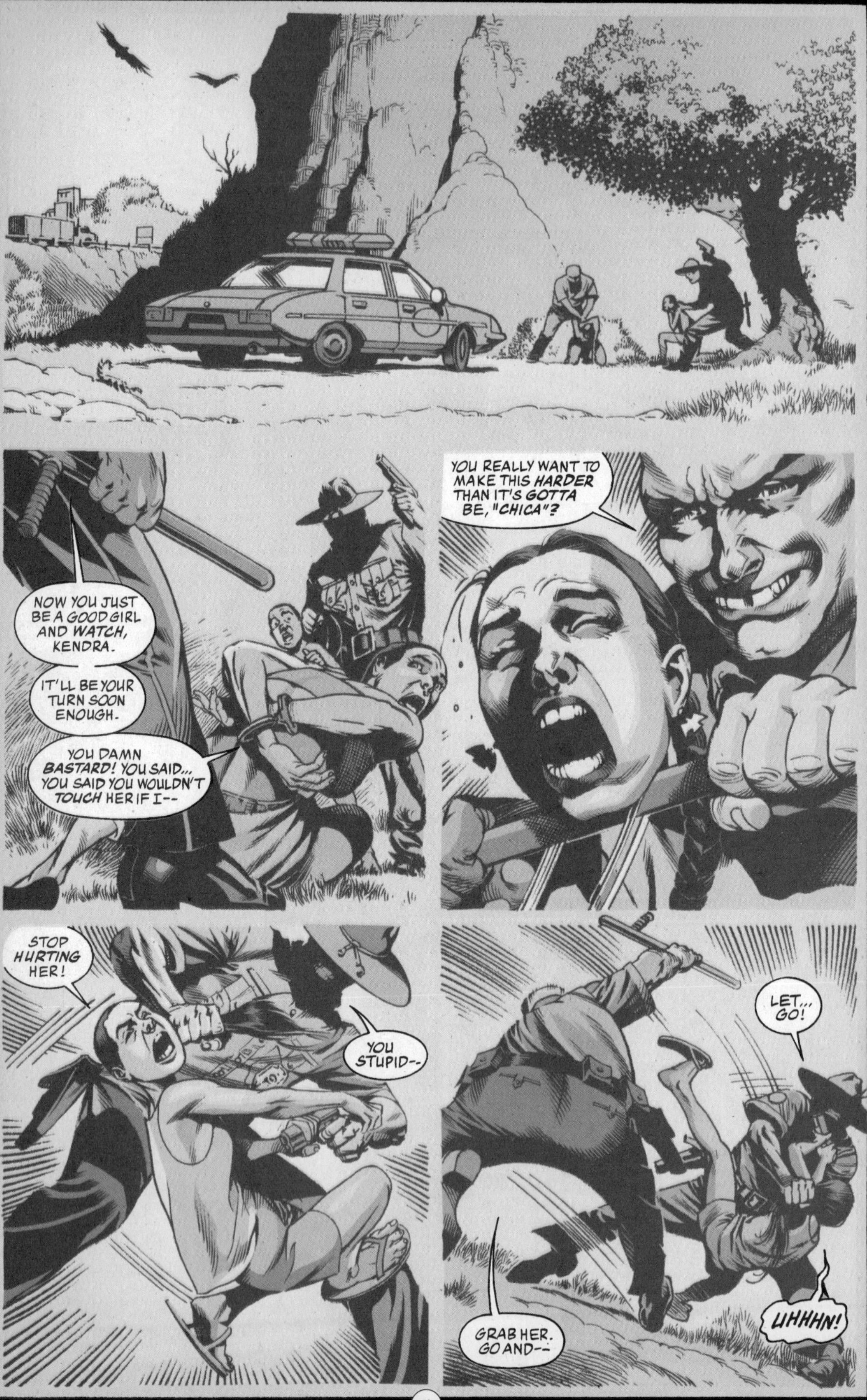

NOW YOU JUST BE A GOOD GIRL AND WATCH, KENDRA.
IT'LL BE YOUR TURN SOON ENOUGH.
YOU DAMN BASTARD! YOU SAID... YOU SAID YOU WOULDN'T TOUCH HER IF I--
YOU REALLY WANT TO MAKE THIS HARDER THAN IT'S GOTTA BE, "CHICA"?
STOP HURTING HER!
YOU STUPID--
LET... GO!
GRAB HER. GO AND--
UHHHN!

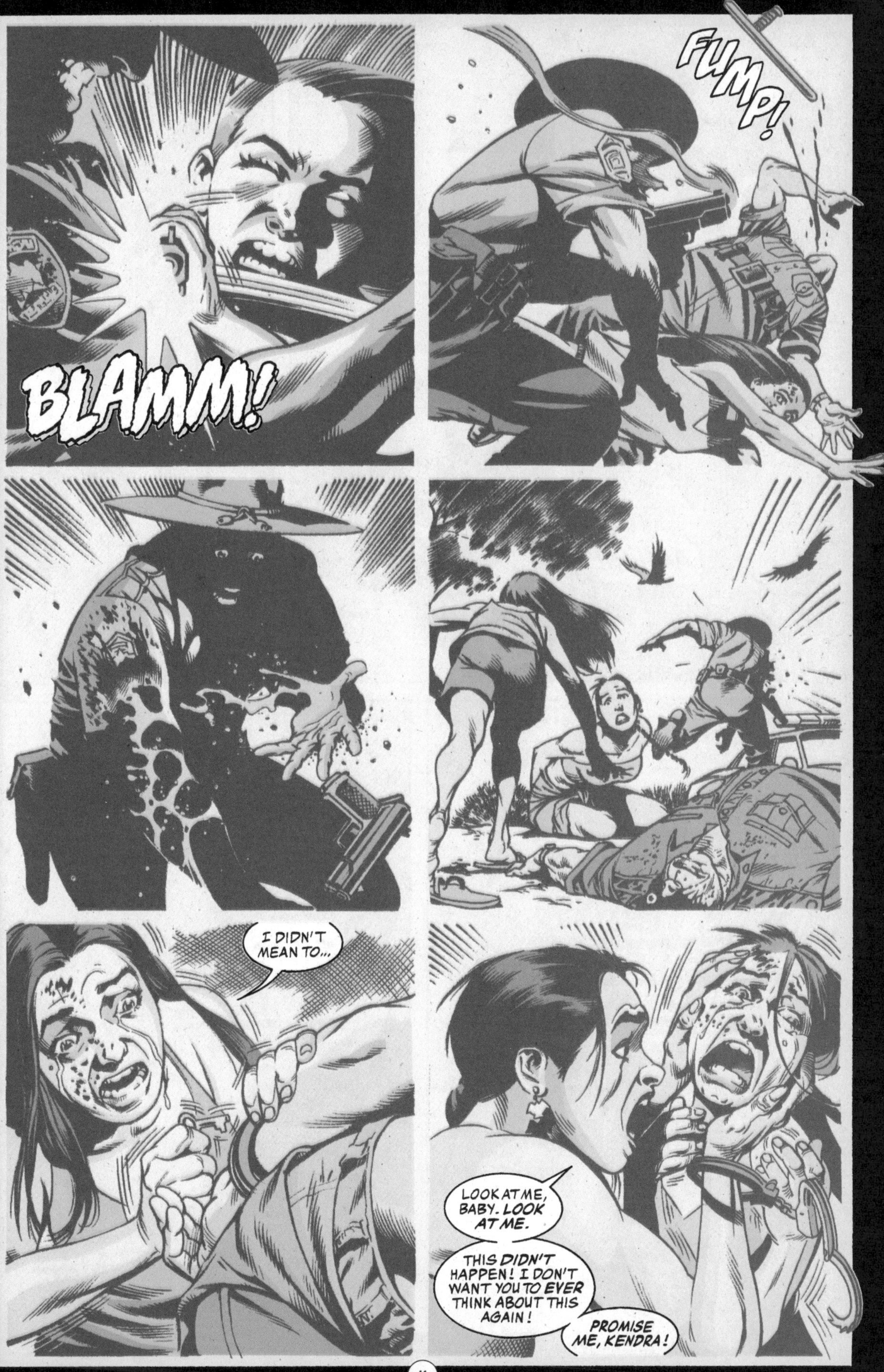
BLAMM!
FUMP!
I DIDN'T MEAN TO...
LOOK AT ME, BABY. LOOK AT ME.
THIS DIDN'T HAPPEN! I DON'T WANT YOU TO EVER THINK ABOUT THIS AGAIN!
PROMISE ME, KENDRA!

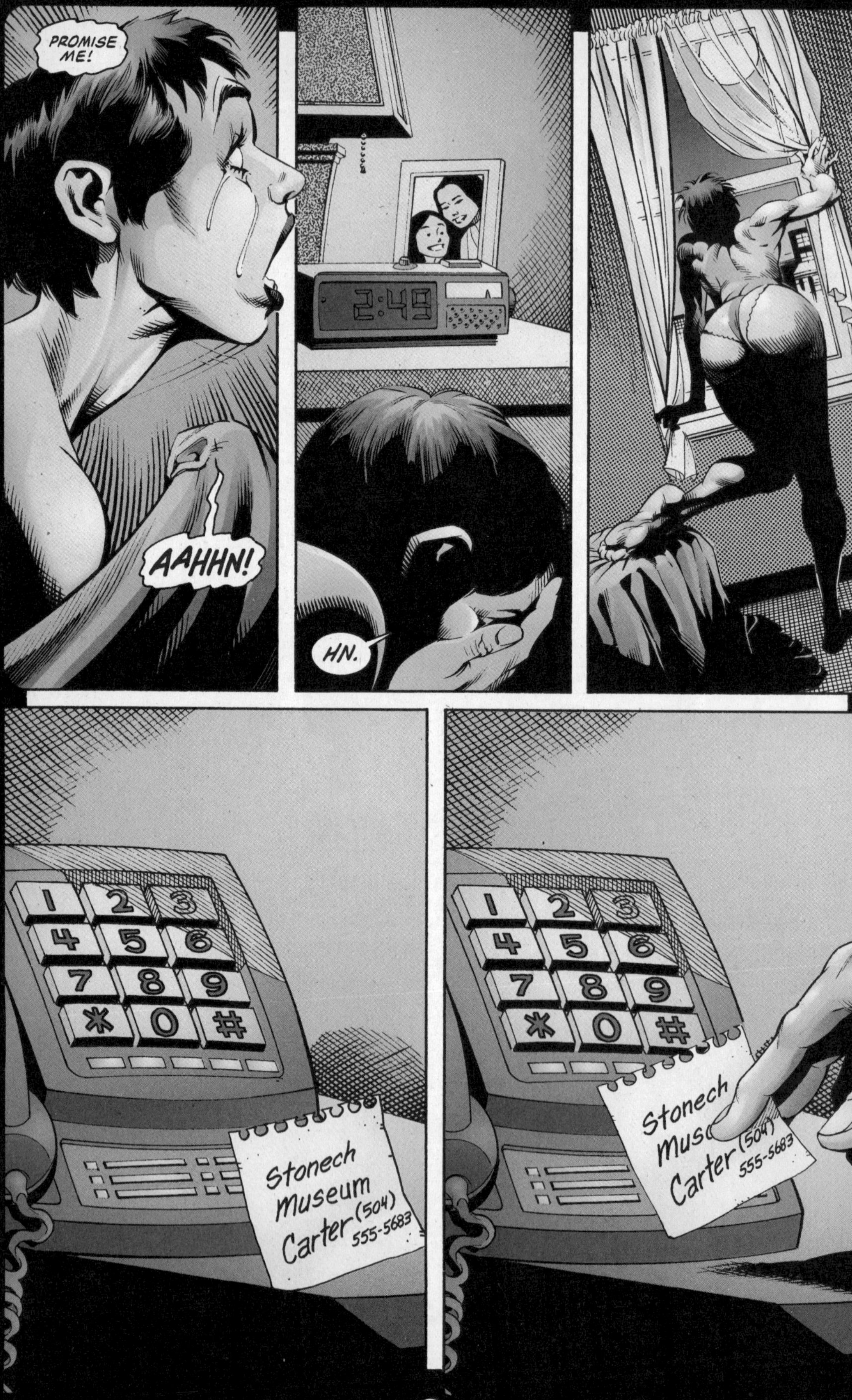
PROMISE ME!
AAHHN!
2:49
HN.
1 2 3
4 5 6
7 8 9
* 0 #
Stonech Museum Carter (504) 555-5683
1 2 3
4 5 6
7 8 9
* 0 #
Stonech Musc Carter (504) 555-5683

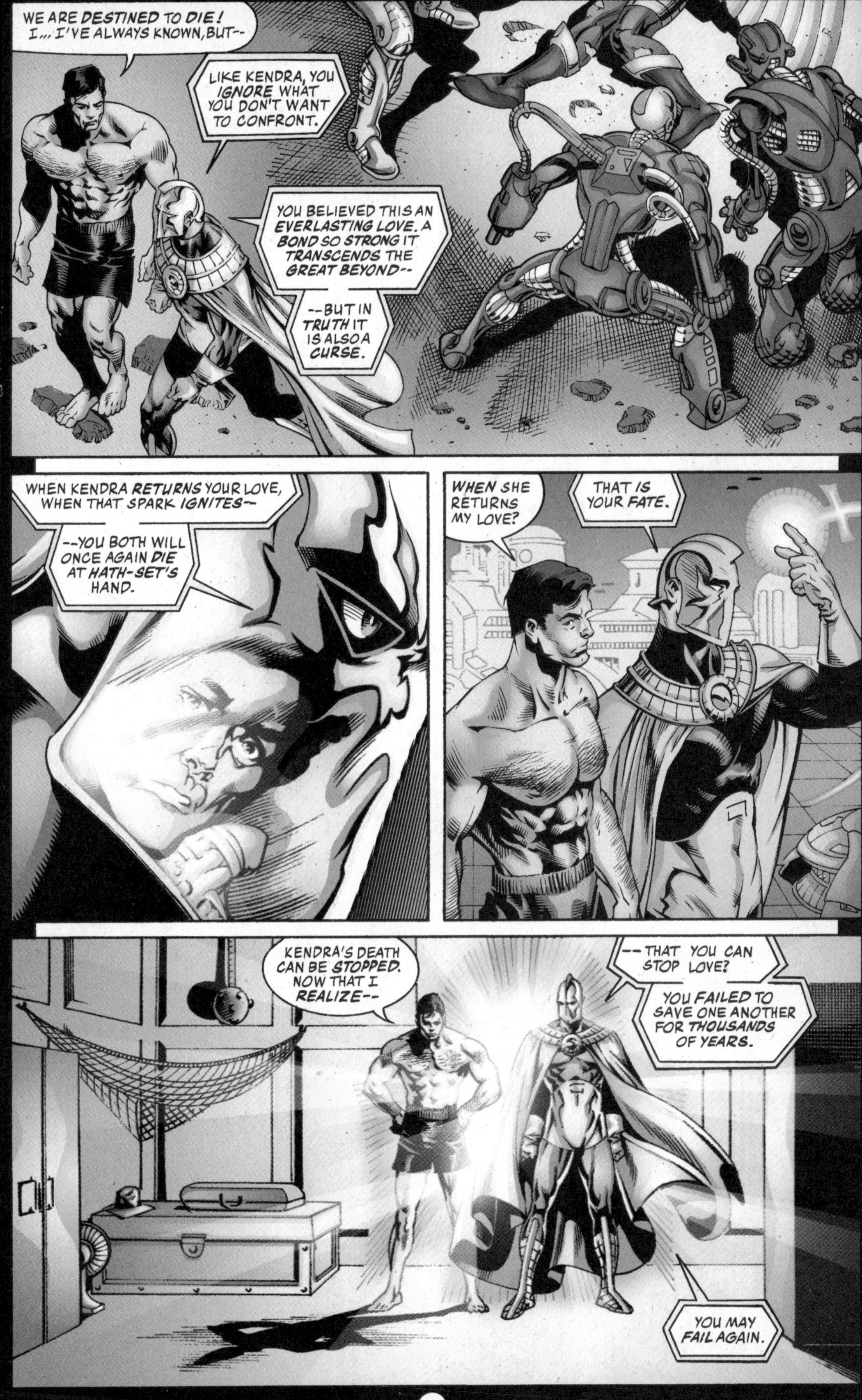

WE ARE DESTINED TO DIE! I... I'VE ALWAYS KNOWN, BUT--
LIKE KENDRA, YOU IGNORE WHAT YOU DON'T WANT TO CONFRONT.
YOU BELIEVED THIS AN EVERLASTING LOVE. A BOND SO STRONG IT TRANSCENDS THE GREAT BEYOND--
--BUT IN TRUTH IT IS ALSO A CURSE.
WHEN KENDRA RETURNS YOUR LOVE, WHEN THAT SPARK IGNITES--
--YOU BOTH WILL ONCE AGAIN DIE AT HATH-SET'S HAND.
WHEN SHE RETURNS MY LOVE?
THAT IS YOUR FATE.
KENDRA'S DEATH CAN BE STOPPED. NOW THAT I REALIZE--
--THAT YOU CAN STOP LOVE?
YOU FAILED TO SAVE ONE ANOTHER FOR THOUSANDS OF YEARS.
YOU MAY FAIL AGAIN.

NABU! LET ME OUT!

HHN. HE WOULDN'T... LET ME OUT. I STILL HAVE TROUBLE...

I'M SORRY, DAD. I WISH I WASN'T THE ONE WHO HAD TO DELIVER THIS.

AND NOW YOU'RE A PART OF THIS CURSED CIRCLE. DESTINED TO BE BORN AGAIN AND AGAIN. TO WARN YOUR OWN PARENTS OF THEIR IMPENDING DESTINY...

YEAH... MY FATE, I GUESS.

WE ALWAYS WANTED A CHILD, BUT FOR SOME REASON... WE NEVER WERE ABLE TO. NOT UNTIL YOU WERE BORN.

I WAITED CENTURIES TO BE A FATHER, HECTOR.

AND DESPITE OUR DIFFERENCES...

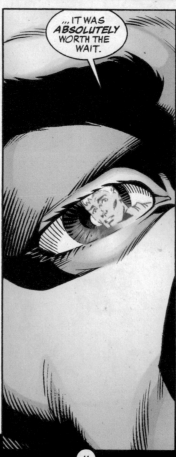

...IT WAS ABSOLUTELY WORTH THE WAIT.

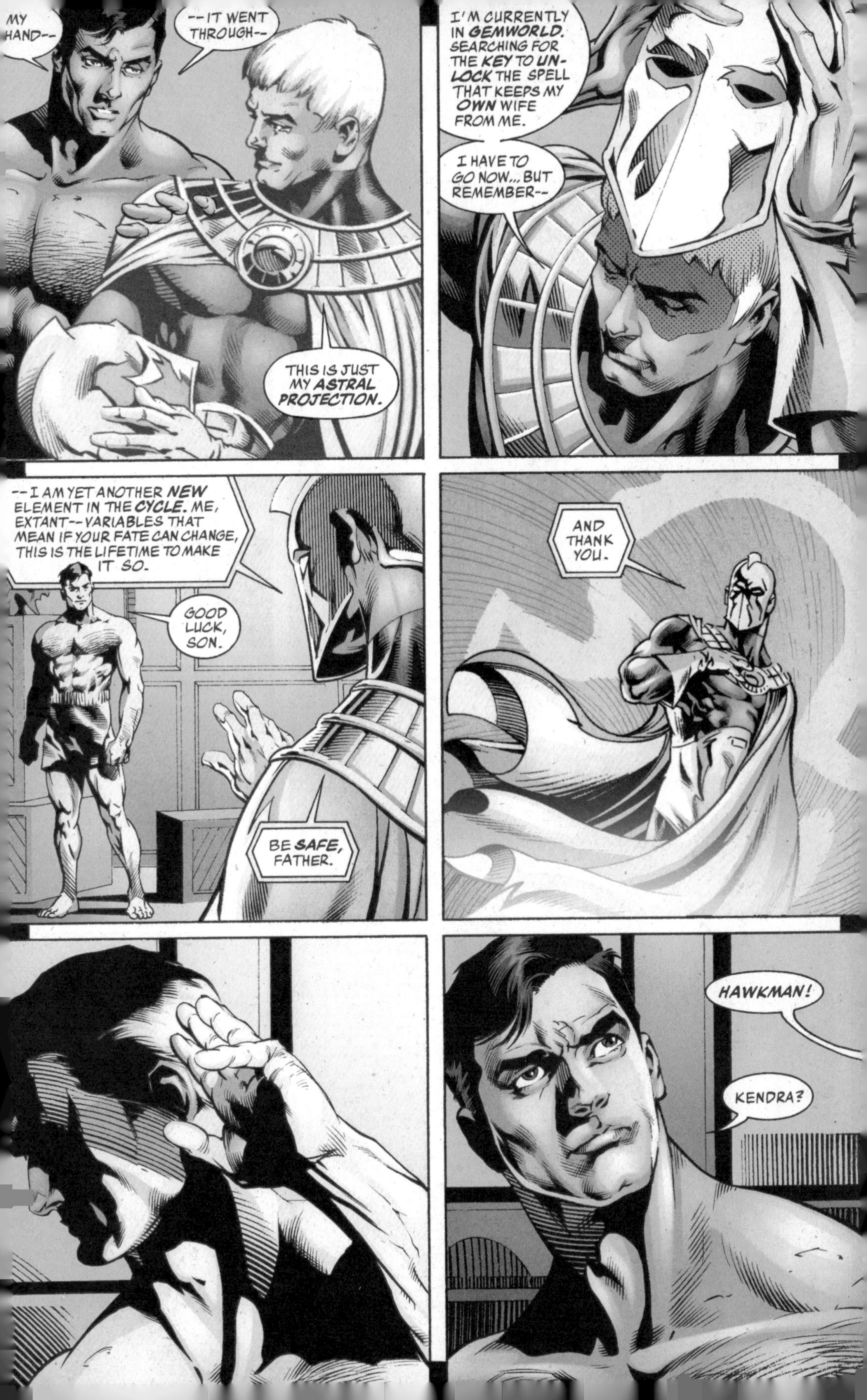
MY HAND--
--IT WENT THROUGH--
THIS IS JUST MY ASTRAL PROJECTION.
I'M CURRENTLY IN GEMWORLD, SEARCHING FOR THE KEY TO UNLOCK THE SPELL THAT KEEPS MY OWN WIFE FROM ME.
I HAVE TO GO NOW... BUT REMEMBER--
--I AM YET ANOTHER NEW ELEMENT IN THE CYCLE. ME, EXTANT--VARIABLES THAT MEAN IF YOUR FATE CAN CHANGE, THIS IS THE LIFETIME TO MAKE IT SO.
GOOD LUCK, SON.
BE SAFE, FATHER.
AND THANK YOU.
HAWKMAN!
KENDRA?

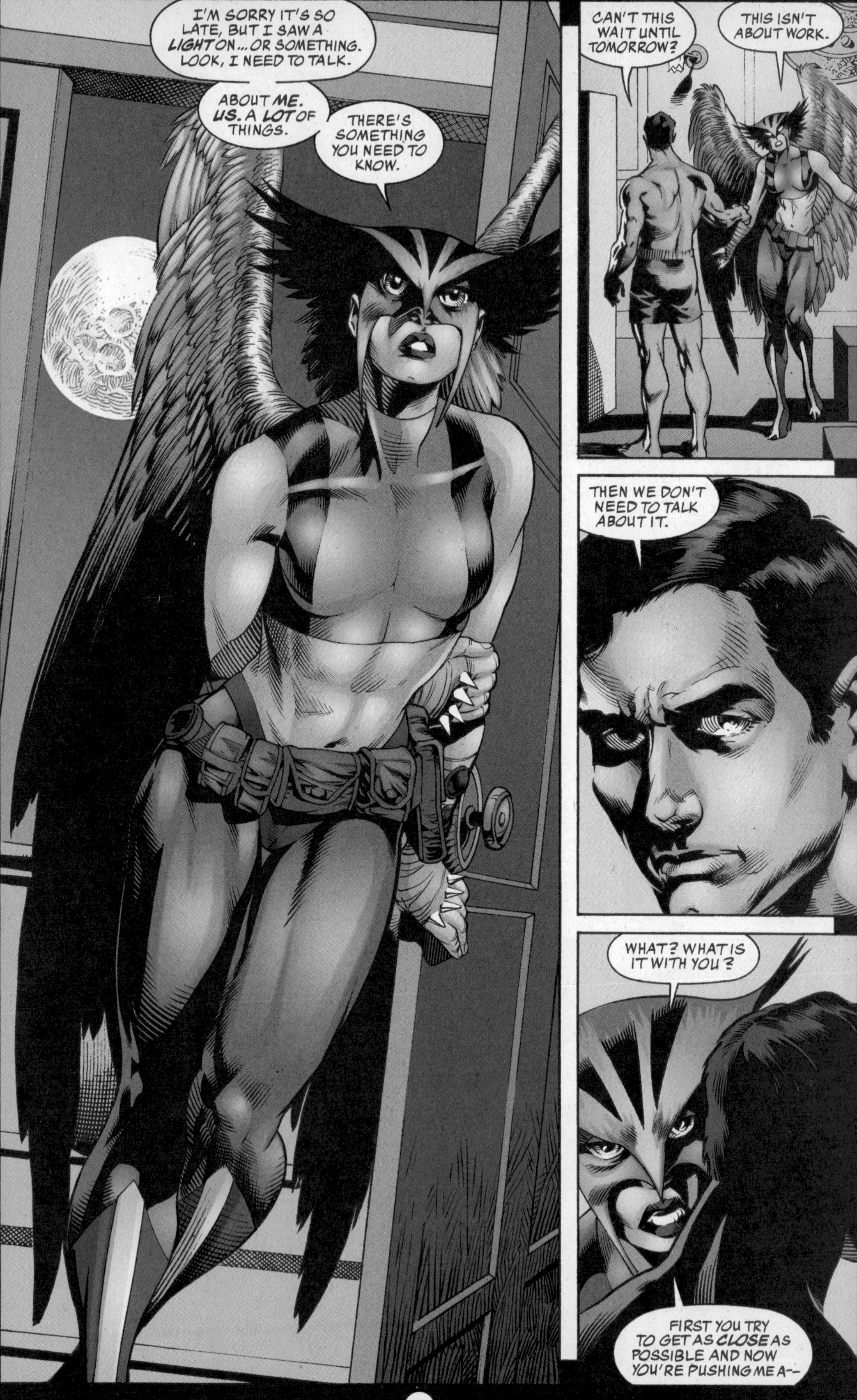

I'M SORRY IT'S SO LATE, BUT I SAW A LIGHT ON... OR SOMETHING. LOOK, I NEED TO TALK.
ABOUT ME. US. A LOT OF THINGS.
THERE'S SOMETHING YOU NEED TO KNOW.
CAN'T THIS WAIT UNTIL TOMORROW?
THIS ISN'T ABOUT WORK.
THEN WE DON'T NEED TO TALK ABOUT IT.
WHAT? WHAT IS IT WITH YOU?
FIRST YOU TRY TO GET AS CLOSE AS POSSIBLE AND NOW YOU'RE PUSHING ME A--

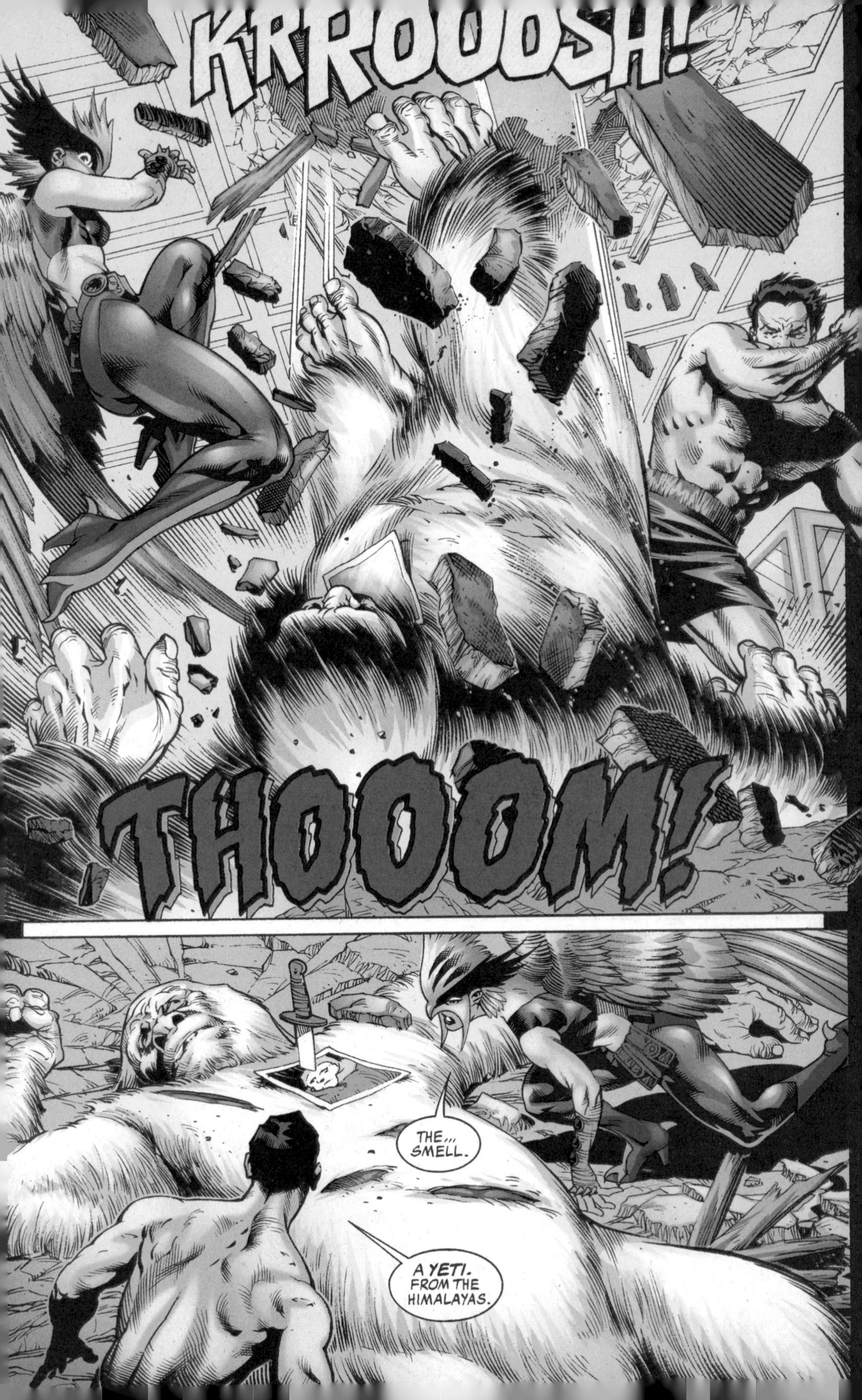
KRROOOSH!
THOOOM!
THE... SMELL.
A YETI. FROM THE HIMALAYAS.

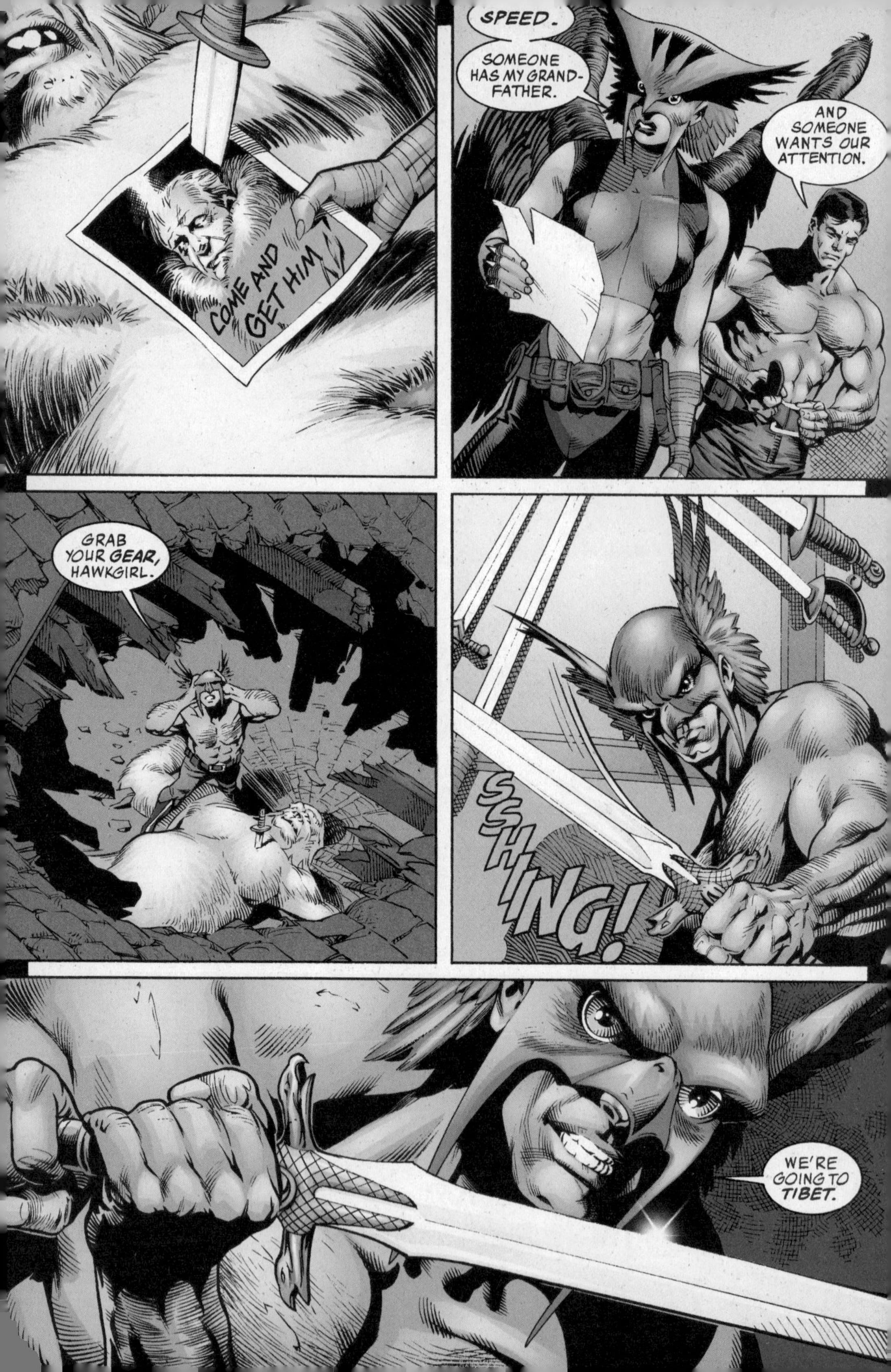
COME AND GET HIM
SPEED.
SOMEONE HAS MY GRAND-FATHER.
AND SOMEONE WANTS OUR ATTENTION.
GRAB YOUR GEAR, HAWKGIRL.
SSHING!
WE'RE GOING TO TIBET.

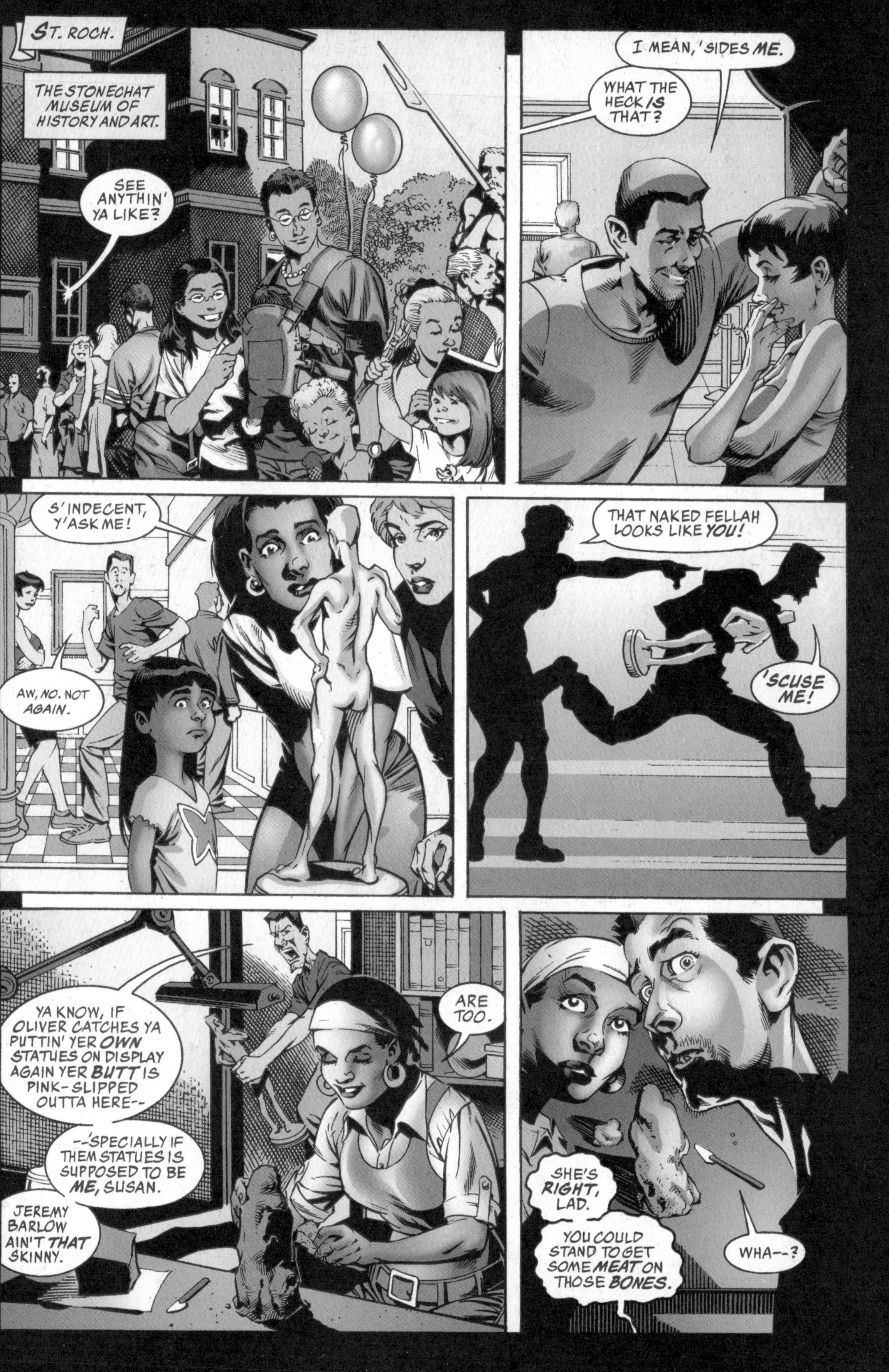
ST. ROCH.
THE STONECHAT MUSEUM OF HISTORY AND ART.
SEE ANYTHIN' YA LIKE?
I MEAN, 'SIDES ME.
WHAT THE HECK IS THAT?
S'INDECENT, Y'ASK ME!
AW, NO. NOT AGAIN.
THAT NAKED FELLAH LOOKS LIKE YOU!
'SCUSE ME!
YA KNOW, IF OLIVER CATCHES YA PUTTIN' YER OWN STATUES ON DISPLAY AGAIN YER BUTT IS PINK-SLIPPED OUTTA HERE--
ARE TOO.
--'SPECIALLY IF THEM STATUES IS SUPPOSED TO BE ME, SUSAN.
JEREMY BARLOW AIN'T THAT SKINNY.
SHE'S RIGHT, LAD.
YOU COULD STAND TO GET SOME MEAT ON THOSE BONES.
WHA--?

Thousands of years ago, an Egyptian Prince and his Princess discovered an alien spacecraft from the planet Thanagar. The ship was powered by a mysterious antigravity element they called Nth metal. The unearthly energies of the Nth metal, enhanced by the strength of their love, transformed the souls of the Prince and Princess. For centuries, they were reincarnated, life after life, destined to meet one another and rekindle their love...until today...Today they are Carter Hall and Kendra Saunders, archaeologists and adventurers. The winged warriors known as HAWKMAN and HAWKGIRL!

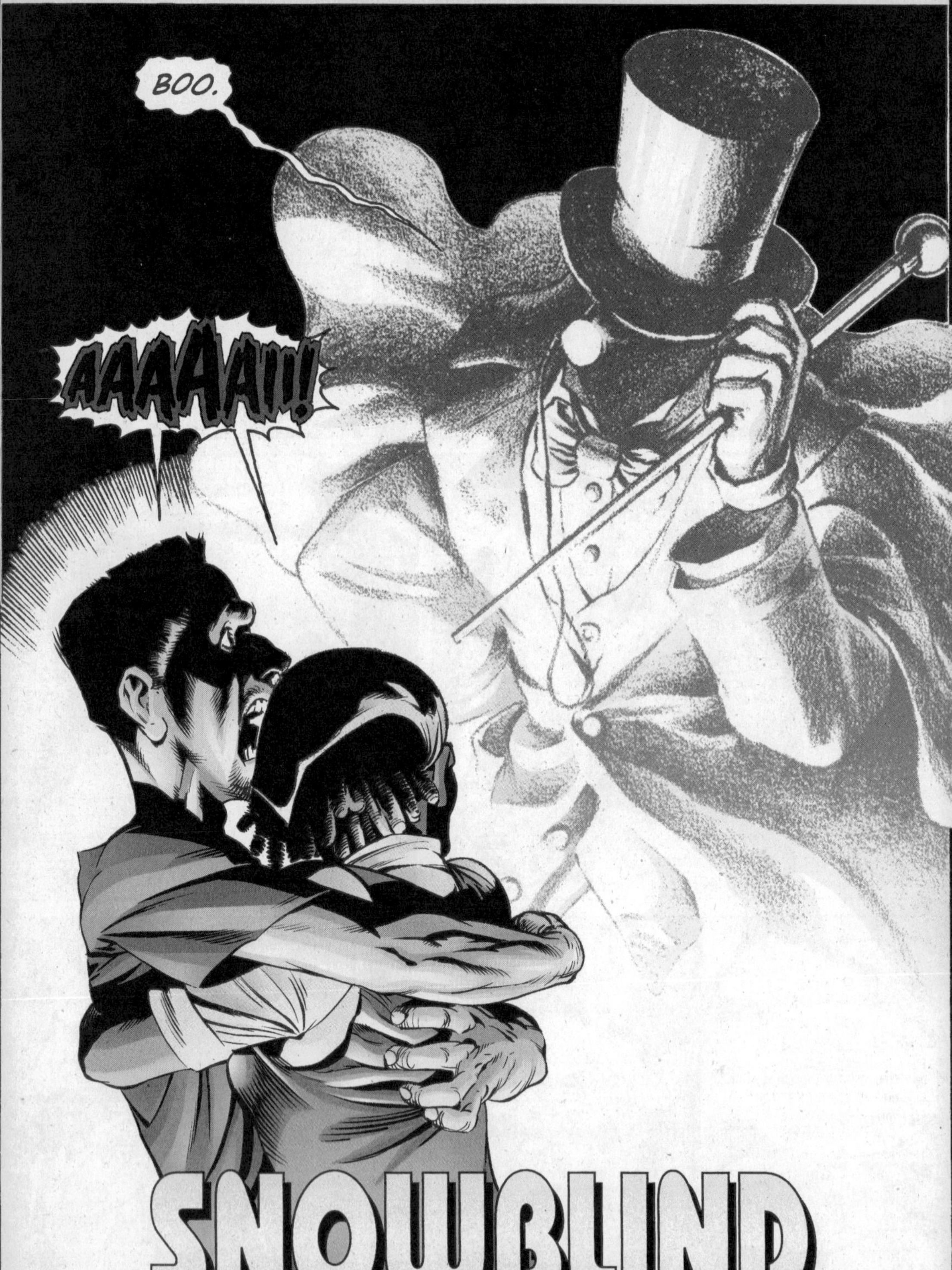
BOO.
AAAAAIII!
SNOWBLIND

GEOFF JOHNS & JAMES ROBINSON *story* · GEOFF JOHNS *words* · RAGS MORALES *penciller* · MICHAEL BAIR *inker* · JOHN KALISZ *colorist* · HEROIC AGE *seps* · BILL OAKLEY *letterer* · VALERIE D'ORAZIO *asst. editor* · PETER TOMASI *editor*

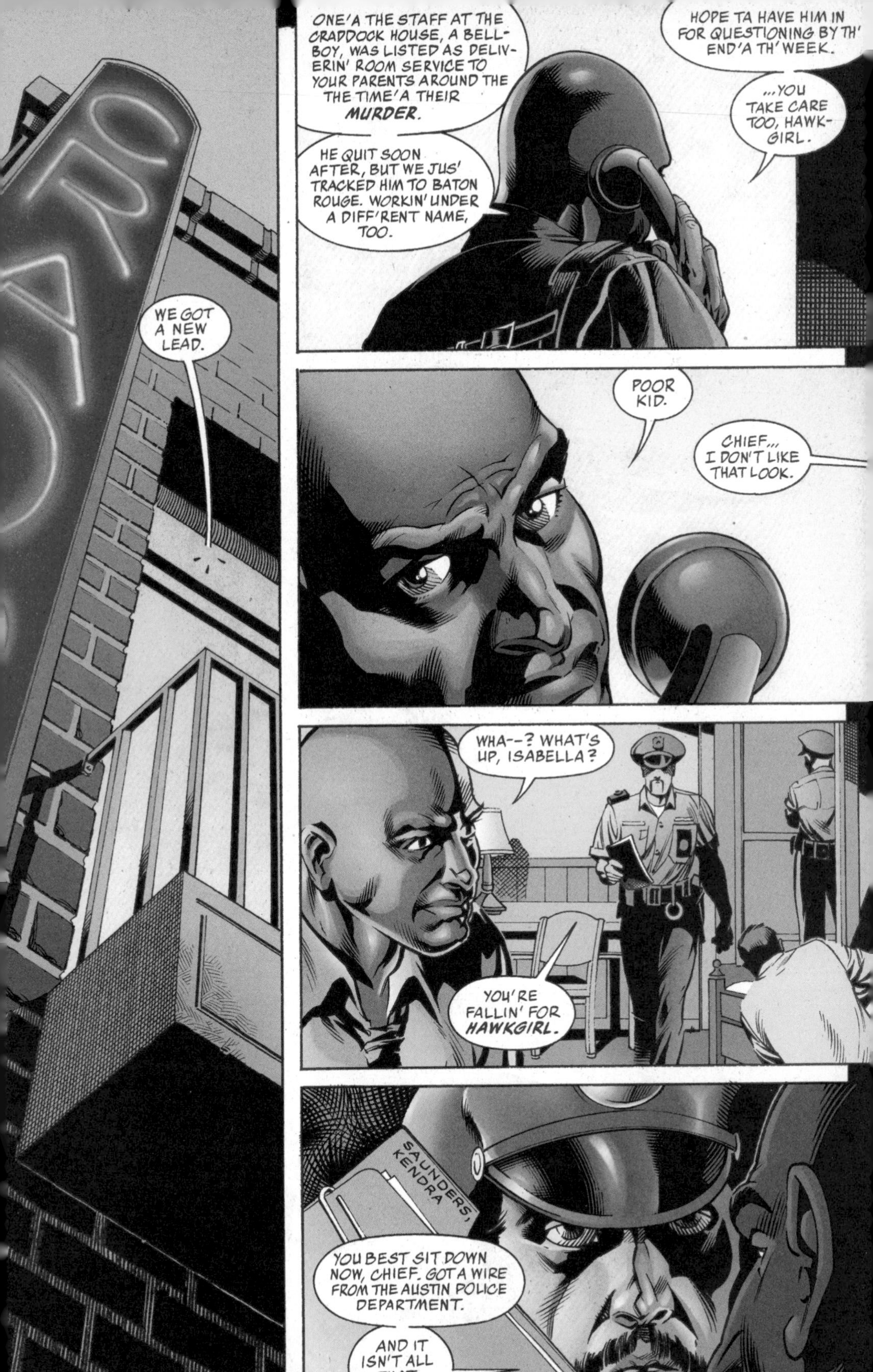
WE GOT A NEW LEAD.
ONE'A THE STAFF AT THE CRADDOCK HOUSE, A BELL-BOY, WAS LISTED AS DELIVERIN' ROOM SERVICE TO YOUR PARENTS AROUND THE THE TIME'A THEIR MURDER.
HE QUIT SOON AFTER, BUT WE JUS' TRACKED HIM TO BATON ROUGE. WORKIN' UNDER A DIFF'RENT NAME, TOO.
HOPE TA HAVE HIM IN FOR QUESTIONING BY TH' END'A TH' WEEK.
...YOU TAKE CARE TOO, HAWK-GIRL.
POOR KID.
CHIEF... I DON'T LIKE THAT LOOK.
WHA--? WHAT'S UP, ISABELLA?
YOU'RE FALLIN' FOR HAWKGIRL.
SAUNDERS, KENDRA
YOU BEST SIT DOWN NOW, CHIEF. GOT A WIRE FROM THE AUSTIN POLICE DEPARTMENT.
AND IT ISN'T ALL THAT GOOD.

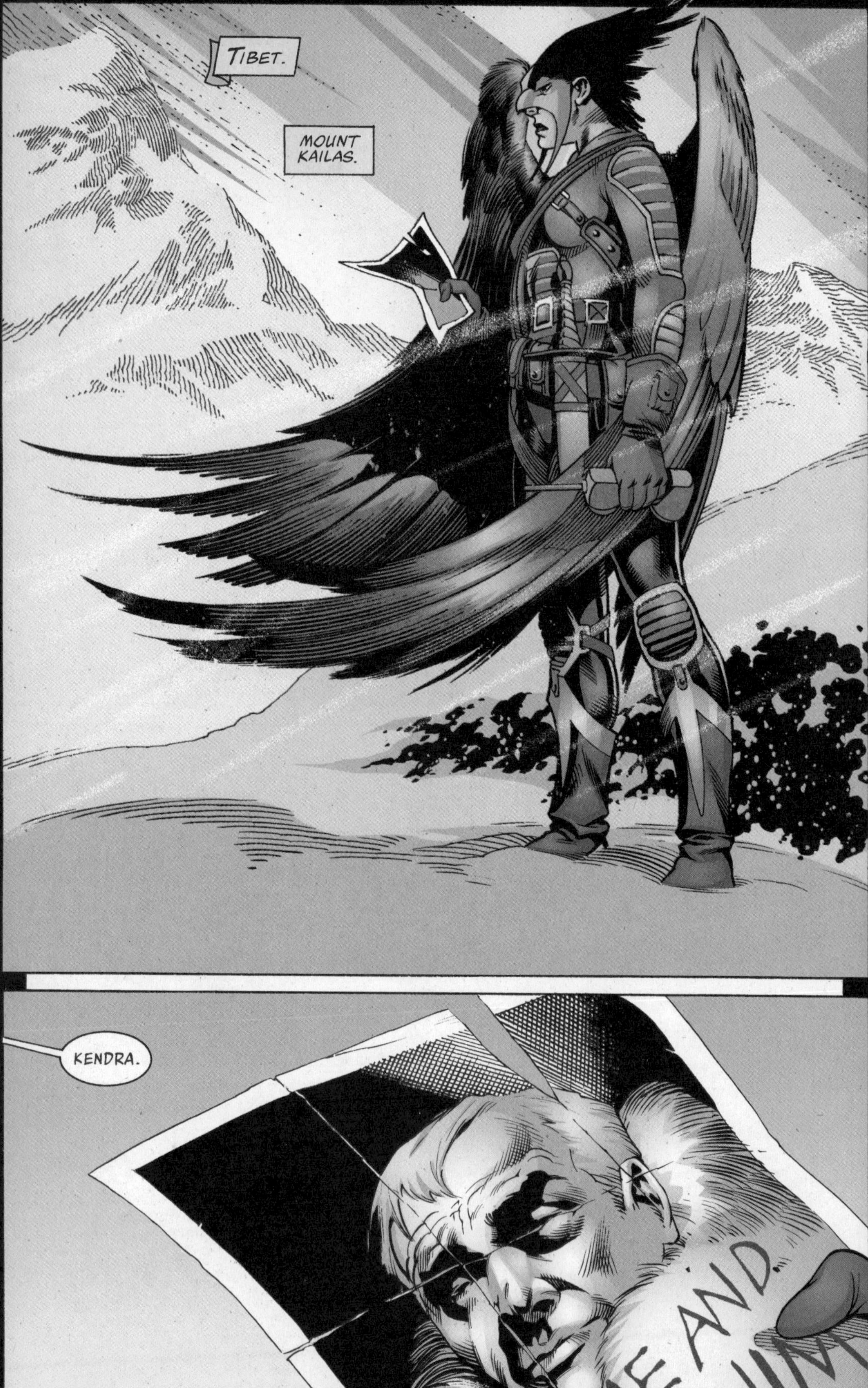
TIBET.
MOUNT KAILAS.
KENDRA.
ME AND.

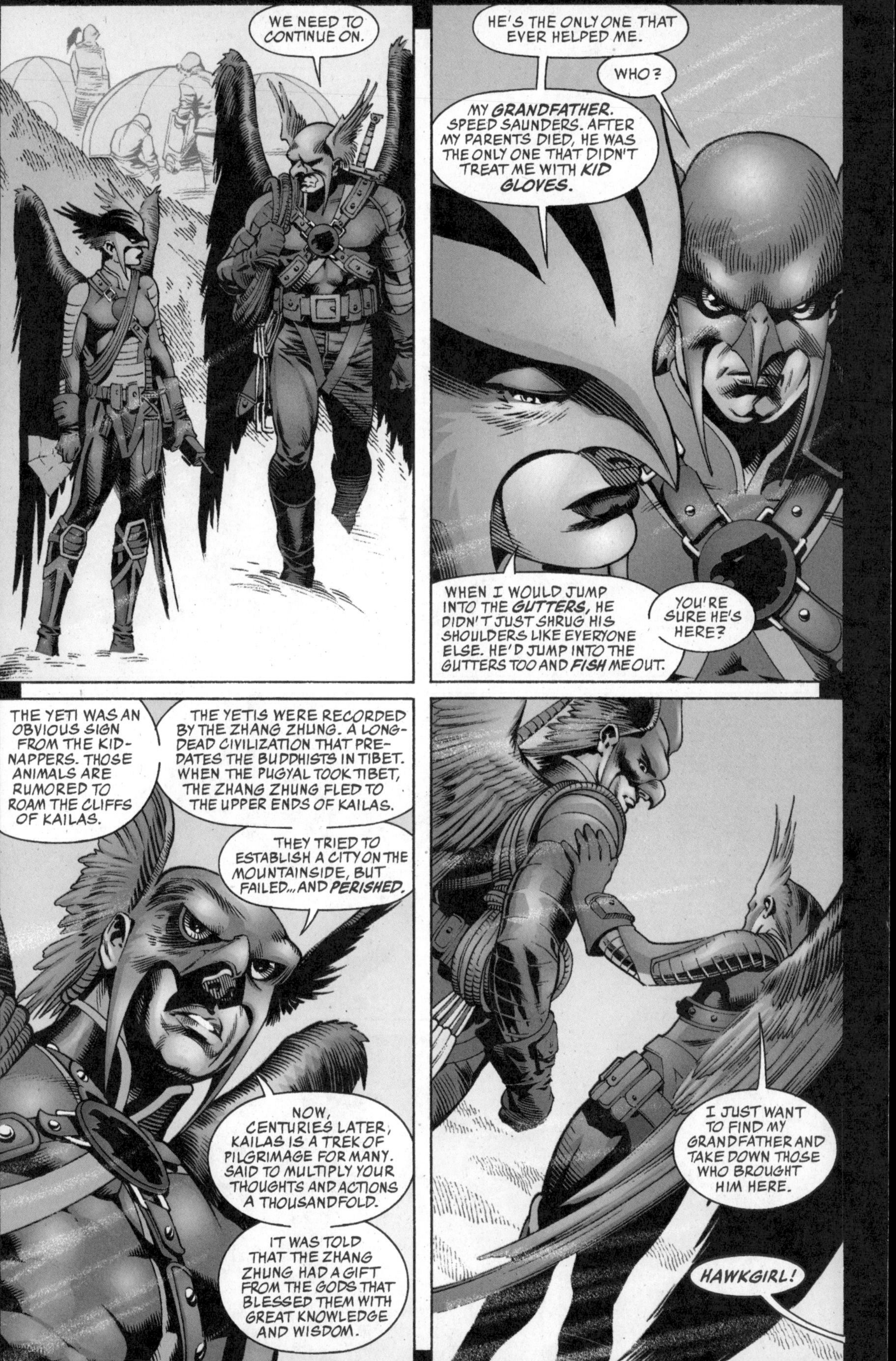
WE NEED TO CONTINUE ON.
HE'S THE ONLY ONE THAT EVER HELPED ME.
WHO?
MY GRANDFATHER. SPEED SAUNDERS. AFTER MY PARENTS DIED, HE WAS THE ONLY ONE THAT DIDN'T TREAT ME WITH KID GLOVES.
WHEN I WOULD JUMP INTO THE GUTTERS, HE DIDN'T JUST SHRUG HIS SHOULDERS LIKE EVERYONE ELSE. HE'D JUMP INTO THE GUTTERS TOO AND FISH ME OUT.
YOU'RE SURE HE'S HERE?
THE YETI WAS AN OBVIOUS SIGN FROM THE KID-NAPPERS. THOSE ANIMALS ARE RUMORED TO ROAM THE CLIFFS OF KAILAS.
THE YETIS WERE RECORDED BY THE ZHANG ZHUNG. A LONG-DEAD CIVILIZATION THAT PRE-DATES THE BUDDHISTS IN TIBET. WHEN THE PUGYAL TOOK TIBET, THE ZHANG ZHUNG FLED TO THE UPPER ENDS OF KAILAS.
THEY TRIED TO ESTABLISH A CITY ON THE MOUNTAINSIDE, BUT FAILED...AND PERISHED.
NOW, CENTURIES LATER, KAILAS IS A TREK OF PILGRIMAGE FOR MANY. SAID TO MULTIPLY YOUR THOUGHTS AND ACTIONS A THOUSANDFOLD.
IT WAS TOLD THAT THE ZHANG ZHUNG HAD A GIFT FROM THE GODS THAT BLESSED THEM WITH GREAT KNOWLEDGE AND WISDOM.
I JUST WANT TO FIND MY GRANDFATHER AND TAKE DOWN THOSE WHO BROUGHT HIM HERE.
HAWKGIRL!

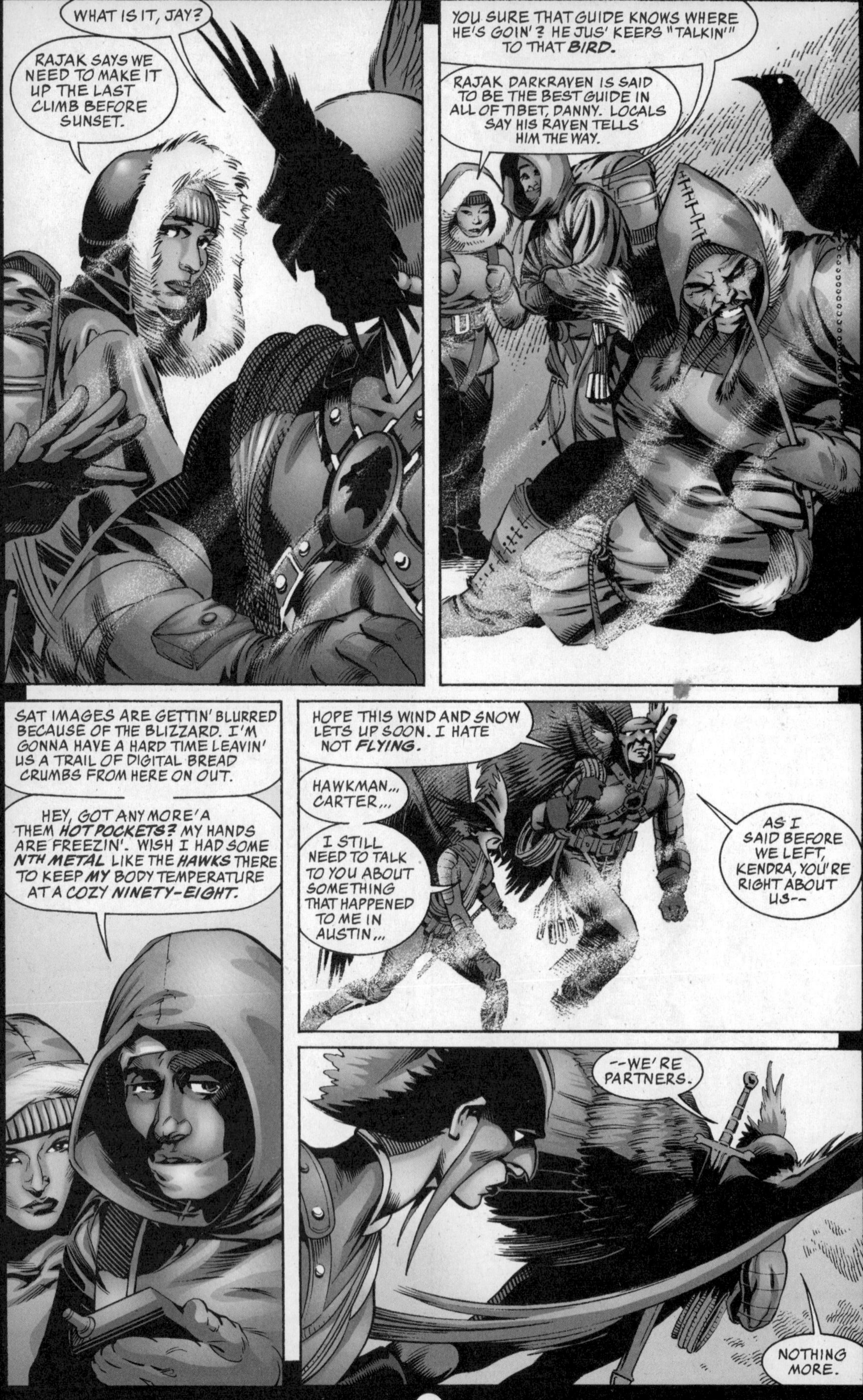

WHAT IS IT, JAY?
RAJAK SAYS WE NEED TO MAKE IT UP THE LAST CLIMB BEFORE SUNSET.
YOU SURE THAT GUIDE KNOWS WHERE HE'S GOIN'? HE JUS' KEEPS "TALKIN'" TO THAT BIRD.
RAJAK DARKRAVEN IS SAID TO BE THE BEST GUIDE IN ALL OF TIBET, DANNY. LOCALS SAY HIS RAVEN TELLS HIM THE WAY.
SAT IMAGES ARE GETTIN' BLURRED BECAUSE OF THE BLIZZARD. I'M GONNA HAVE A HARD TIME LEAVIN' US A TRAIL OF DIGITAL BREAD CRUMBS FROM HERE ON OUT.
HEY, GOT ANY MORE'A THEM HOT POCKETS? MY HANDS ARE FREEZIN'. WISH I HAD SOME NTH METAL LIKE THE HAWKS THERE TO KEEP MY BODY TEMPERATURE AT A COZY NINETY-EIGHT.
HOPE THIS WIND AND SNOW LETS UP SOON. I HATE NOT FLYING.
HAWKMAN... CARTER...
I STILL NEED TO TALK TO YOU ABOUT SOMETHING THAT HAPPENED TO ME IN AUSTIN...
AS I SAID BEFORE WE LEFT, KENDRA, YOU'RE RIGHT ABOUT US--
--WE'RE PARTNERS.
NOTHING MORE.

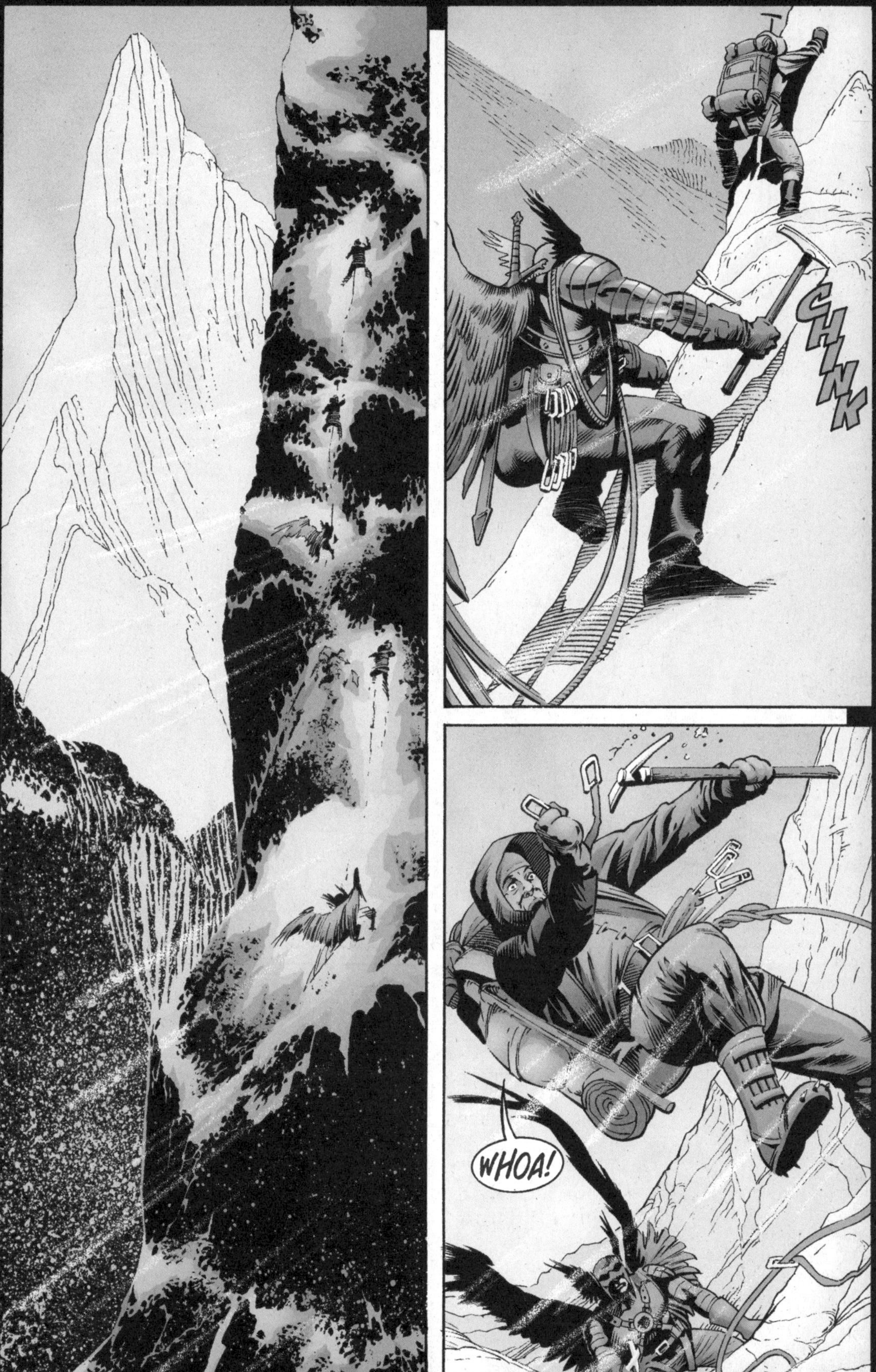
CHINK
WHOA!

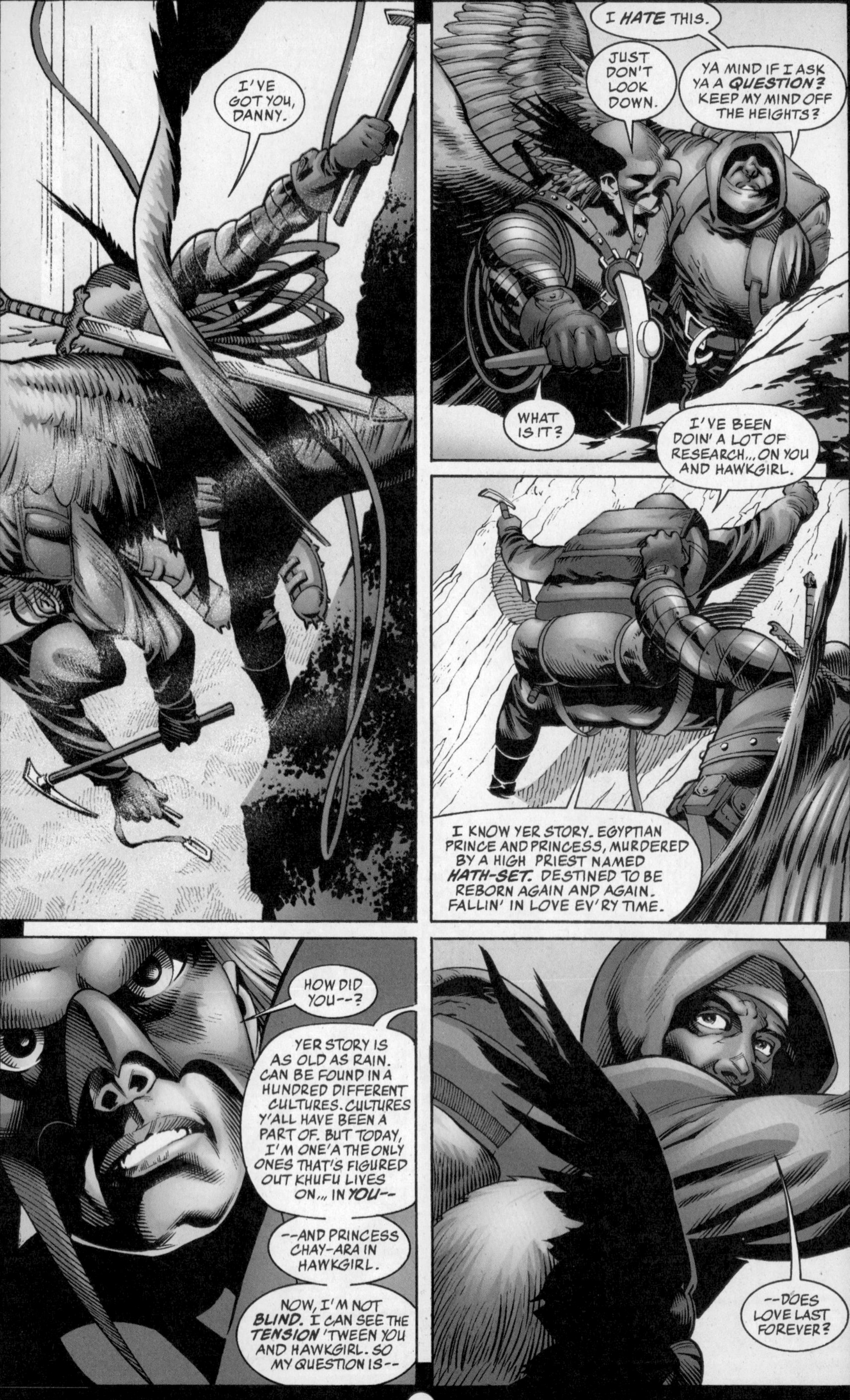

I'VE GOT YOU, DANNY.
I HATE THIS.
JUST DON'T LOOK DOWN.
YA MIND IF I ASK YA A QUESTION? KEEP MY MIND OFF THE HEIGHTS?
WHAT IS IT?
I'VE BEEN DOIN' A LOT OF RESEARCH... ON YOU AND HAWKGIRL.
I KNOW YER STORY. EGYPTIAN PRINCE AND PRINCESS, MURDERED BY A HIGH PRIEST NAMED HATH-SET. DESTINED TO BE REBORN AGAIN AND AGAIN. FALLIN' IN LOVE EV'RY TIME.
HOW DID YOU--?
YER STORY IS AS OLD AS RAIN. CAN BE FOUND IN A HUNDRED DIFFERENT CULTURES. CULTURES Y'ALL HAVE BEEN A PART OF. BUT TODAY, I'M ONE'A THE ONLY ONES THAT'S FIGURED OUT KHUFU LIVES ON... IN YOU--
--AND PRINCESS CHAY-ARA IN HAWKGIRL.
NOW, I'M NOT BLIND. I CAN SEE THE TENSION 'TWEEN YOU AND HAWKGIRL. SO MY QUESTION IS--
--DOES LOVE LAST FOREVER?

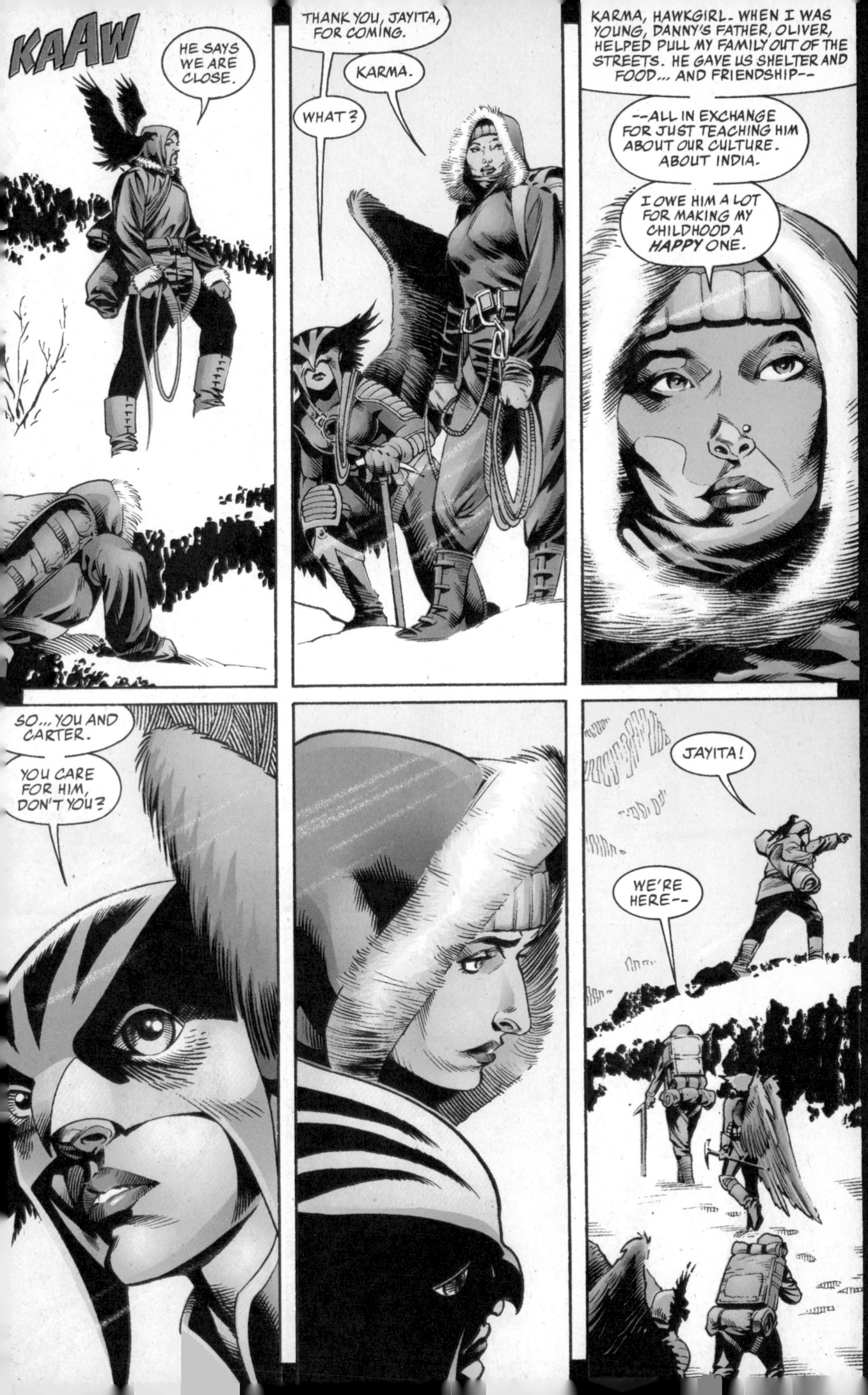
KAAW
HE SAYS WE ARE CLOSE.
THANK YOU, JAYITA, FOR COMING.
KARMA.
WHAT?
KARMA, HAWKGIRL. WHEN I WAS YOUNG, DANNY'S FATHER, OLIVER, HELPED PULL MY FAMILY OUT OF THE STREETS. HE GAVE US SHELTER AND FOOD... AND FRIENDSHIP--
--ALL IN EXCHANGE FOR JUST TEACHING HIM ABOUT OUR CULTURE. ABOUT INDIA.
I OWE HIM A LOT FOR MAKING MY CHILDHOOD A HAPPY ONE.
SO... YOU AND CARTER.
YOU CARE FOR HIM, DON'T YOU?
JAYITA!
WE'RE HERE--

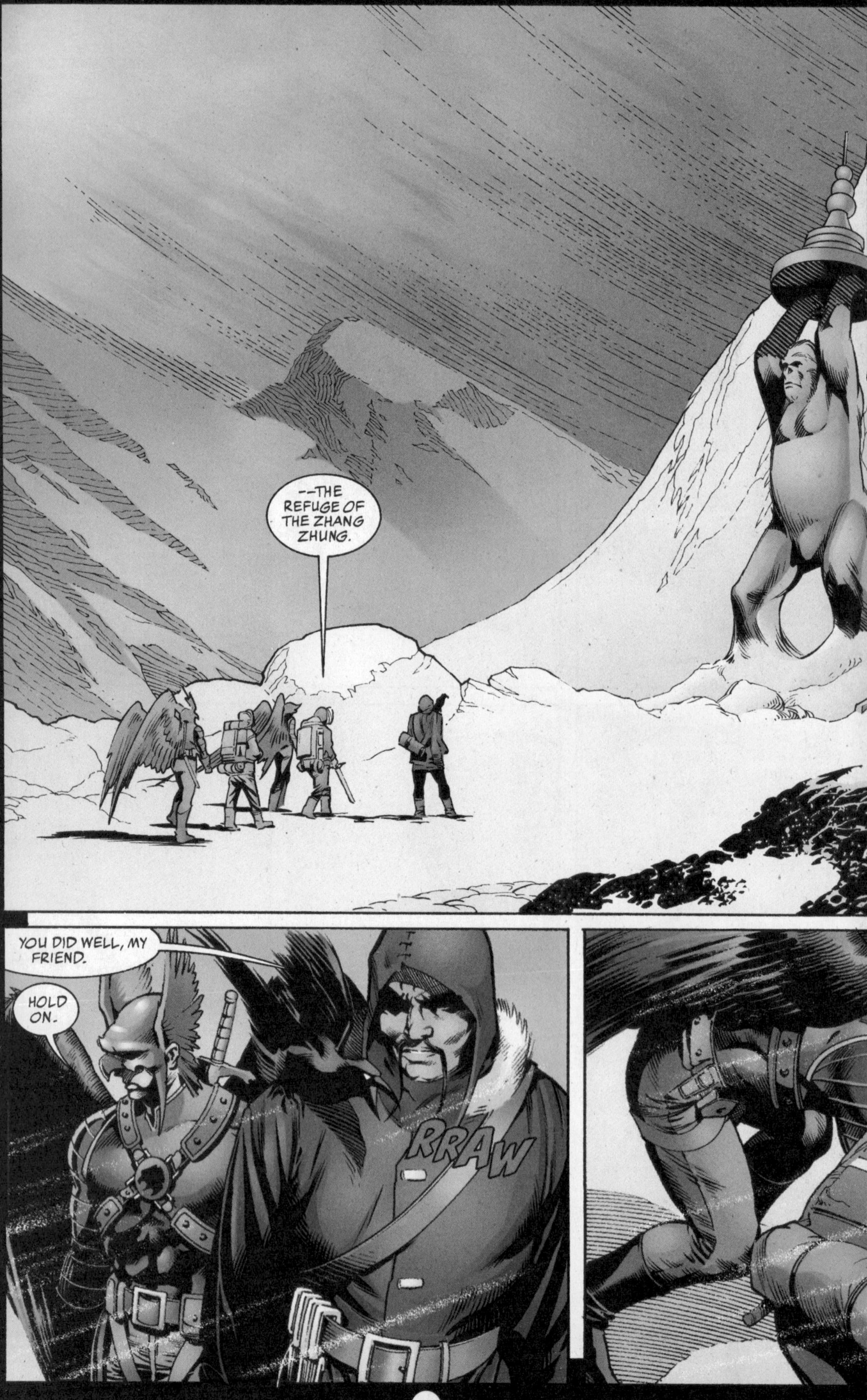
--THE REFUGE OF THE ZHANG ZHUNG.
YOU DID WELL, MY FRIEND.
HOLD ON.
RRAW

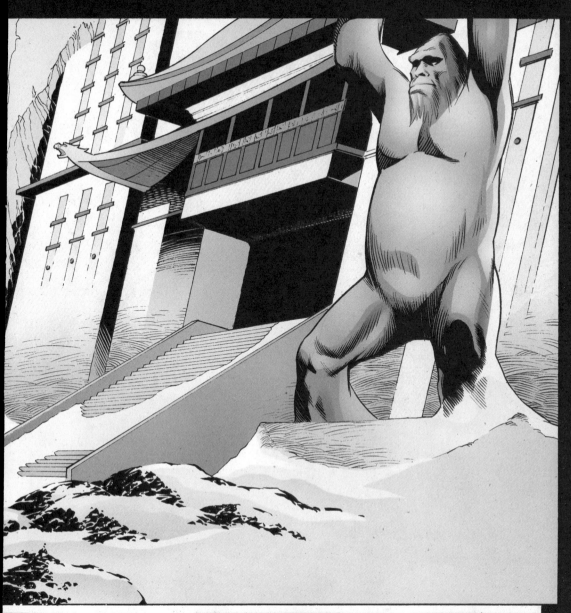

WHAT IS IT?

TROUBLE.

RRRRRRRRUUUUUUUUUU

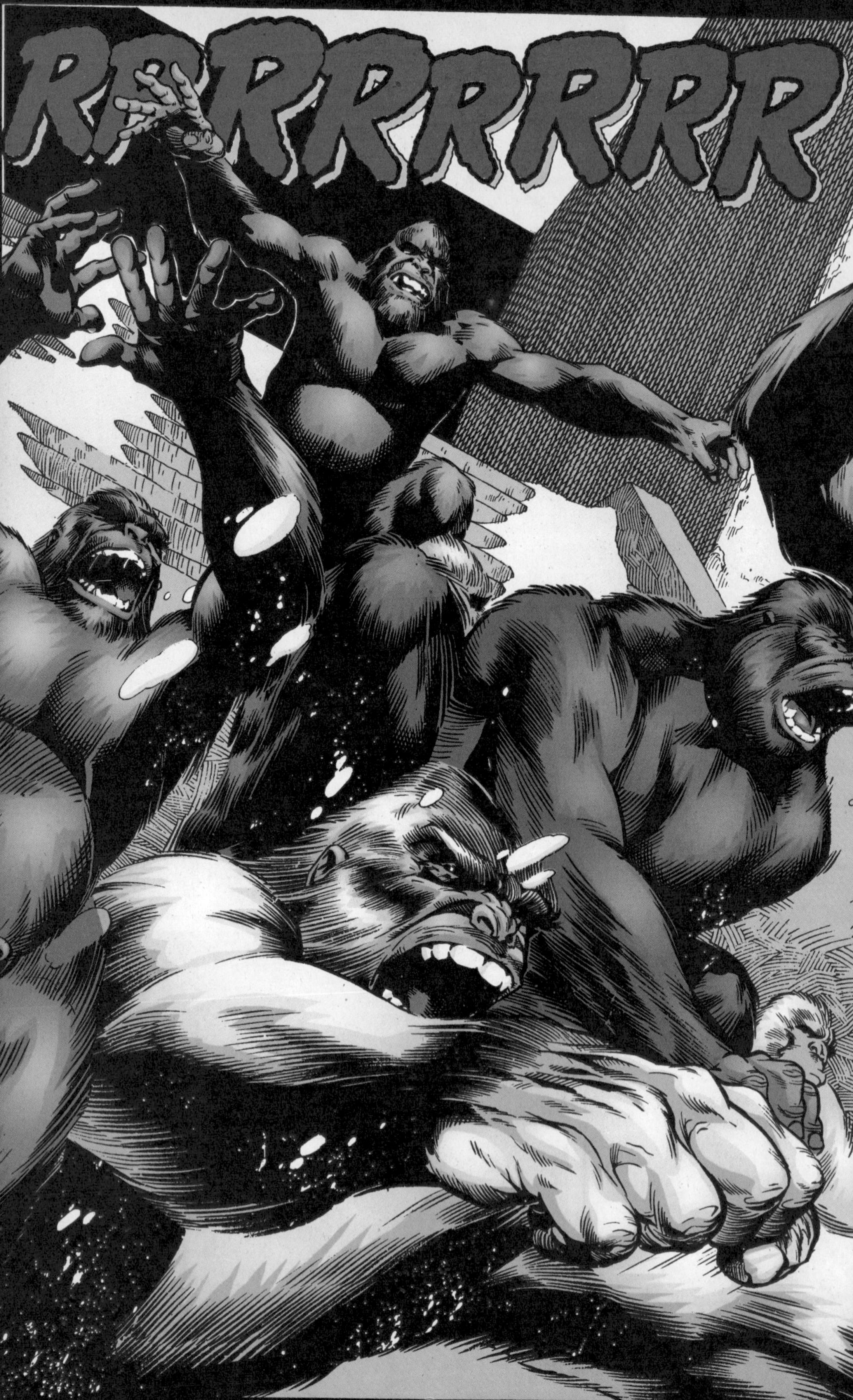
RRRRRRRRR

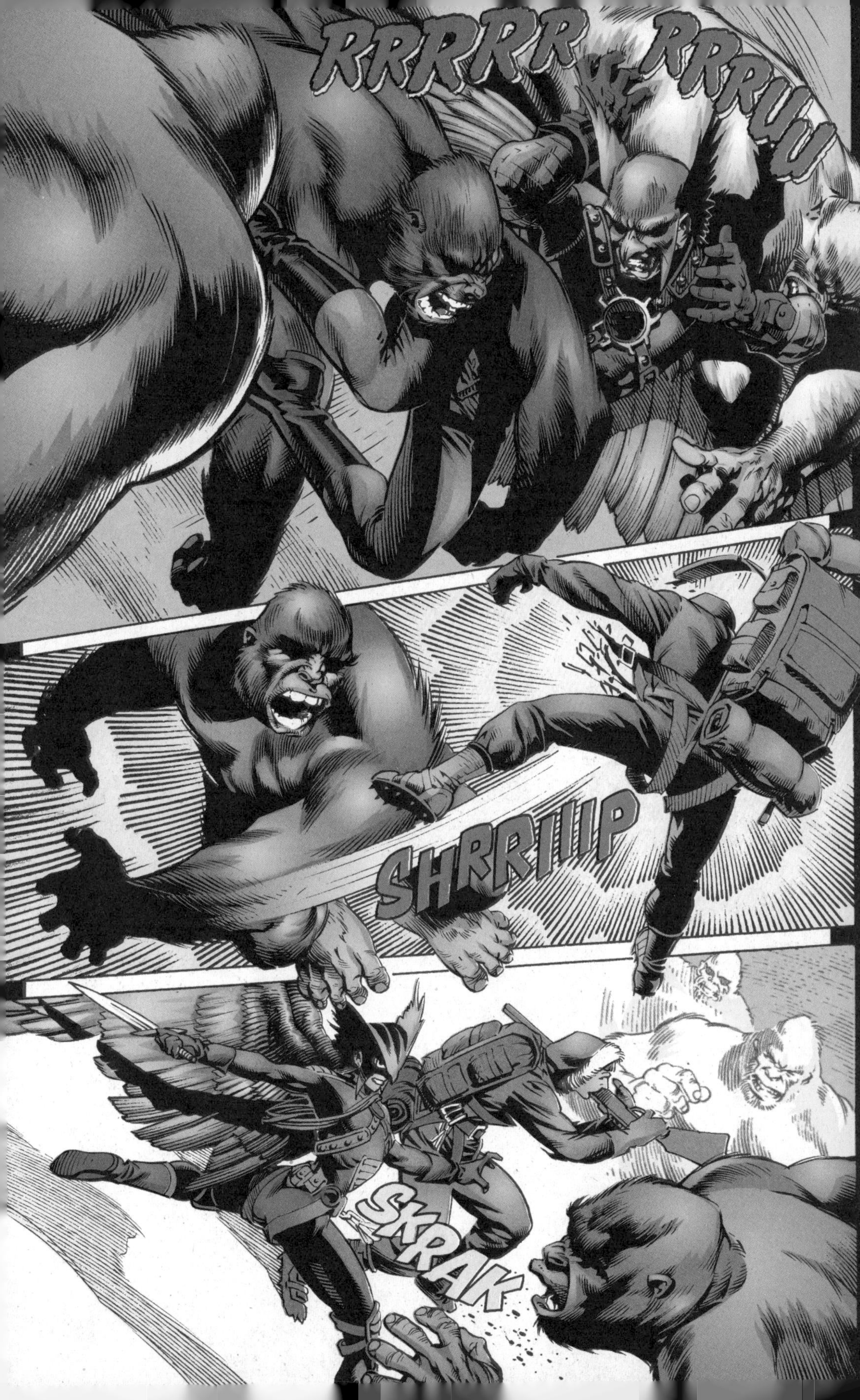

RRRRR
RRRUU
SHRRIIIP
SKRAK

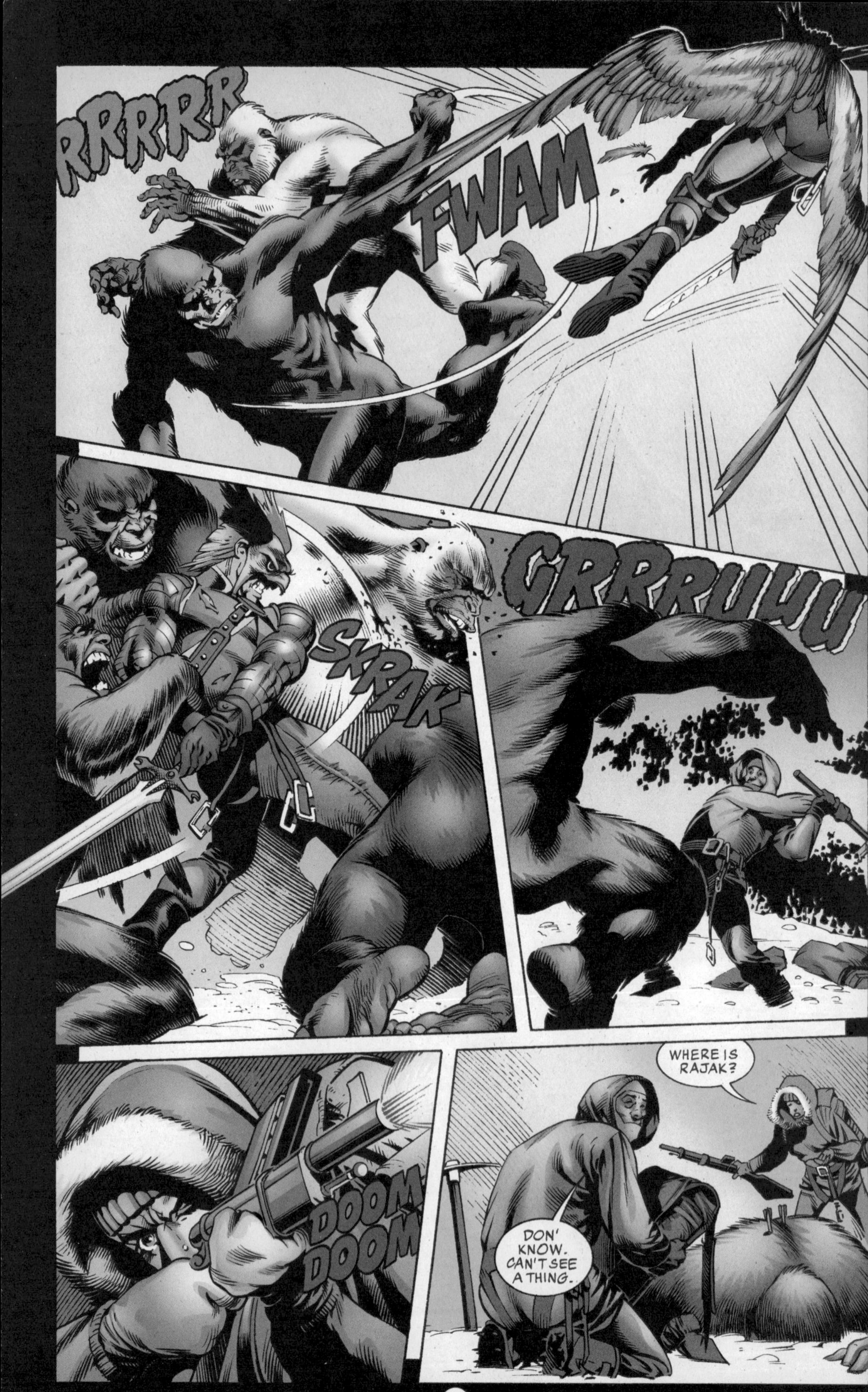
RRRRR
FWAM
GRRRUUU
SKRAK
DOOM DOOM
WHERE IS RAJAK?
DON' KNOW. CAN'T SEE A THING.

KENDRA?!
RRRRRRRRRRRR
WHAT DO THEY WANT?!
FWOOM!
WARM BLOOD, I'D GUESS!
FWAM
FWAM

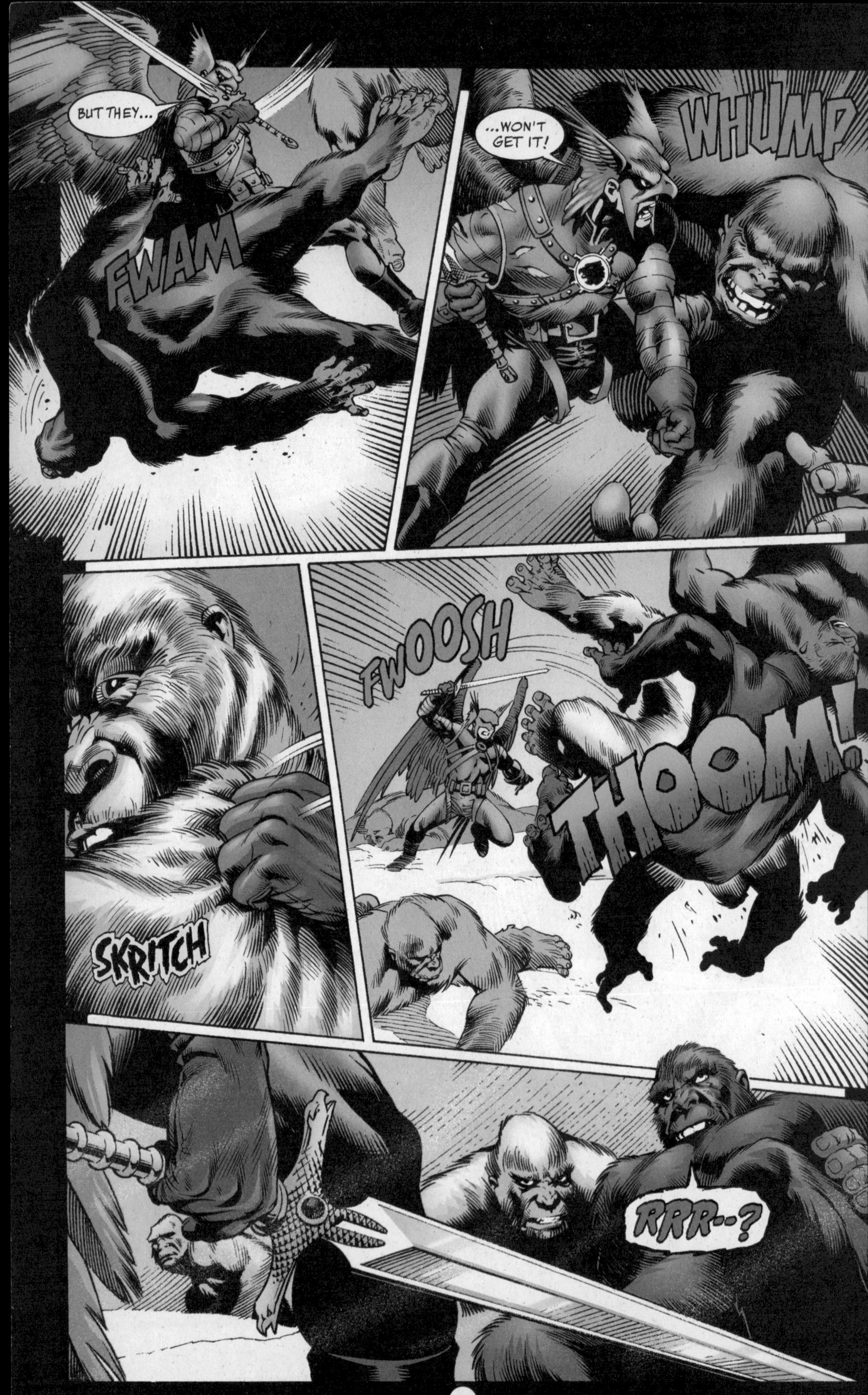
BUT THEY...
FWAM
...WON'T GET IT!
WHUMP
SKRITCH
FWOOSH
THOOM!
RRR--?

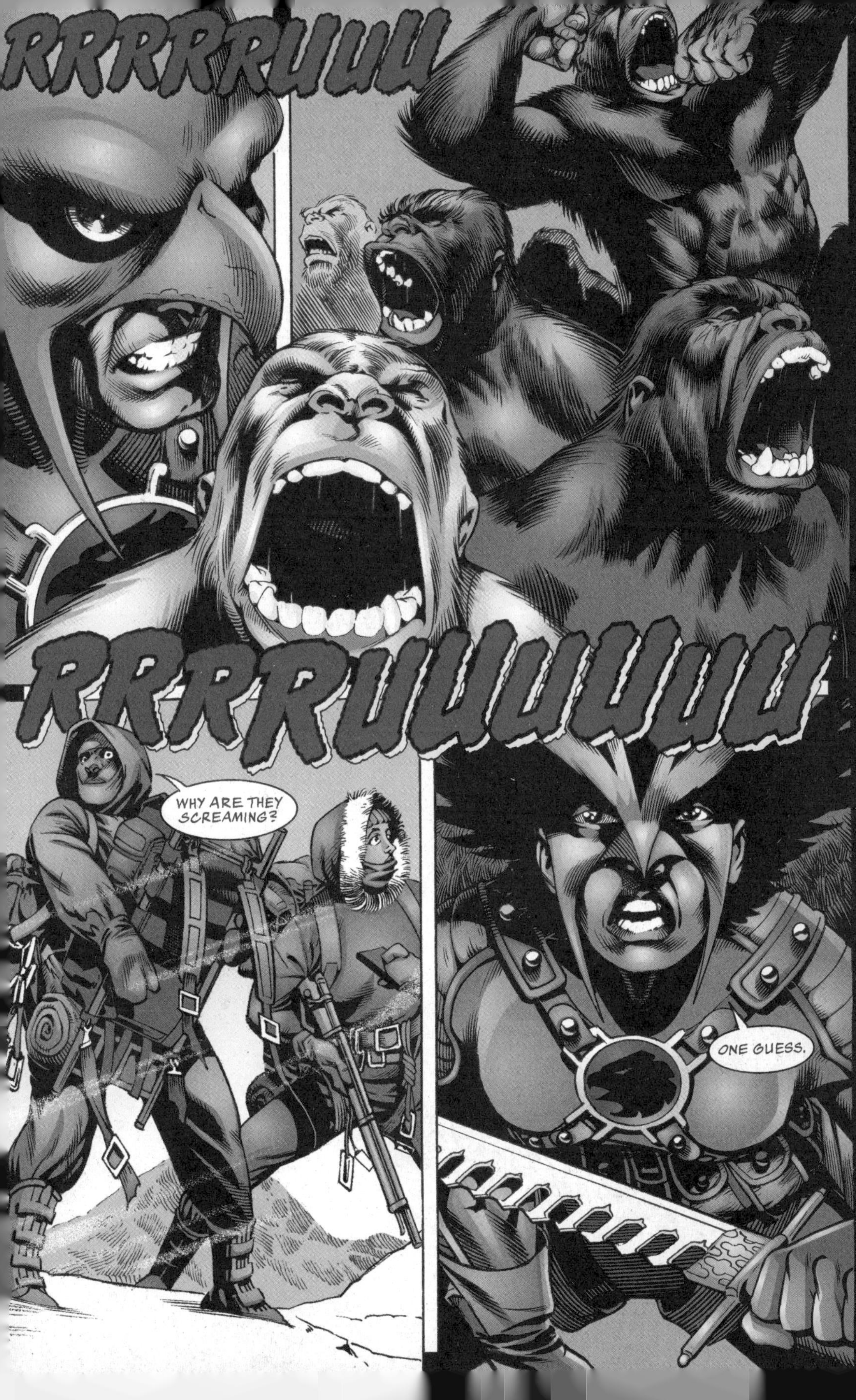

RRRRRUUU
RRRRUUUUUU
WHY ARE THEY SCREAMING?
ONE GUESS.

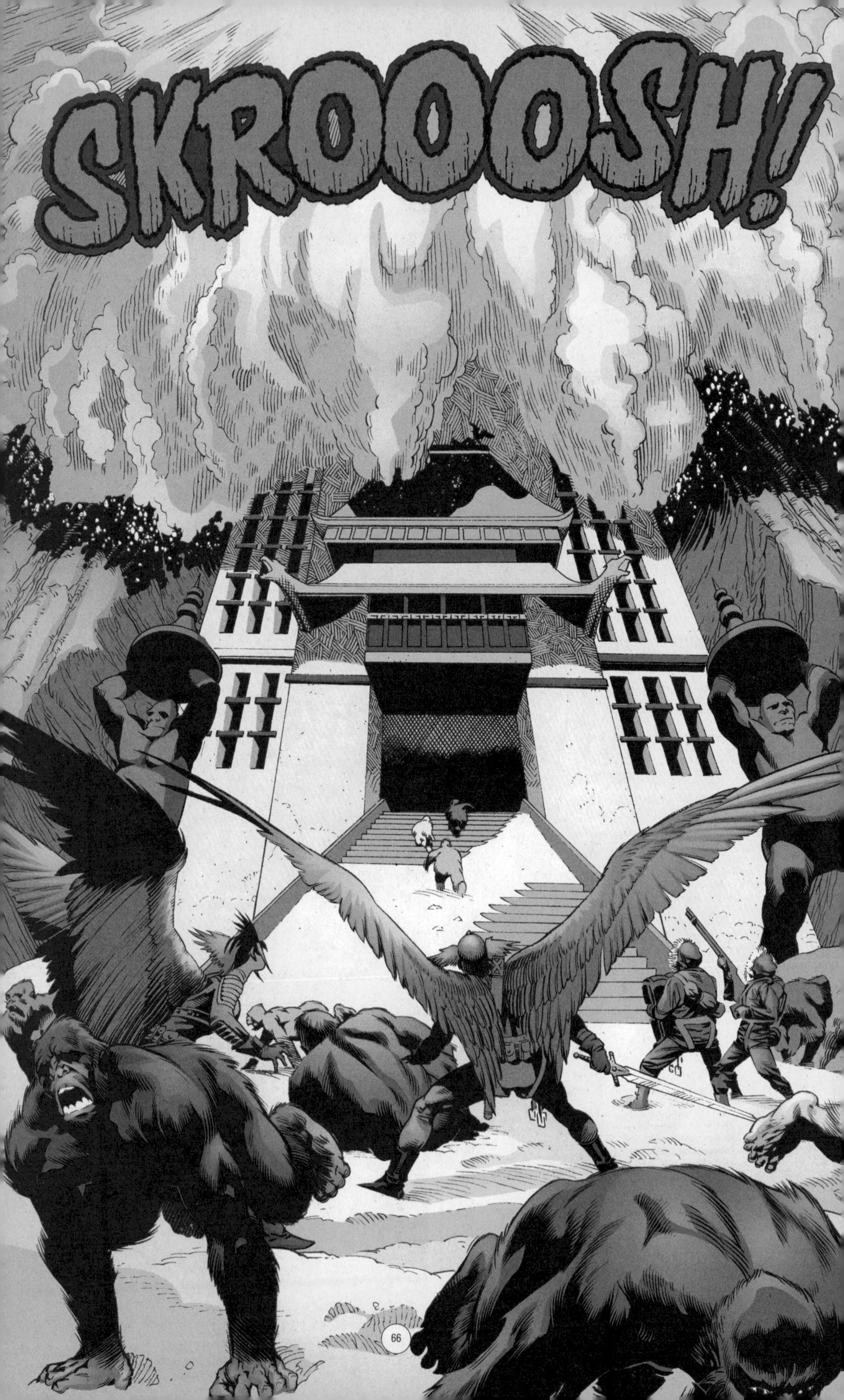
SKROOOSH!

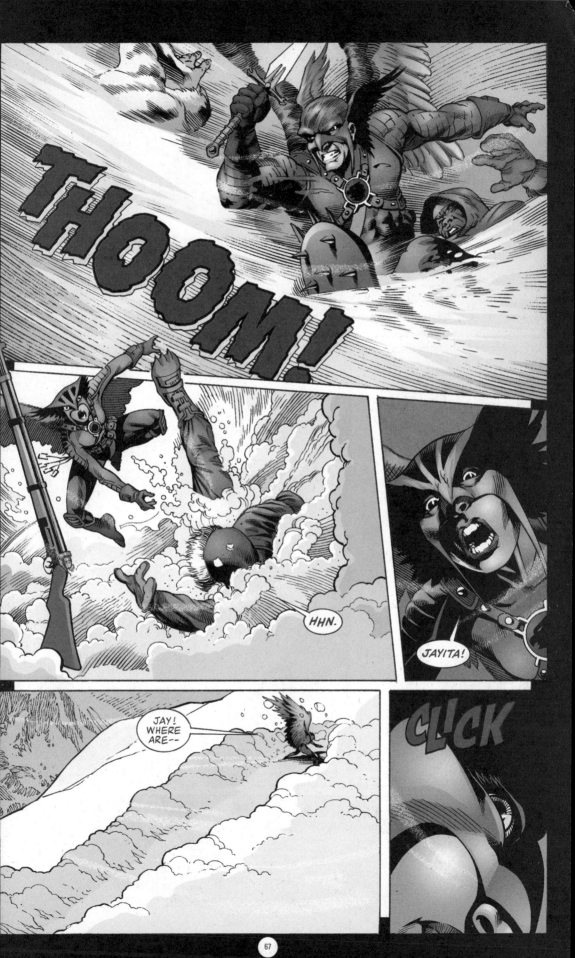

THOOM!

HHN.

JAYITA!

JAY! WHERE ARE--

CLICK

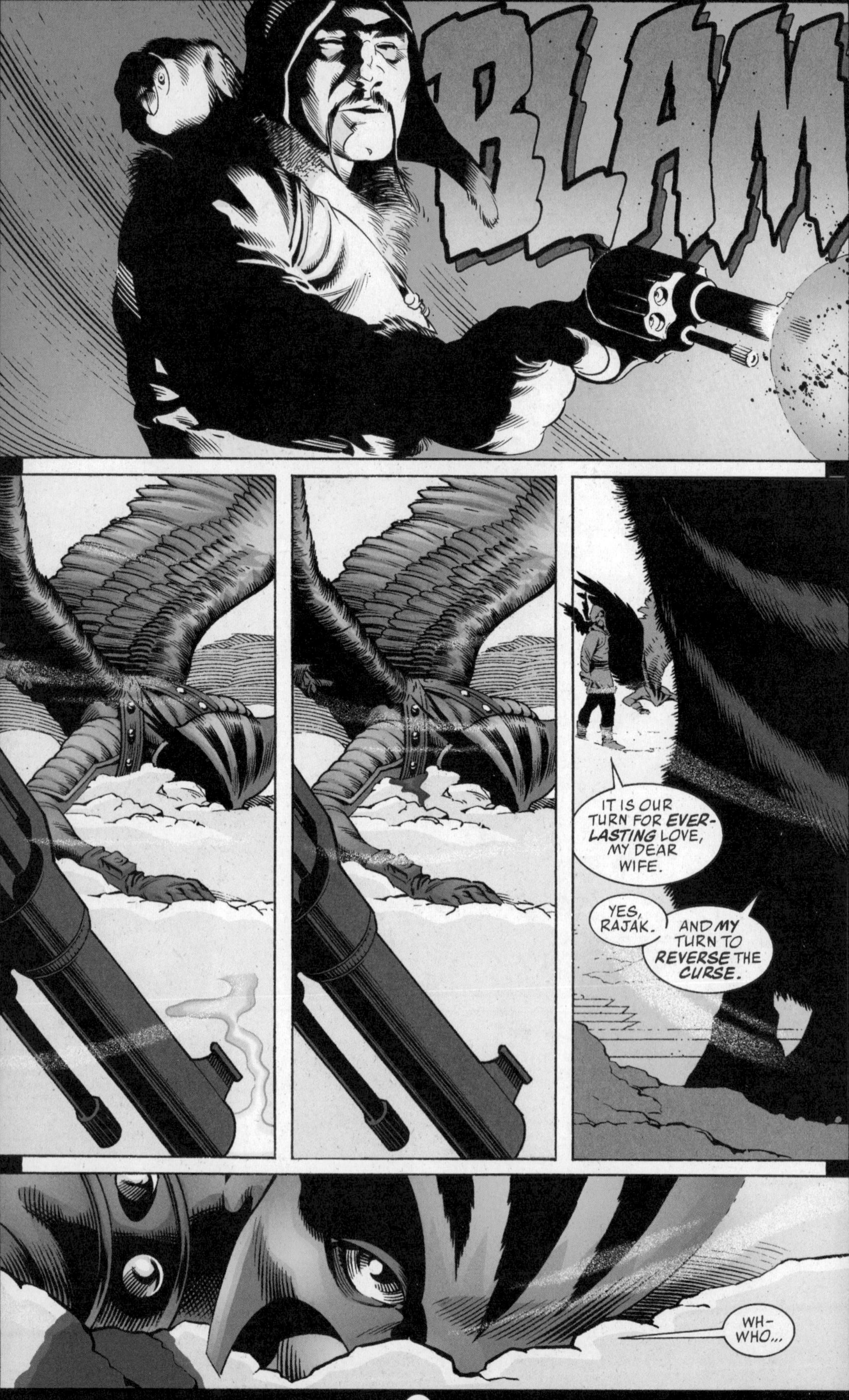
BLAM
IT IS OUR TURN FOR EVER-LASTING LOVE, MY DEAR WIFE.
YES, RAJAK.
AND MY TURN TO REVERSE THE CURSE.
WH- WHO...

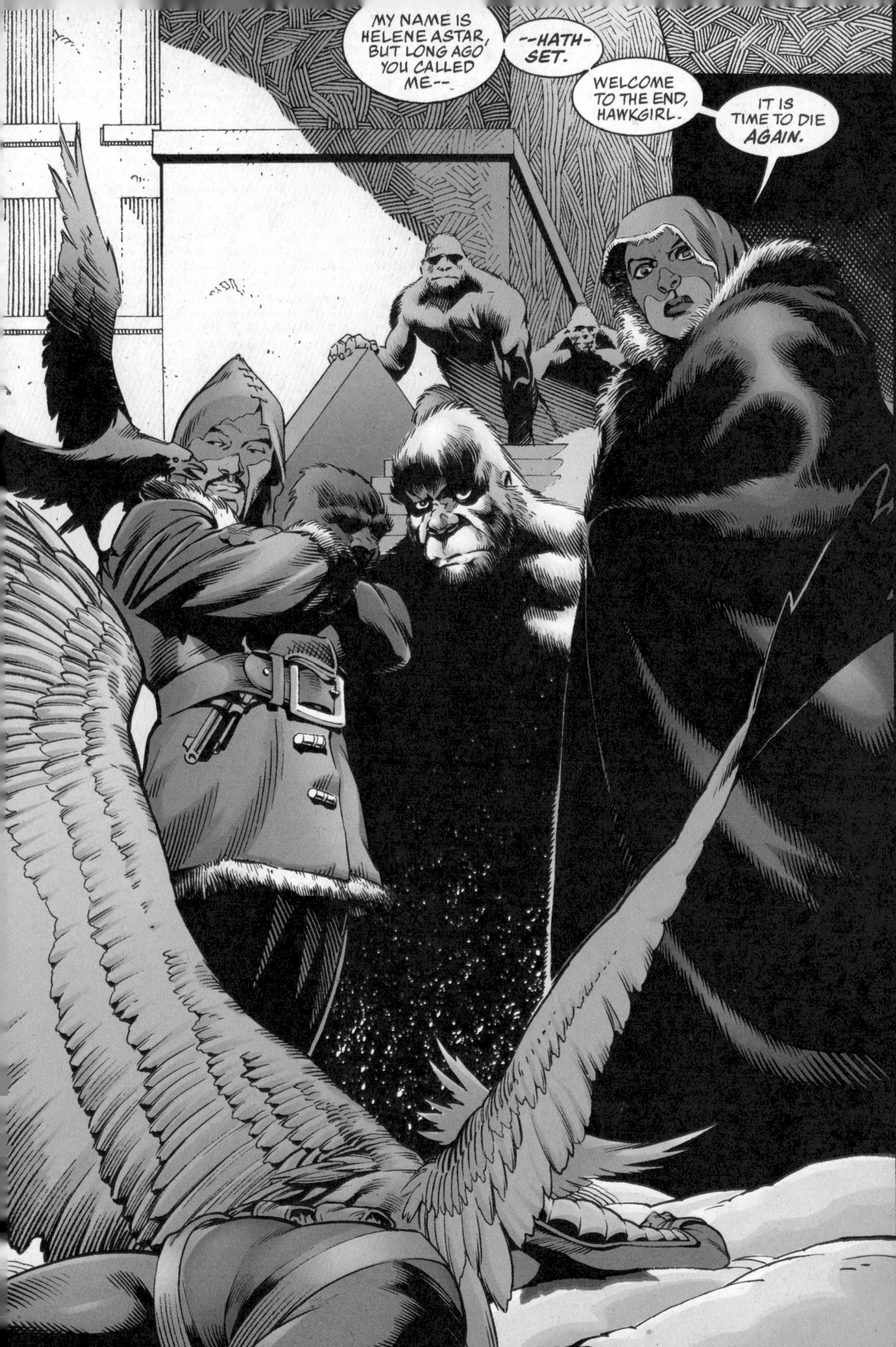
MY NAME IS HELENE ASTAR, BUT LONG AGO YOU CALLED ME--
--HATH-SET.
WELCOME TO THE END, HAWKGIRL.
IT IS TIME TO DIE AGAIN.

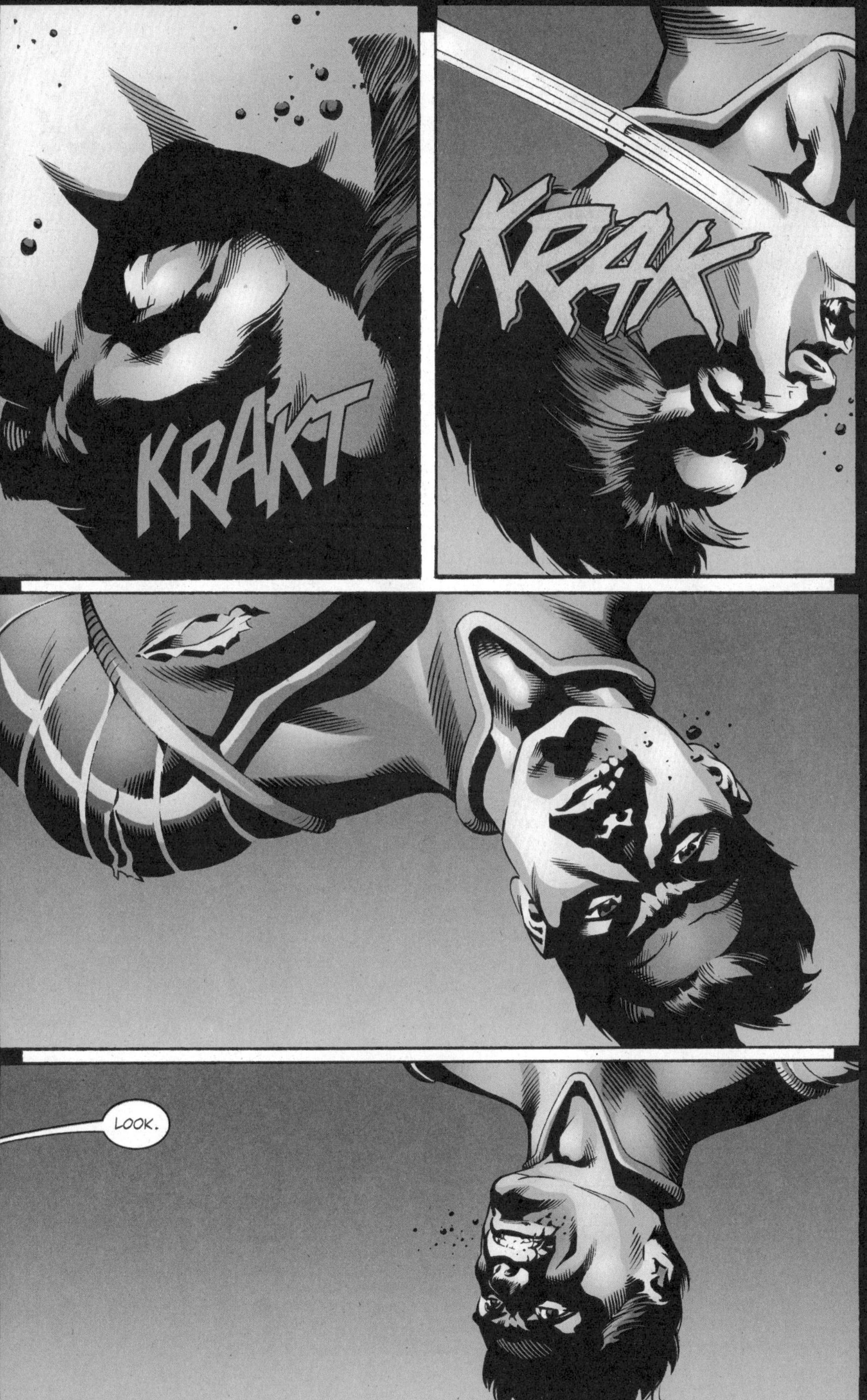
KRAKT
KRAK
LOOK.

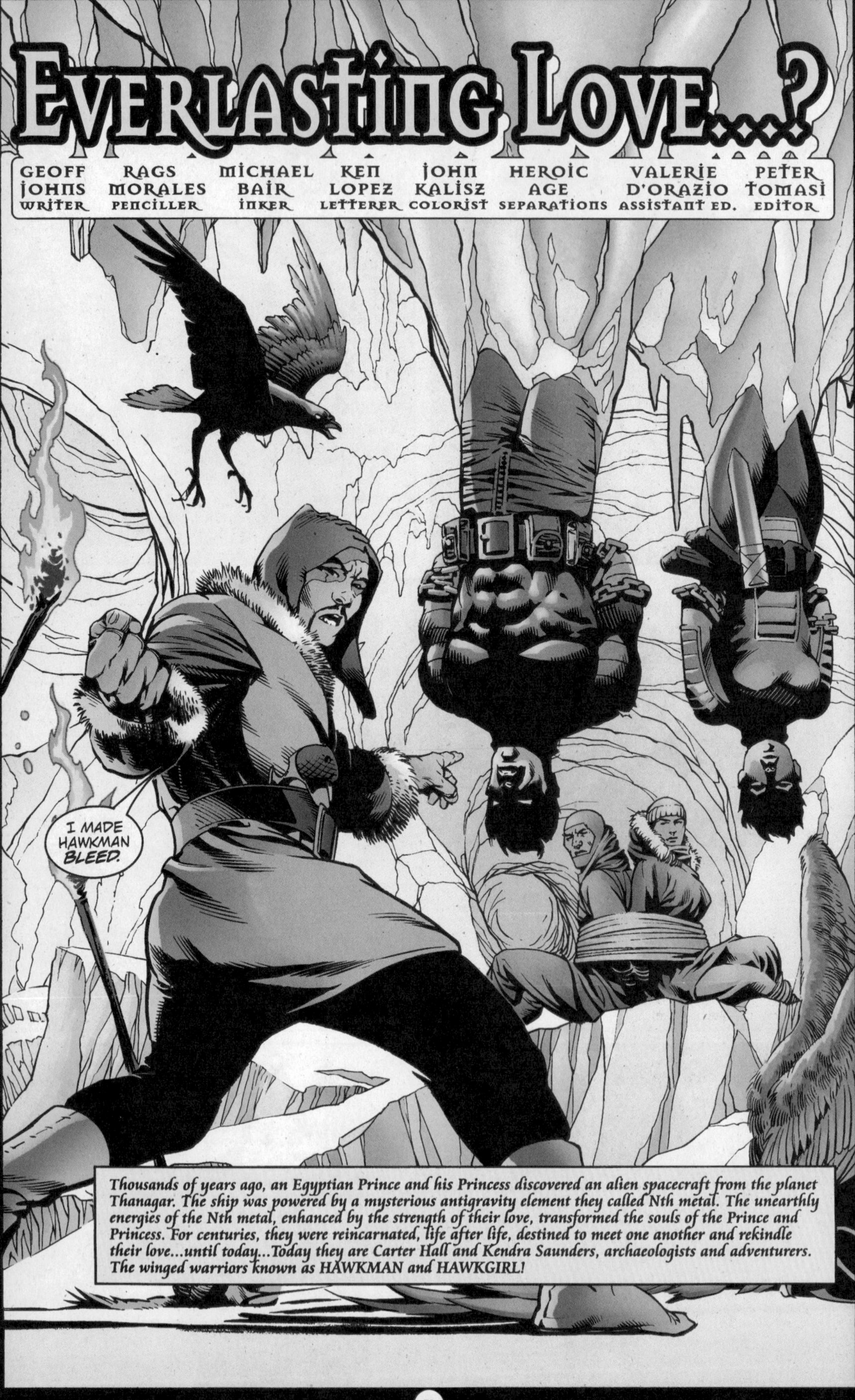
EVERLASTING LOVE...?
GEOFF JOHNS WRITER
RAGS MORALES PENCILLER
MICHAEL BAIR INKER
KEN LOPEZ LETTERER
JOHN KALISZ COLORIST
HEROIC AGE SEPARATIONS
VALERIE D'ORAZIO ASSISTANT ED.
PETER TOMASI EDITOR
I MADE HAWKMAN BLEED.
Thousands of years ago, an Egyptian Prince and his Princess discovered an alien spacecraft from the planet Thanagar. The ship was powered by a mysterious antigravity element they called Nth metal. The unearthly energies of the Nth metal, enhanced by the strength of their love, transformed the souls of the Prince and Princess. For centuries, they were reincarnated, life after life, destined to meet one another and rekindle their love...until today...Today they are Carter Hall and Kendra Saunders, archaeologists and adventurers. The winged warriors known as HAWKMAN and HAWKGIRL!

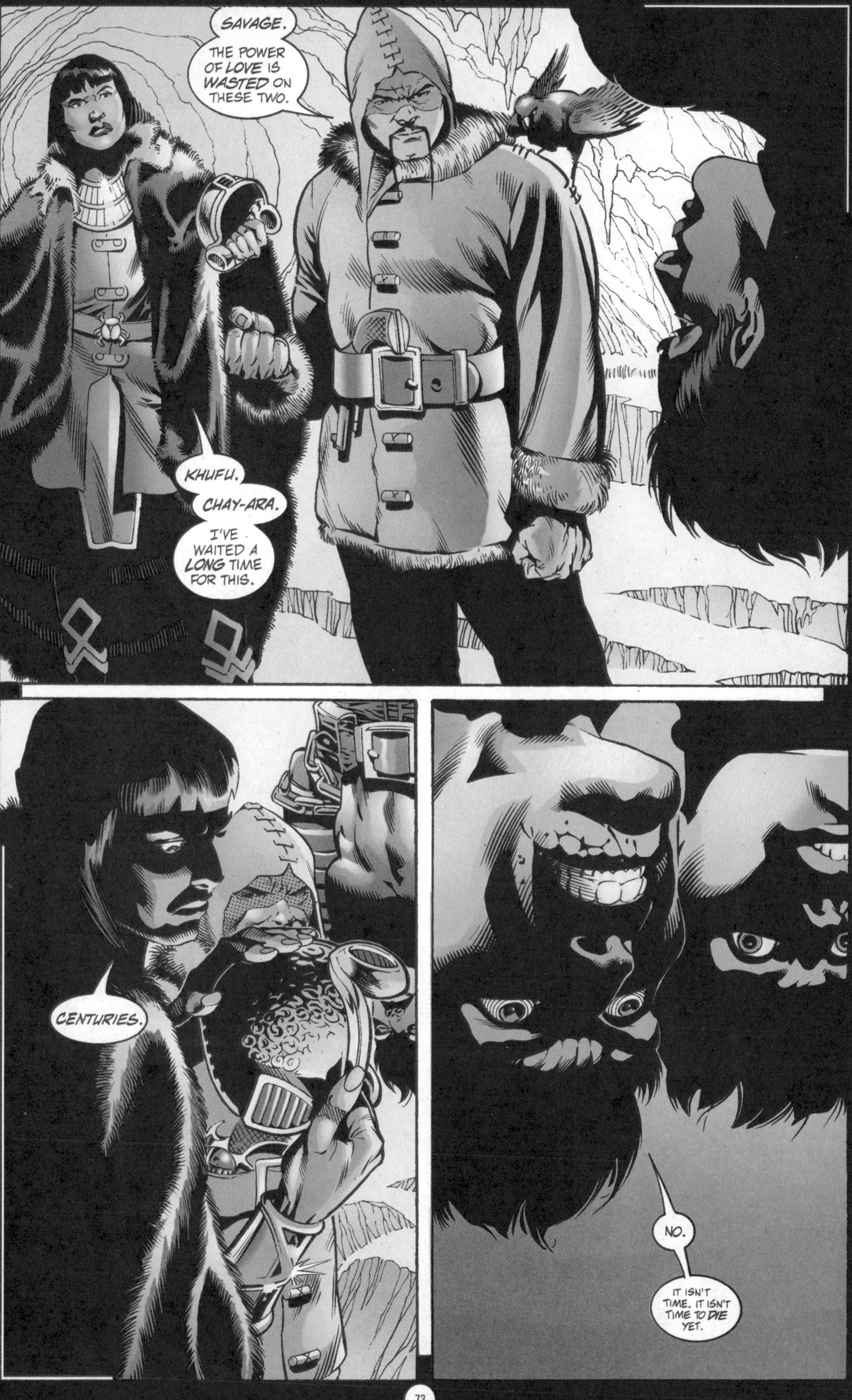
SAVAGE.
THE POWER OF LOVE IS WASTED ON THESE TWO.
KHUFU.
CHAY-ARA.
I'VE WAITED A LONG TIME FOR THIS.
CENTURIES.
NO.
IT ISN'T TIME. IT ISN'T TIME TO DIE YET.

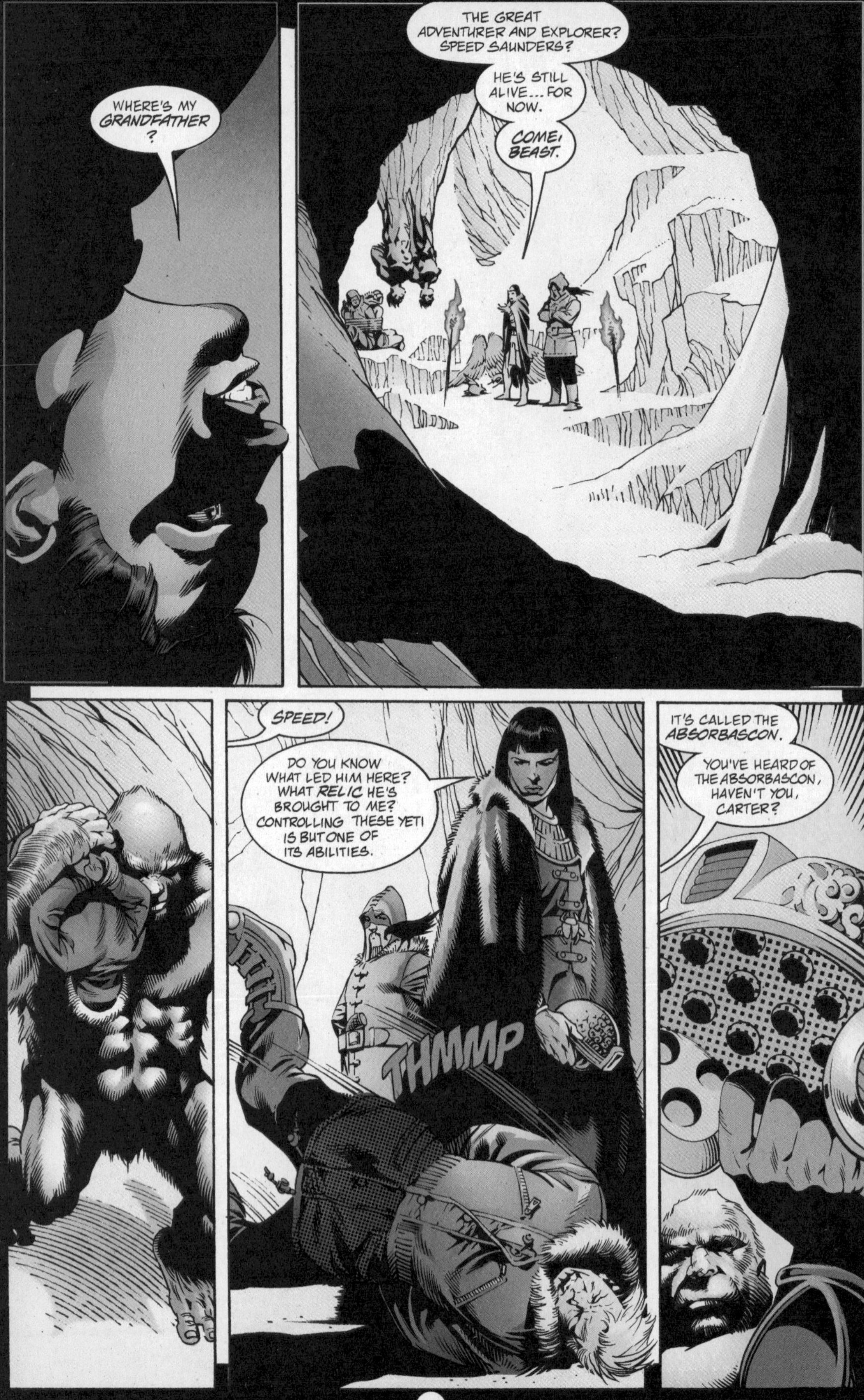
WHERE'S MY GRANDFATHER ?
THE GREAT ADVENTURER AND EXPLORER? SPEED SAUNDERS?
HE'S STILL ALIVE... FOR NOW.
COME, BEAST.
SPEED!
DO YOU KNOW WHAT LED HIM HERE? WHAT RELIC HE'S BROUGHT TO ME? CONTROLLING THESE YETI IS BUT ONE OF ITS ABILITIES.
THMMP
IT'S CALLED THE ABSORBASCON.
YOU'VE HEARD OF THE ABSORBASCON, HAVEN'T YOU, CARTER?

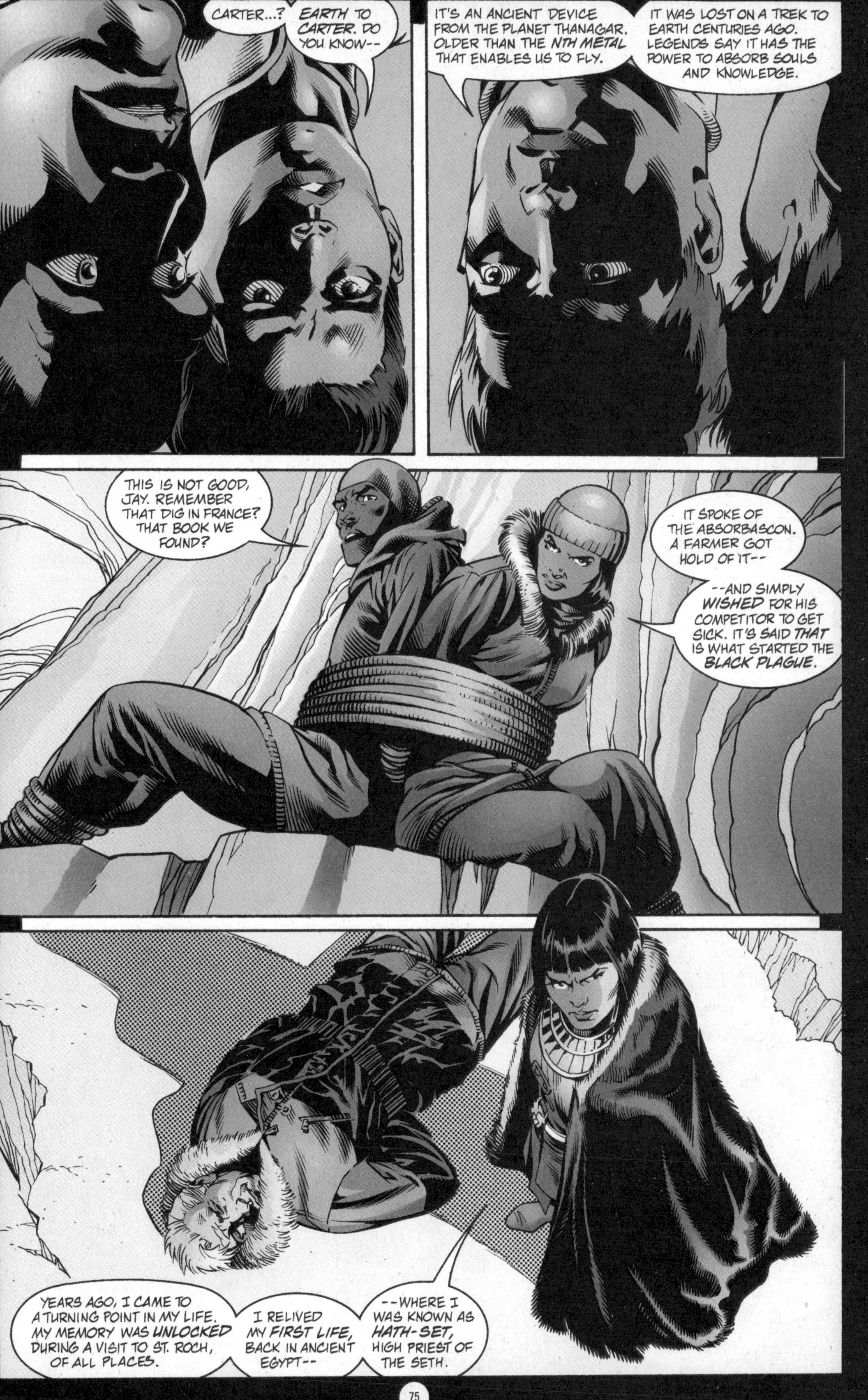

CARTER...? EARTH TO CARTER. DO YOU KNOW--
IT'S AN ANCIENT DEVICE FROM THE PLANET THANAGAR. OLDER THAN THE NTH METAL THAT ENABLES US TO FLY.
IT WAS LOST ON A TREK TO EARTH CENTURIES AGO. LEGENDS SAY IT HAS THE POWER TO ABSORB SOULS AND KNOWLEDGE.
THIS IS NOT GOOD, JAY. REMEMBER THAT DIG IN FRANCE? THAT BOOK WE FOUND?
IT SPOKE OF THE ABSORBASCON. A FARMER GOT HOLD OF IT--
--AND SIMPLY WISHED FOR HIS COMPETITOR TO GET SICK. IT'S SAID THAT IS WHAT STARTED THE BLACK PLAGUE.
YEARS AGO, I CAME TO A TURNING POINT IN MY LIFE. MY MEMORY WAS UNLOCKED DURING A VISIT TO ST. ROCH, OF ALL PLACES.
I RELIVED MY FIRST LIFE, BACK IN ANCIENT EGYPT--
--WHERE I WAS KNOWN AS HATH-SET, HIGH PRIEST OF THE SETH.

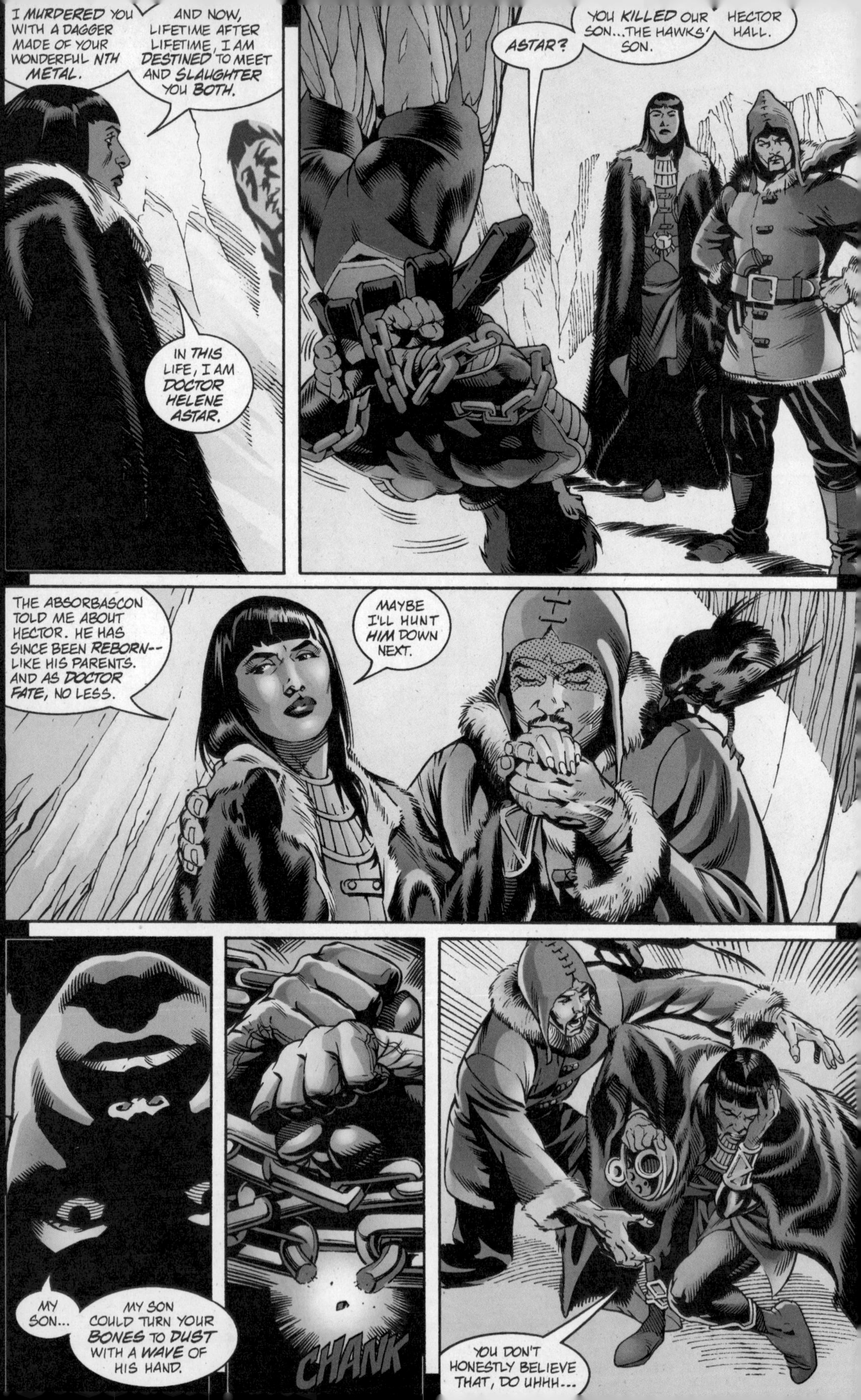
I MURDERED YOU WITH A DAGGER MADE OF YOUR WONDERFUL NTH METAL.
AND NOW, LIFETIME AFTER LIFETIME, I AM DESTINED TO MEET AND SLAUGHTER YOU BOTH.
IN THIS LIFE, I AM DOCTOR HELENE ASTAR.
ASTAR?
YOU KILLED OUR SON...THE HAWKS' SON.
HECTOR HALL.
THE ABSORBASCON TOLD ME ABOUT HECTOR. HE HAS SINCE BEEN REBORN-- LIKE HIS PARENTS. AND AS DOCTOR FATE, NO LESS.
MAYBE I'LL HUNT HIM DOWN NEXT.
MY SON...
MY SON COULD TURN YOUR BONES TO DUST WITH A WAVE OF HIS HAND.
CHANK
YOU DON'T HONESTLY BELIEVE THAT, DO UHHH...

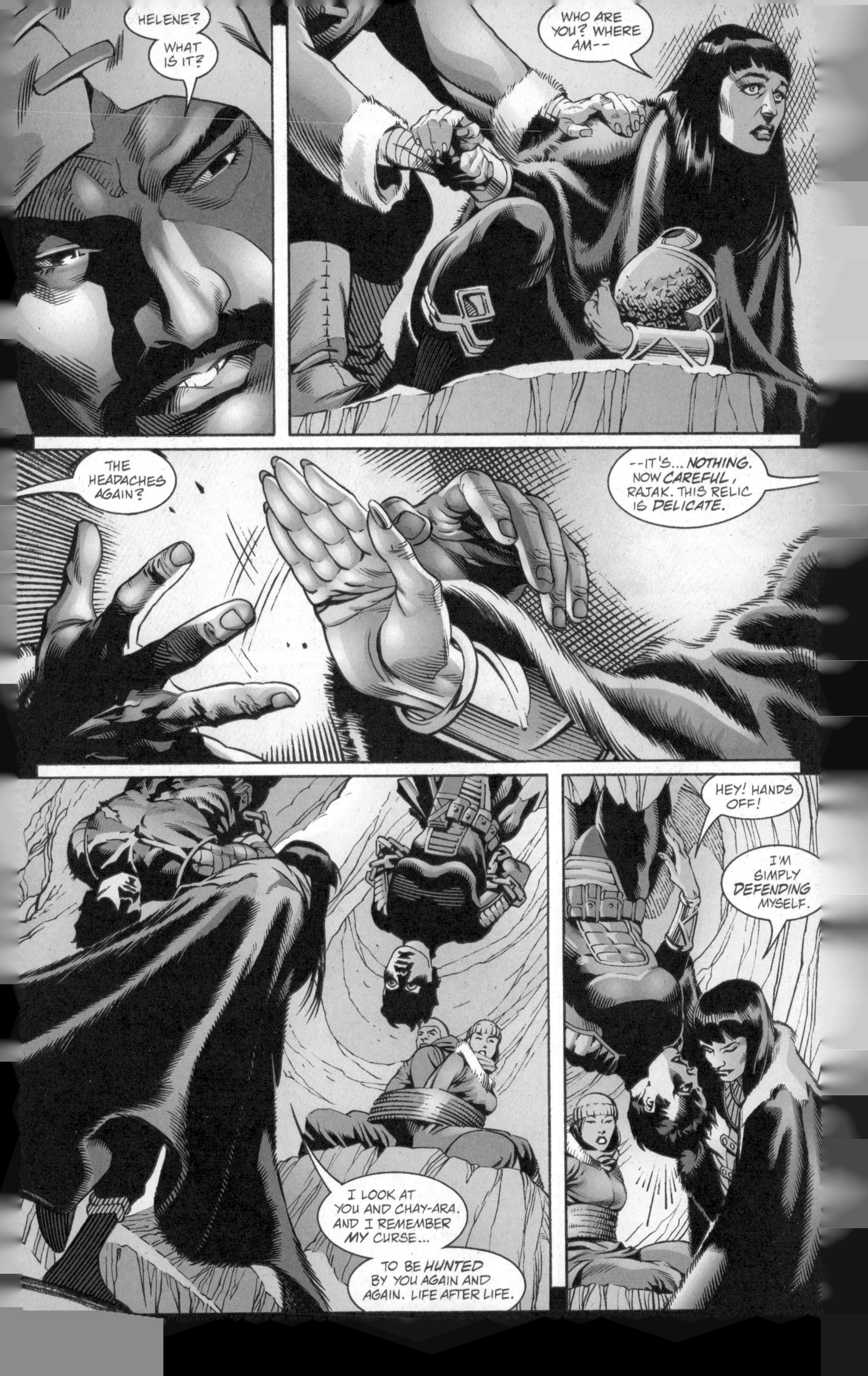
HELENE?
WHAT IS IT?
WHO ARE YOU? WHERE AM--
THE HEADACHES AGAIN?
--IT'S... NOTHING. NOW CAREFUL, RAJAK. THIS RELIC IS DELICATE.
I LOOK AT YOU AND CHAY-ARA. AND I REMEMBER MY CURSE...
TO BE HUNTED BY YOU AGAIN AND AGAIN. LIFE AFTER LIFE.
HEY! HANDS OFF!
I'M SIMPLY DEFENDING MYSELF.

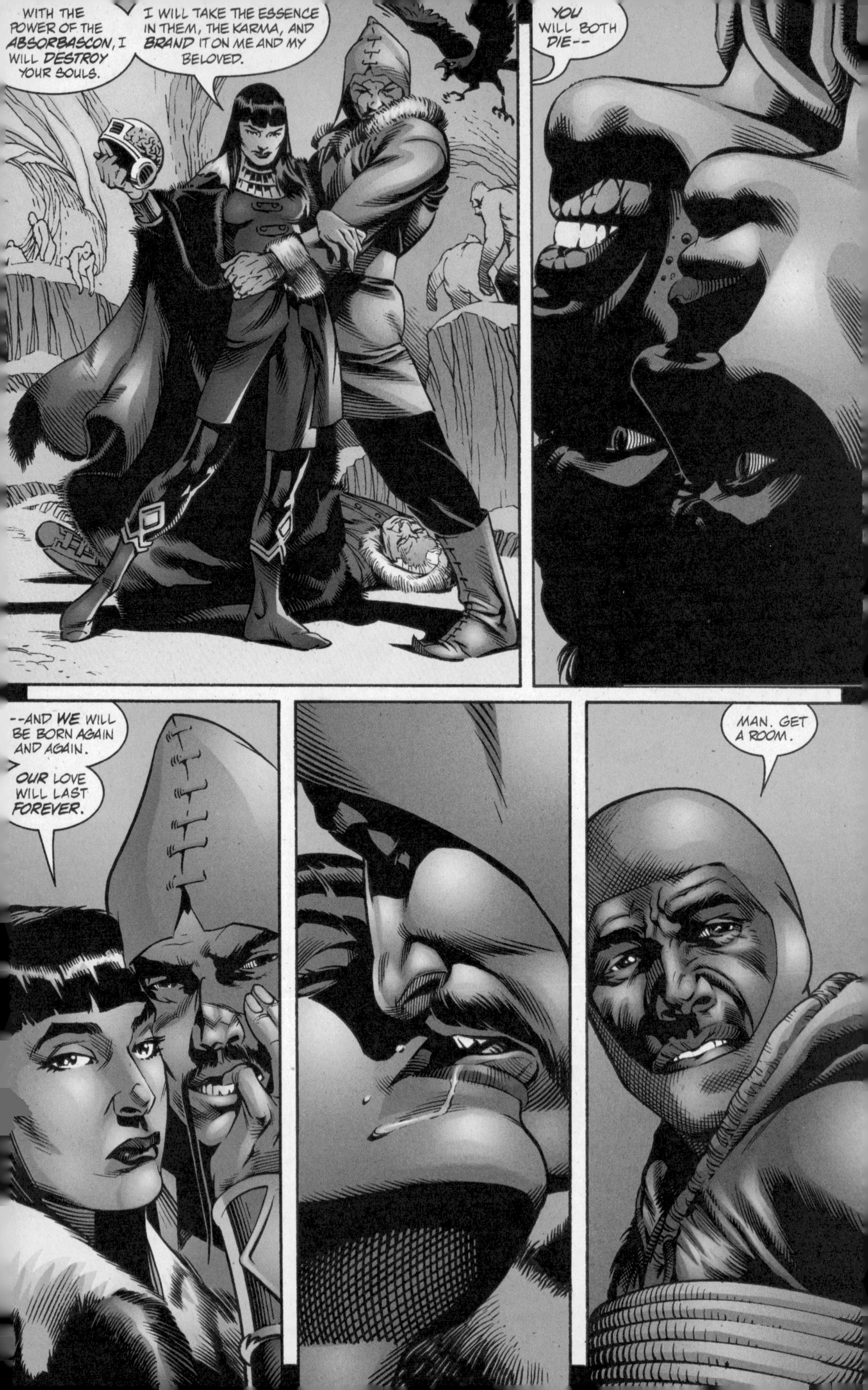
WITH THE POWER OF THE ABSORBASCON, I WILL DESTROY YOUR SOULS.
I WILL TAKE THE ESSENCE IN THEM, THE KARMA, AND BRAND IT ON ME AND MY BELOVED.
YOU WILL BOTH DIE--
--AND WE WILL BE BORN AGAIN AND AGAIN.
OUR LOVE WILL LAST FOREVER.
MAN. GET A ROOM.

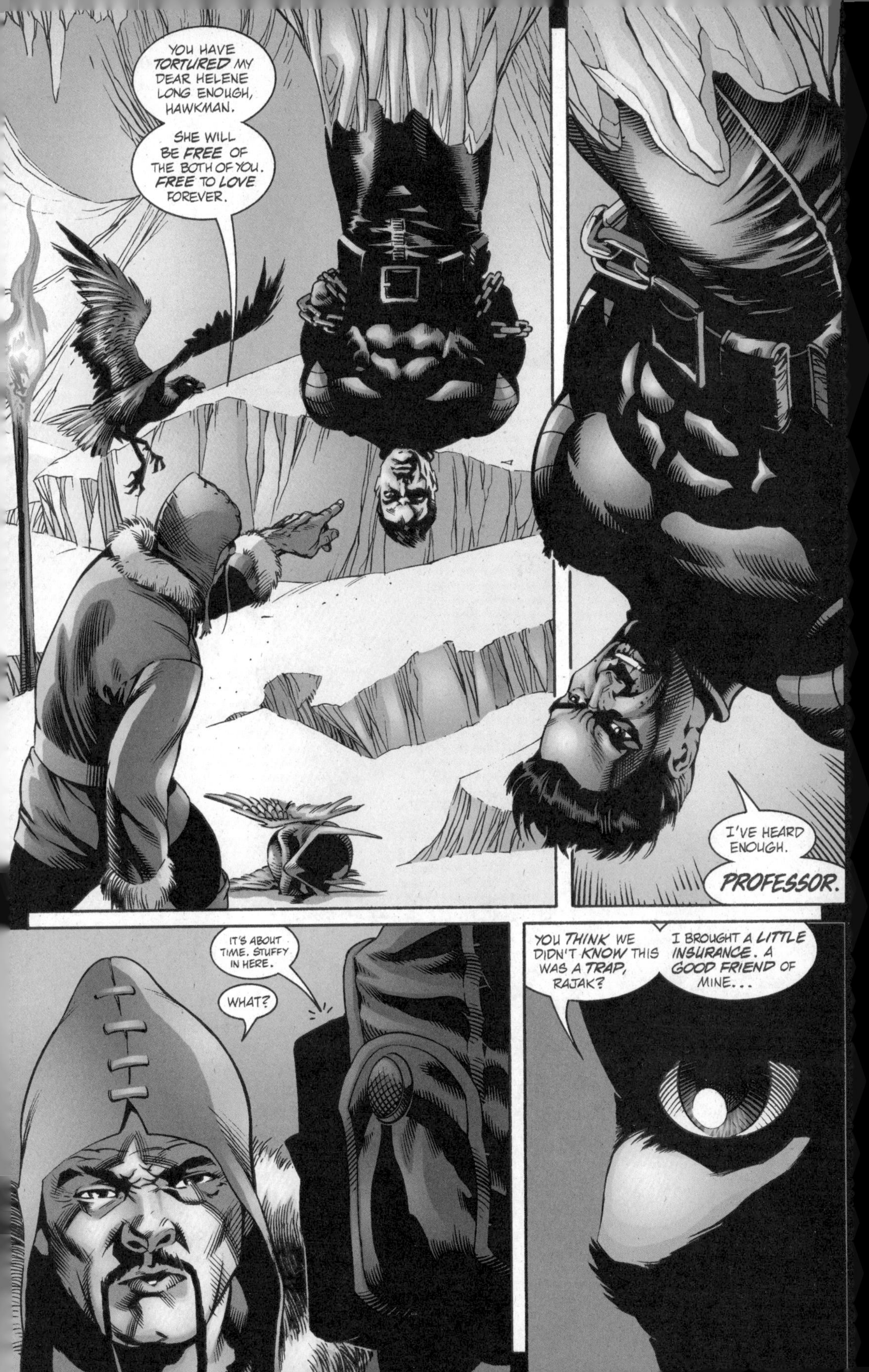

YOU HAVE TORTURED MY DEAR HELENE LONG ENOUGH, HAWKMAN.
SHE WILL BE FREE OF THE BOTH OF YOU. FREE TO LOVE FOREVER.
I'VE HEARD ENOUGH.
PROFESSOR.
IT'S ABOUT TIME. STUFFY IN HERE.
WHAT?
YOU THINK WE DIDN'T KNOW THIS WAS A TRAP, RAJAK?
I BROUGHT A LITTLE INSURANCE. A GOOD FRIEND OF MINE...

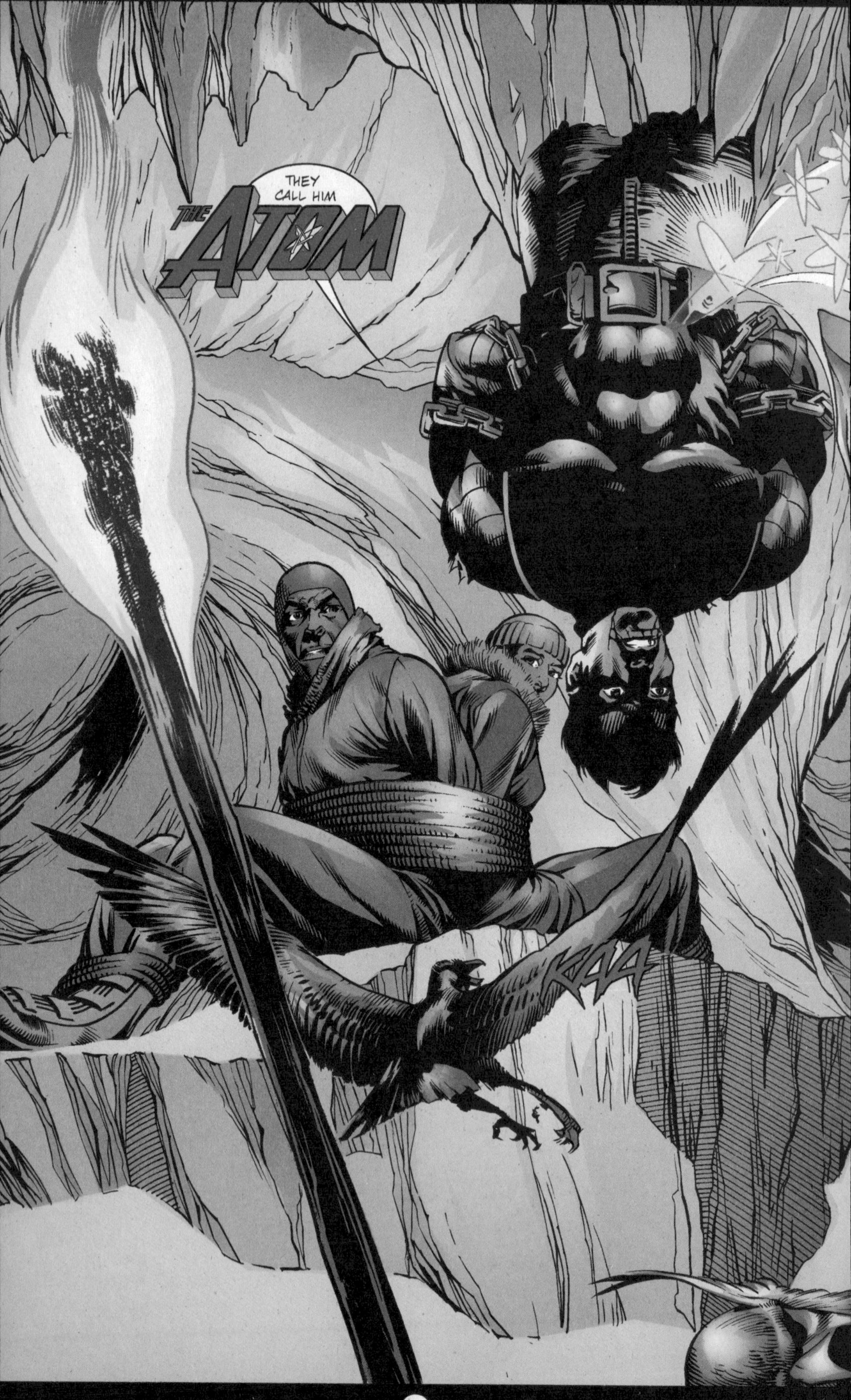
THEY CALL HIM
THE ATOM
KAA

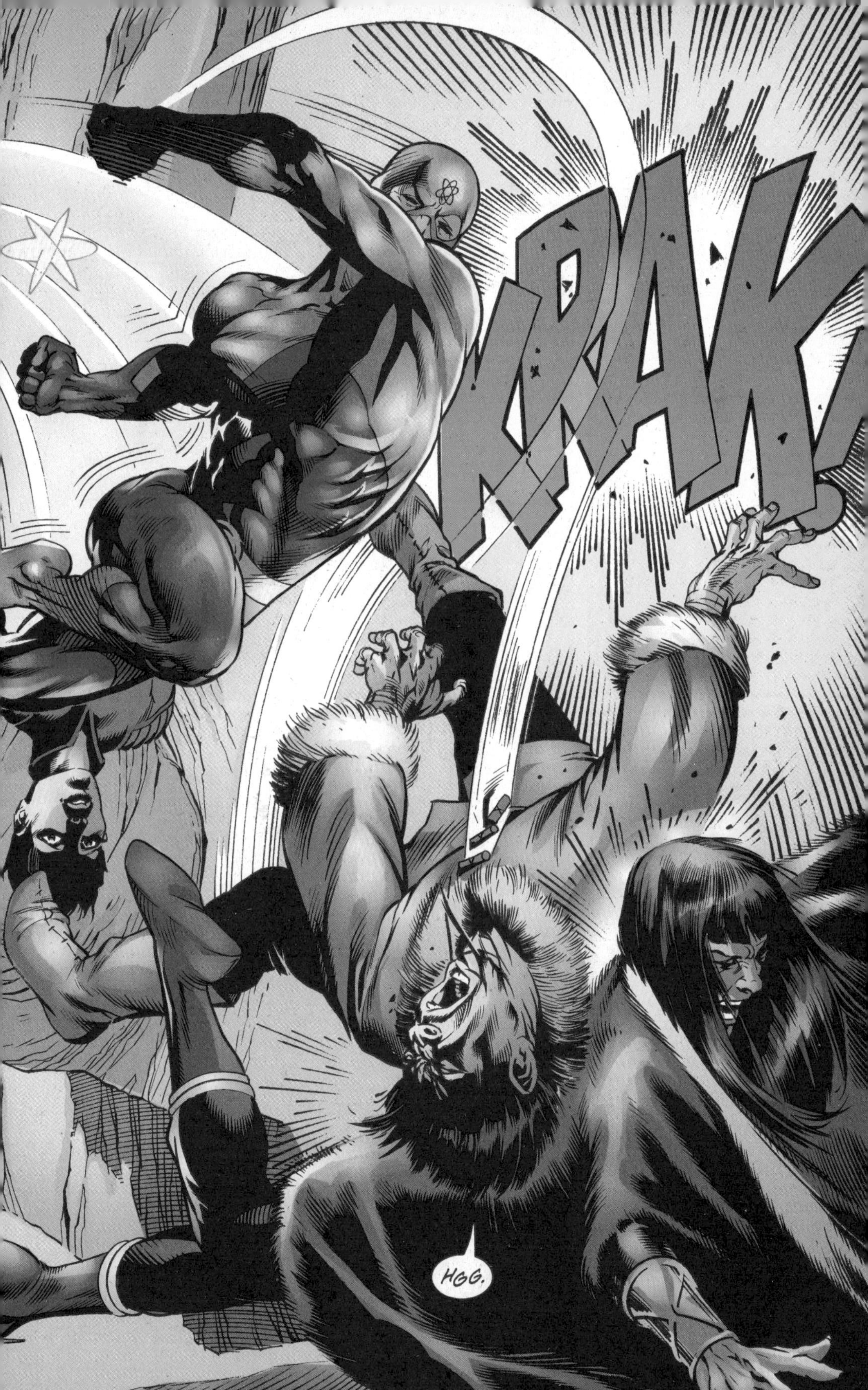
KRAK!
HGG.

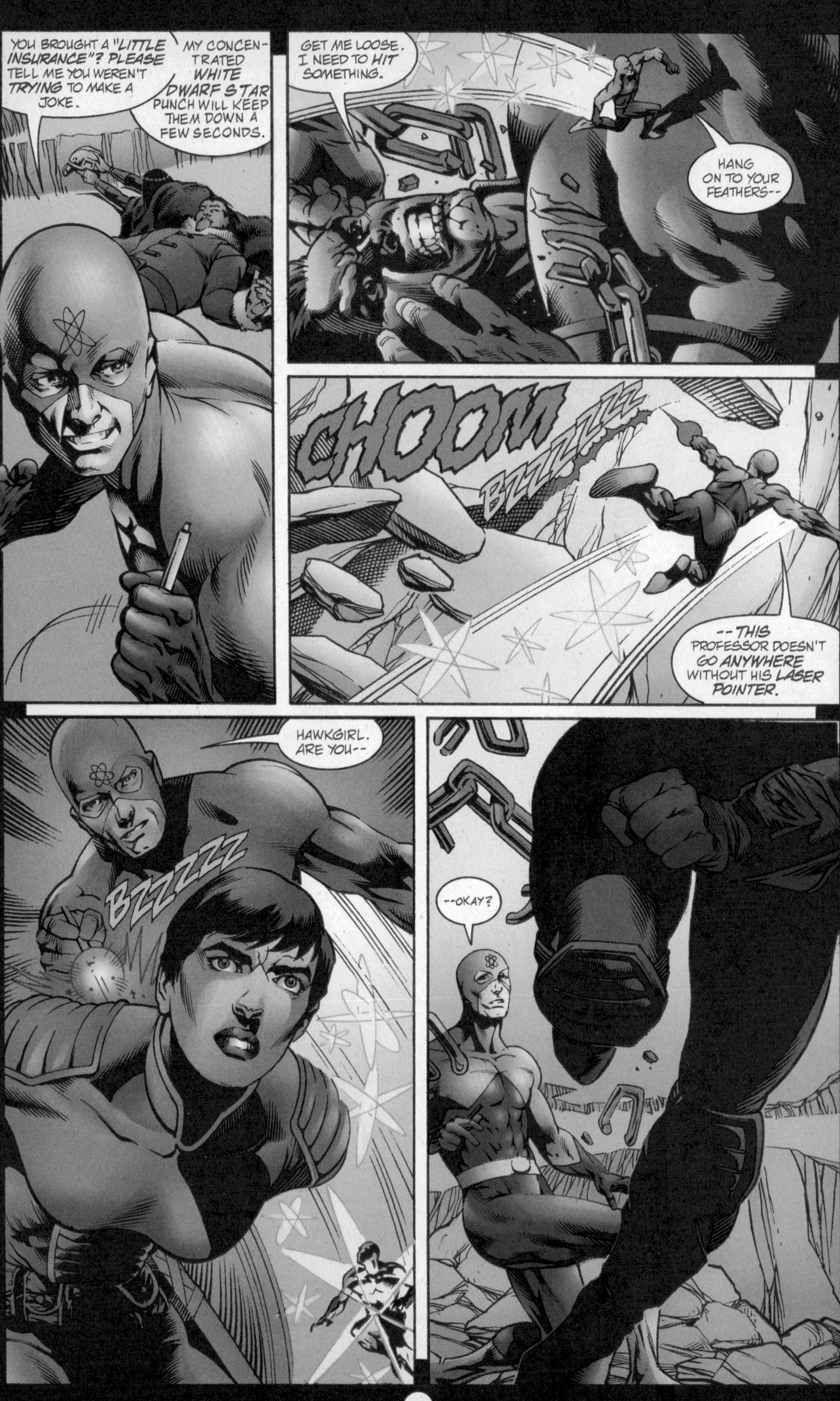
YOU BROUGHT A "LITTLE INSURANCE"? PLEASE TELL ME YOU WEREN'T TRYING TO MAKE A JOKE.
MY CONCEN-TRATED WHITE DWARF STAR PUNCH WILL KEEP THEM DOWN A FEW SECONDS.
GET ME LOOSE. I NEED TO HIT SOMETHING.
HANG ON TO YOUR FEATHERS--
CHOOM
BZZZZZZ
--THIS PROFESSOR DOESN'T GO ANYWHERE WITHOUT HIS LASER POINTER.
HAWKGIRL. ARE YOU--
BZZZZZ
--OKAY?

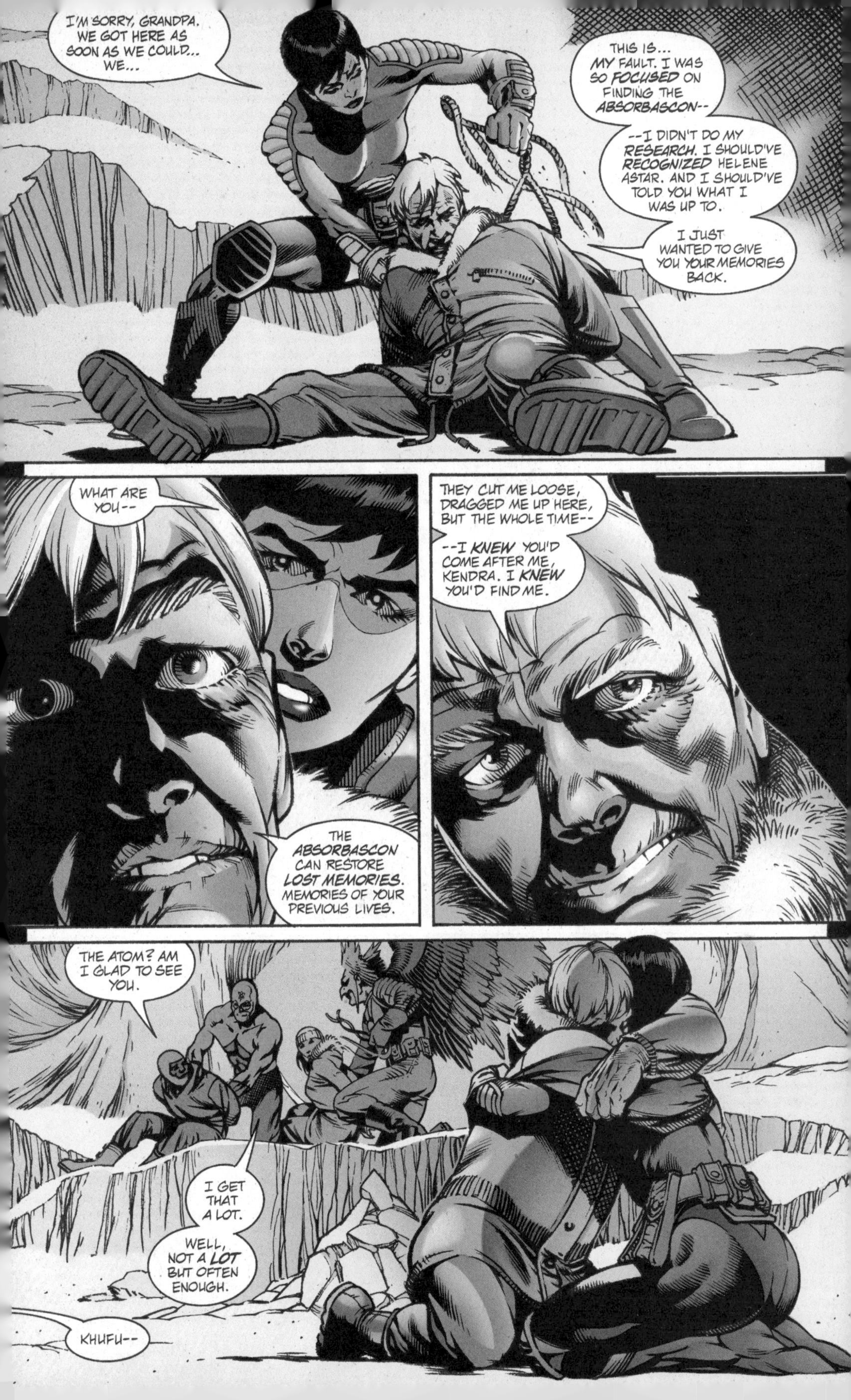
I'M SORRY, GRANDPA. WE GOT HERE AS SOON AS WE COULD... WE...
THIS IS... MY FAULT. I WAS SO FOCUSED ON FINDING THE ABSORBASCON--
--I DIDN'T DO MY RESEARCH. I SHOULD'VE RECOGNIZED HELENE ASTAR. AND I SHOULD'VE TOLD YOU WHAT I WAS UP TO.
I JUST WANTED TO GIVE YOU YOUR MEMORIES BACK.
WHAT ARE YOU--
THE ABSORBASCON CAN RESTORE LOST MEMORIES. MEMORIES OF YOUR PREVIOUS LIVES.
THEY CUT ME LOOSE, DRAGGED ME UP HERE, BUT THE WHOLE TIME--
--I KNEW YOU'D COME AFTER ME, KENDRA. I KNEW YOU'D FIND ME.
THE ATOM? AM I GLAD TO SEE YOU.
I GET THAT A LOT.
WELL, NOT A LOT BUT OFTEN ENOUGH.
KHUFU--

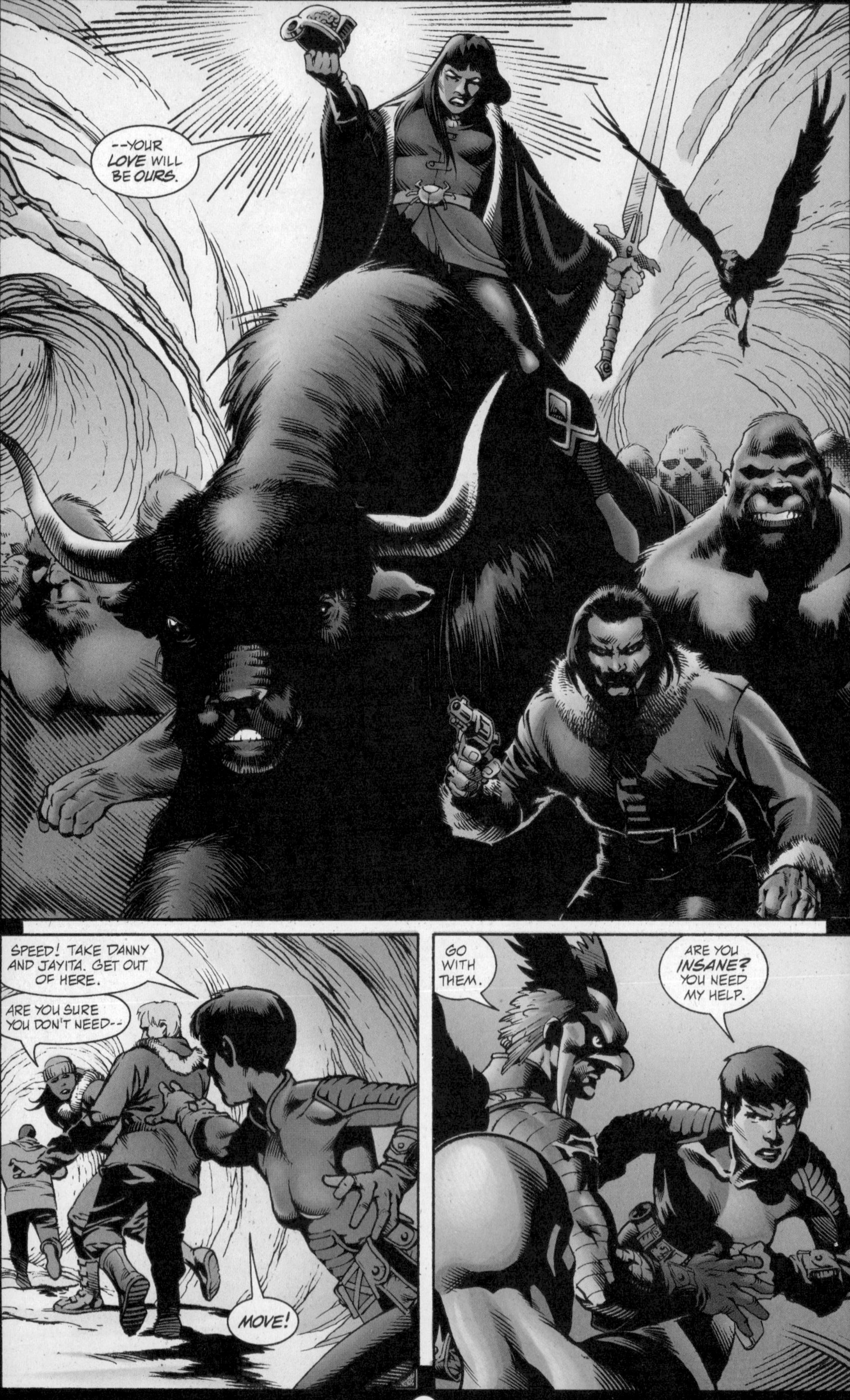
--YOUR LOVE WILL BE OURS.
SPEED! TAKE DANNY AND JAYITA. GET OUT OF HERE.
ARE YOU SURE YOU DON'T NEED--
MOVE!
GO WITH THEM.
ARE YOU INSANE? YOU NEED MY HELP.

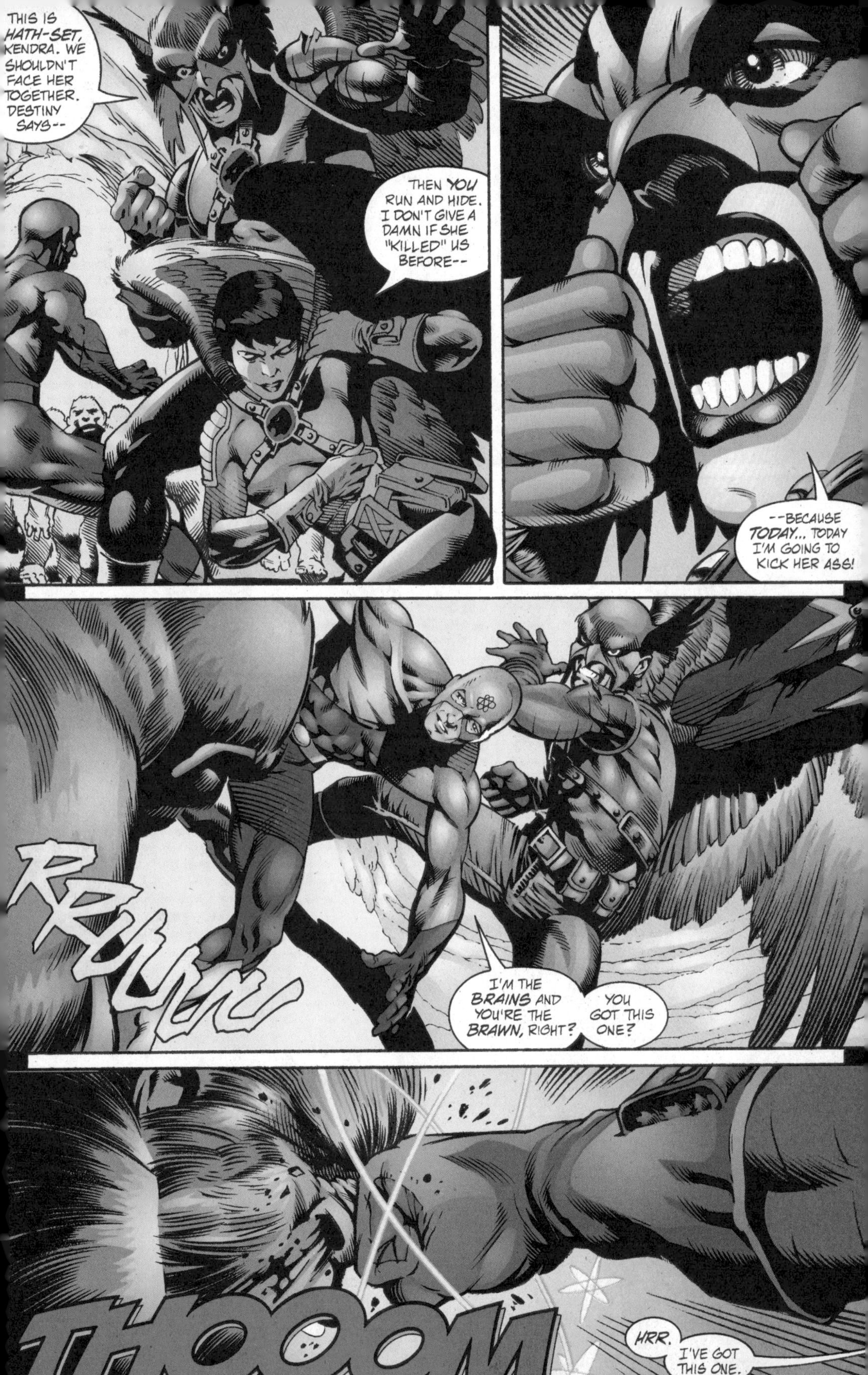
THIS IS HATH-SET, KENDRA. WE SHOULDN'T FACE HER TOGETHER. DESTINY SAYS--
THEN YOU RUN AND HIDE. I DON'T GIVE A DAMN IF SHE "KILLED" US BEFORE--
--BECAUSE TODAY... TODAY I'M GOING TO KICK HER ASS!
RRUUUU
I'M THE BRAINS AND YOU'RE THE BRAWN, RIGHT?
YOU GOT THIS ONE?
THOOOM
HRR.
I'VE GOT THIS ONE.

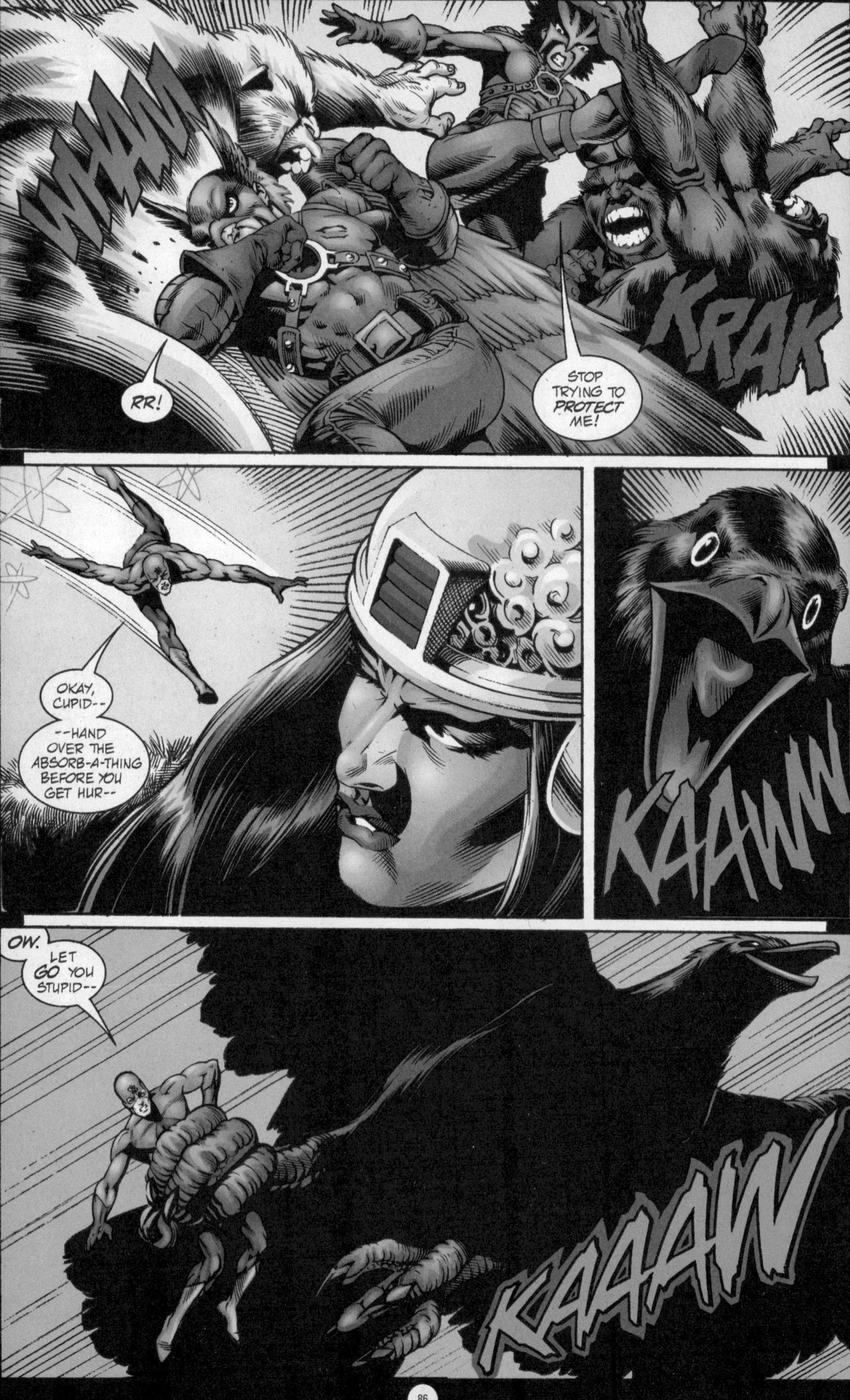
WHAM
RR!
STOP TRYING TO PROTECT ME!
KRAK
OKAY, CUPID--
--HAND OVER THE ABSORB-A-THING BEFORE YOU GET HUR--
KAAWW
OW.
LET GO YOU STUPID--
KAAAW

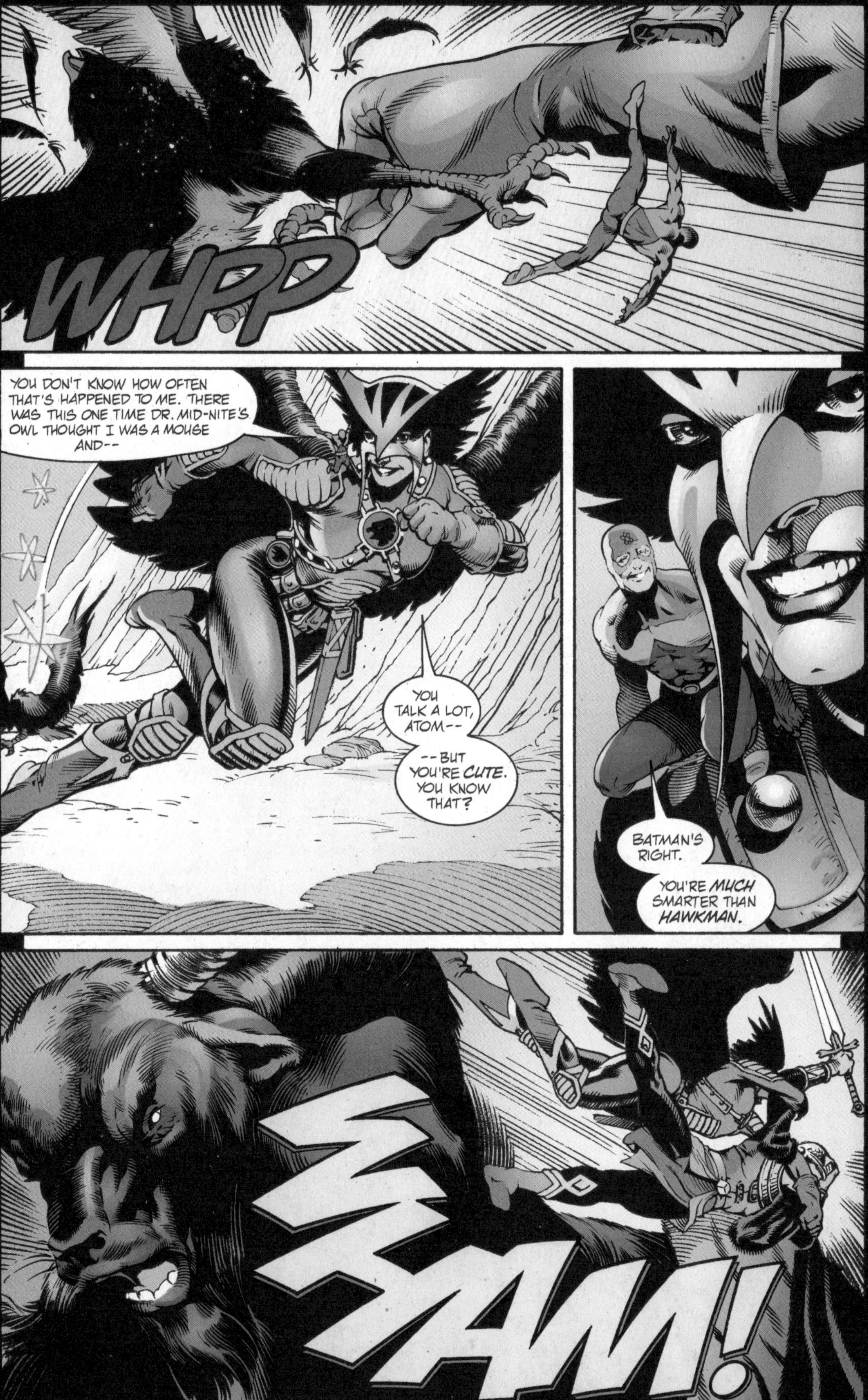

WHPP
YOU DON'T KNOW HOW OFTEN THAT'S HAPPENED TO ME. THERE WAS THIS ONE TIME DR. MID-NITE'S OWL THOUGHT I WAS A MOUSE AND--
YOU TALK A LOT, ATOM--
--BUT YOU'RE CUTE. YOU KNOW THAT?
BATMAN'S RIGHT.
YOU'RE MUCH SMARTER THAN HAWKMAN.
WHAM!

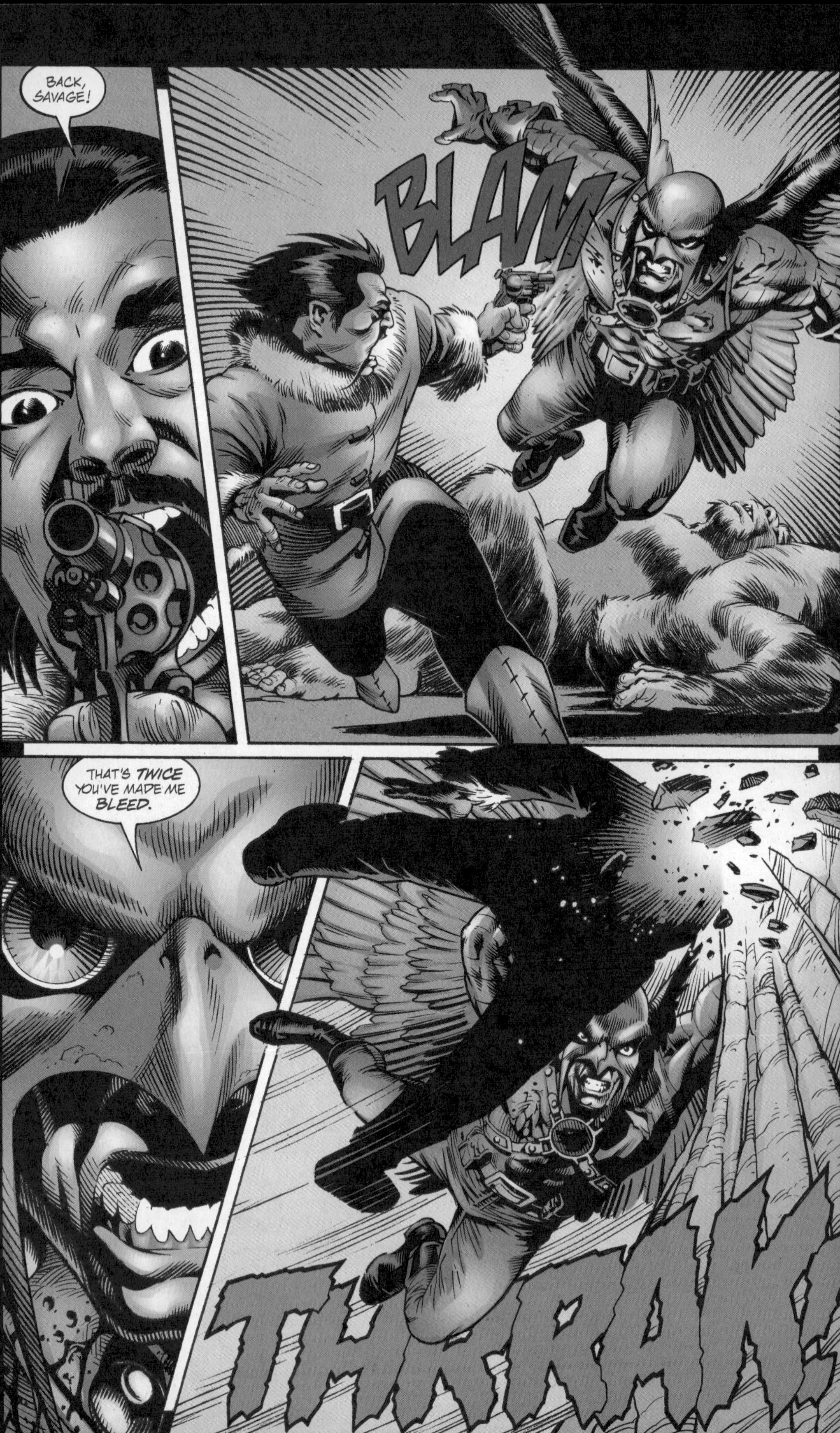
BACK, SAVAGE!
BLAM
THAT'S TWICE YOU'VE MADE ME BLEED.
THRAK!

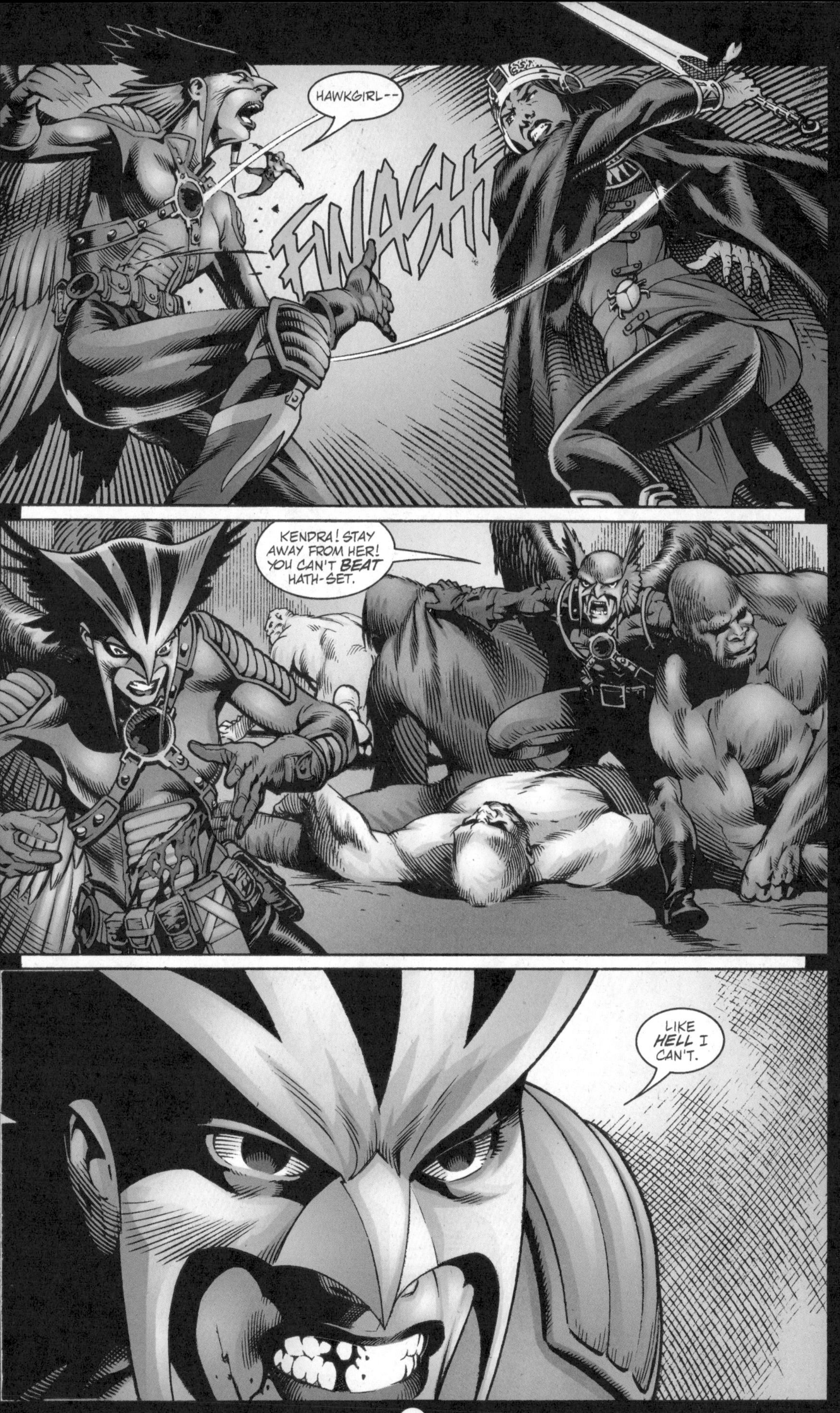
HAWKGIRL--
FWASH
KENDRA! STAY AWAY FROM HER! YOU CAN'T BEAT HATH-SET.
LIKE HELL I CAN'T.

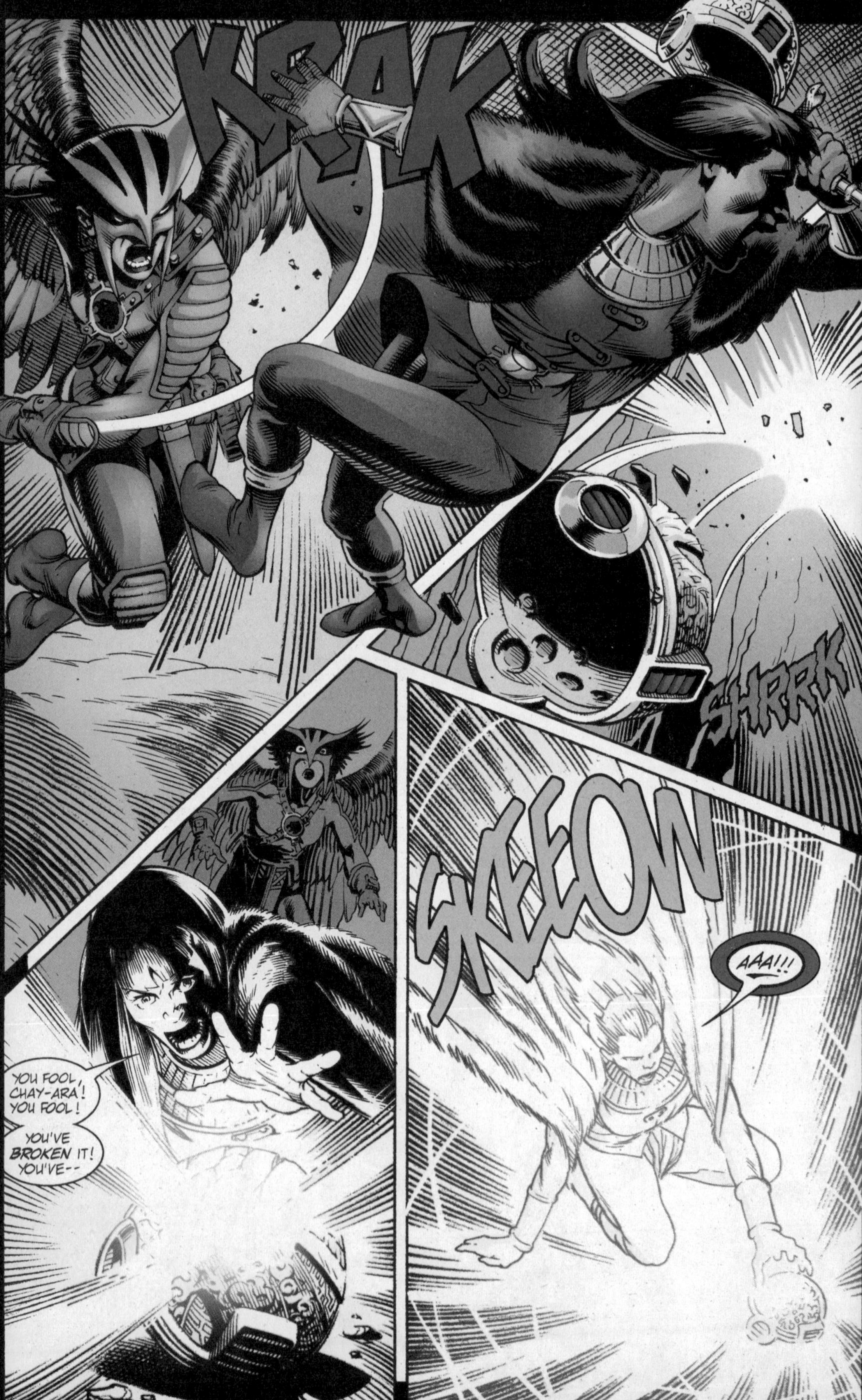
KRAK
SHRRK
SKEEOW
AAA!!!
YOU FOOL, CHAY-ARA! YOU FOOL!
YOU'VE BROKEN IT! YOU'VE--

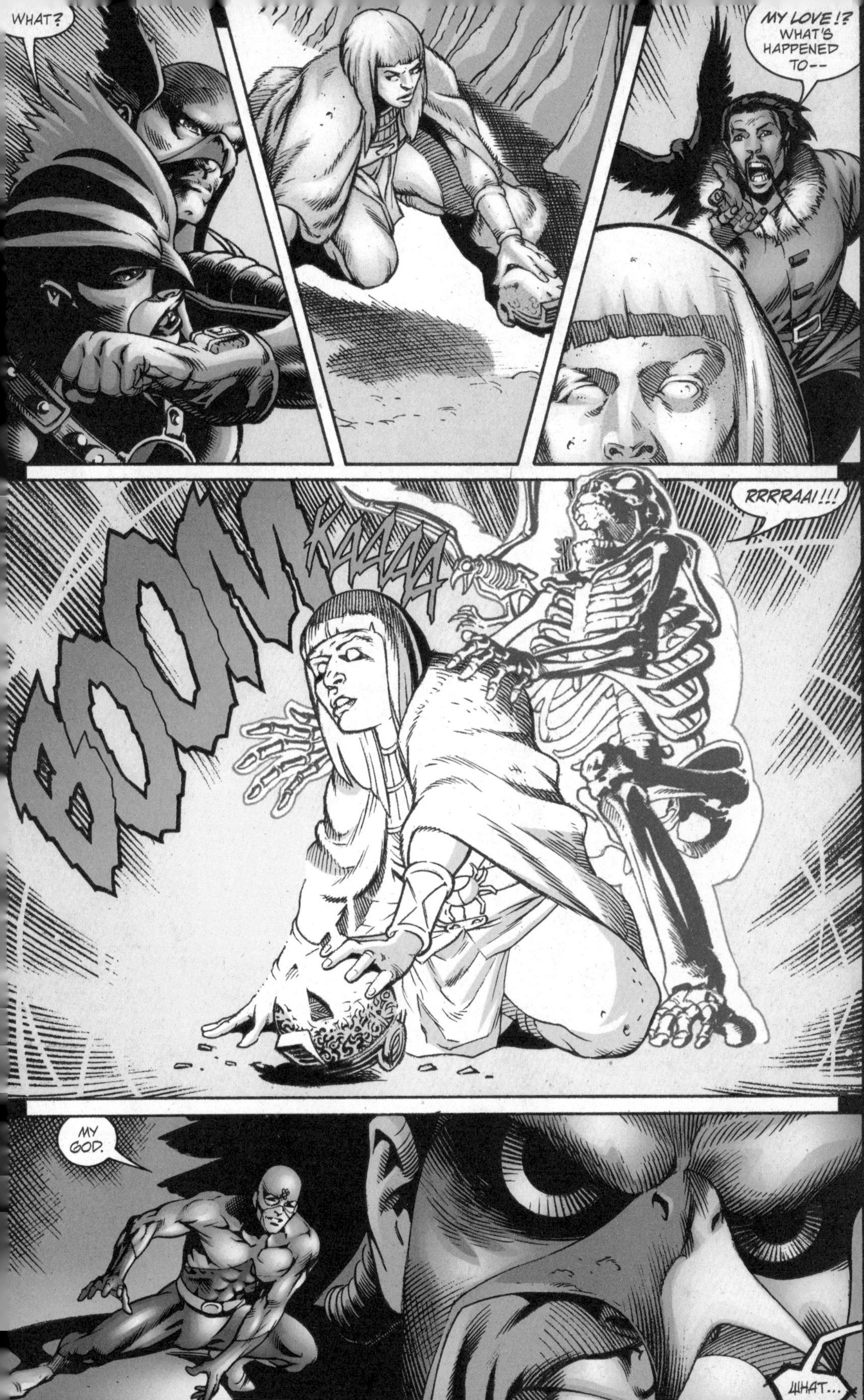
WHAT?
MY LOVE!? WHAT'S HAPPENED TO--
BOOM
KAAAA
RRRRAAI!!!
MY GOD.
WHAT...

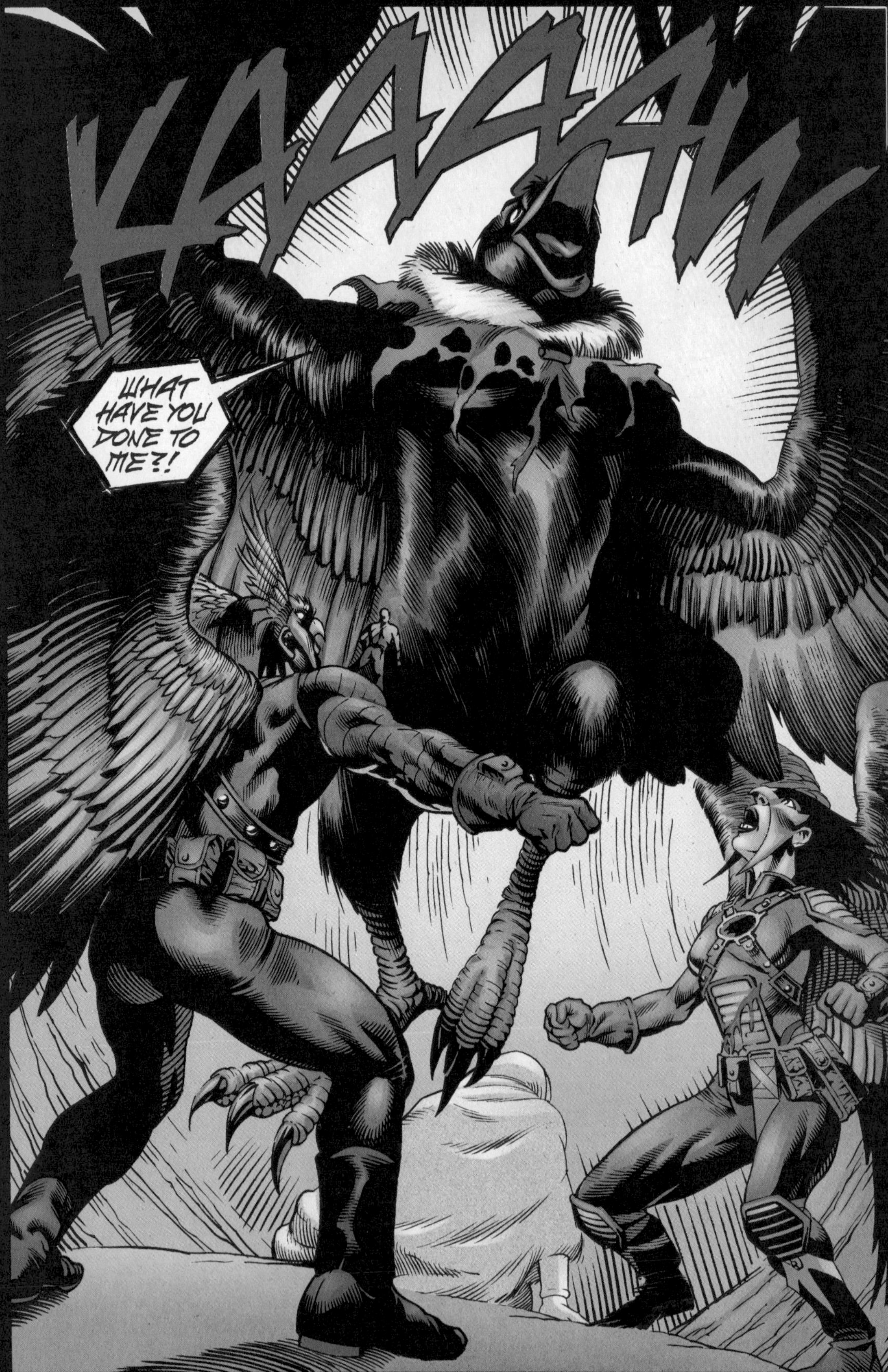
KAAAAW
WHAT HAVE YOU DONE TO ME?!

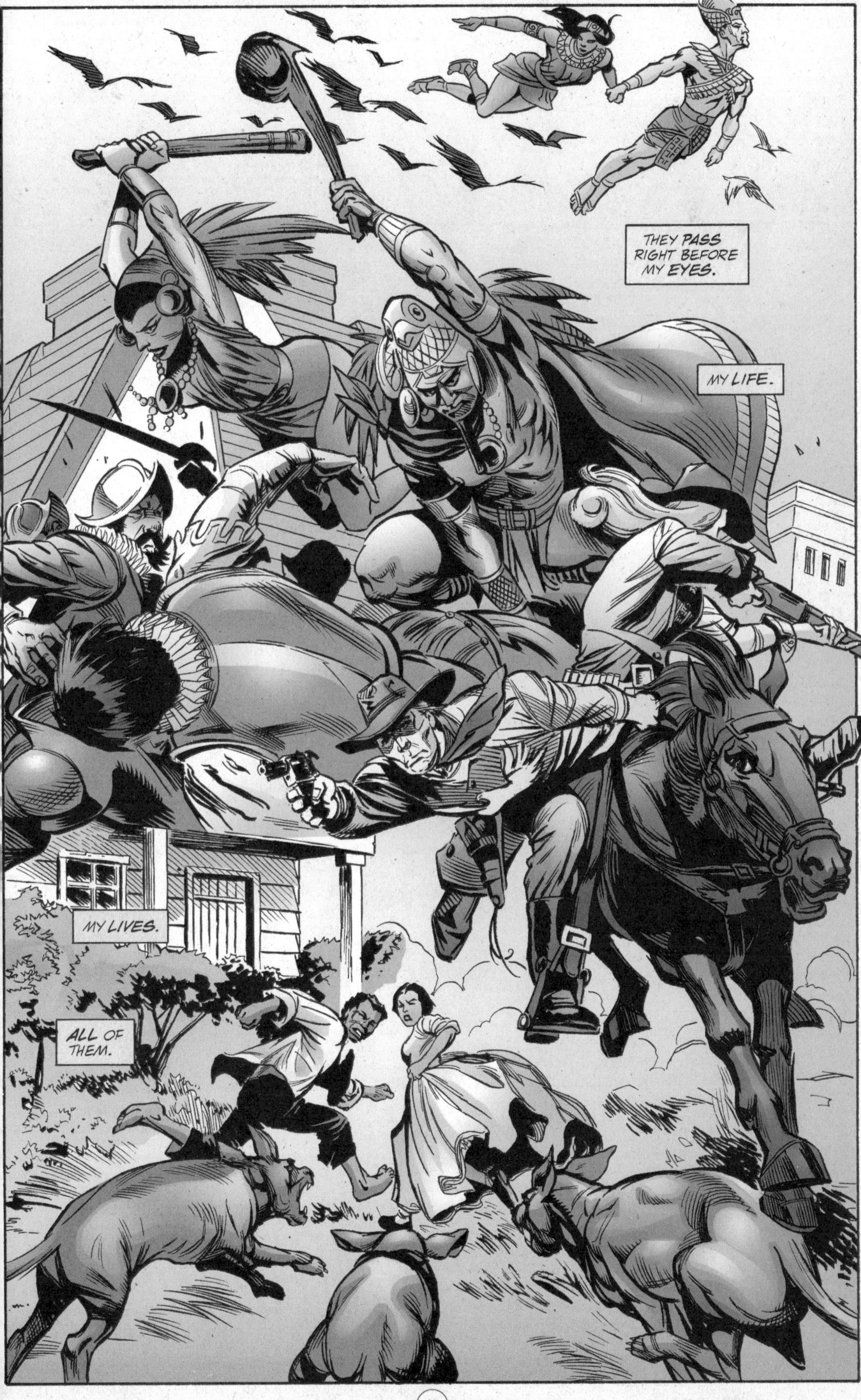
THEY PASS RIGHT BEFORE MY EYES.
MY LIFE.
MY LIVES.
ALL OF THEM.

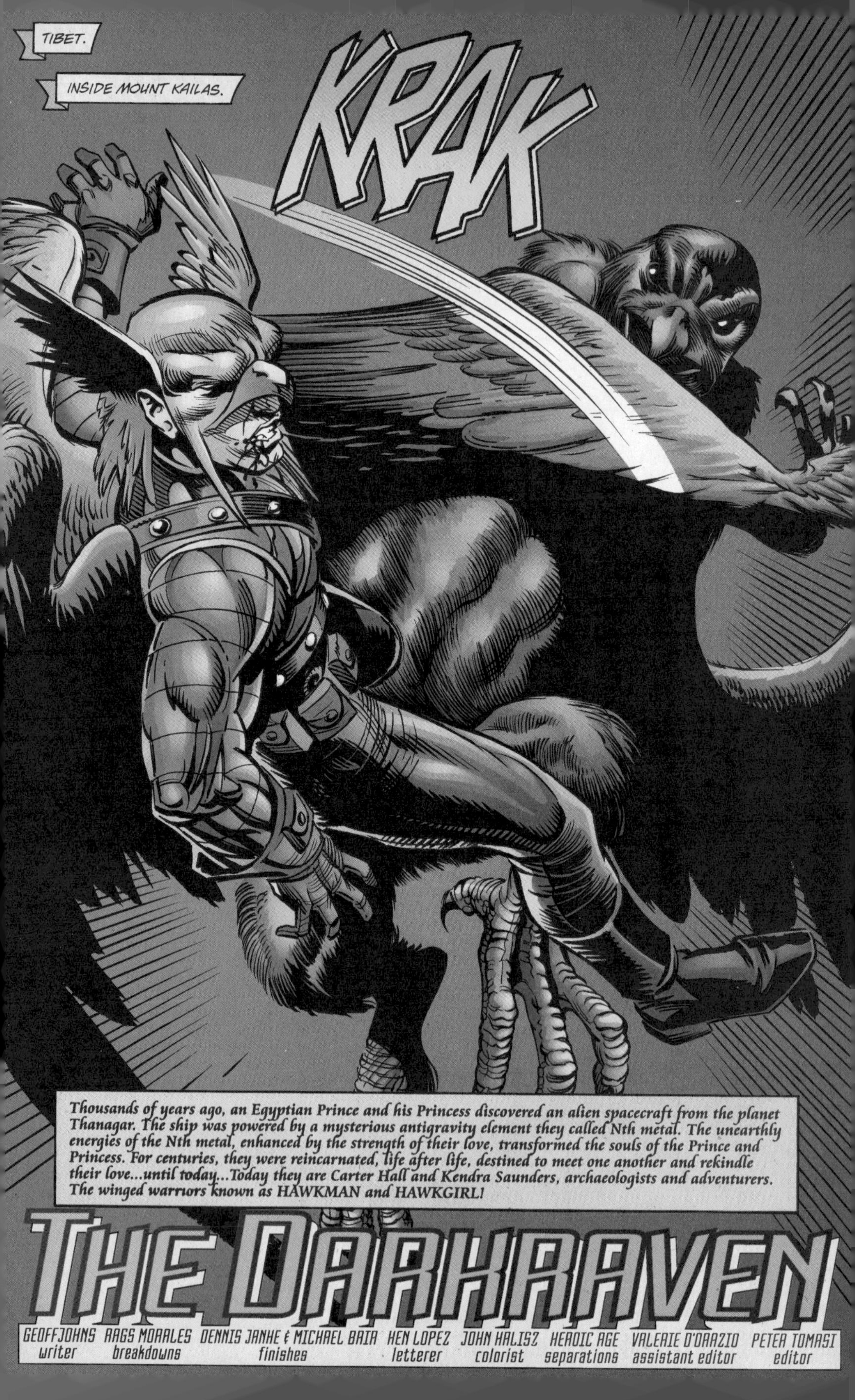
TIBET.
INSIDE MOUNT KAILAS.
KRAK
Thousands of years ago, an Egyptian Prince and his Princess discovered an alien spacecraft from the planet Thanagar. The ship was powered by a mysterious antigravity element they called Nth metal. The unearthly energies of the Nth metal, enhanced by the strength of their love, transformed the souls of the Prince and Princess. For centuries, they were reincarnated, life after life, destined to meet one another and rekindle their love...until today...Today they are Carter Hall and Kendra Saunders, archaeologists and adventurers. The winged warriors known as HAWKMAN and HAWKGIRL!
THE DARKRAVEN
GEOFF JOHNS writer
RAGS MORALES breakdowns
DENNIS JANKE & MICHAEL BAIR finishes
KEN LOPEZ letterer
JOHN KALISZ colorist
HEROIC AGE separations
VALERIE D'ORAZIO assistant editor
PETER TOMASI editor

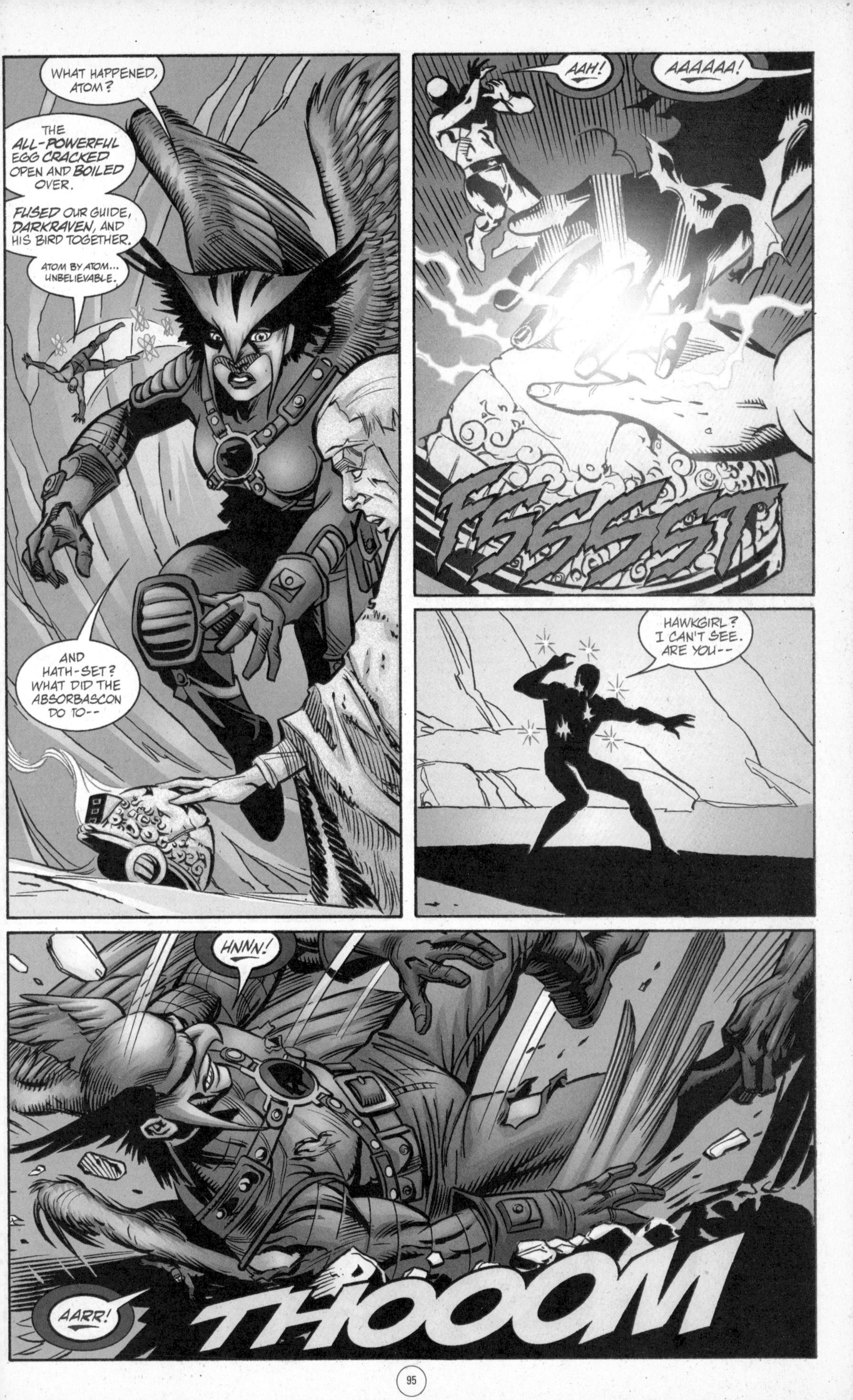
WHAT HAPPENED, ATOM?
THE ALL-POWERFUL EGG CRACKED OPEN AND BOILED OVER.
FUSED OUR GUIDE, DARKRAVEN, AND HIS BIRD TOGETHER.
ATOM BY ATOM... UNBELIEVABLE.
AND HATH-SET? WHAT DID THE ABSORBASCON DO TO--
AAH!
AAAAAA!
FSSSST
HAWKGIRL? I CAN'T SEE. ARE YOU--
HNNN!
AARR!
THOOOM

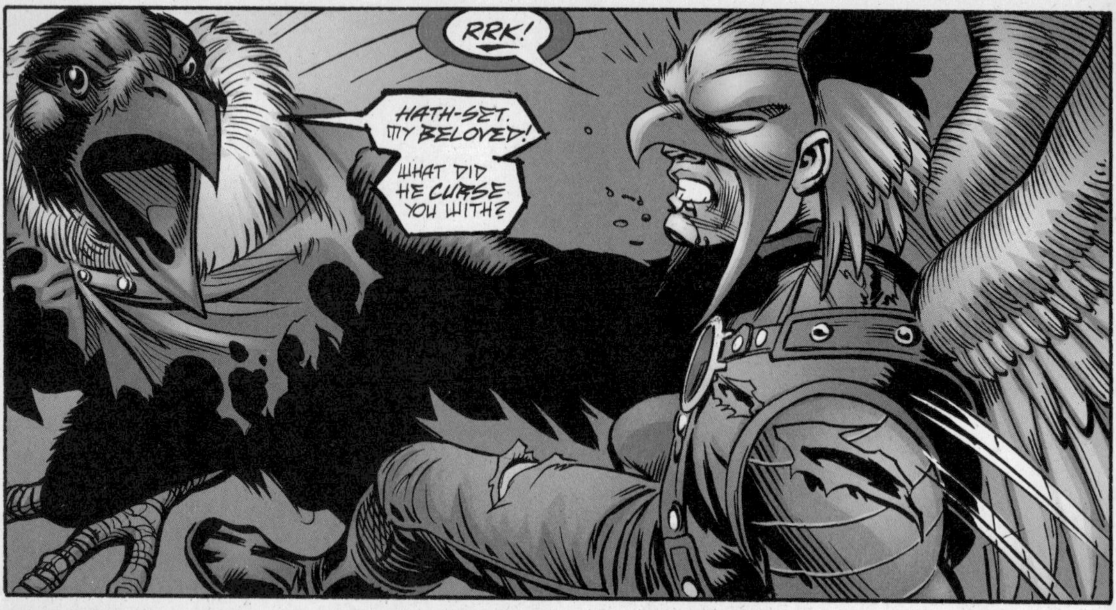
RRK!
HATH-SET. MY BELOVED!
WHAT DID HE CURSE YOU WITH?

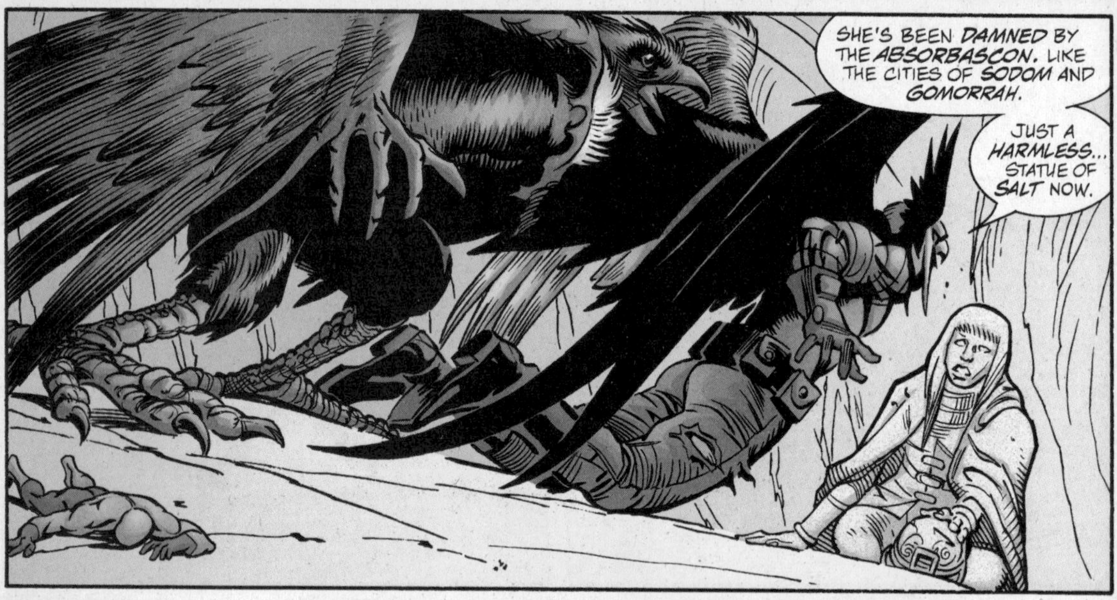
SHE'S BEEN DAMNED BY THE ABSORBASCON. LIKE THE CITIES OF SODOM AND GOMORRAH.
JUST A HARMLESS... STATUE OF SALT NOW.

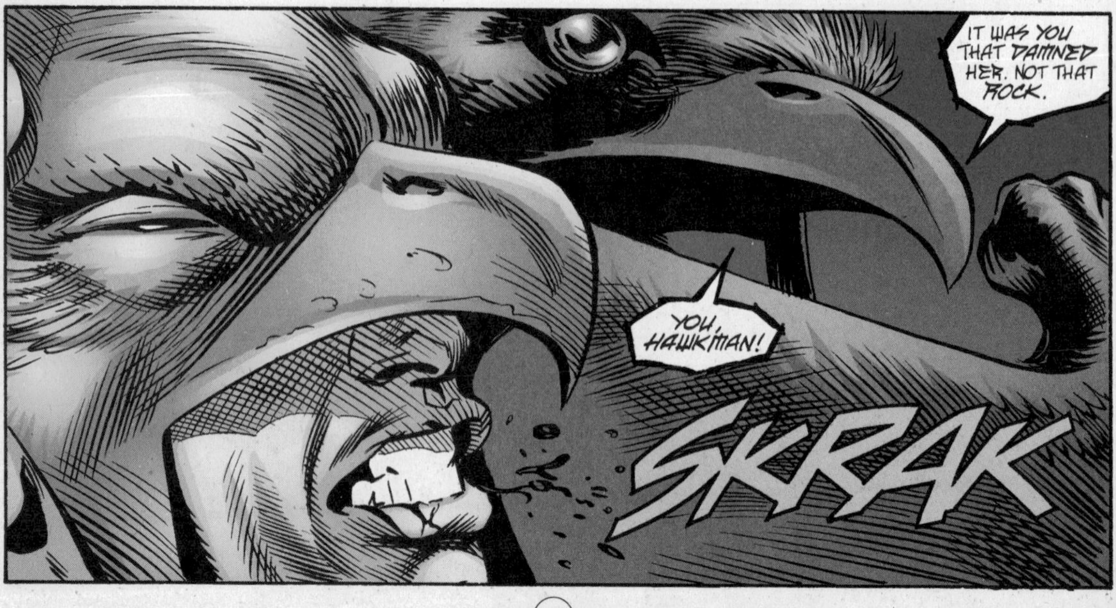
IT WAS YOU THAT DAMNED HER. NOT THAT ROCK.
YOU, HAWKMAN!
SKRAK

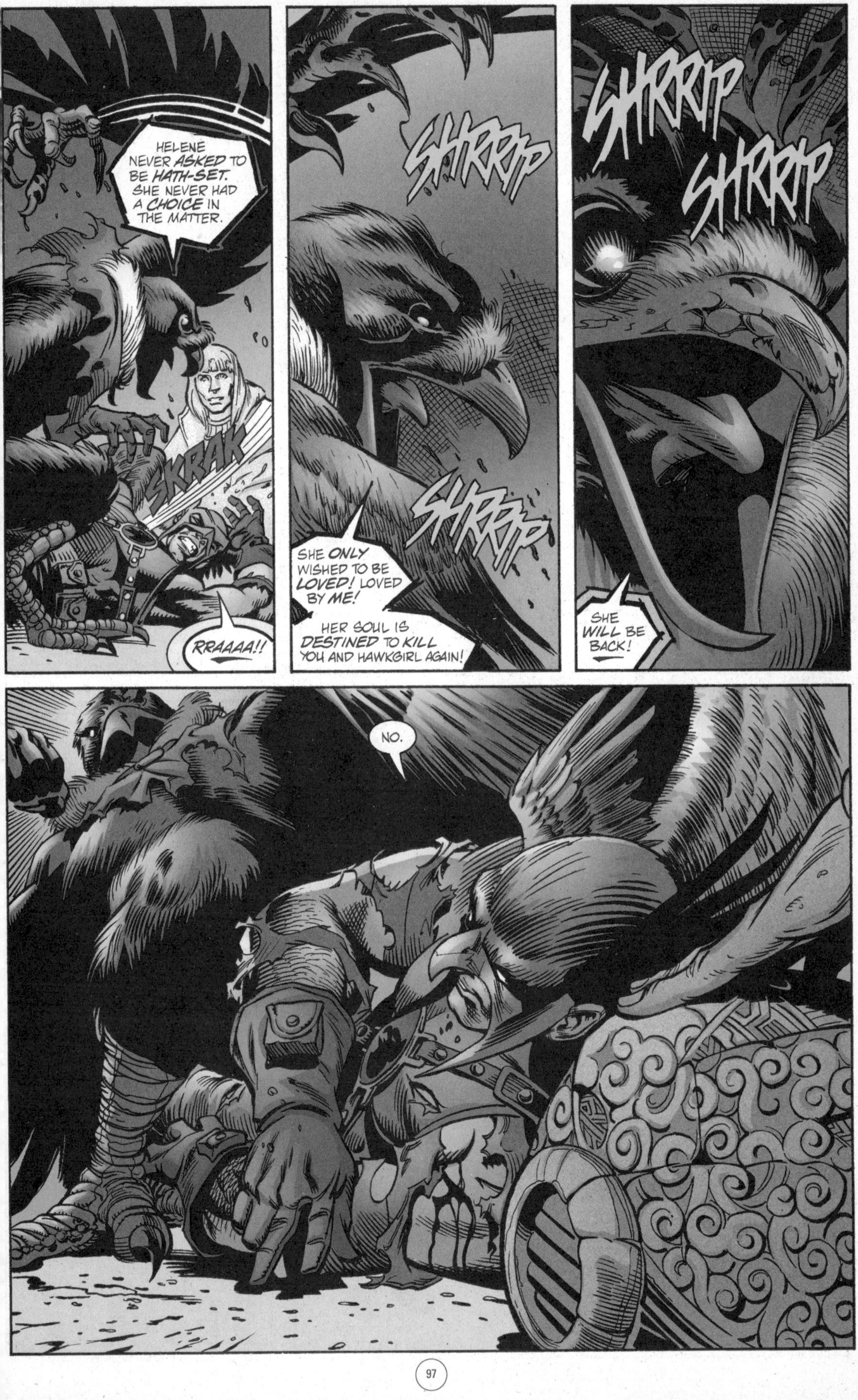
HELENE NEVER ASKED TO BE HATH-SET. SHE NEVER HAD A CHOICE IN THE MATTER.
SKRAK
RRAAAA!!
SHRRIP
SHRRIP
SHE ONLY WISHED TO BE LOVED! LOVED BY ME!
HER SOUL IS DESTINED TO KILL YOU AND HAWKGIRL AGAIN!
SHRRIP
SHRRIP
SHE WILL BE BACK!
NO.

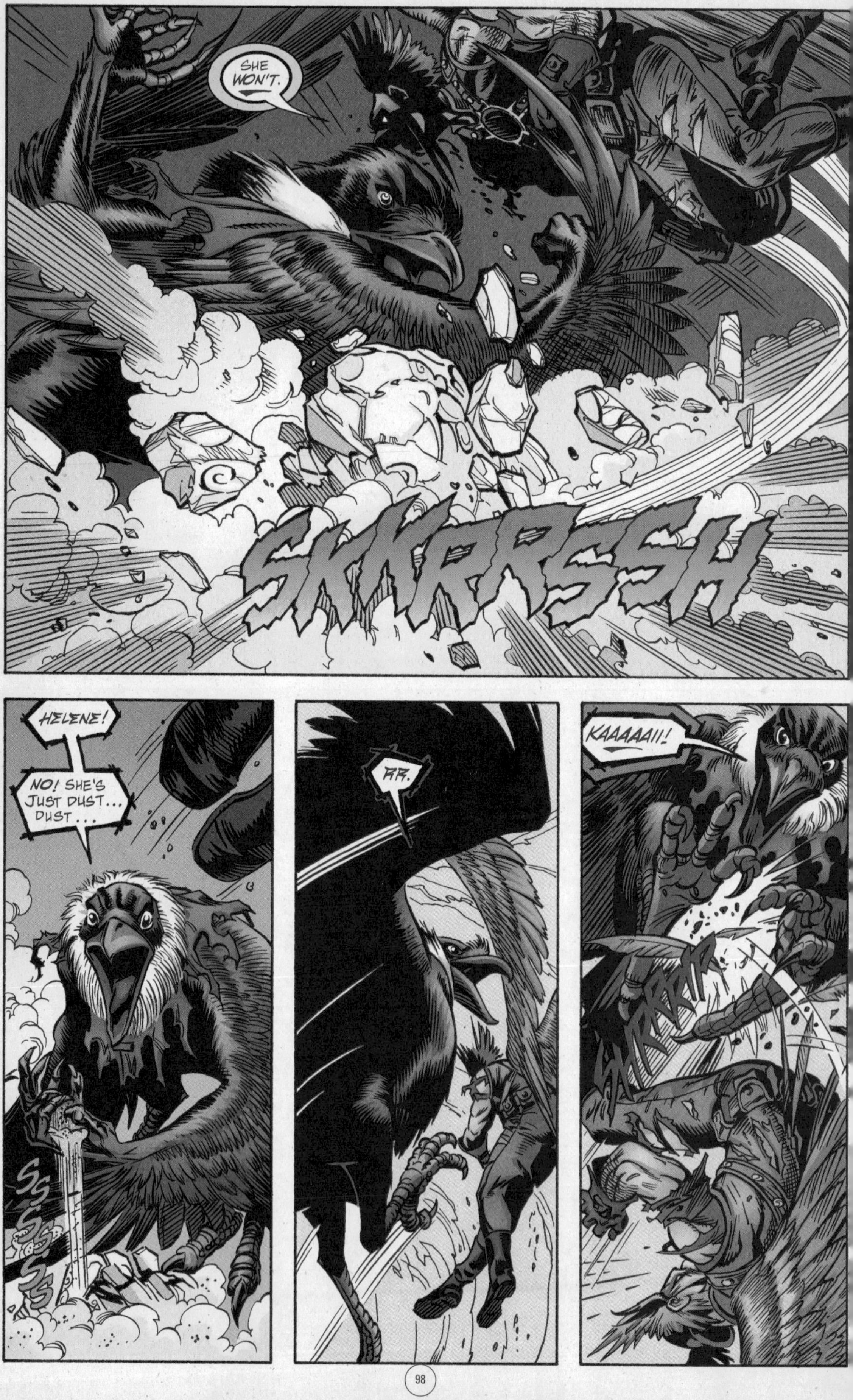
SHE WON'T.
SKRRSSH
HELENE!
NO! SHE'S JUST DUST... DUST...
RR.
KAAAAAII!

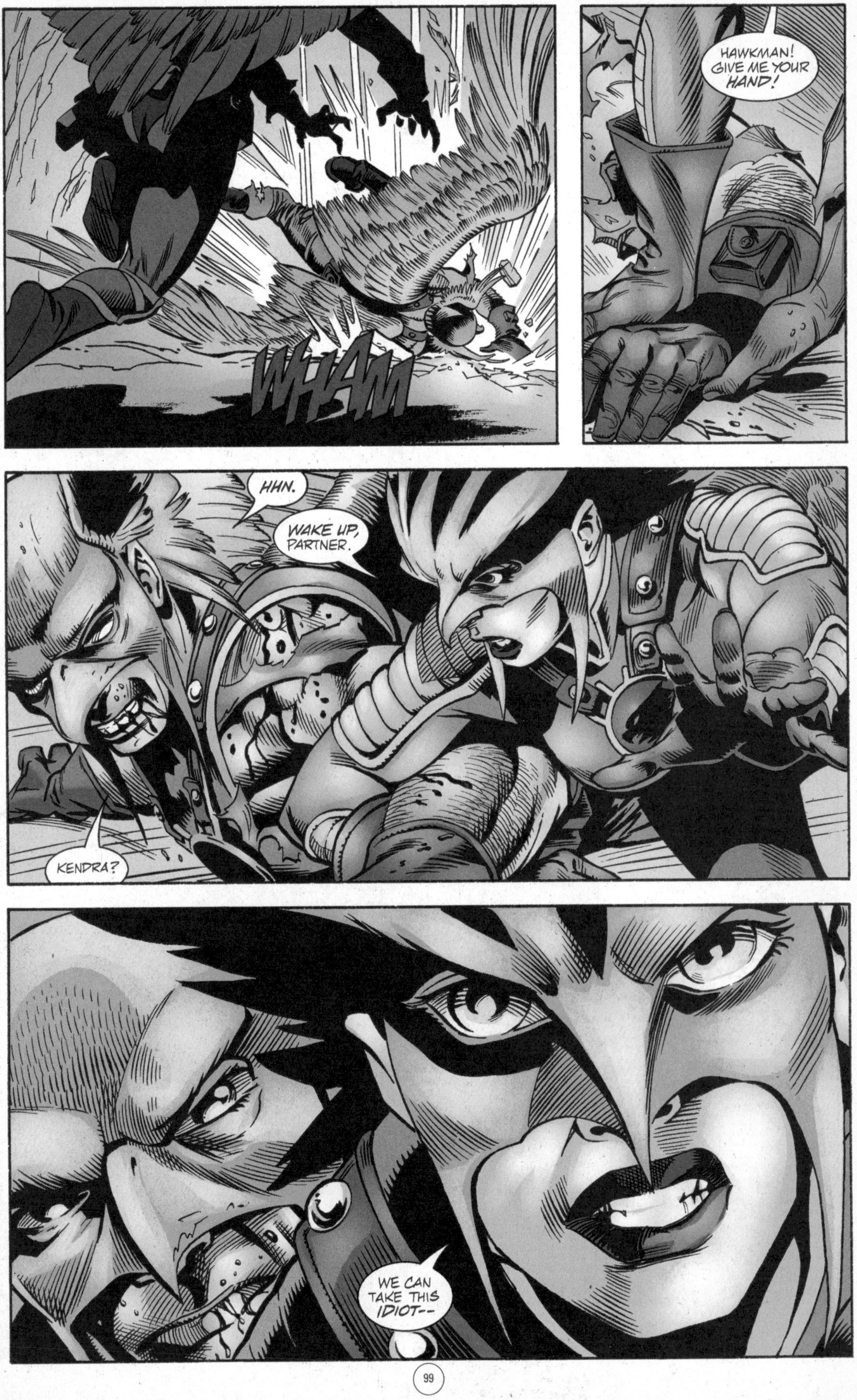
WHAM
HAWKMAN! GIVE ME YOUR HAND!
HHN.
WAKE UP, PARTNER.
KENDRA?
WE CAN TAKE THIS IDIOT--

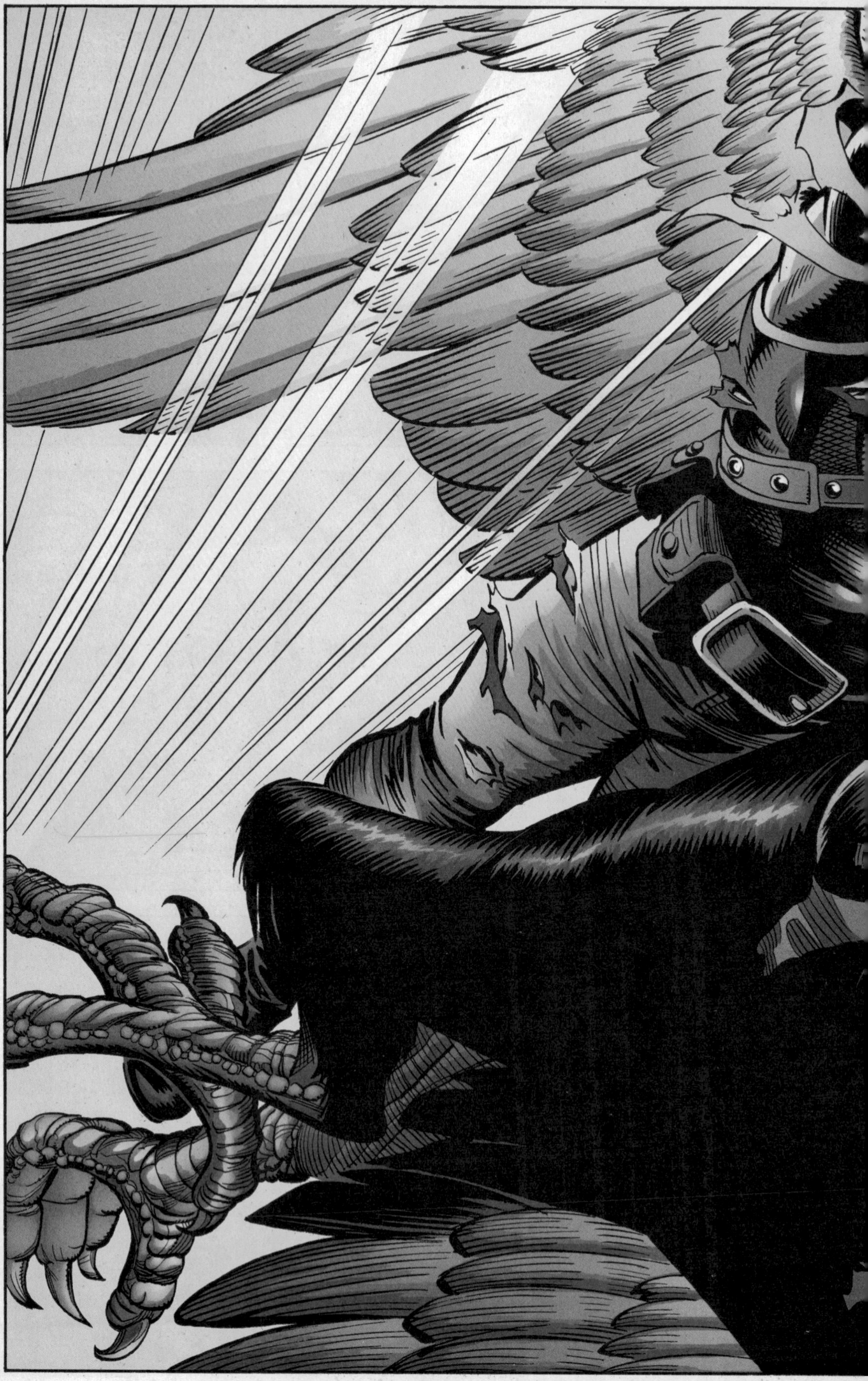

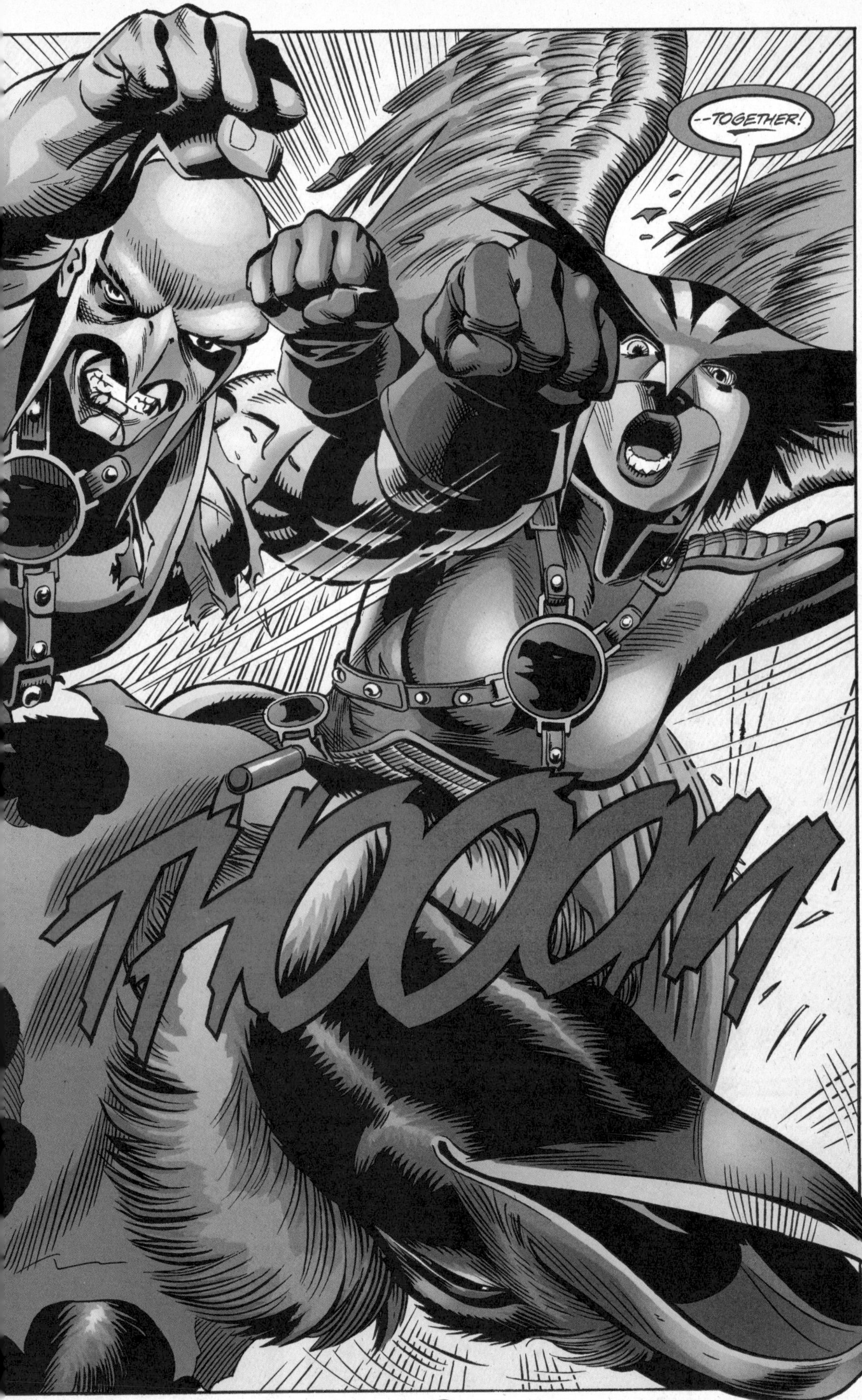
--TOGETHER!
THOOOM

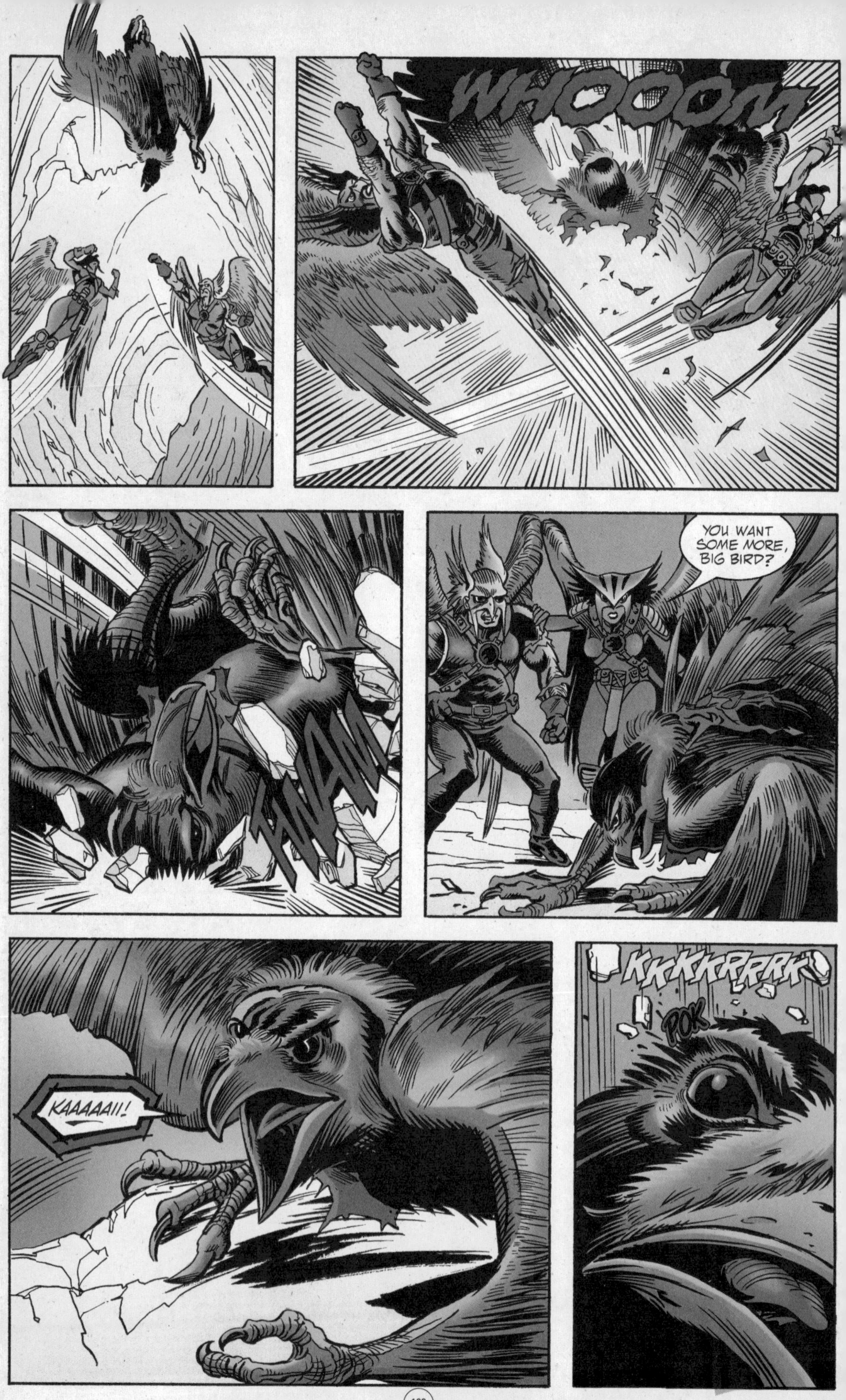
WHOOOOM
THAM
YOU WANT SOME MORE, BIG BIRD?
KAAAAAII!
KKKKRRRK
POK

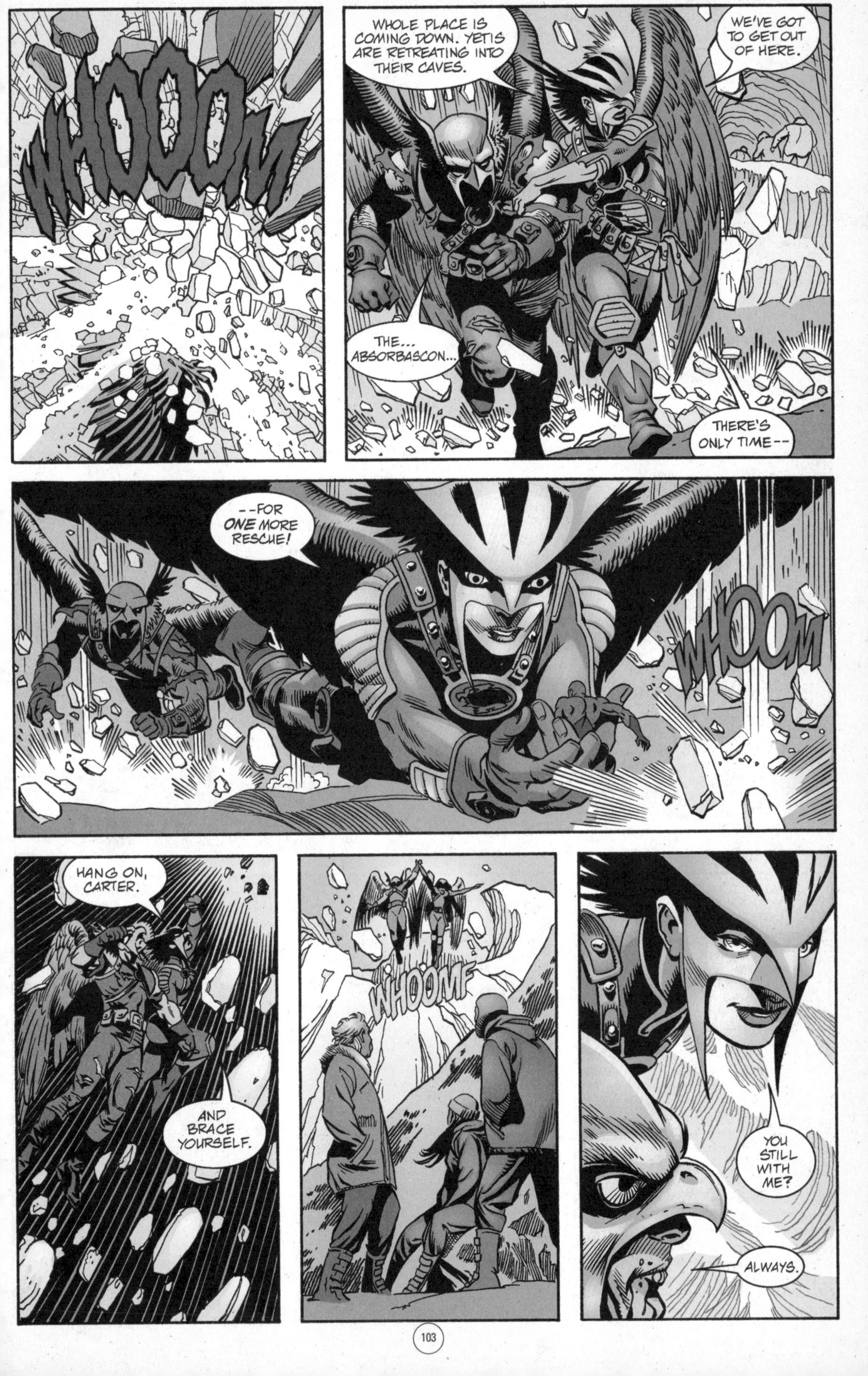
WHOOOM
WHOLE PLACE IS COMING DOWN. YETIS ARE RETREATING INTO THEIR CAVES.
WE'VE GOT TO GET OUT OF HERE.
THE... ABSORBASCON...
THERE'S ONLY TIME--
--FOR ONE MORE RESCUE!
WHOOM
HANG ON, CARTER.
AND BRACE YOURSELF.
WHOOMF
YOU STILL WITH ME?
ALWAYS.

STRANGE. NO ONE'S ANSWERING THE MUSEUM PHONE.

YOU'RE SURE YOU'RE ALL RIGHT TO *FLY?*

MY *WOUNDS* ARE ALREADY CLOSING, ATOM. THE *NTH METAL.*

SPEEDS UP THE HEALING PROCESS TOO?

I *DO* WANT TO *STUDY* THIS. AND YOU OWE ME A *DINNER.* WHEN YOU HAVE A SPARE MOMENT, OF COURSE.

A SPARE MOMENT?

WITH HATH-SET *GONE*... THANKS TO HAWKGIRL--

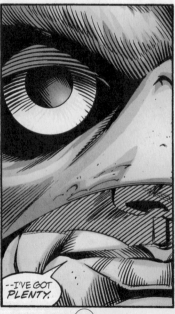

--I'VE GOT *PLENTY.*

KENDRA'S *DETERMINATION* IS UNBELIEVABLE.

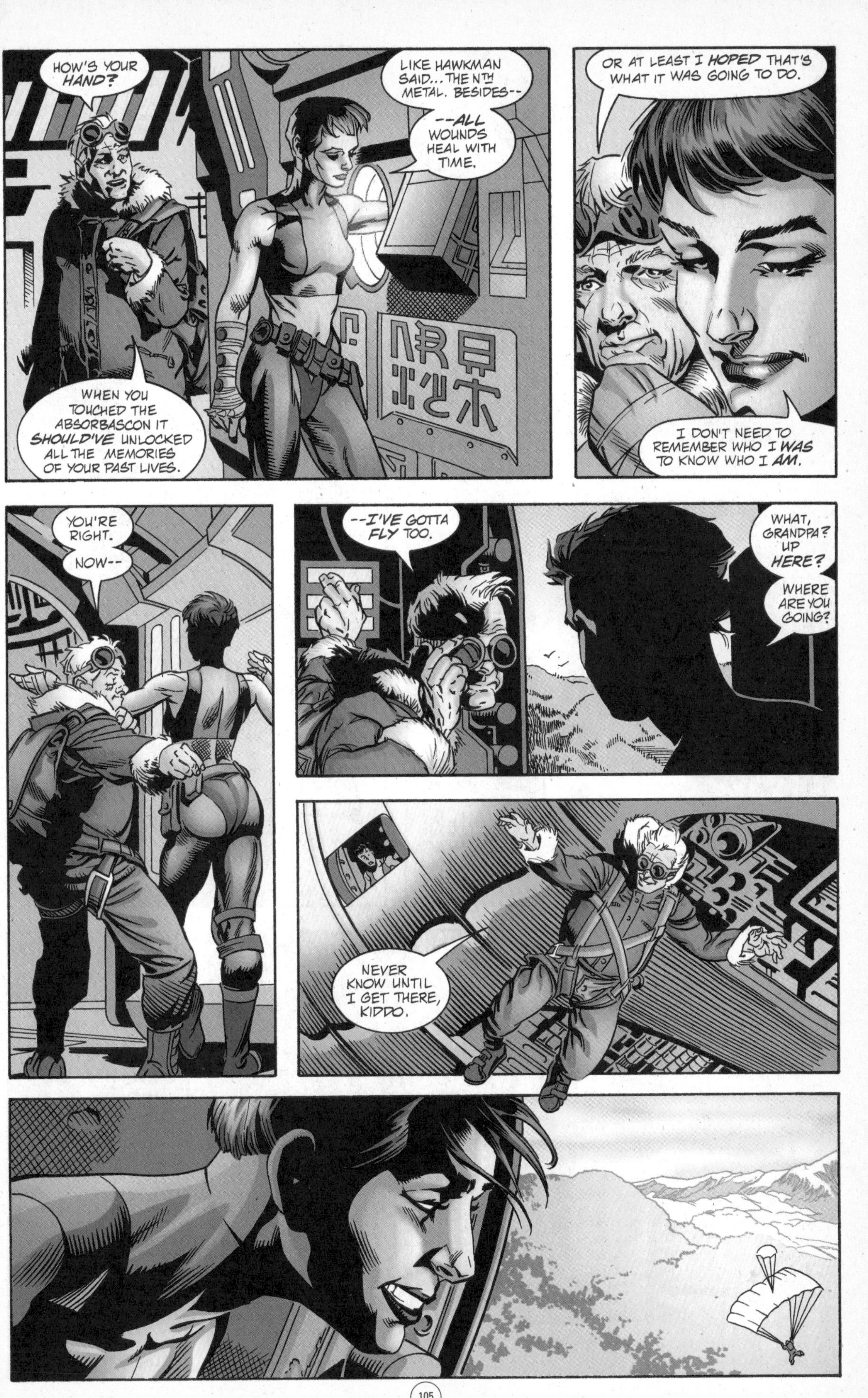
HOW'S YOUR HAND?
LIKE HAWKMAN SAID... THE NTH METAL. BESIDES--
--ALL WOUNDS HEAL WITH TIME.
WHEN YOU TOUCHED THE ABSORBASCON IT SHOULD'VE UNLOCKED ALL THE MEMORIES OF YOUR PAST LIVES.
OR AT LEAST I HOPED THAT'S WHAT IT WAS GOING TO DO.
I DON'T NEED TO REMEMBER WHO I WAS TO KNOW WHO I AM.
YOU'RE RIGHT.
NOW--
--I'VE GOTTA FLY TOO.
WHAT, GRANDPA? UP HERE?
WHERE ARE YOU GOING?
NEVER KNOW UNTIL I GET THERE, KIDDO.

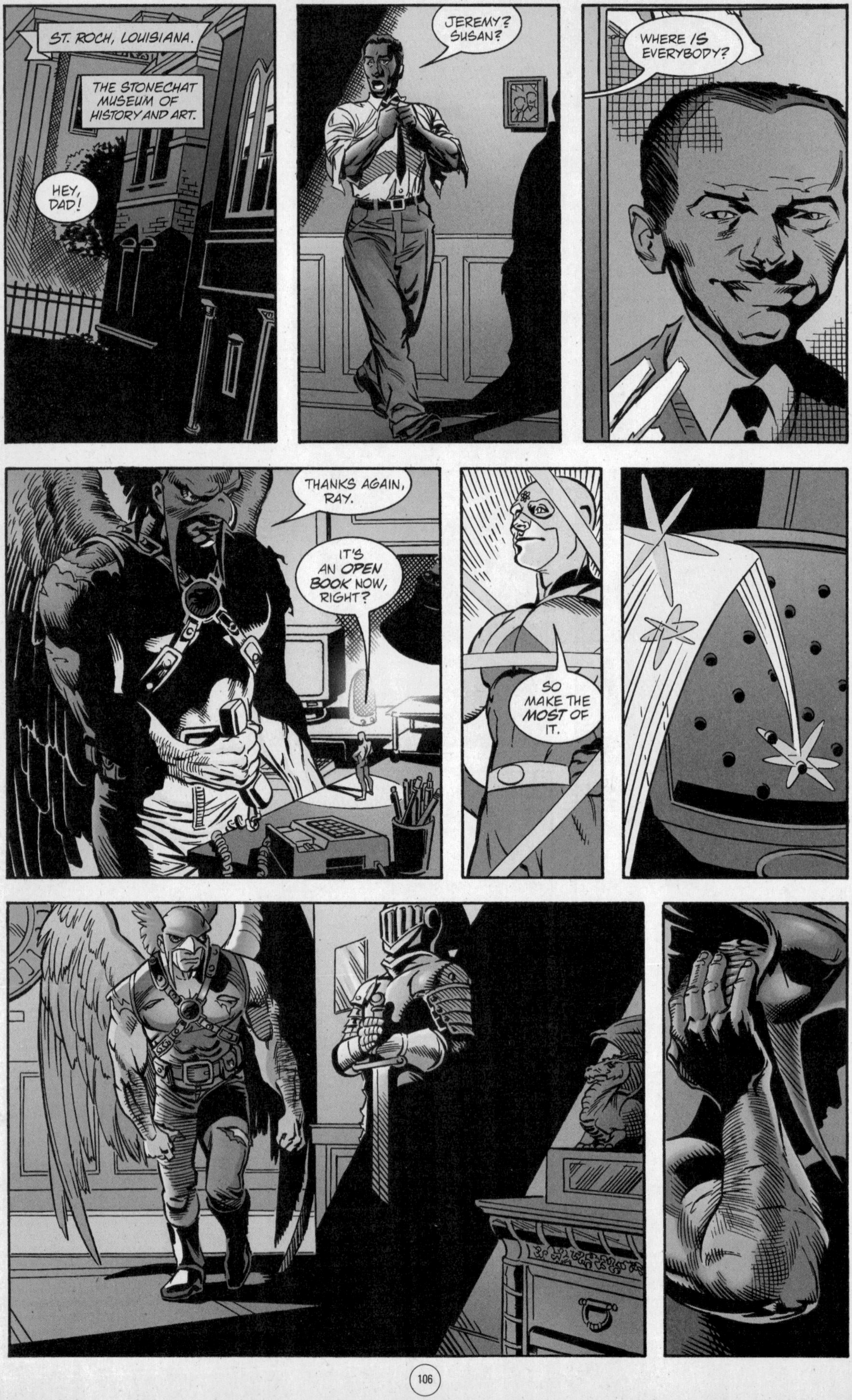

ST. ROCH, LOUISIANA.
THE STONECHAT MUSEUM OF HISTORY AND ART.
HEY, DAD!
JEREMY? SUSAN?
WHERE IS EVERYBODY?
THANKS AGAIN, RAY.
IT'S AN OPEN BOOK NOW, RIGHT?
SO MAKE THE MOST OF IT.

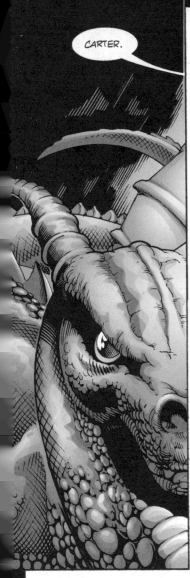

CARTER.

KENDRA.

I WAS JUST... THINKING.

ABOUT THE PAST?

YES.

AND THE FUTURE.

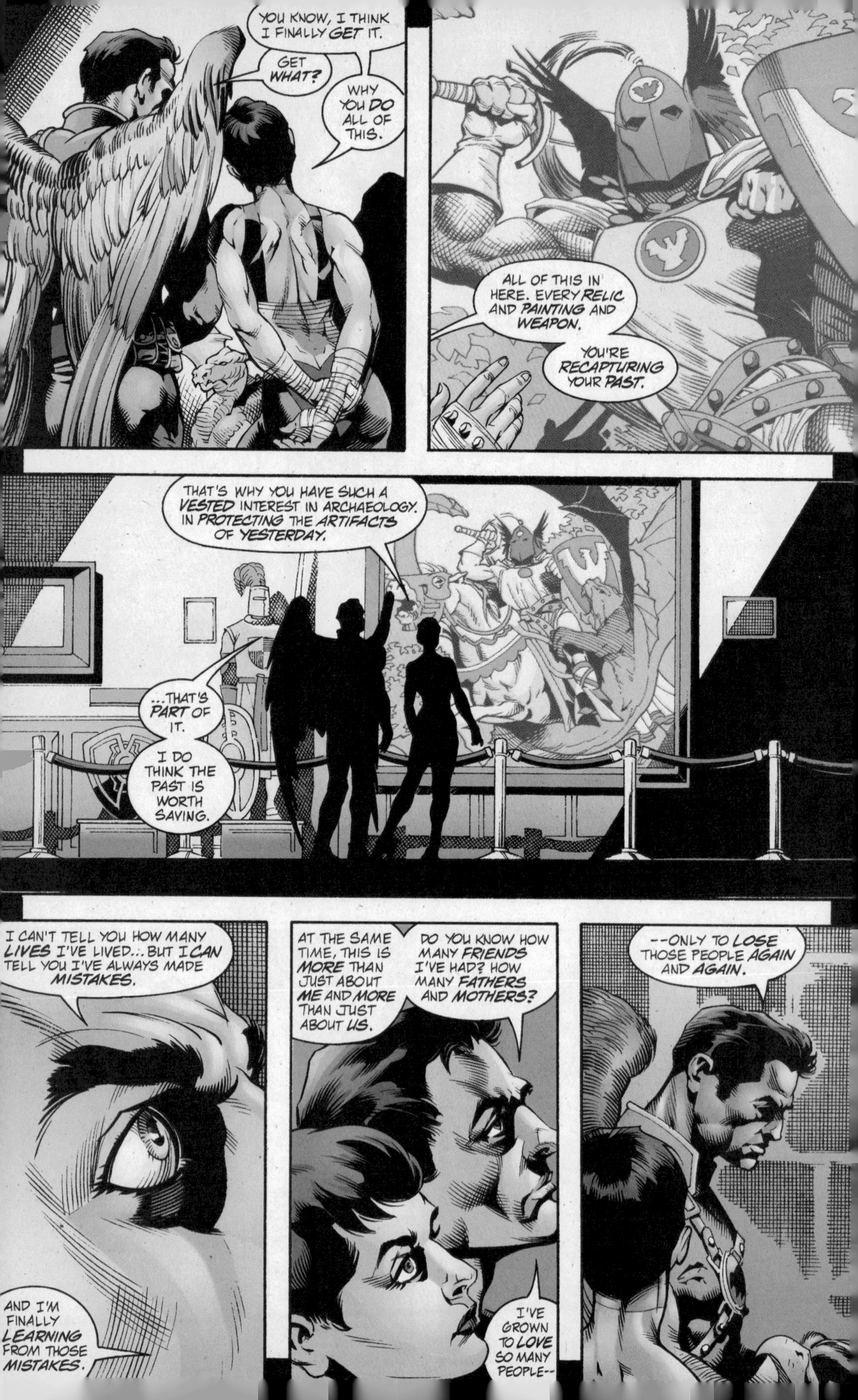
YOU KNOW, I THINK I FINALLY GET IT.
GET WHAT?
WHY YOU DO ALL OF THIS.
ALL OF THIS IN HERE. EVERY RELIC AND PAINTING AND WEAPON.
YOU'RE RECAPTURING YOUR PAST.
THAT'S WHY YOU HAVE SUCH A VESTED INTEREST IN ARCHAEOLOGY. IN PROTECTING THE ARTIFACTS OF YESTERDAY.
...THAT'S PART OF IT.
I DO THINK THE PAST IS WORTH SAVING.
I CAN'T TELL YOU HOW MANY LIVES I'VE LIVED... BUT I CAN TELL YOU I'VE ALWAYS MADE MISTAKES.
AND I'M FINALLY LEARNING FROM THOSE MISTAKES.
AT THE SAME TIME, THIS IS MORE THAN JUST ABOUT ME AND MORE THAN JUST ABOUT US.
DO YOU KNOW HOW MANY FRIENDS I'VE HAD? HOW MANY FATHERS AND MOTHERS?
I'VE GROWN TO LOVE SO MANY PEOPLE--
--ONLY TO LOSE THOSE PEOPLE AGAIN AND AGAIN.

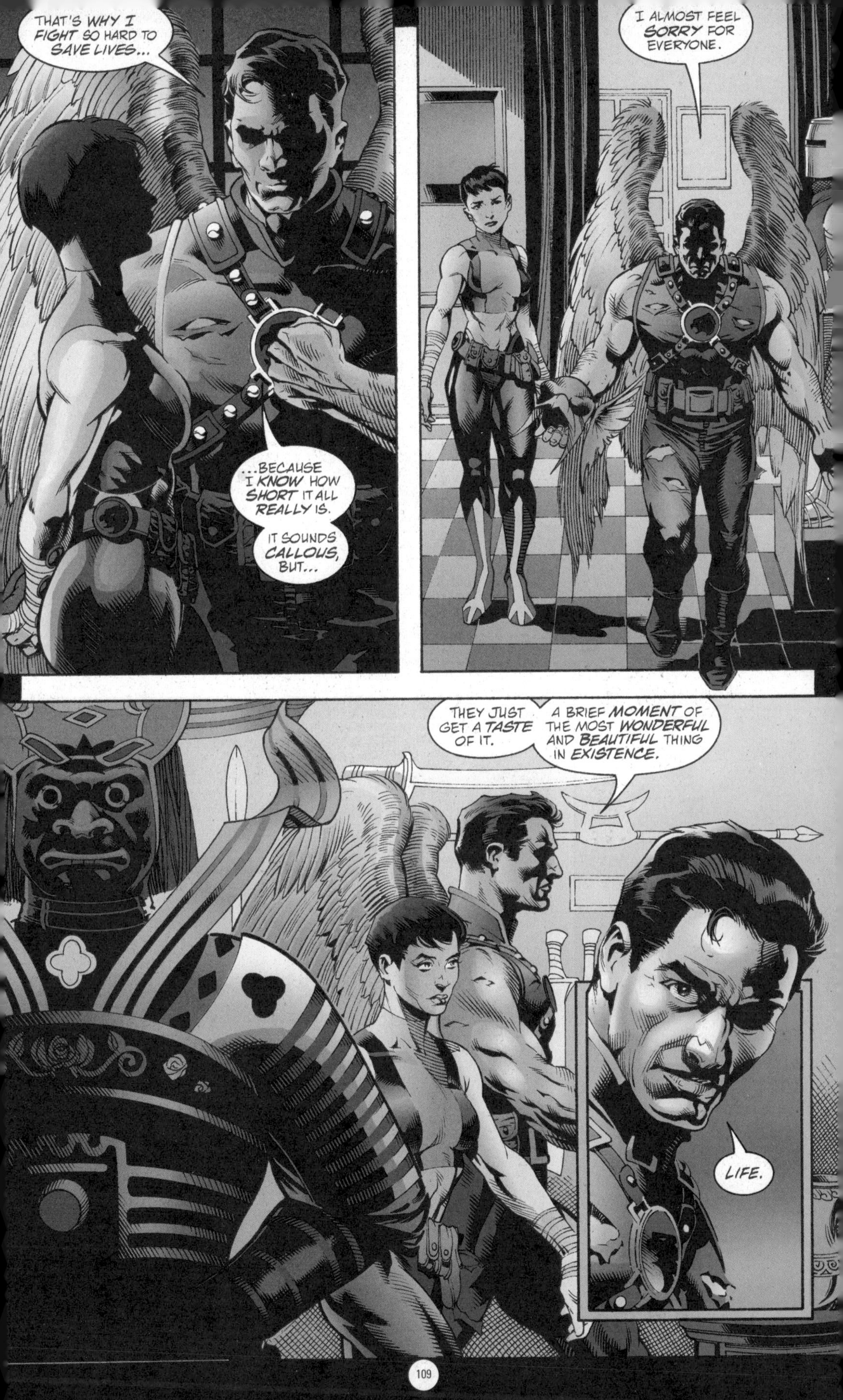
THAT'S WHY I FIGHT SO HARD TO SAVE LIVES...
...BECAUSE I KNOW HOW SHORT IT ALL REALLY IS.
IT SOUNDS CALLOUS, BUT...
I ALMOST FEEL SORRY FOR EVERYONE.
THEY JUST GET A TASTE OF IT.
A BRIEF MOMENT OF THE MOST WONDERFUL AND BEAUTIFUL THING IN EXISTENCE.
LIFE.

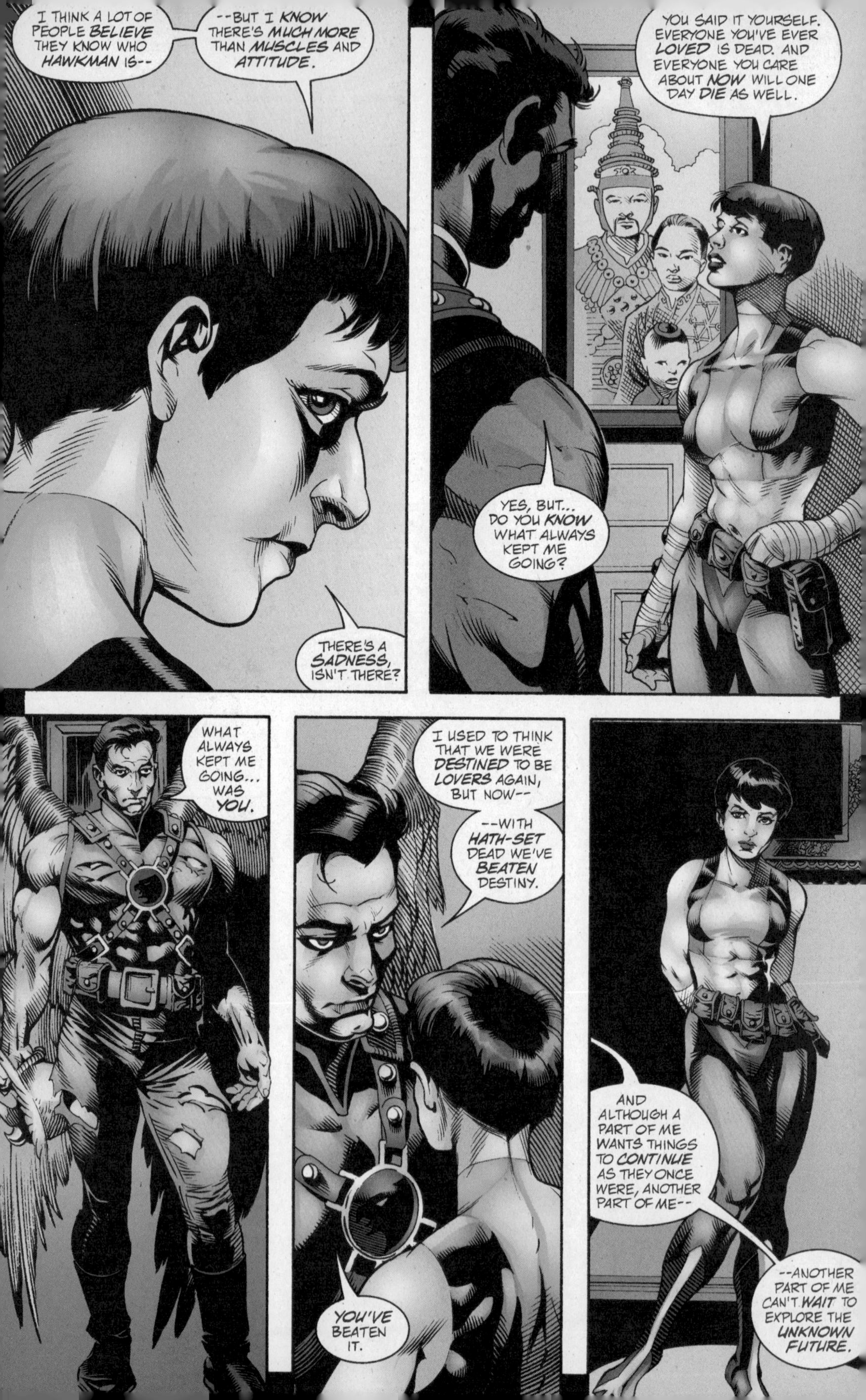
I THINK A LOT OF PEOPLE BELIEVE THEY KNOW WHO HAWKMAN IS--
--BUT I KNOW THERE'S MUCH MORE THAN MUSCLES AND ATTITUDE.
THERE'S A SADNESS, ISN'T THERE?
YOU SAID IT YOURSELF. EVERYONE YOU'VE EVER LOVED IS DEAD. AND EVERYONE YOU CARE ABOUT NOW WILL ONE DAY DIE AS WELL.
YES, BUT... DO YOU KNOW WHAT ALWAYS KEPT ME GOING?
WHAT ALWAYS KEPT ME GOING... WAS YOU.
I USED TO THINK THAT WE WERE DESTINED TO BE LOVERS AGAIN, BUT NOW--
--WITH HATH-SET DEAD WE'VE BEATEN DESTINY.
YOU'VE BEATEN IT.
AND ALTHOUGH A PART OF ME WANTS THINGS TO CONTINUE AS THEY ONCE WERE, ANOTHER PART OF ME--
--ANOTHER PART OF ME CAN'T WAIT TO EXPLORE THE UNKNOWN FUTURE.

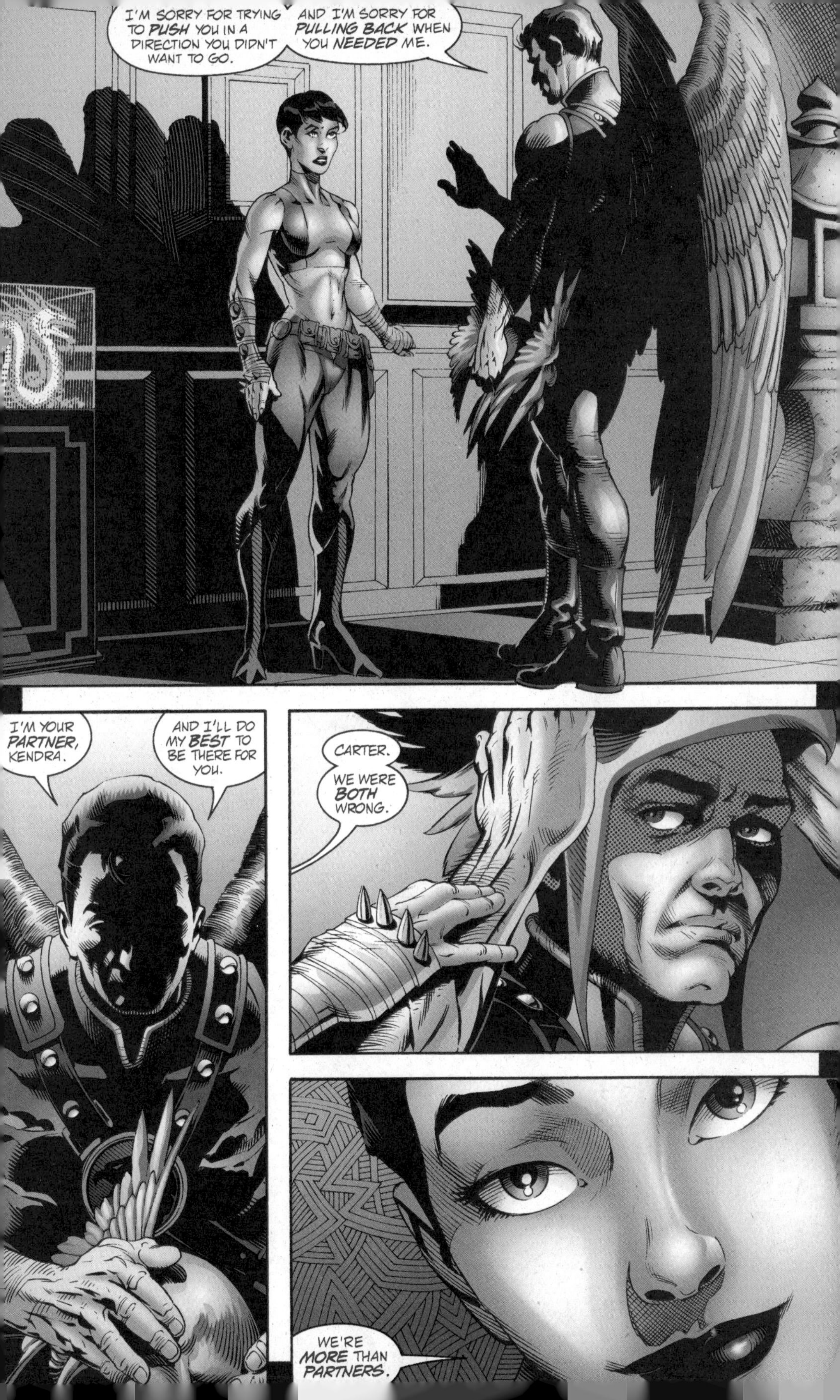
I'M SORRY FOR TRYING TO PUSH YOU IN A DIRECTION YOU DIDN'T WANT TO GO.
AND I'M SORRY FOR PULLING BACK WHEN YOU NEEDED ME.
I'M YOUR PARTNER, KENDRA.
AND I'LL DO MY BEST TO BE THERE FOR YOU.
CARTER.
WE WERE BOTH WRONG.
WE'RE MORE THAN PARTNERS.

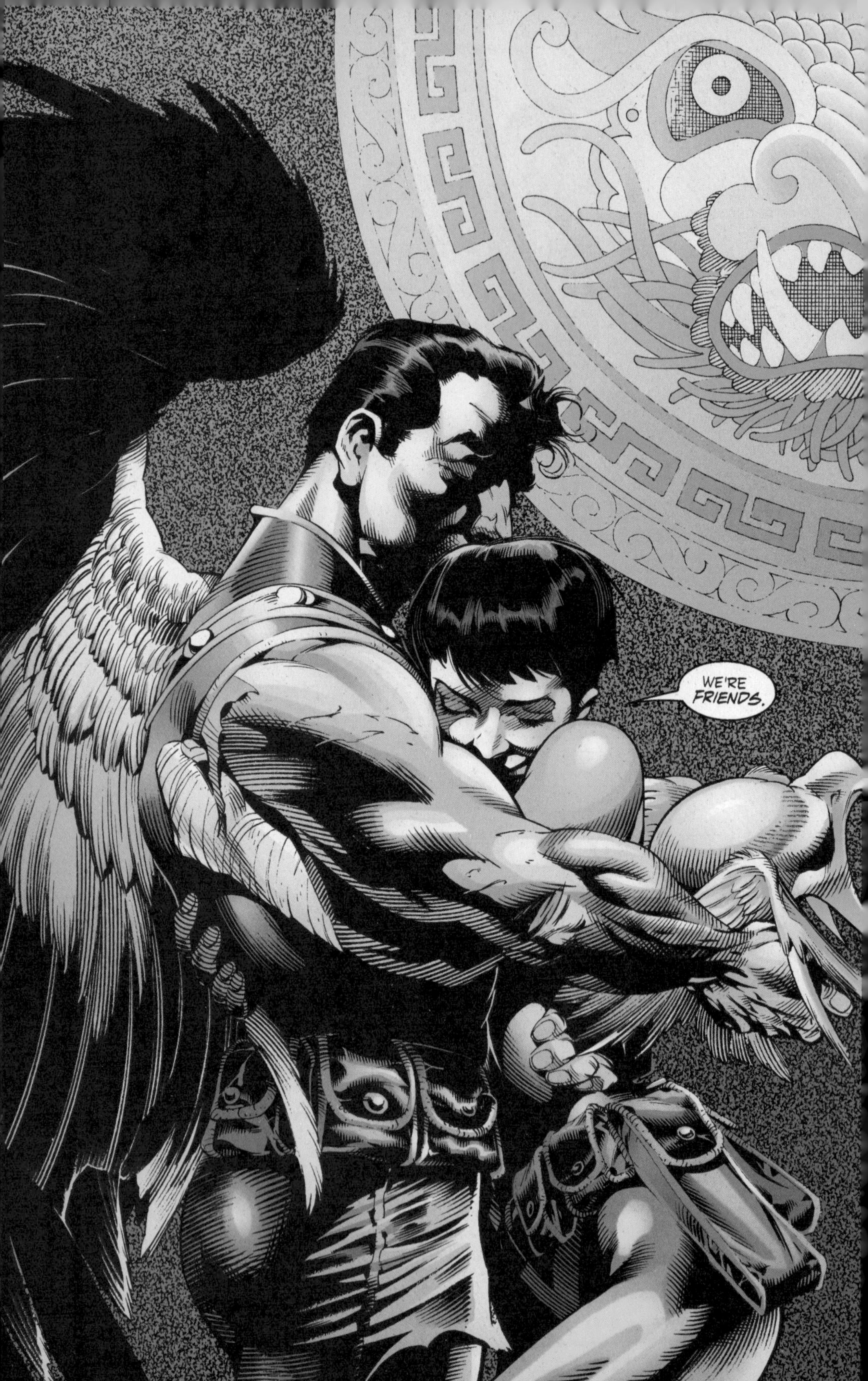
WE'RE FRIENDS.

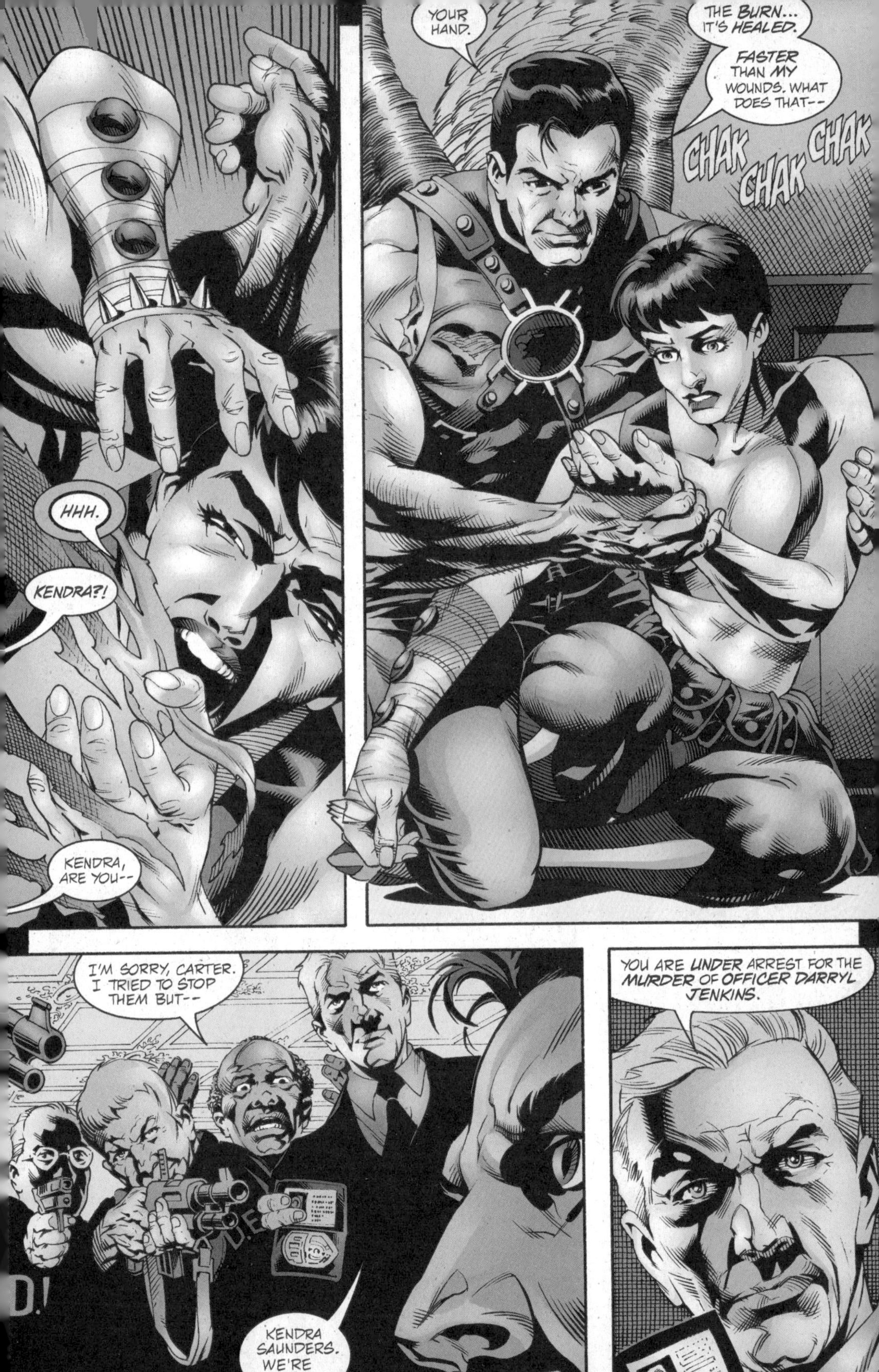
HHH.
KENDRA?!
KENDRA, ARE YOU--
YOUR HAND.
THE BURN... IT'S HEALED.
FASTER THAN MY WOUNDS. WHAT DOES THAT--
CHAK CHAK CHAK
I'M SORRY, CARTER. I TRIED TO STOP THEM BUT--
D!
KENDRA SAUNDERS. WE'RE D.E.O.
YOU ARE UNDER ARREST FOR THE MURDER OF OFFICER DARRYL JENKINS.

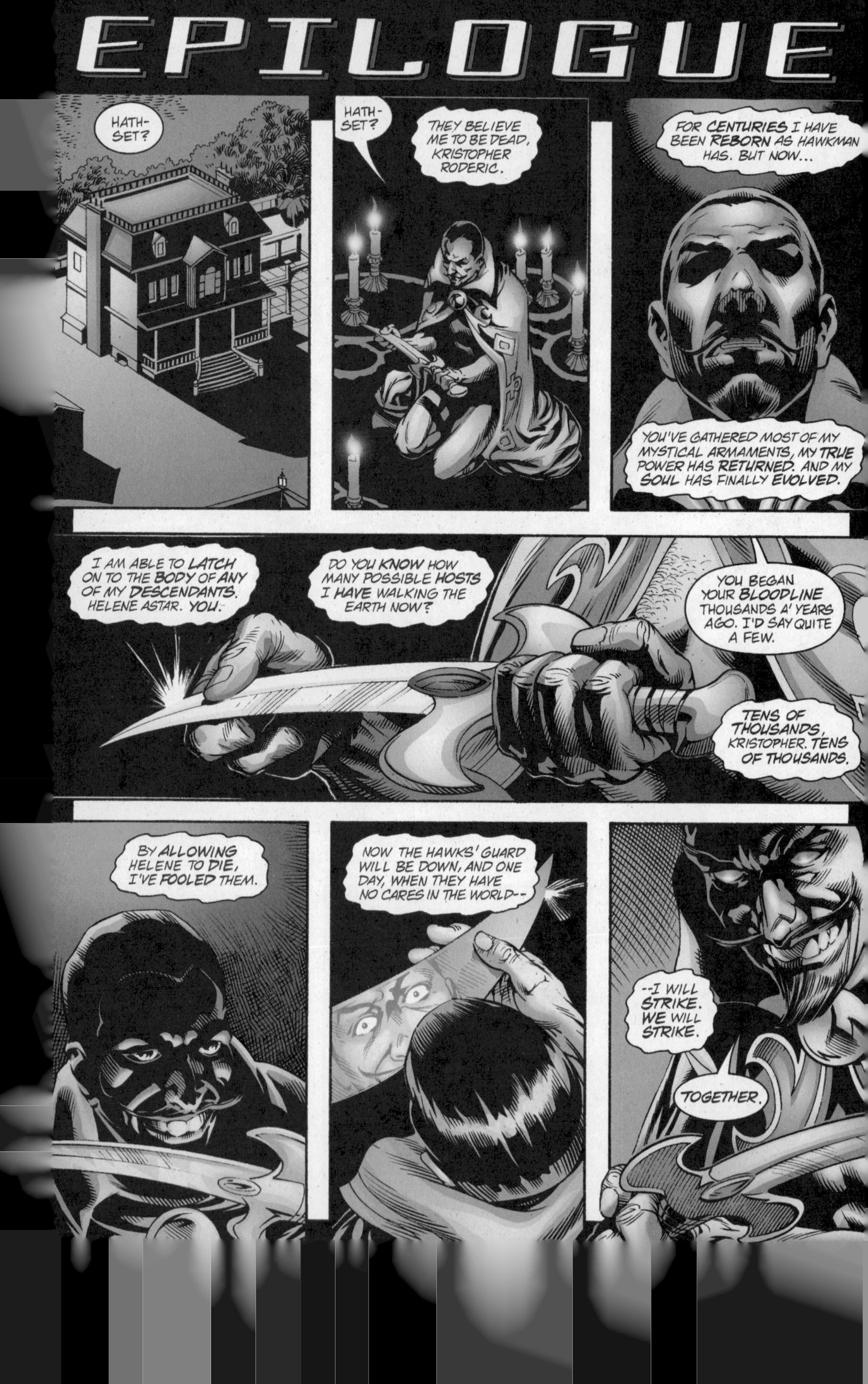
EPILOGUE
HATH-SET?
HATH-SET?
THEY BELIEVE ME TO BE DEAD, KRISTOPHER RODERIC.
FOR CENTURIES I HAVE BEEN REBORN AS HAWKMAN HAS. BUT NOW...
YOU'VE GATHERED MOST OF MY MYSTICAL ARMAMENTS, MY TRUE POWER HAS RETURNED. AND MY SOUL HAS FINALLY EVOLVED.
I AM ABLE TO LATCH ON TO THE BODY OF ANY OF MY DESCENDANTS. HELENE ASTAR. YOU.
DO YOU KNOW HOW MANY POSSIBLE HOSTS I HAVE WALKING THE EARTH NOW?
YOU BEGAN YOUR BLOODLINE THOUSANDS A' YEARS AGO. I'D SAY QUITE A FEW.
TENS OF THOUSANDS, KRISTOPHER. TENS OF THOUSANDS.
BY ALLOWING HELENE TO DIE, I'VE FOOLED THEM.
NOW THE HAWKS' GUARD WILL BE DOWN, AND ONE DAY, WHEN THEY HAVE NO CARES IN THE WORLD--
--I WILL STRIKE. WE WILL STRIKE.
TOGETHER.

YOU COME OUTTA THE SETTING SUN, *JUST* LIKE THEM DIME STORE BOOKS SAID YOU DONE.

RIDIN' TOWARDS THE NIGHT THEY SAID. EAGER FOR DARKNESS AND ITS *TERRORS* YOU'D DRAW BACK THE HAMMER ON.

OH YES, SIR, YOU DONE COME OUTTA A SUNSET ALL BURNT BLACK AND RUBY RED LIKE JAM FROM BERRY PIE.

'COURSE NO ONE KNEW YOU WAS RUNNING *FROM* SOMETHING.

MAYBE 'CAUSE YOU DIDN'T RIGHTLY KNOW THAT YOURSELF.

BUT YOU WAS AFRAID. JUST A LITTLE. SOMEWHERE IN THE PART OF YOUR HEAD YOU DIDN'T LIKE TO DWELL FOR MORE'N A *MITE* O'TIME.

TO THEM'AT SAW YOU, YOU WAS ALL *N'MORE* WHAT YOU SEEMED TO BE.

YOU WAS A MASK N'A GUN N'BRIGHT DEEDS IN DARK HOURS.

YOUR BIRTH NAME MIGHT'A BEEN ONE THING--*HAWKES* --FOR THE *FEW* WHO CARED TO KNOW AND THE *FEWER* STILL THAT YOU TOLD.

BUT YOUR MONIKER TO THEM'AT CROSSED YOU-- THEM'AT DREW AND DROPPED-- *THAT* WAS THE NAME YOU LET THE FOLKS HAVE TO CALL YOU.

TO THEM YOU WAS *NIGHTHAWK.* N'THERE WEREN'T BUT A *FEW* GUNS AS GOOD AS YOURS.

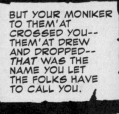

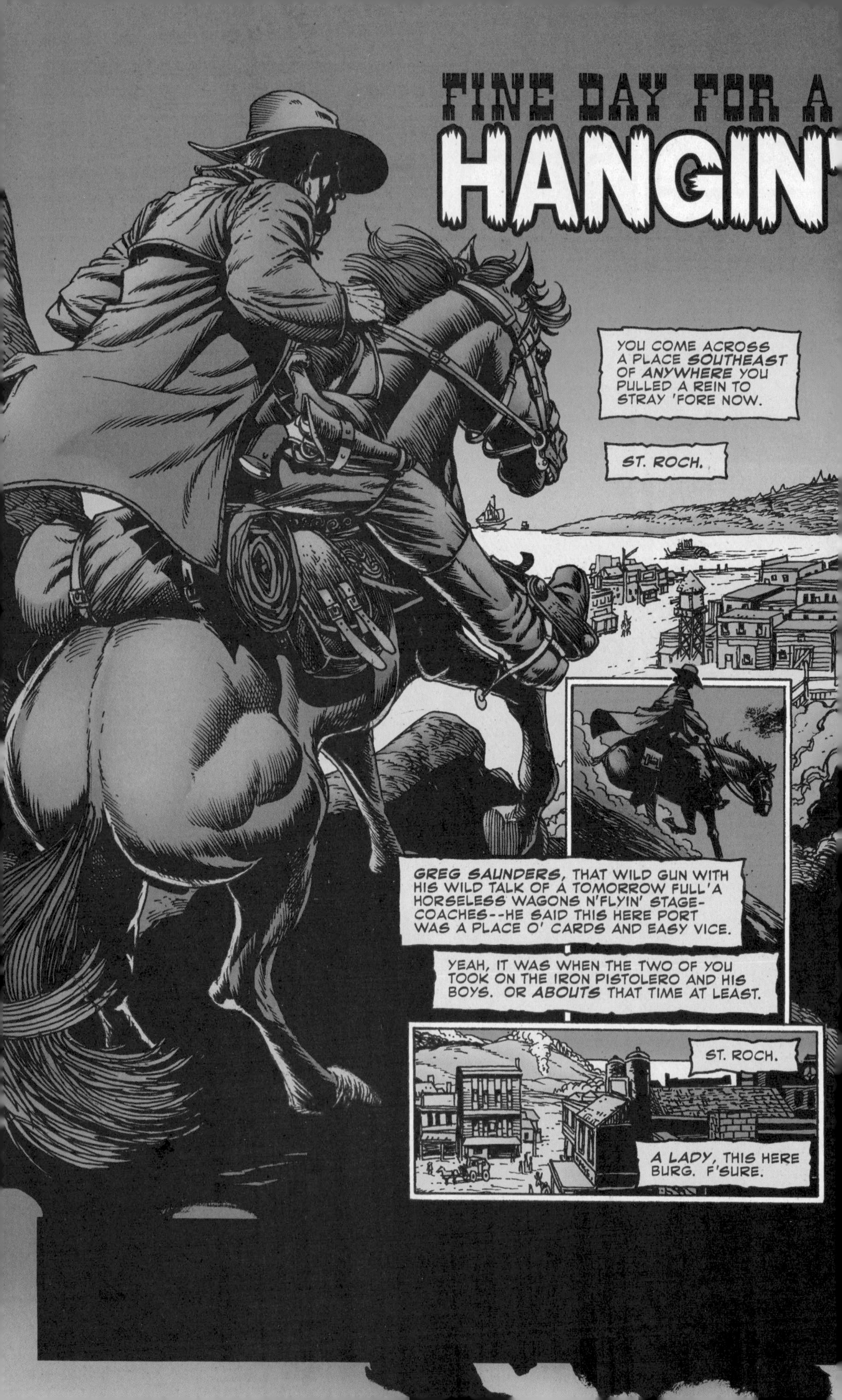
FINE DAY FOR A HANGIN'
YOU COME ACROSS A PLACE SOUTHEAST OF ANYWHERE YOU PULLED A REIN TO STRAY 'FORE NOW.
ST. ROCH.
GREG SAUNDERS, THAT WILD GUN WITH HIS WILD TALK OF A TOMORROW FULL'A HORSELESS WAGONS N'FLYIN' STAGE-COACHES--HE SAID THIS HERE PORT WAS A PLACE O' CARDS AND EASY VICE.
YEAH, IT WAS WHEN THE TWO OF YOU TOOK ON THE IRON PISTOLERO AND HIS BOYS. OR ABOUTS THAT TIME AT LEAST.
ST. ROCH.
A LADY, THIS HERE BURG. F'SURE.

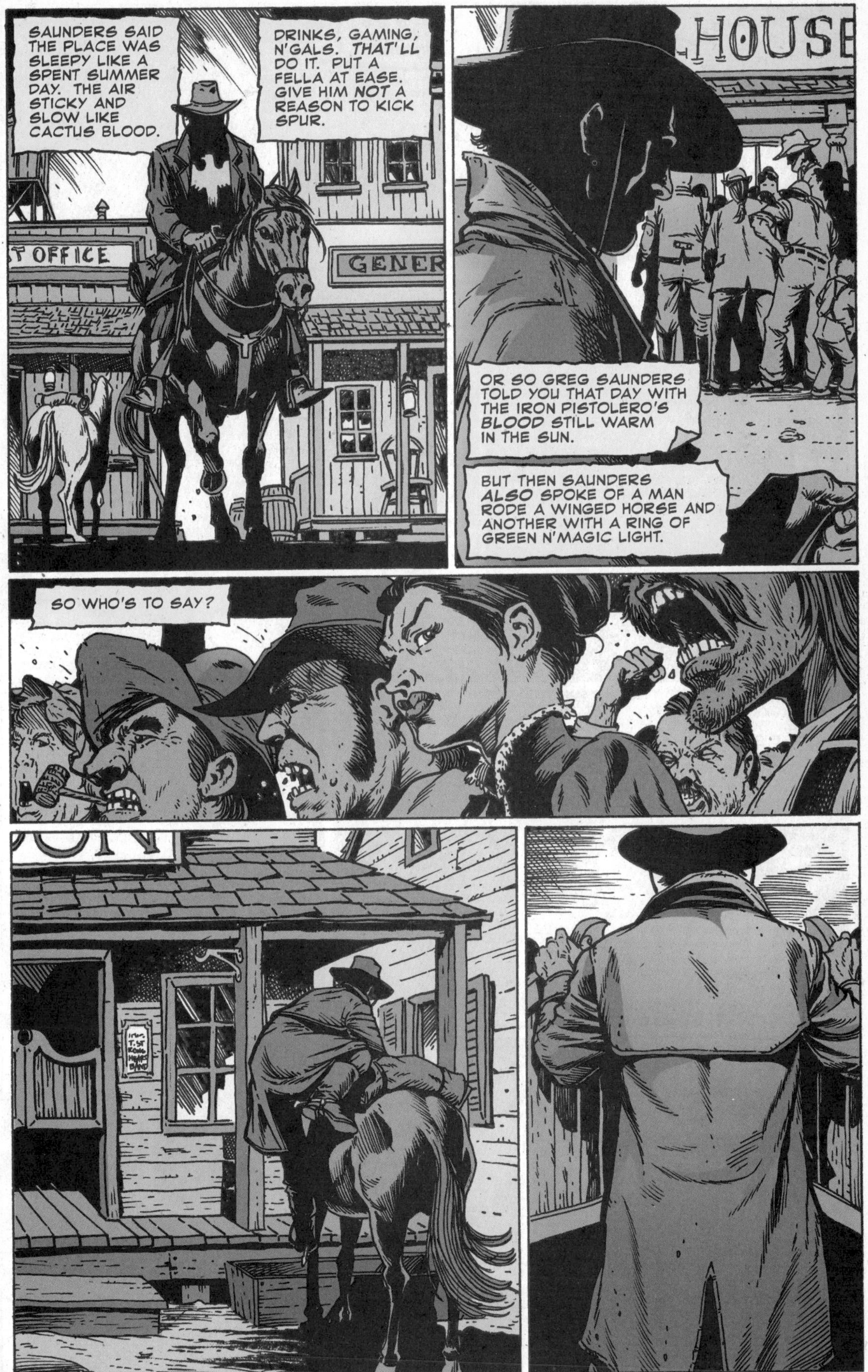

SAUNDERS SAID THE PLACE WAS SLEEPY LIKE A SPENT SUMMER DAY. THE AIR STICKY AND SLOW LIKE CACTUS BLOOD.
DRINKS, GAMING, N'GALS. THAT'LL DO IT. PUT A FELLA AT EASE. GIVE HIM NOT A REASON TO KICK SPUR.
T OFFICE
GENER
HOUSE
OR SO GREG SAUNDERS TOLD YOU THAT DAY WITH THE IRON PISTOLERO'S BLOOD STILL WARM IN THE SUN.
BUT THEN SAUNDERS ALSO SPOKE OF A MAN RODE A WINGED HORSE AND ANOTHER WITH A RING OF GREEN N'MAGIC LIGHT.
SO WHO'S TO SAY?

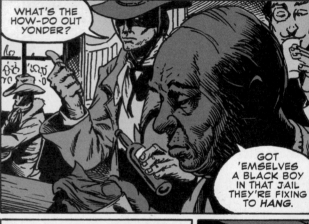

WHISKEY.

GLASS OR BOTTLE?

TAKE A WILD GUESS.

WHAT'S THE HOW-DO OUT YONDER?

GOT 'EMSELVES A BLACK BOY IN THAT JAIL THEY'RE FIXING TO *HANG*.

MANY'S THE BOY, WHITE N'BLACK, GOT 'EMSELVES THE WRONG SIDE OF A MARSHAL'S STAR. WHYFORE THE CROWD?

I JUST SERVE DRINKS.

NICE.

IT'S THE *CLIMATE,* DEAR FELLOW...

IT MAKES ONE TESTY, EVEN THIS NORMALLY RIBALD BARKEEP. YOUR QUESTION HAD MERIT. ALLOW ME TO SHED LIGHT UPON DARKNESS.

THE UNFORTUNATE WITHIN NEARBY GAOL IS NAMED *CYRUS EVANS.* HIS EMPLOYER, *BOIS GARVEY* GOT HIMSELF SHOT IN SOME VOLATILE BODY PARTS. THE OLD MAN DIED.

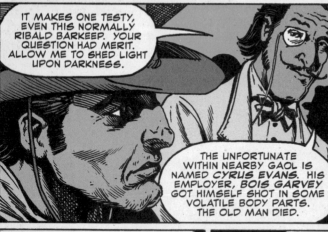

WORD GOT OUT FROM GARVEY'S LEGAL REPRESENTATION THAT EVANS IS THE *HEIR* ON ACCOUNT OF HIM BEING THE *ONLY ONE* WHO GAVE A TINKER'S CUSS FOR THE OLD MAN WHEN HIS WALK GOT SLOW AND HIS BLADDER WEAK.

EVANS' PEOPLE WERE SLAVES OF THE GARVEYS FOR GENERATIONS. BUT BOIS GARVEY CAUSED QUITE THE WAVE OF WHISPERS WHEN HE FREED THEM ALL...

I CALL BOIS GARVEY A GOOD MAN.

SO DID MOST PEOPLE. THAT'S WHY HIS MURDER HAS GOT THEM ALL HOT UNDER THE NECK-SCARVES.

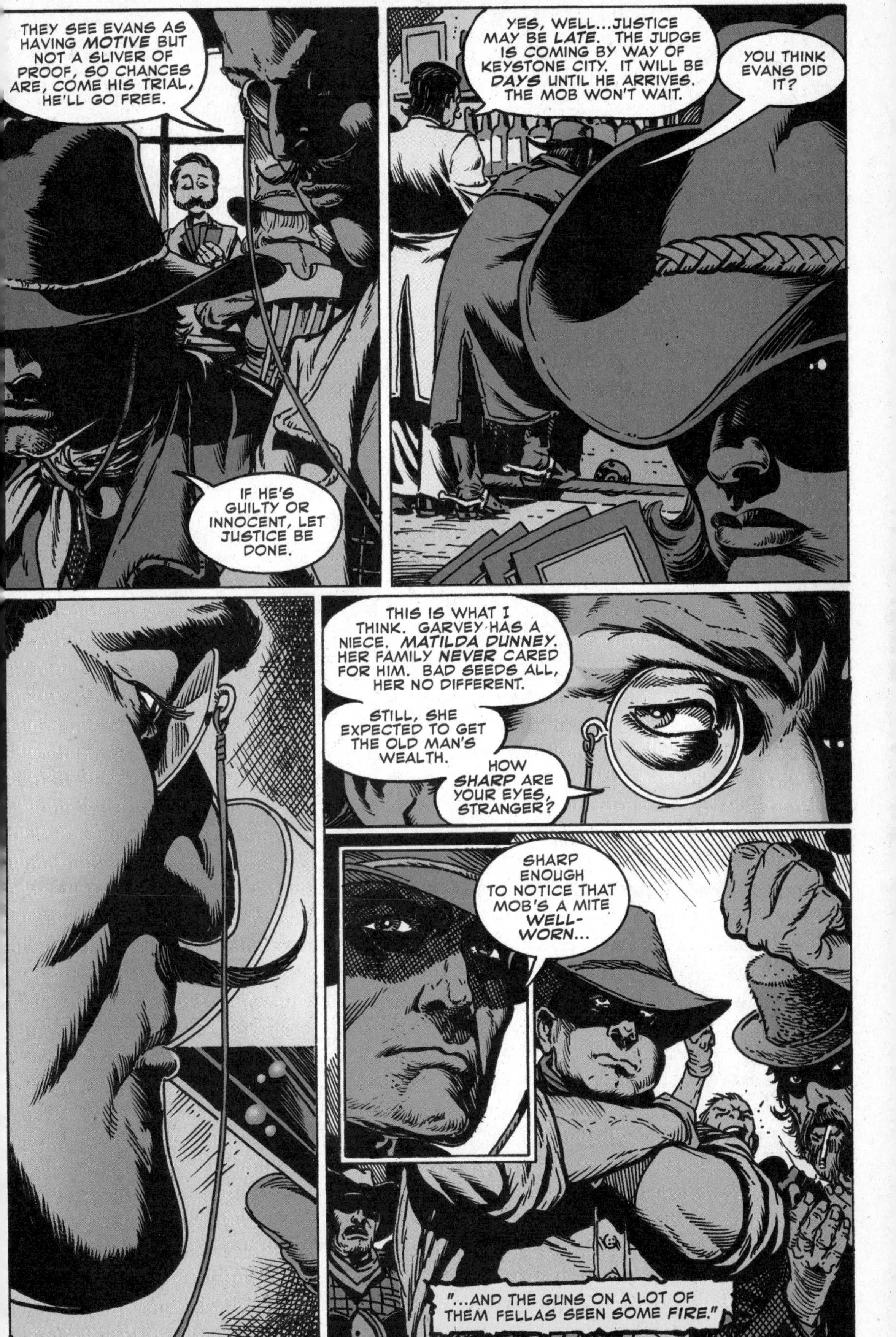
THEY SEE EVANS AS HAVING MOTIVE BUT NOT A SLIVER OF PROOF, SO CHANCES ARE, COME HIS TRIAL, HE'LL GO FREE.
IF HE'S GUILTY OR INNOCENT, LET JUSTICE BE DONE.
YES, WELL...JUSTICE MAY BE LATE. THE JUDGE IS COMING BY WAY OF KEYSTONE CITY. IT WILL BE DAYS UNTIL HE ARRIVES. THE MOB WON'T WAIT.
YOU THINK EVANS DID IT?
THIS IS WHAT I THINK. GARVEY HAS A NIECE. MATILDA DUNNEY. HER FAMILY NEVER CARED FOR HIM. BAD SEEDS ALL, HER NO DIFFERENT.
STILL, SHE EXPECTED TO GET THE OLD MAN'S WEALTH.
HOW SHARP ARE YOUR EYES, STRANGER?
SHARP ENOUGH TO NOTICE THAT MOB'S A MITE WELL-WORN...
"...AND THE GUNS ON A LOT OF THEM FELLAS SEEN SOME FIRE."

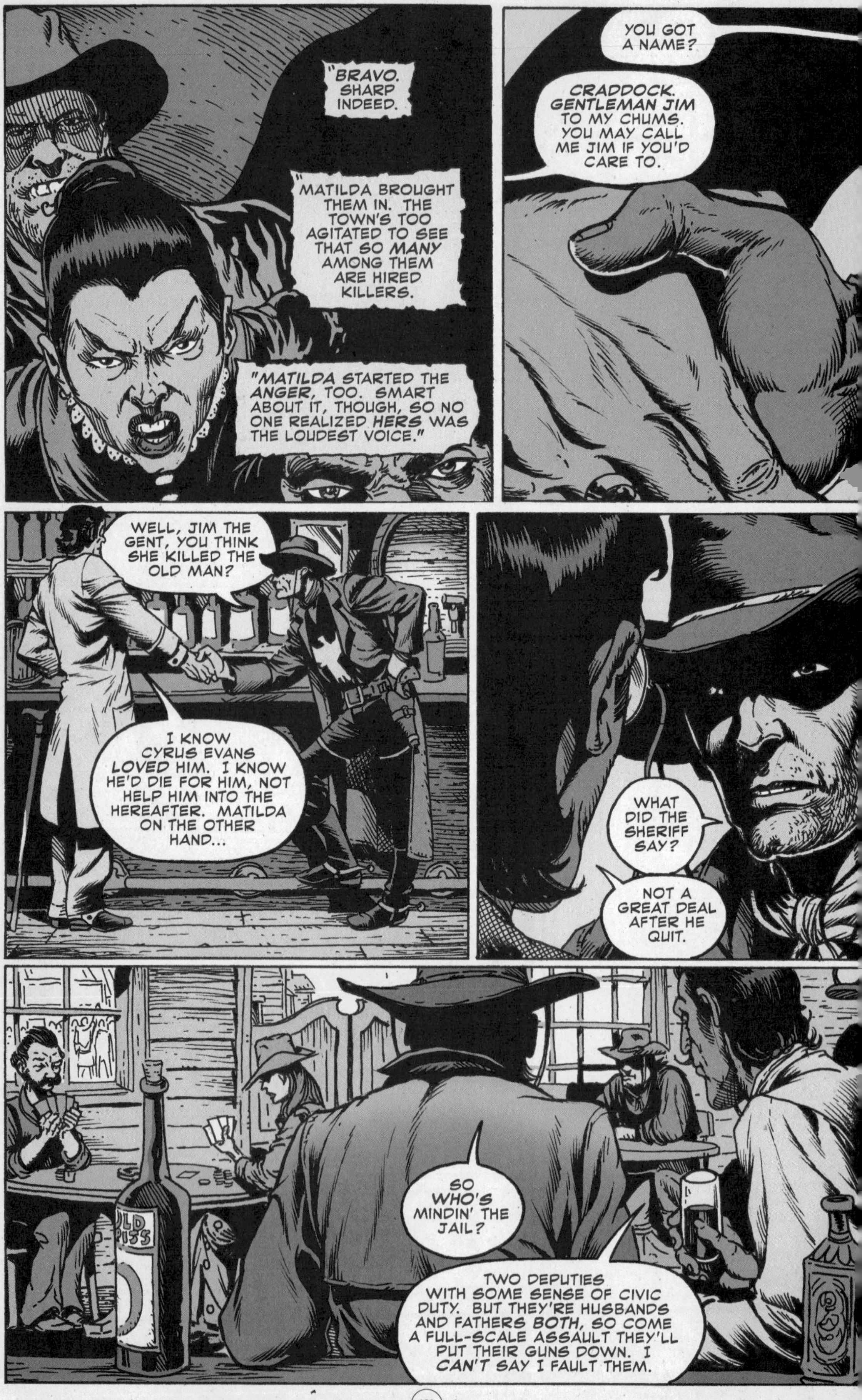
"BRAVO. SHARP INDEED.
"MATILDA BROUGHT THEM IN. THE TOWN'S TOO AGITATED TO SEE THAT SO MANY AMONG THEM ARE HIRED KILLERS.
"MATILDA STARTED THE ANGER, TOO. SMART ABOUT IT, THOUGH, SO NO ONE REALIZED HERS WAS THE LOUDEST VOICE."
YOU GOT A NAME?
CRADDOCK. GENTLEMAN JIM TO MY CHUMS. YOU MAY CALL ME JIM IF YOU'D CARE TO.
WELL, JIM THE GENT, YOU THINK SHE KILLED THE OLD MAN?
I KNOW CYRUS EVANS LOVED HIM. I KNOW HE'D DIE FOR HIM, NOT HELP HIM INTO THE HEREAFTER. MATILDA ON THE OTHER HAND...
WHAT DID THE SHERIFF SAY?
NOT A GREAT DEAL AFTER HE QUIT.
SO WHO'S MINDIN' THE JAIL?
TWO DEPUTIES WITH SOME SENSE OF CIVIC DUTY. BUT THEY'RE HUSBANDS AND FATHERS BOTH, SO COME A FULL-SCALE ASSAULT THEY'LL PUT THEIR GUNS DOWN. I CAN'T SAY I FAULT THEM.

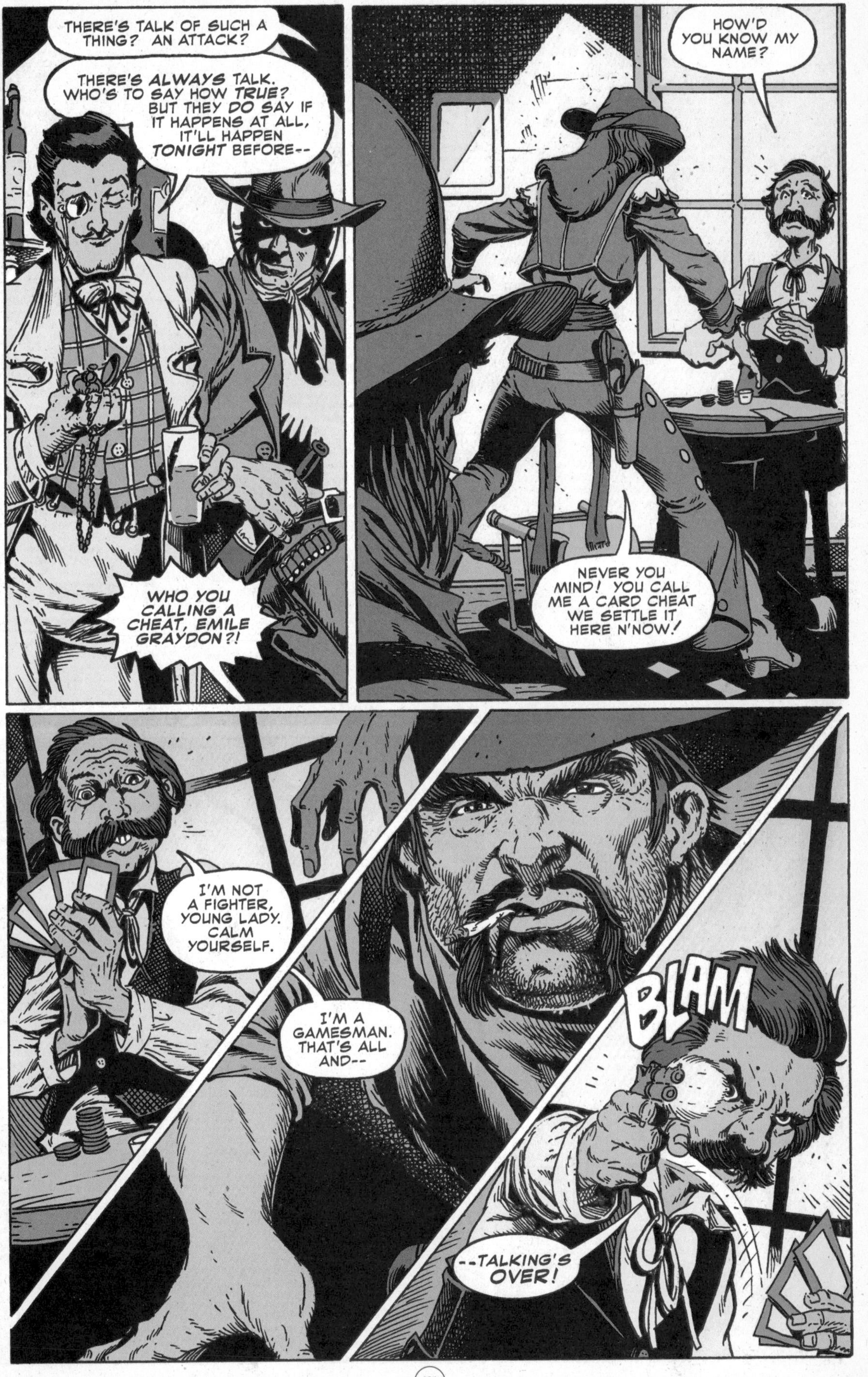
THERE'S TALK OF SUCH A THING? AN ATTACK?
THERE'S ALWAYS TALK. WHO'S TO SAY HOW TRUE? BUT THEY DO SAY IF IT HAPPENS AT ALL, IT'LL HAPPEN TONIGHT BEFORE--
WHO YOU CALLING A CHEAT, EMILE GRAYDON?!
HOW'D YOU KNOW MY NAME?
NEVER YOU MIND! YOU CALL ME A CARD CHEAT WE SETTLE IT HERE N'NOW!
I'M NOT A FIGHTER, YOUNG LADY. CALM YOURSELF.
I'M A GAMESMAN. THAT'S ALL AND--
BLAM
--TALKING'S OVER!

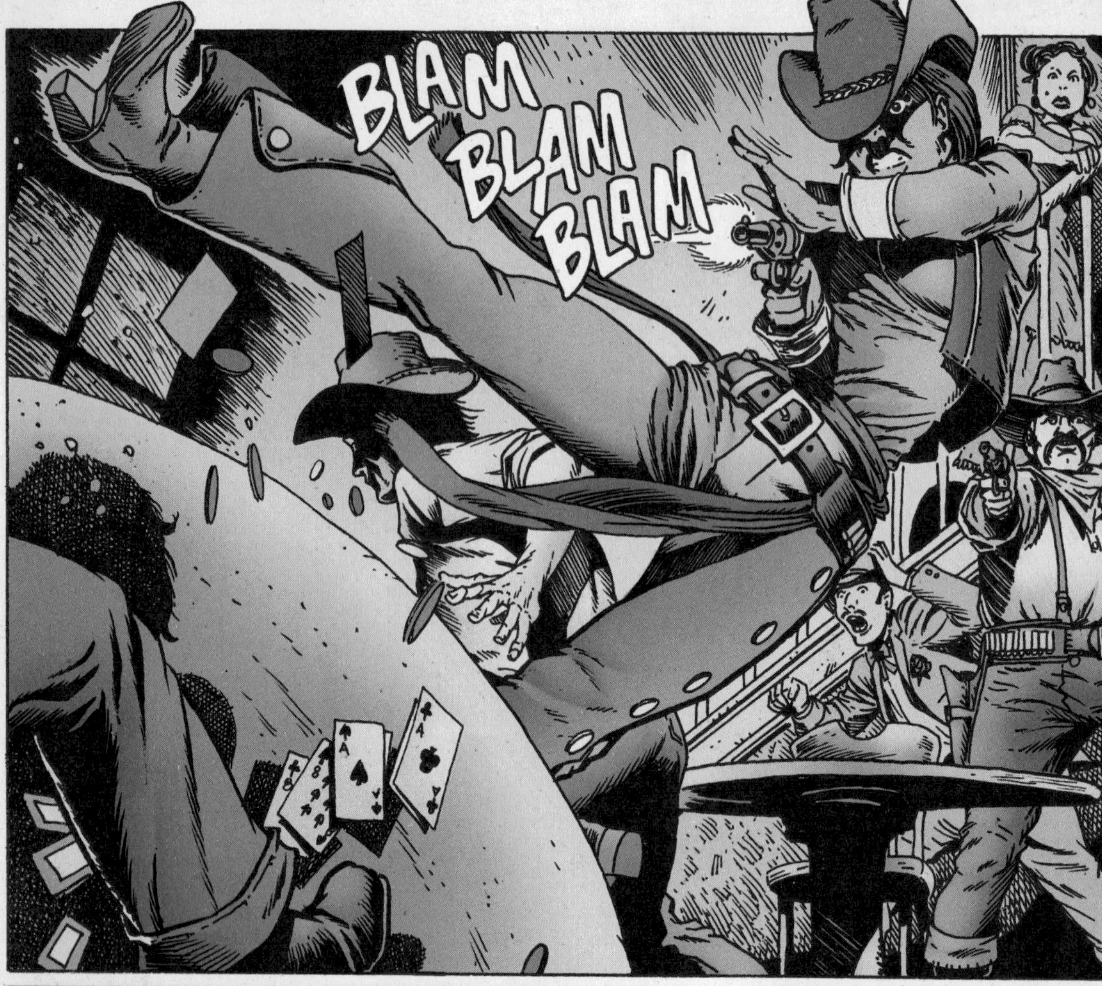
BLAM
BLAM
BLAM

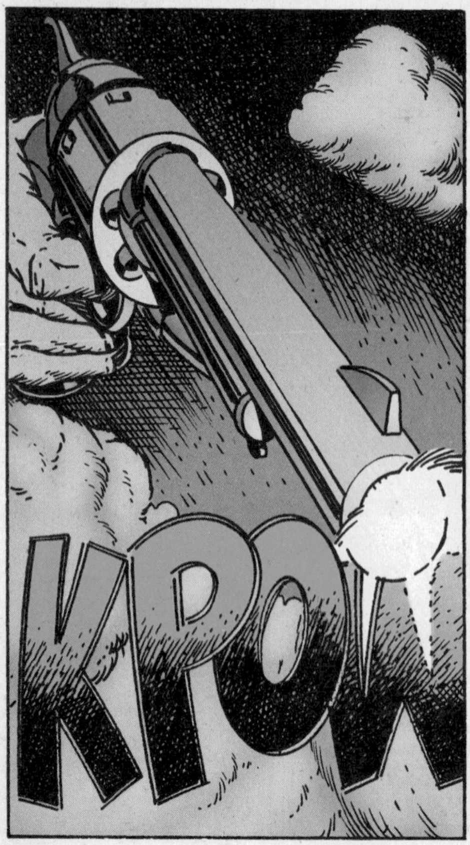
KPOW

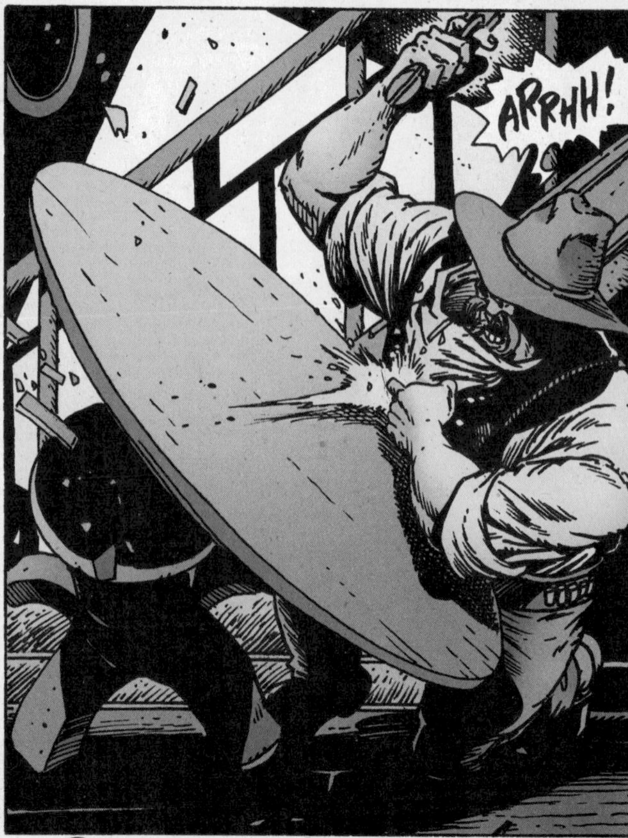
ARRHH!

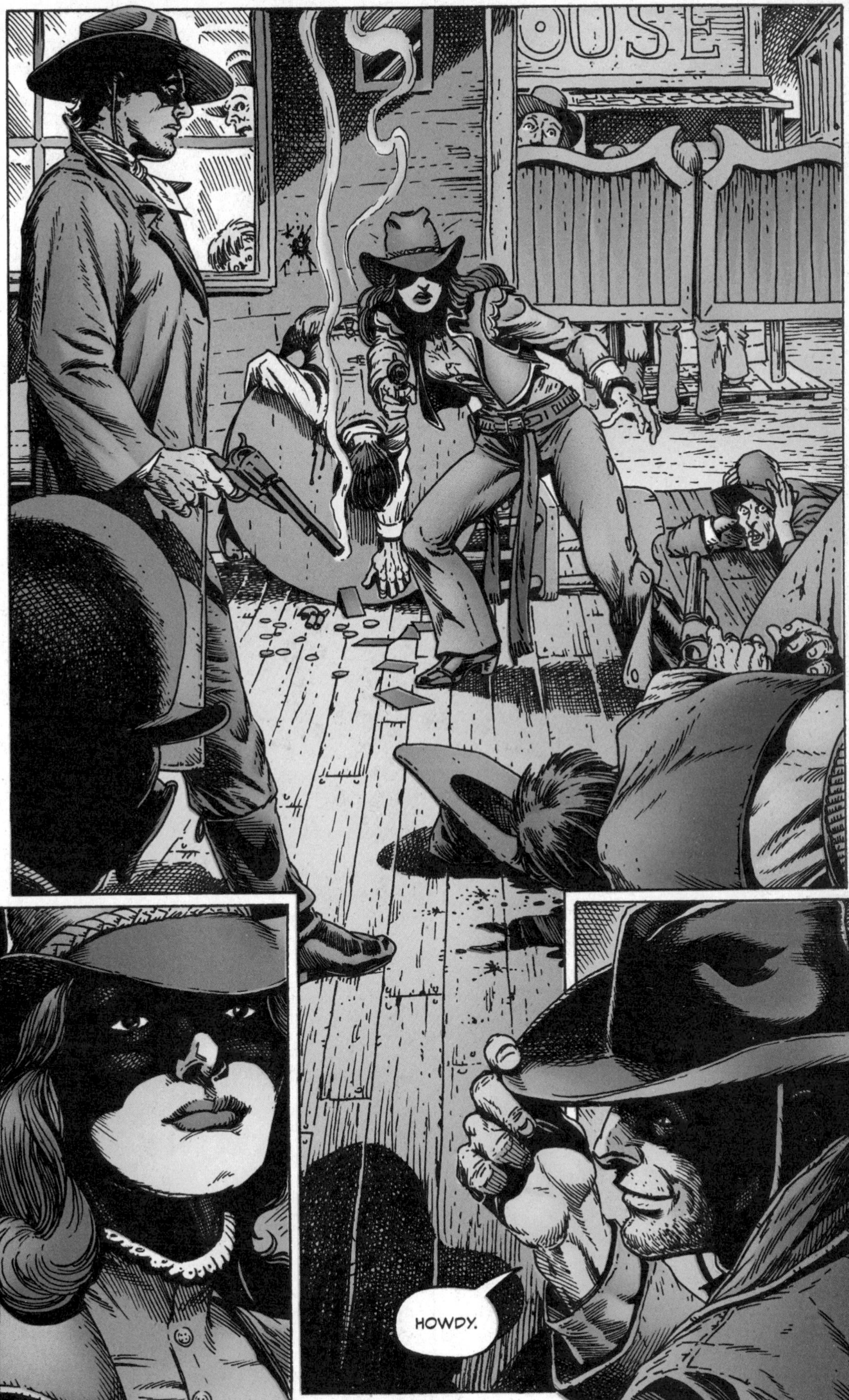
HOWDY.

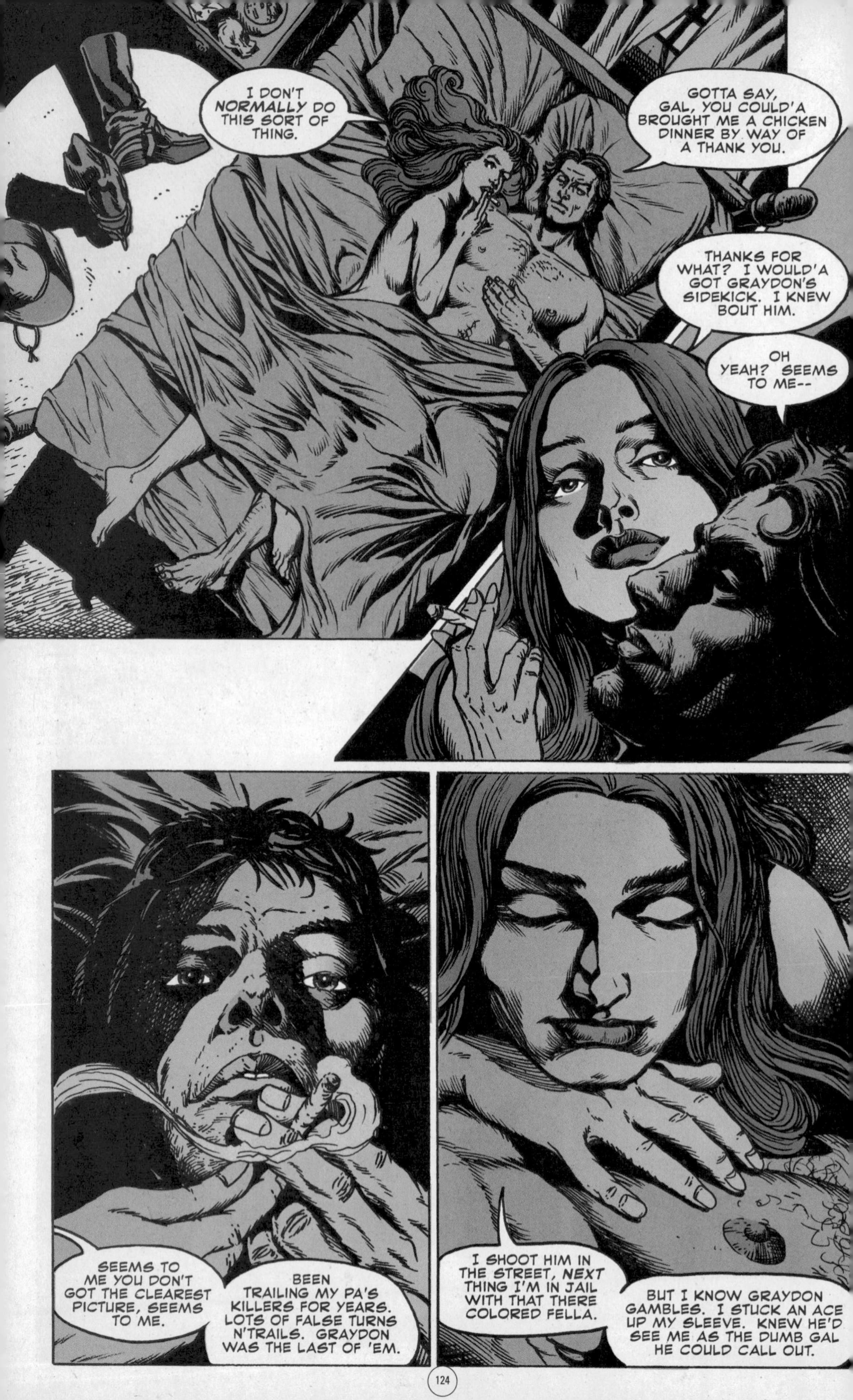
I DON'T NORMALLY DO THIS SORT OF THING.
GOTTA SAY, GAL, YOU COULD'A BROUGHT ME A CHICKEN DINNER BY WAY OF A THANK YOU.
THANKS FOR WHAT? I WOULD'A GOT GRAYDON'S SIDEKICK. I KNEW BOUT HIM.
OH YEAH? SEEMS TO ME--
SEEMS TO ME YOU DON'T GOT THE CLEAREST PICTURE, SEEMS TO ME.
BEEN TRAILING MY PA'S KILLERS FOR YEARS. LOTS OF FALSE TURNS N'TRAILS. GRAYDON WAS THE LAST OF 'EM.
I SHOOT HIM IN THE STREET, NEXT THING I'M IN JAIL WITH THAT THERE COLORED FELLA.
BUT I KNOW GRAYDON GAMBLES. I STUCK AN ACE UP MY SLEEVE. KNEW HE'D SEE ME AS THE DUMB GAL HE COULD CALL OUT.

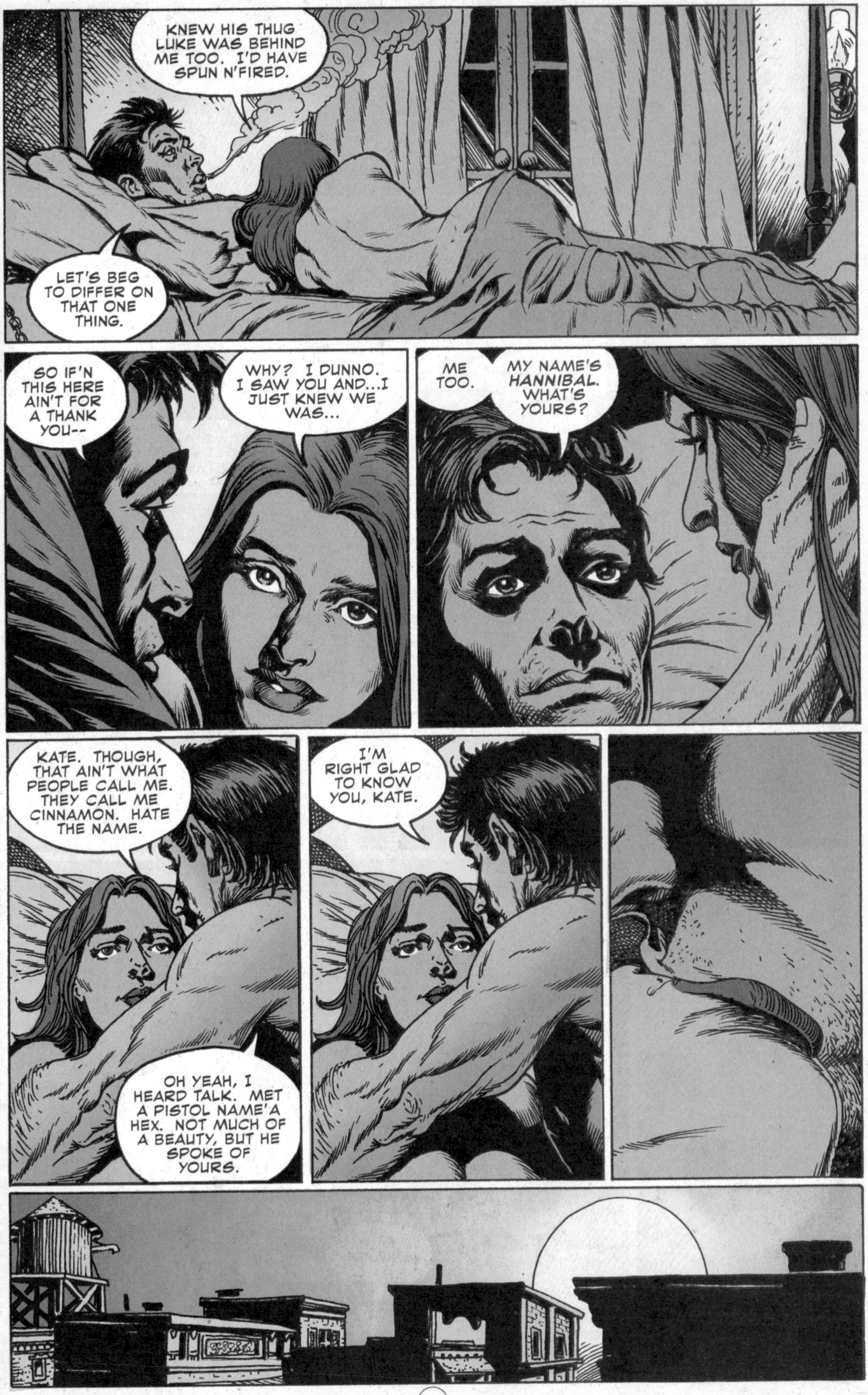
KNEW HIS THUG LUKE WAS BEHIND ME TOO. I'D HAVE SPUN N'FIRED.
LET'S BEG TO DIFFER ON THAT ONE THING.
SO IF'N THIS HERE AIN'T FOR A THANK YOU--
WHY? I DUNNO. I SAW YOU AND...I JUST KNEW WE WAS...
ME TOO.
MY NAME'S HANNIBAL. WHAT'S YOURS?
KATE. THOUGH, THAT AIN'T WHAT PEOPLE CALL ME. THEY CALL ME CINNAMON. HATE THE NAME.
OH YEAH, I HEARD TALK. MET A PISTOL NAME'A HEX. NOT MUCH OF A BEAUTY, BUT HE SPOKE OF YOURS.
I'M RIGHT GLAD TO KNOW YOU, KATE.

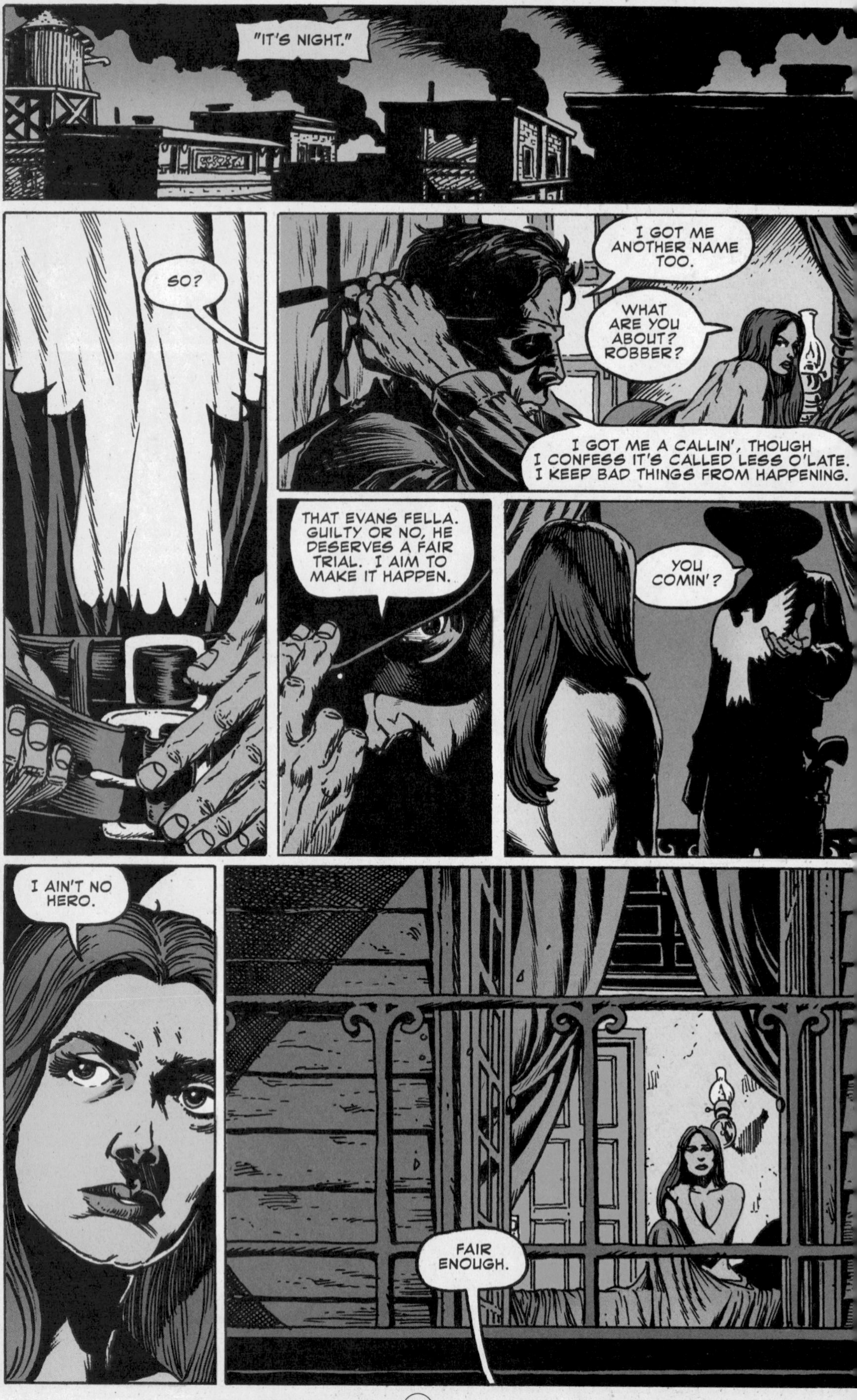
"IT'S NIGHT."
SO?
I GOT ME ANOTHER NAME TOO.
WHAT ARE YOU ABOUT? ROBBER?
I GOT ME A CALLIN', THOUGH I CONFESS IT'S CALLED LESS O'LATE. I KEEP BAD THINGS FROM HAPPENING.
THAT EVANS FELLA. GUILTY OR NO, HE DESERVES A FAIR TRIAL. I AIM TO MAKE IT HAPPEN.
YOU COMIN'?
I AIN'T NO HERO.
FAIR ENOUGH.

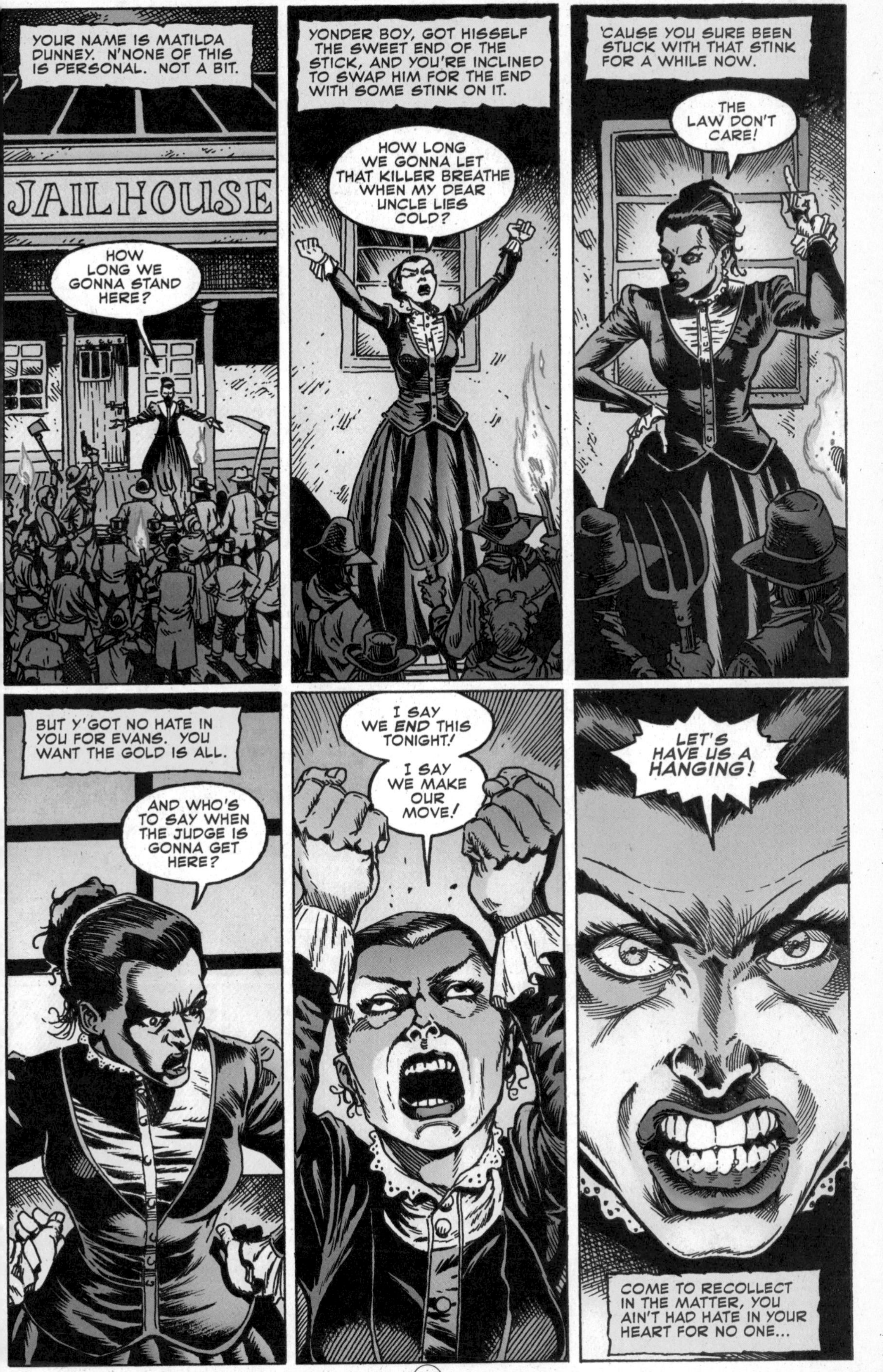
YOUR NAME IS MATILDA DUNNEY. N'NONE OF THIS IS PERSONAL. NOT A BIT.
JAILHOUSE
HOW LONG WE GONNA STAND HERE?
YONDER BOY, GOT HISSELF THE SWEET END OF THE STICK, AND YOU'RE INCLINED TO SWAP HIM FOR THE END WITH SOME STINK ON IT.
HOW LONG WE GONNA LET THAT KILLER BREATHE WHEN MY DEAR UNCLE LIES COLD?
'CAUSE YOU SURE BEEN STUCK WITH THAT STINK FOR A WHILE NOW.
THE LAW DON'T CARE!
BUT Y'GOT NO HATE IN YOU FOR EVANS. YOU WANT THE GOLD IS ALL.
AND WHO'S TO SAY WHEN THE JUDGE IS GONNA GET HERE?
I SAY WE END THIS TONIGHT!
I SAY WE MAKE OUR MOVE!
LET'S HAVE US A HANGING!
COME TO RECOLLECT IN THE MATTER, YOU AIN'T HAD HATE IN YOUR HEART FOR NO ONE...

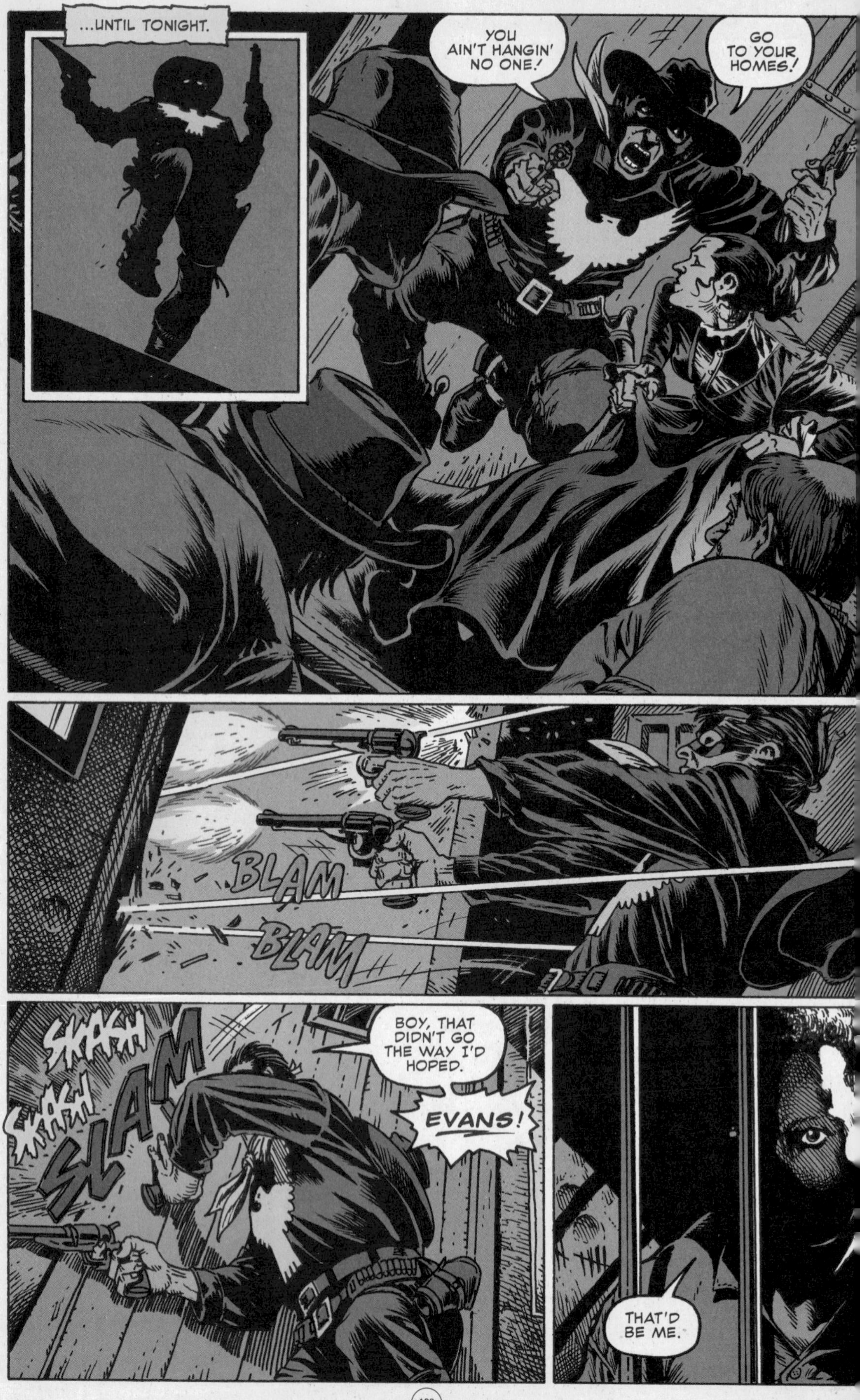
...UNTIL TONIGHT.
YOU AIN'T HANGIN' NO ONE!
GO TO YOUR HOMES!
BLAM
BLAM
SKASH
SKASH
SLAM
BOY, THAT DIDN'T GO THE WAY I'D HOPED.
EVANS!
THAT'D BE ME.

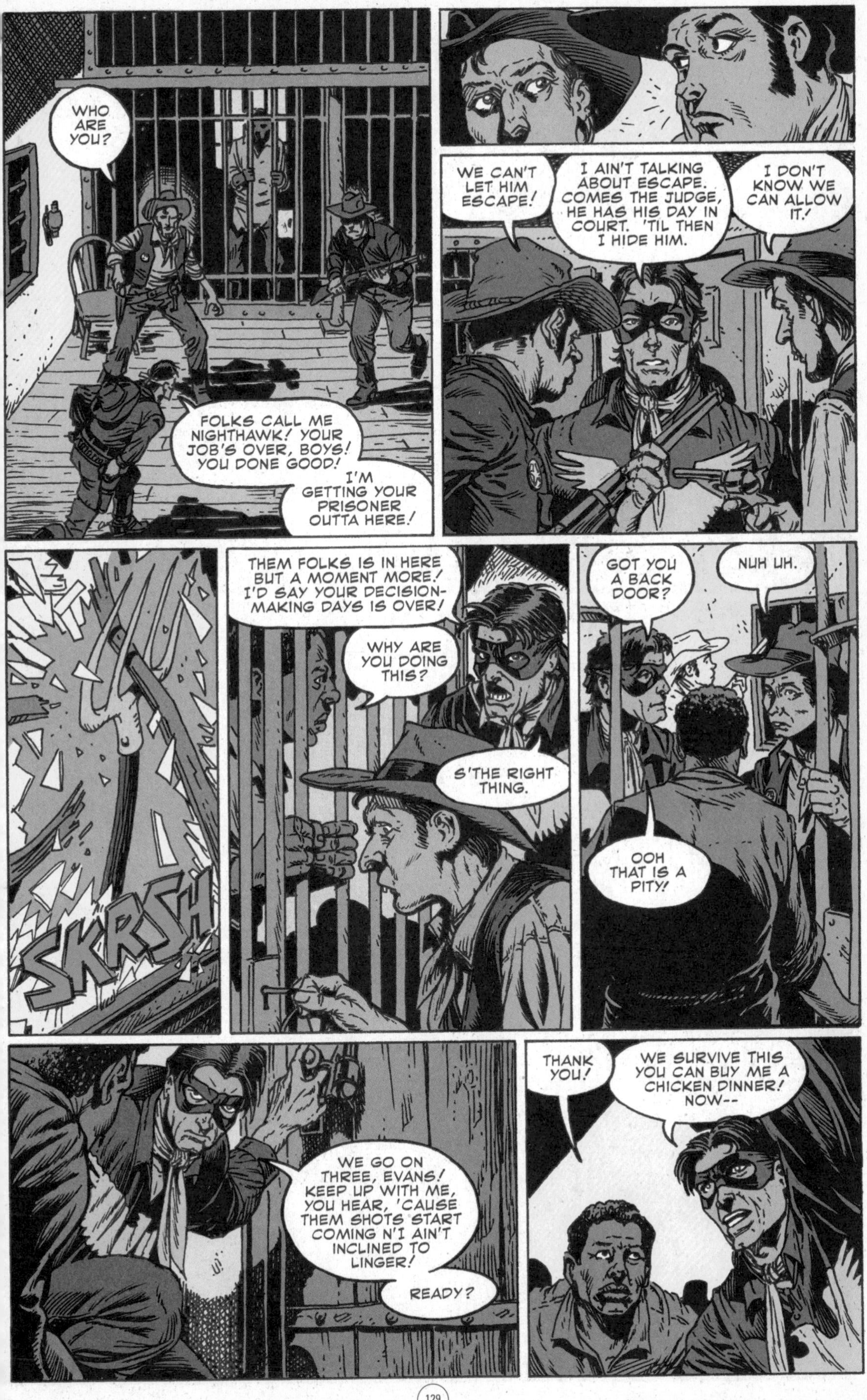
WHO ARE YOU?
FOLKS CALL ME NIGHTHAWK! YOUR JOB'S OVER, BOYS! YOU DONE GOOD!
I'M GETTING YOUR PRISONER OUTTA HERE!
WE CAN'T LET HIM ESCAPE!
I AIN'T TALKING ABOUT ESCAPE. COMES THE JUDGE, HE HAS HIS DAY IN COURT. 'TIL THEN I HIDE HIM.
I DON'T KNOW WE CAN ALLOW IT!
SKRSH
THEM FOLKS IS IN HERE BUT A MOMENT MORE! I'D SAY YOUR DECISION-MAKING DAYS IS OVER!
WHY ARE YOU DOING THIS?
S'THE RIGHT THING.
GOT YOU A BACK DOOR?
NUH UH.
OOH THAT IS A PITY!
WE GO ON THREE, EVANS! KEEP UP WITH ME, YOU HEAR, 'CAUSE THEM SHOTS START COMING N'I AIN'T INCLINED TO LINGER!
READY?
THANK YOU!
WE SURVIVE THIS YOU CAN BUY ME A CHICKEN DINNER! NOW--

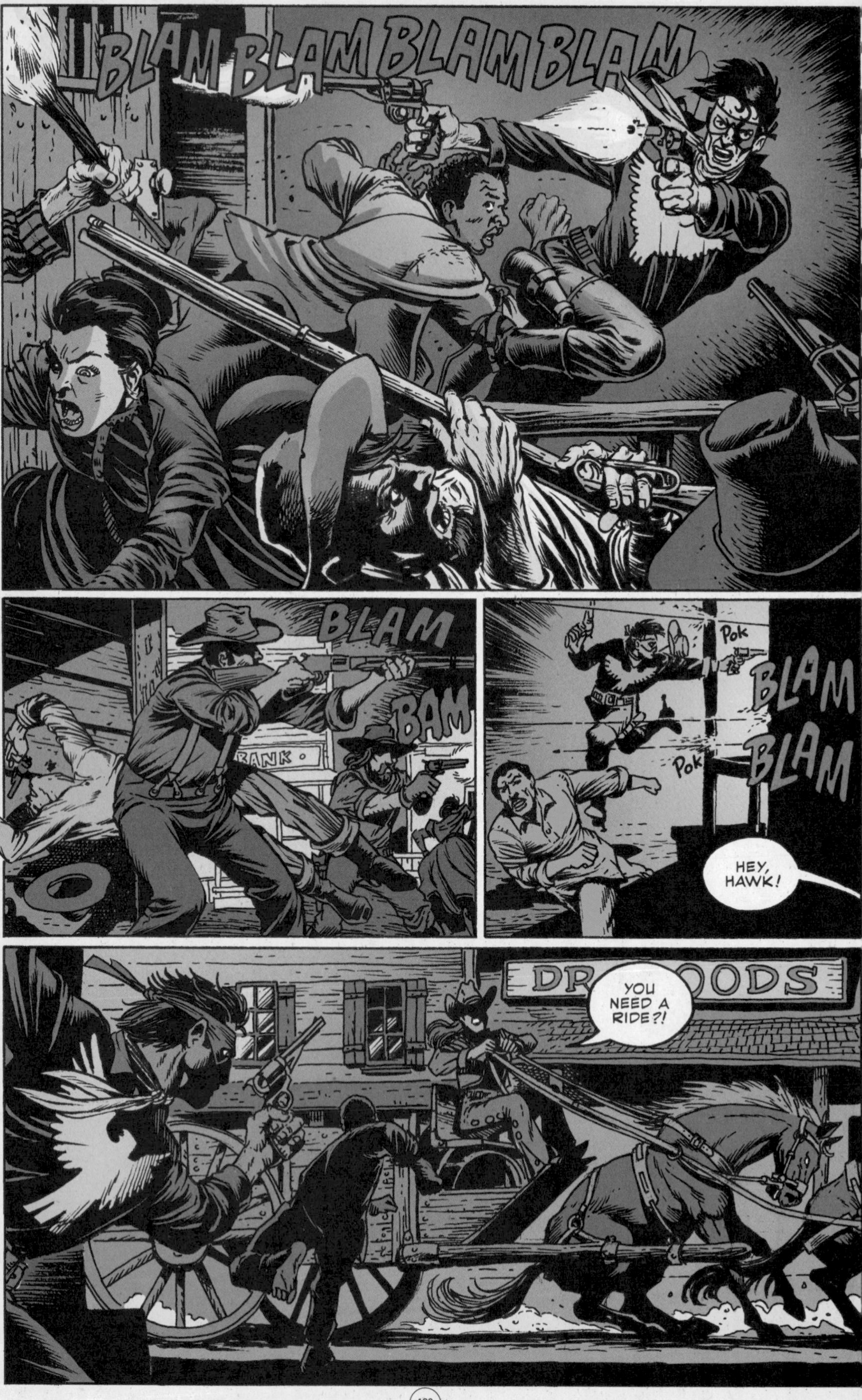
BLAM BLAM BLAM BLAM
BLAM
BAM
BANK
Pok
BLAM
BLAM
Pok
HEY, HAWK!
DR OODS
YOU NEED A RIDE?!

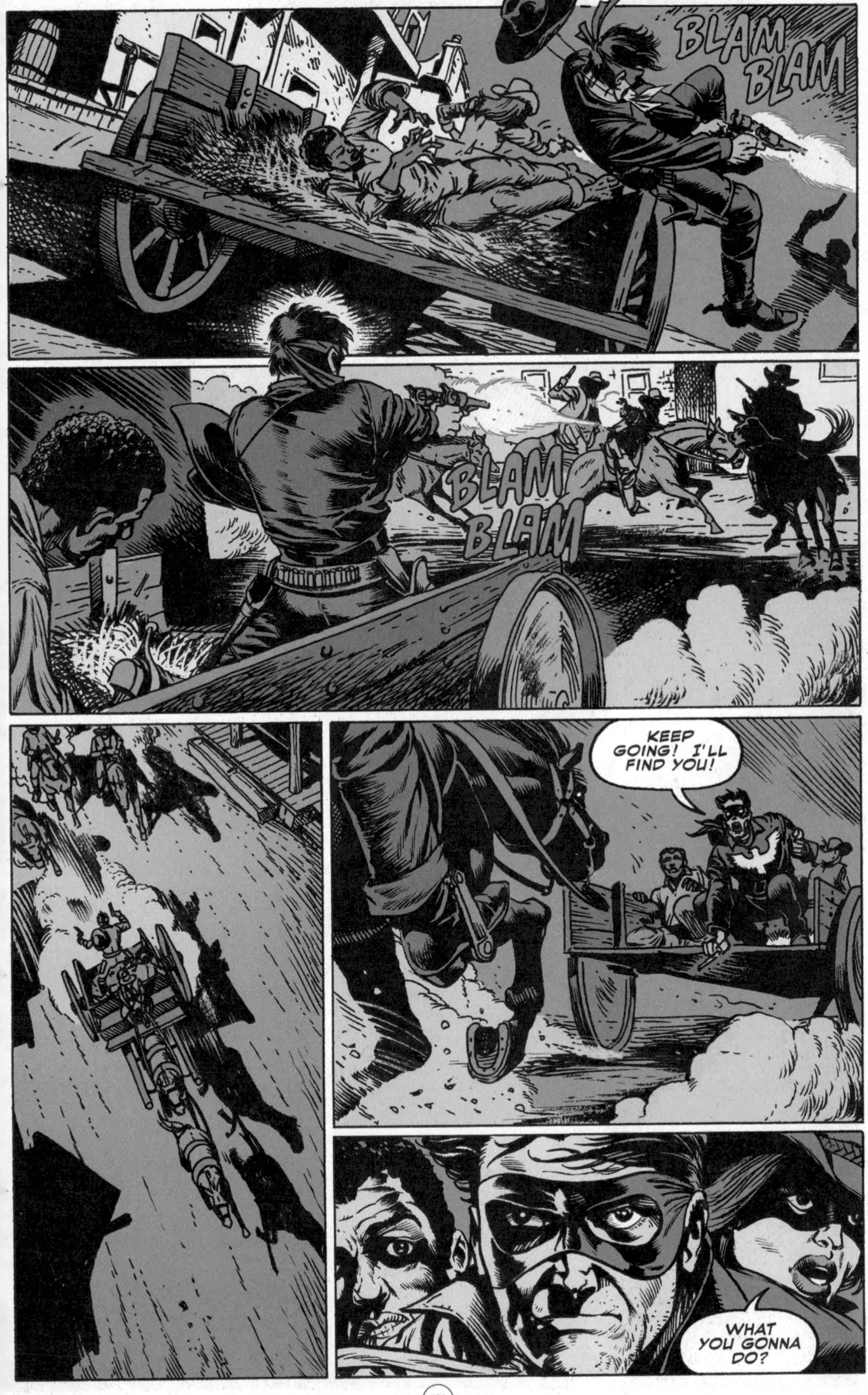
BLAM
BLAM
BLAM
BLAM
KEEP GOING! I'LL FIND YOU!
WHAT YOU GONNA DO?

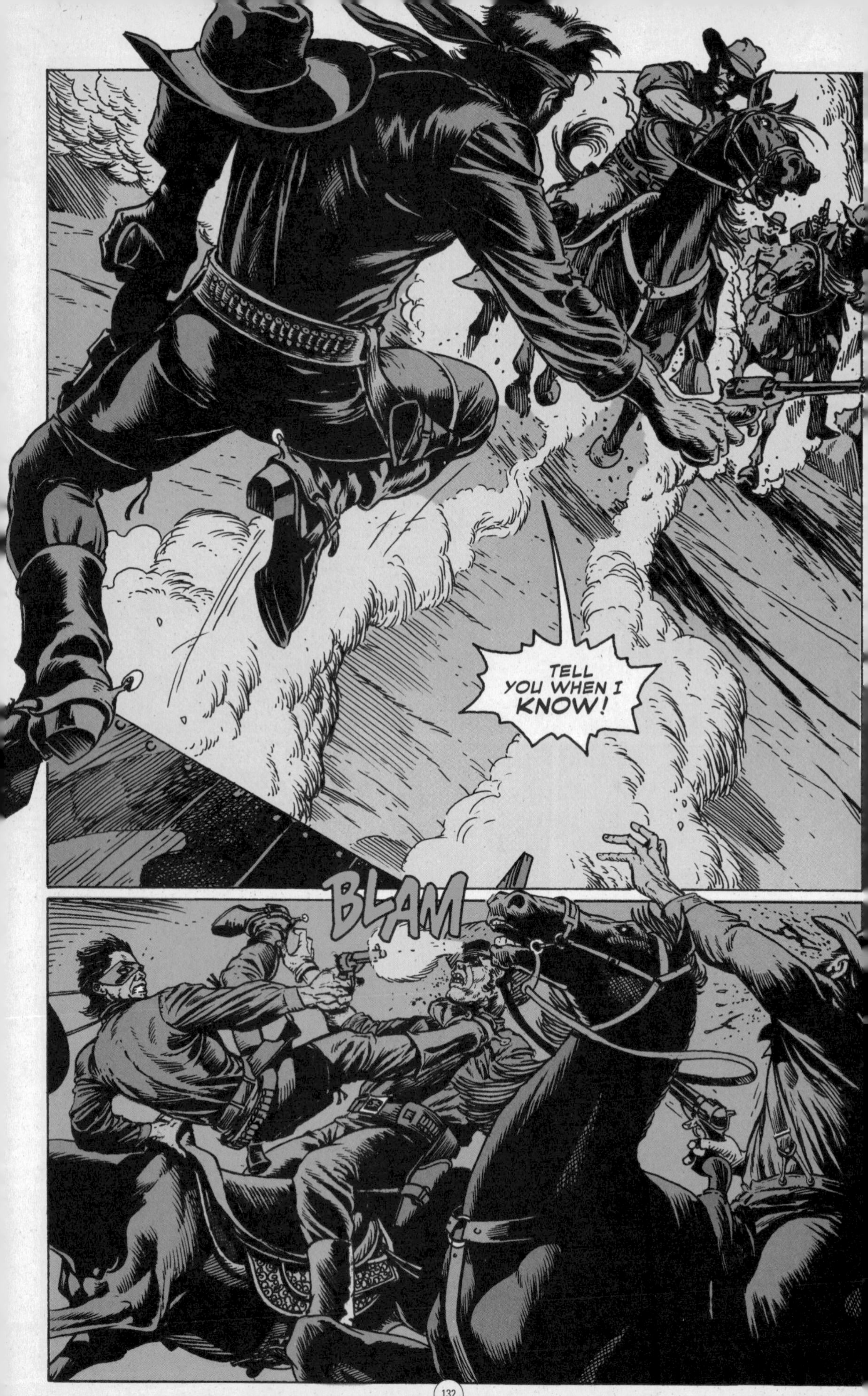
TELL YOU WHEN I KNOW!
BLAM

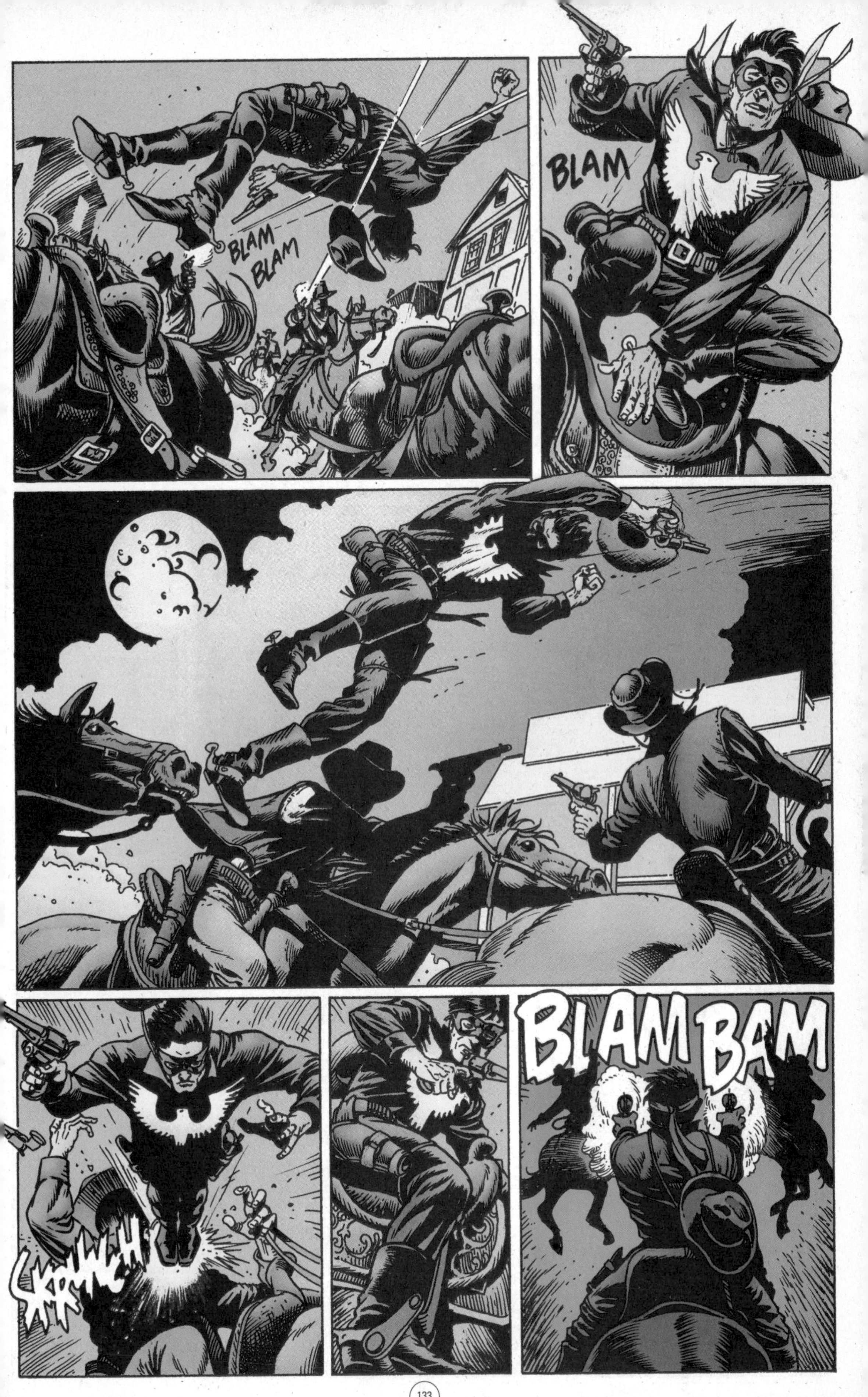
BLAM
BLAM
BLAM
BLAM BAM

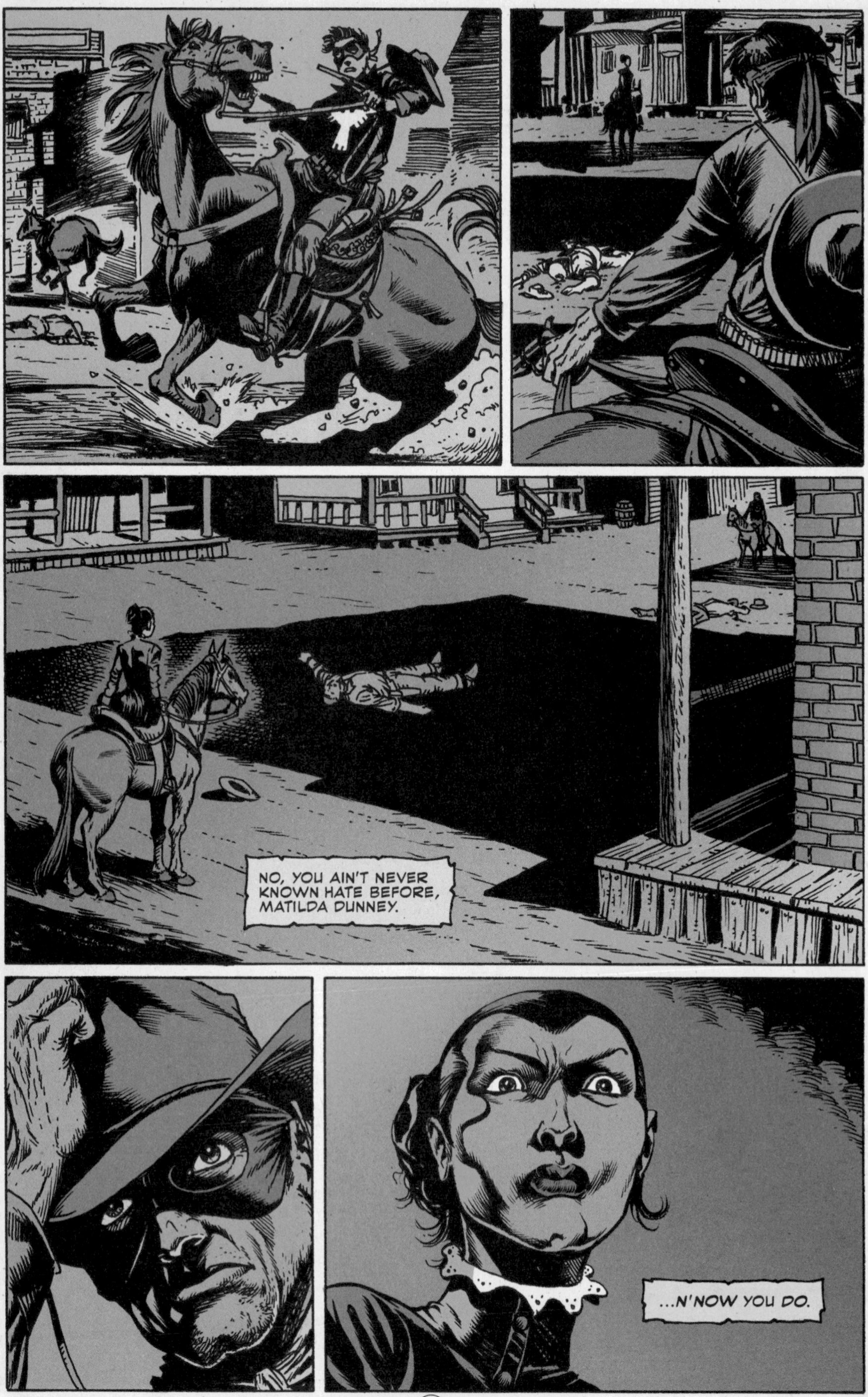
NO, YOU AIN'T NEVER KNOWN HATE BEFORE, MATILDA DUNNEY.
...N'NOW YOU DO.

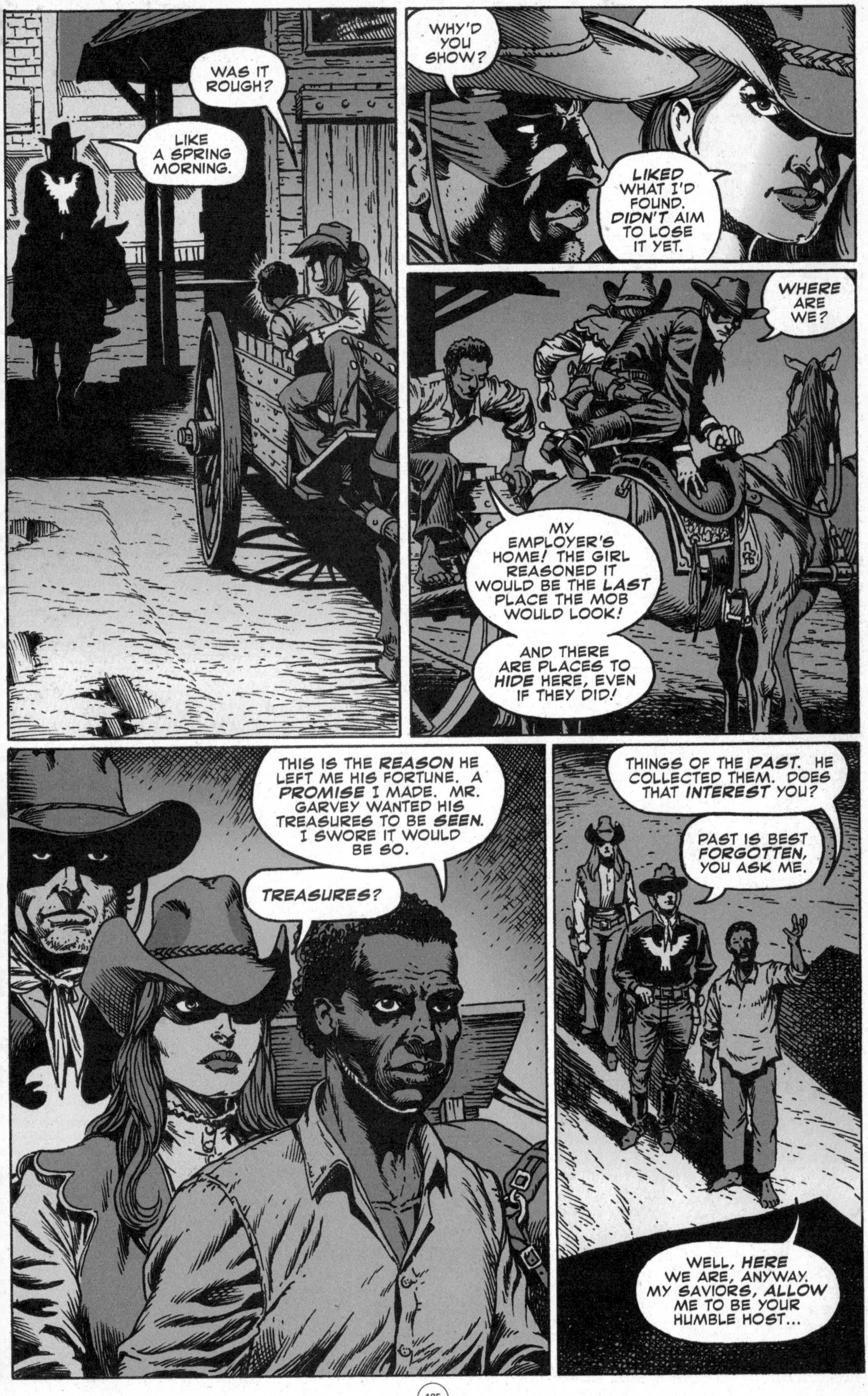

WAS IT ROUGH?
LIKE A SPRING MORNING.
WHY'D YOU SHOW?
LIKED WHAT I'D FOUND. DIDN'T AIM TO LOSE IT YET.
WHERE ARE WE?
MY EMPLOYER'S HOME! THE GIRL REASONED IT WOULD BE THE LAST PLACE THE MOB WOULD LOOK!
AND THERE ARE PLACES TO HIDE HERE, EVEN IF THEY DID!
THIS IS THE REASON HE LEFT ME HIS FORTUNE. A PROMISE I MADE. MR. GARVEY WANTED HIS TREASURES TO BE SEEN. I SWORE IT WOULD BE SO.
TREASURES?
THINGS OF THE PAST. HE COLLECTED THEM. DOES THAT INTEREST YOU?
PAST IS BEST FORGOTTEN, YOU ASK ME.
WELL, HERE WE ARE, ANYWAY. MY SAVIORS, ALLOW ME TO BE YOUR HUMBLE HOST...

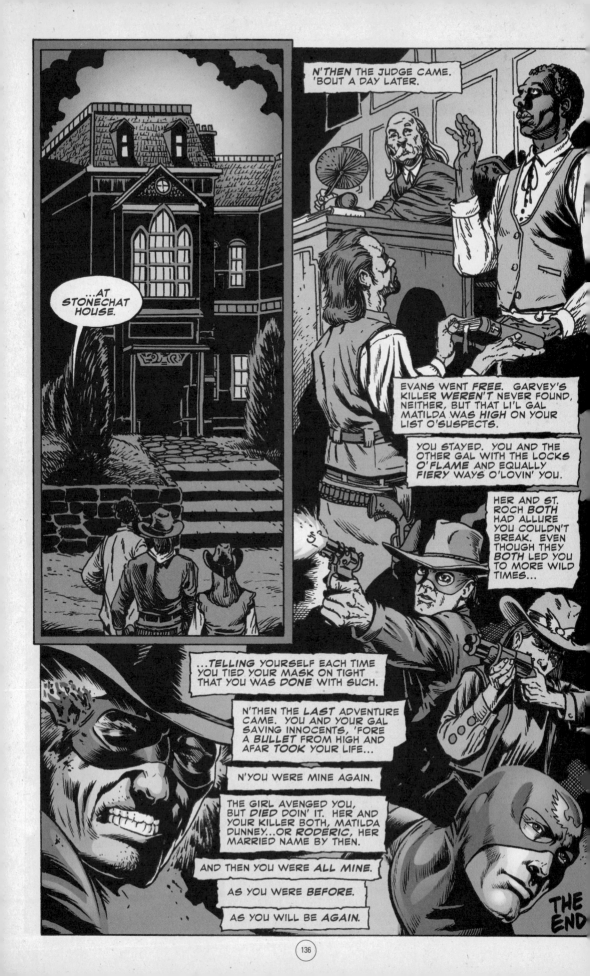

...AT STONECHAT HOUSE.

N'THEN THE JUDGE CAME. 'BOUT A DAY LATER.

EVANS WENT *FREE.* GARVEY'S KILLER *WEREN'T* NEVER FOUND, NEITHER, BUT THAT LI'L GAL MATILDA WAS *HIGH* ON YOUR LIST O'SUSPECTS.

YOU STAYED. YOU AND THE OTHER GAL WITH THE LOCKS O'*FLAME* AND EQUALLY *FIERY* WAYS O'LOVIN' YOU.

HER AND ST. ROCH *BOTH* HAD ALLURE YOU COULDN'T BREAK. EVEN THOUGH THEY *BOTH* LED YOU TO MORE WILD TIMES...

...*TELLING* YOURSELF EACH TIME YOU TIED YOUR MASK ON TIGHT THAT YOU WAS *DONE* WITH SUCH.

N'THEN THE *LAST* ADVENTURE CAME. YOU AND YOUR GAL SAVING INNOCENTS, 'FORE A *BULLET* FROM HIGH AND AFAR *TOOK* YOUR LIFE...

N'YOU WERE MINE AGAIN.

THE GIRL AVENGED YOU, BUT *DIED DOIN'* IT. HER AND YOUR KILLER BOTH, MATILDA DUNNEY...OR *RODERIC,* HER MARRIED NAME BY THEN.

AND THEN YOU WERE *ALL* MINE.

AS YOU WERE *BEFORE.*

AS YOU WILL BE *AGAIN.*

THE END

136

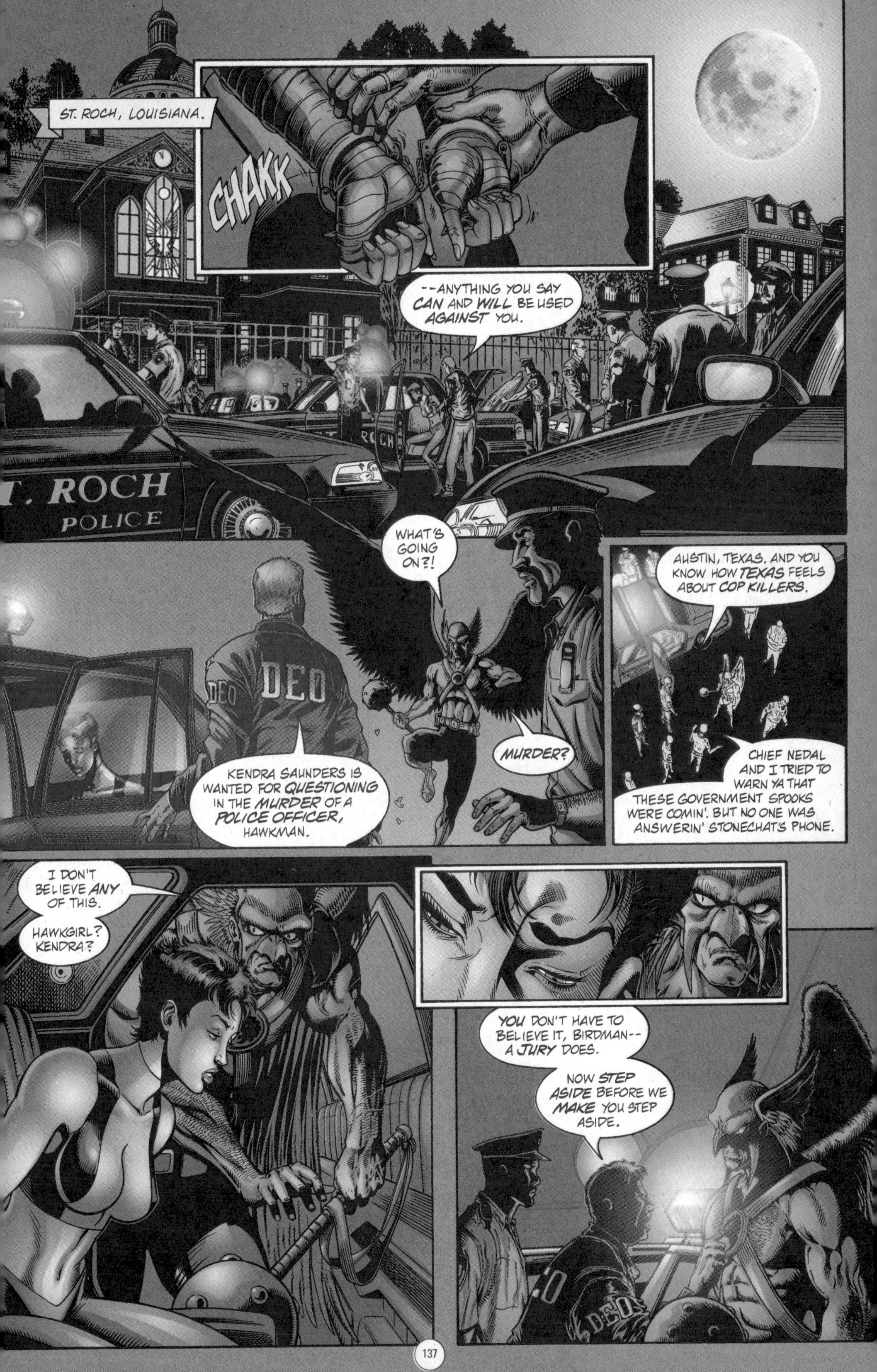

ST. ROCH, LOUISIANA.
CHAKK
--ANYTHING YOU SAY CAN AND WILL BE USED AGAINST YOU.
ST. ROCH POLICE
WHAT'S GOING ON?!
DEO
KENDRA SAUNDERS IS WANTED FOR QUESTIONING IN THE MURDER OF A POLICE OFFICER, HAWKMAN.
MURDER?
AUSTIN, TEXAS. AND YOU KNOW HOW TEXAS FEELS ABOUT COP KILLERS.
CHIEF NEDAL AND I TRIED TO WARN YA THAT THESE GOVERNMENT SPOOKS WERE COMIN'. BUT NO ONE WAS ANSWERIN' STONECHAT'S PHONE.
I DON'T BELIEVE ANY OF THIS.
HAWKGIRL? KENDRA?
YOU DON'T HAVE TO BELIEVE IT, BIRDMAN-- A JURY DOES.
NOW STEP ASIDE BEFORE WE MAKE YOU STEP ASIDE.

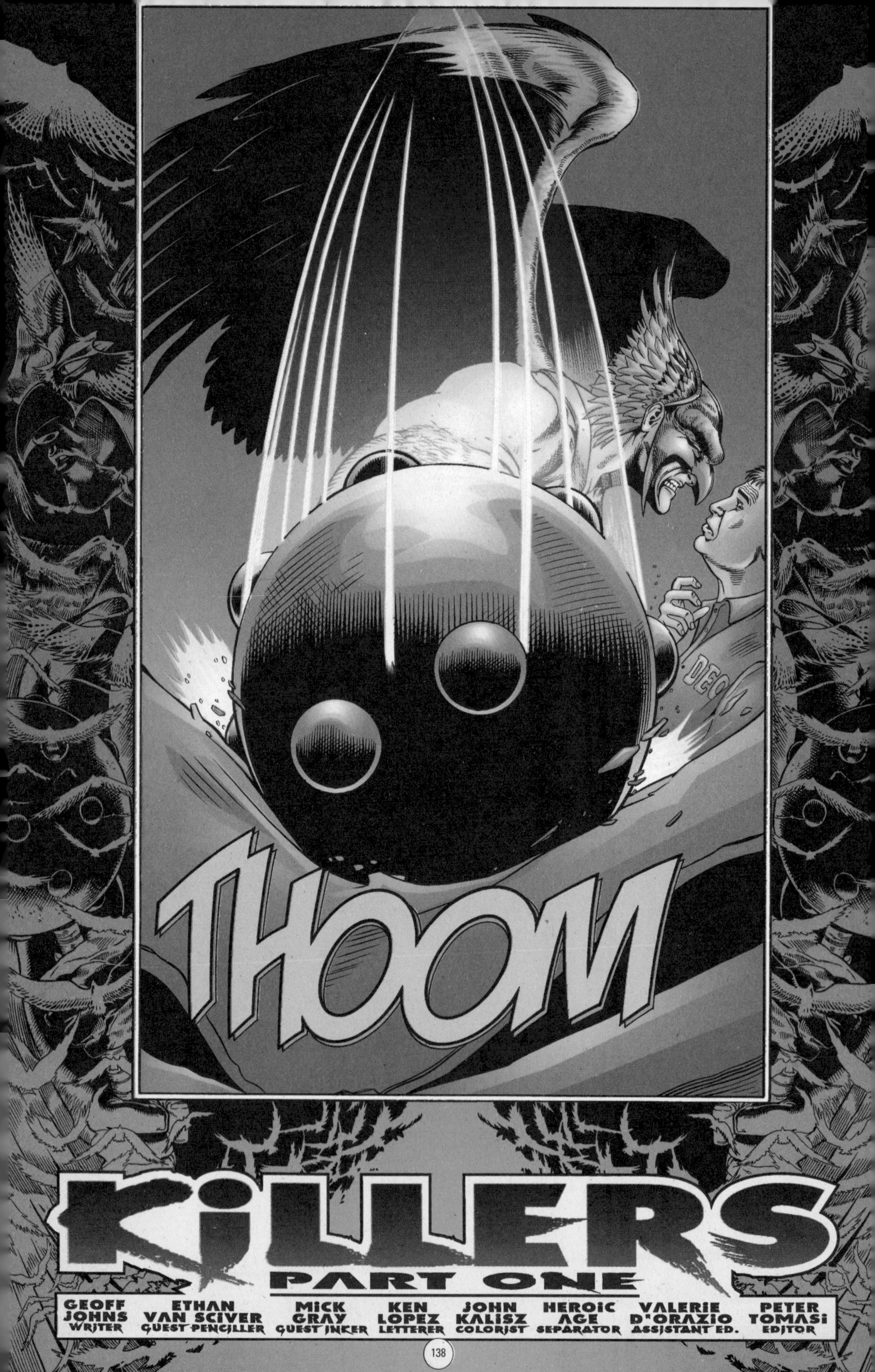
THOOM
DEO
KILLERS
PART ONE
GEOFF JOHNS WRITER
ETHAN VAN SCIVER GUEST PENCILLER
MICK GRAY GUEST INKER
KEN LOPEZ LETTERER
JOHN KALISZ COLORIST
HEROIC AGE SEPARATOR
VALERIE D'ORAZIO ASSISTANT ED.
PETER TOMASI EDITOR

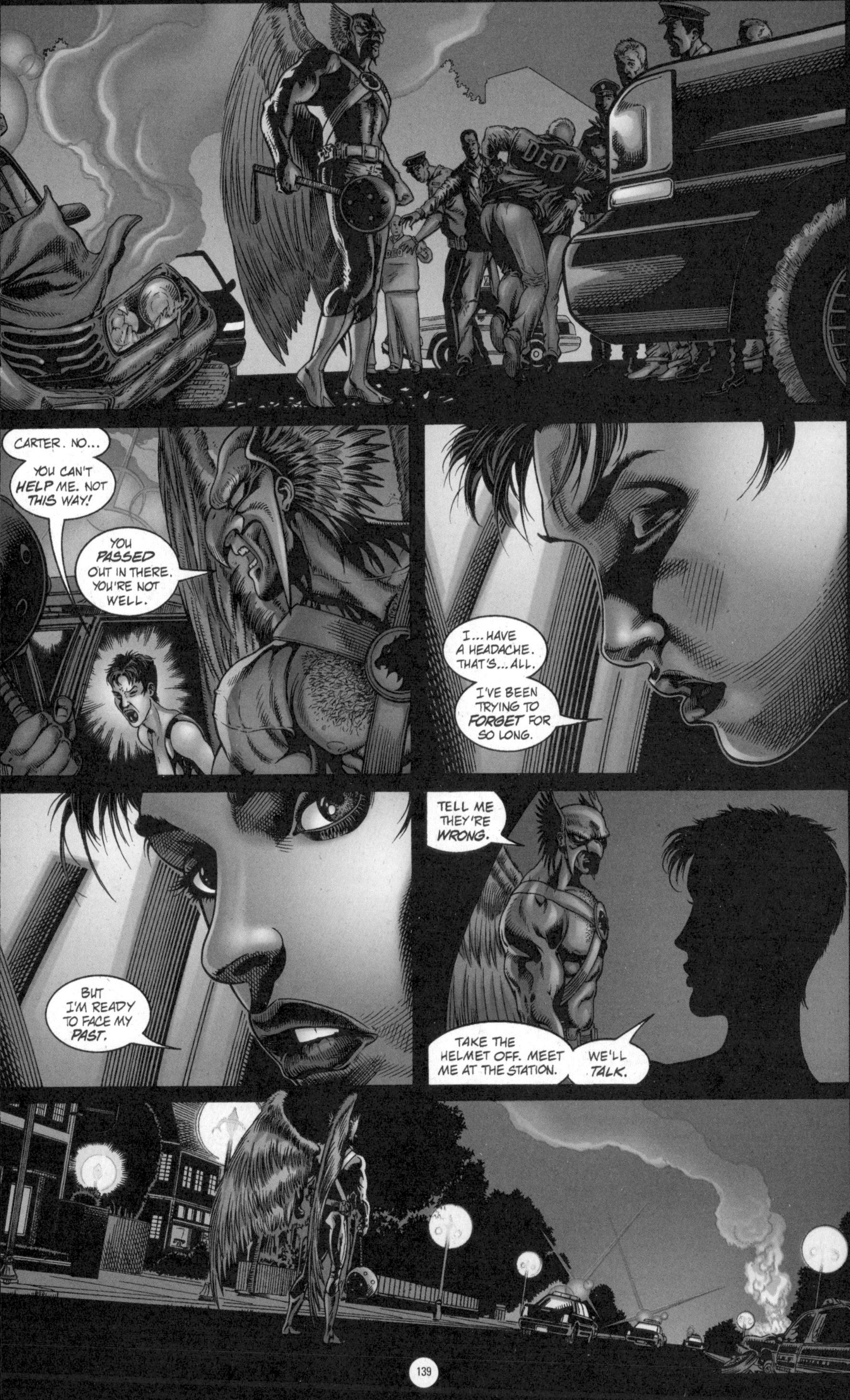

CARTER. NO...
YOU CAN'T HELP ME. NOT THIS WAY!
YOU PASSED OUT IN THERE. YOU'RE NOT WELL.
I... HAVE A HEADACHE. THAT'S... ALL.
I'VE BEEN TRYING TO FORGET FOR SO LONG.
BUT I'M READY TO FACE MY PAST.
TELL ME THEY'RE WRONG.
TAKE THE HELMET OFF. MEET ME AT THE STATION.
WE'LL TALK.

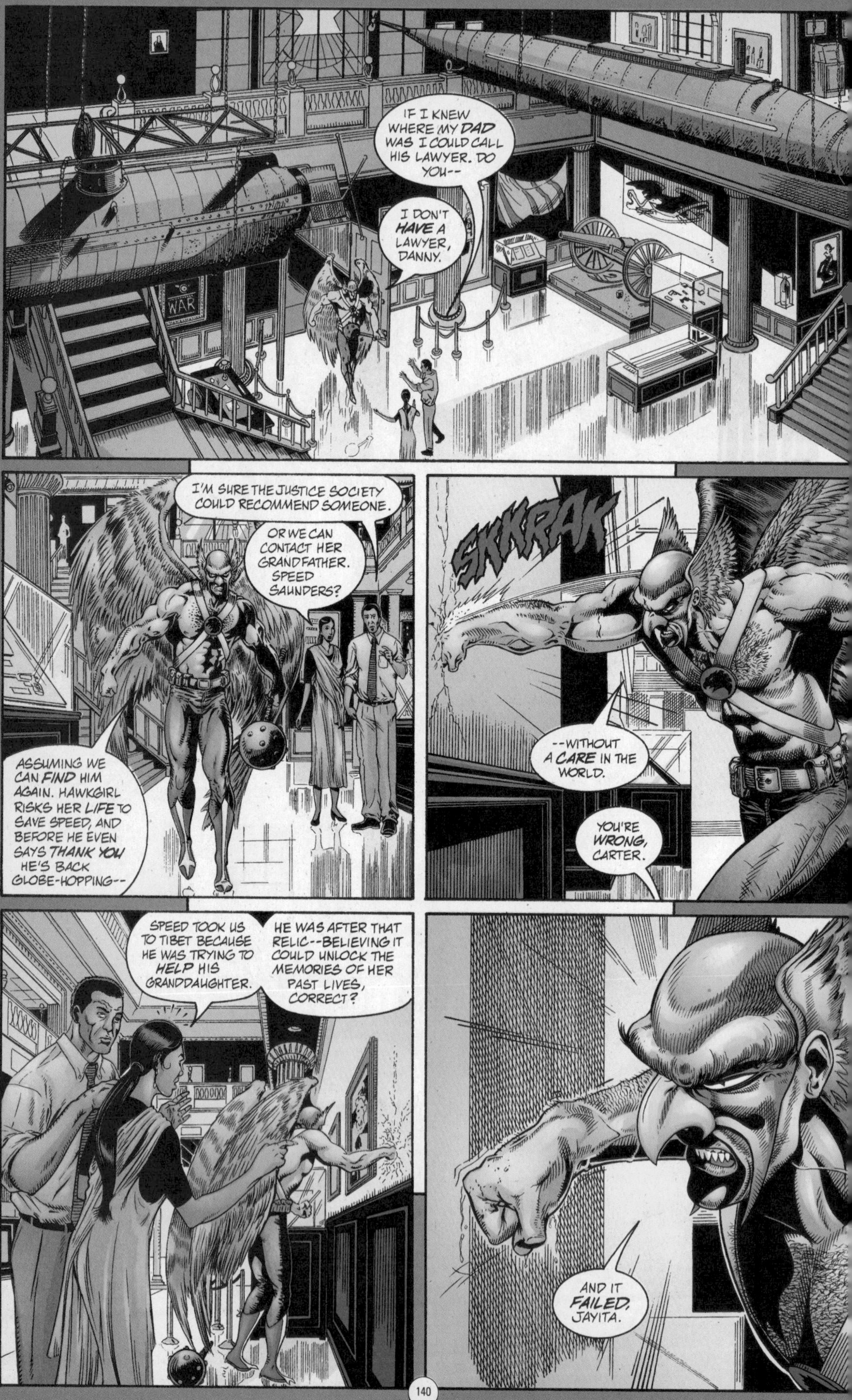
IF I KNEW WHERE MY DAD WAS I COULD CALL HIS LAWYER. DO YOU--
I DON'T HAVE A LAWYER, DANNY.
I'M SURE THE JUSTICE SOCIETY COULD RECOMMEND SOMEONE.
OR WE CAN CONTACT HER GRANDFATHER. SPEED SAUNDERS?
ASSUMING WE CAN FIND HIM AGAIN. HAWKGIRL RISKS HER LIFE TO SAVE SPEED, AND BEFORE HE EVEN SAYS THANK YOU HE'S BACK GLOBE-HOPPING--
SKKRAK
--WITHOUT A CARE IN THE WORLD.
YOU'RE WRONG, CARTER.
SPEED TOOK US TO TIBET BECAUSE HE WAS TRYING TO HELP HIS GRANDDAUGHTER.
HE WAS AFTER THAT RELIC--BELIEVING IT COULD UNLOCK THE MEMORIES OF HER PAST LIVES, CORRECT?
AND IT FAILED, JAYITA.

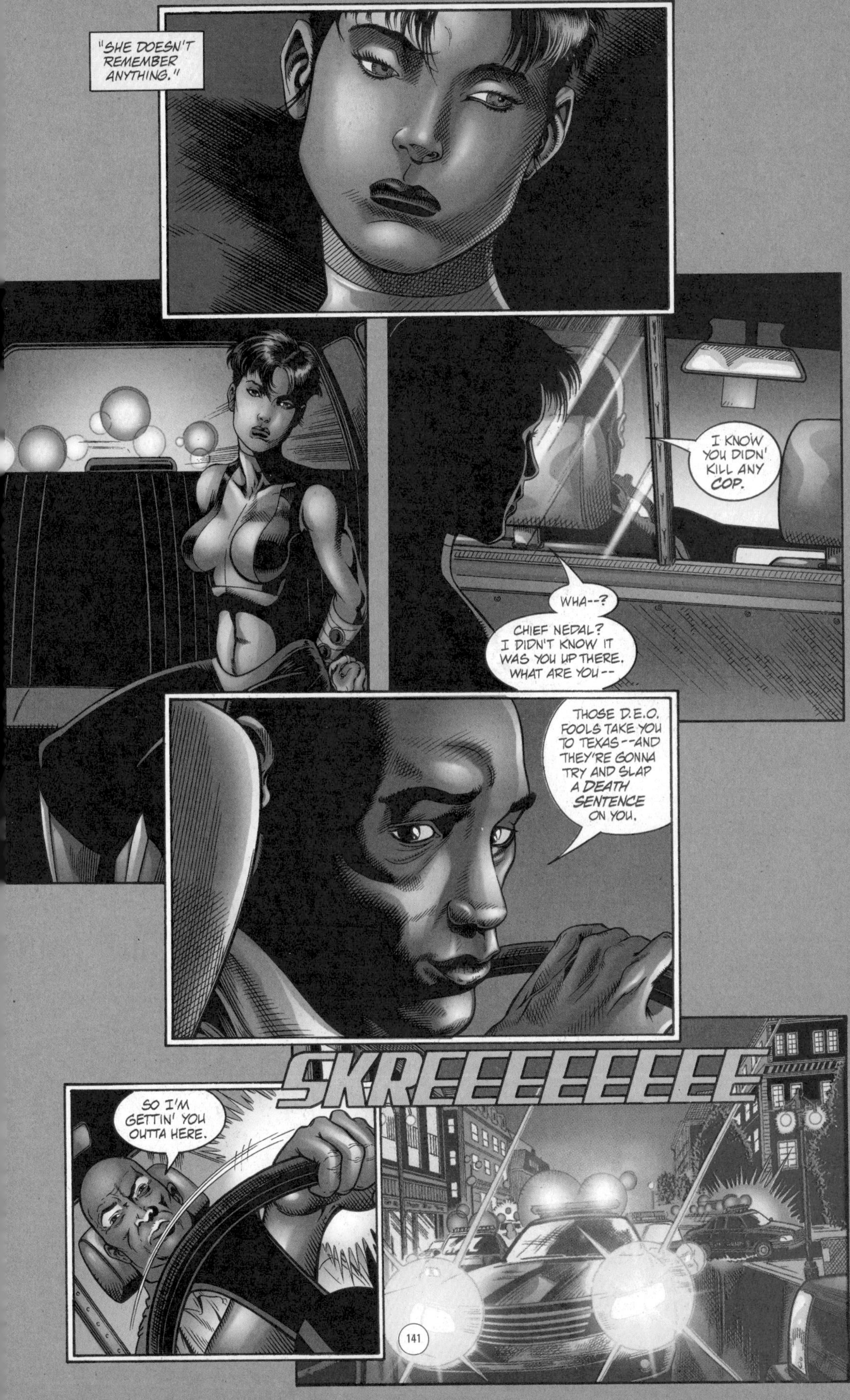
"SHE DOESN'T REMEMBER ANYTHING."
I KNOW YOU DIDN' KILL ANY COP.
WHA--?
CHIEF NEDAL? I DIDN'T KNOW IT WAS YOU UP THERE. WHAT ARE YOU--
THOSE D.E.O. FOOLS TAKE YOU TO TEXAS--AND THEY'RE GONNA TRY AND SLAP A DEATH SENTENCE ON YOU.
SKREEEEEEEEE
SO I'M GETTIN' YOU OUTTA HERE.

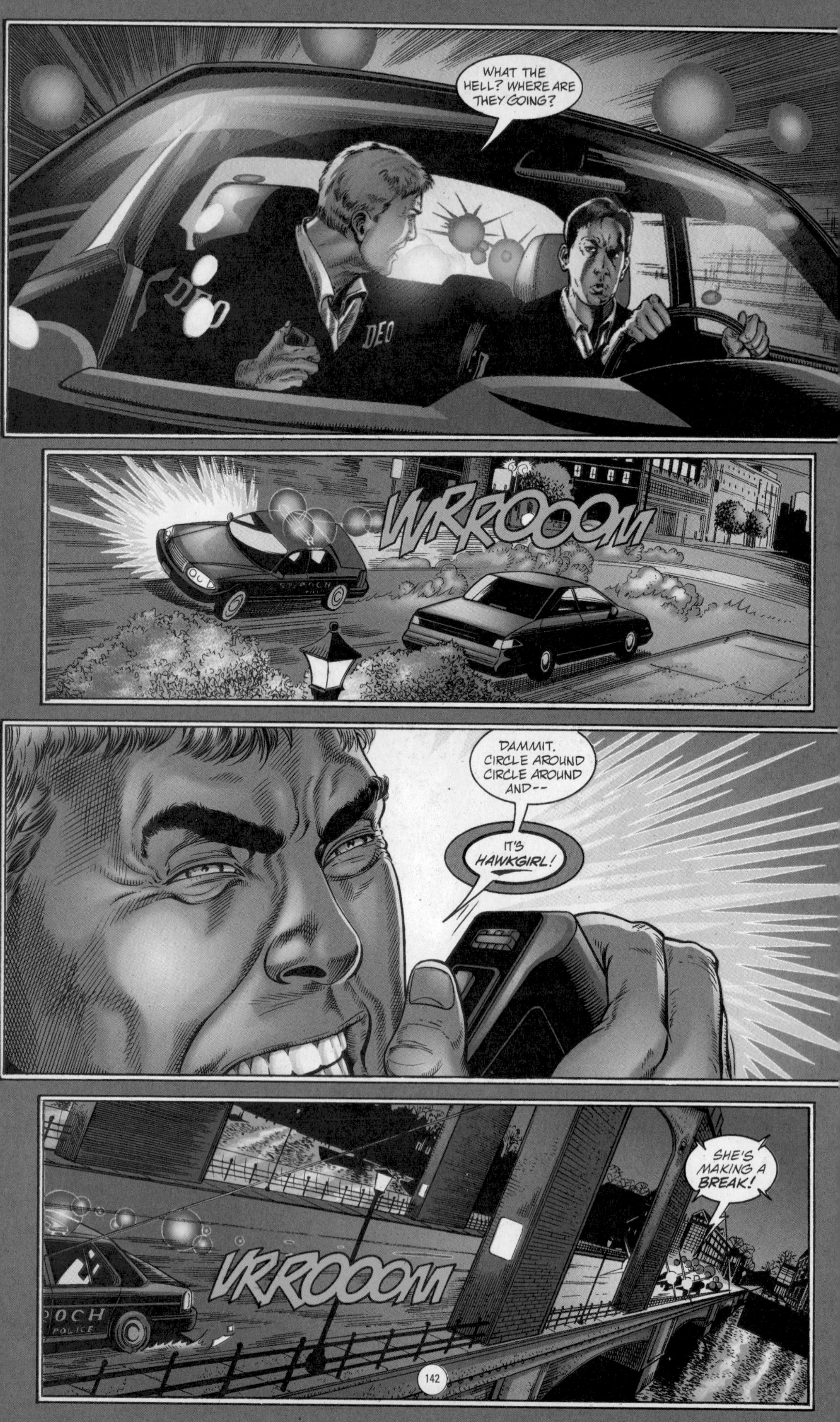

WHAT THE HELL? WHERE ARE THEY GOING?
DEO
DEO
WRROOOM
DAMMIT. CIRCLE AROUND CIRCLE AROUND AND--
IT'S HAWKGIRL!
SHE'S MAKING A BREAK!
VRROOOM
POLICE

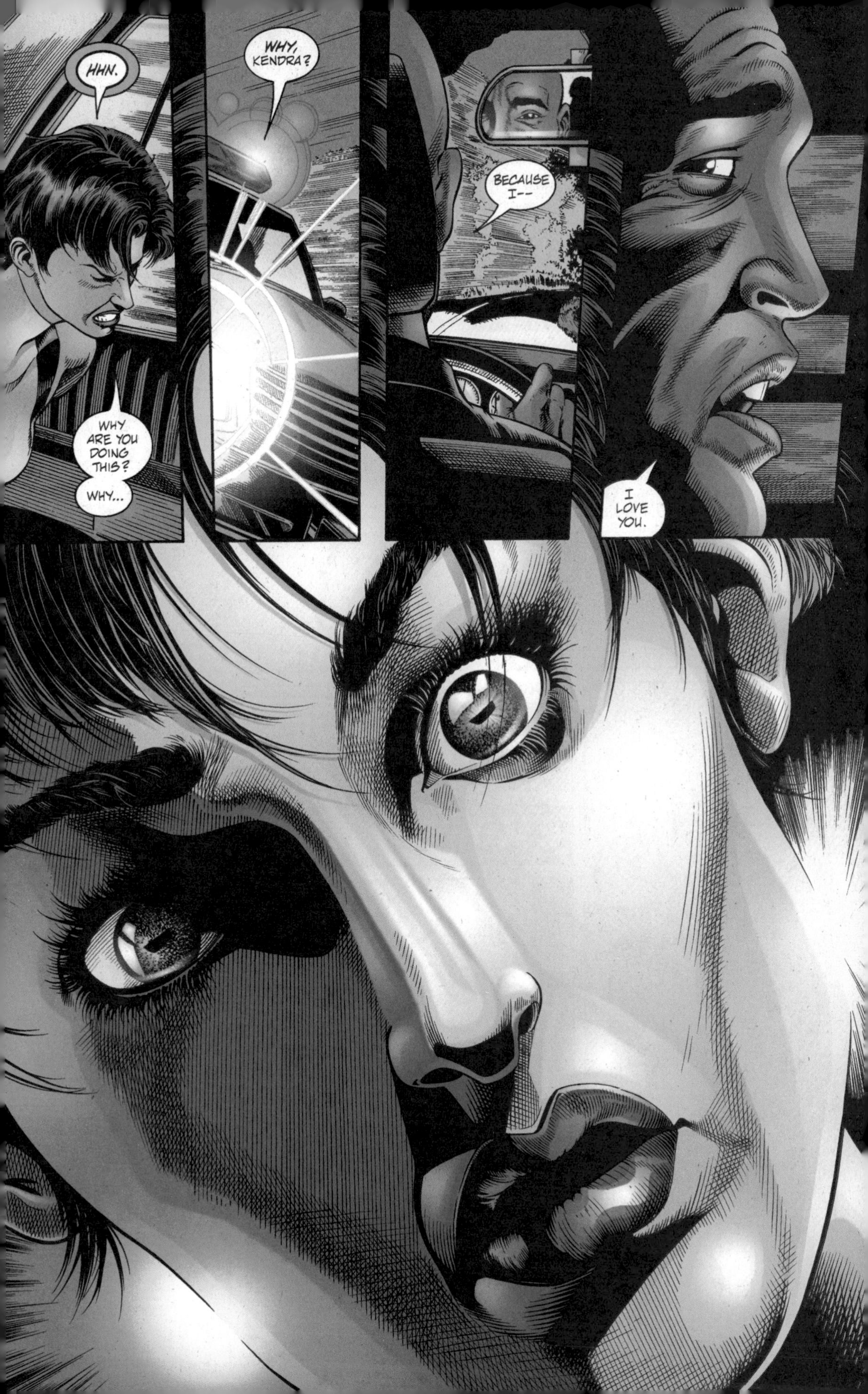
HHN.
WHY ARE YOU DOING THIS?
WHY...
WHY, KENDRA?
BECAUSE I--
I LOVE YOU.

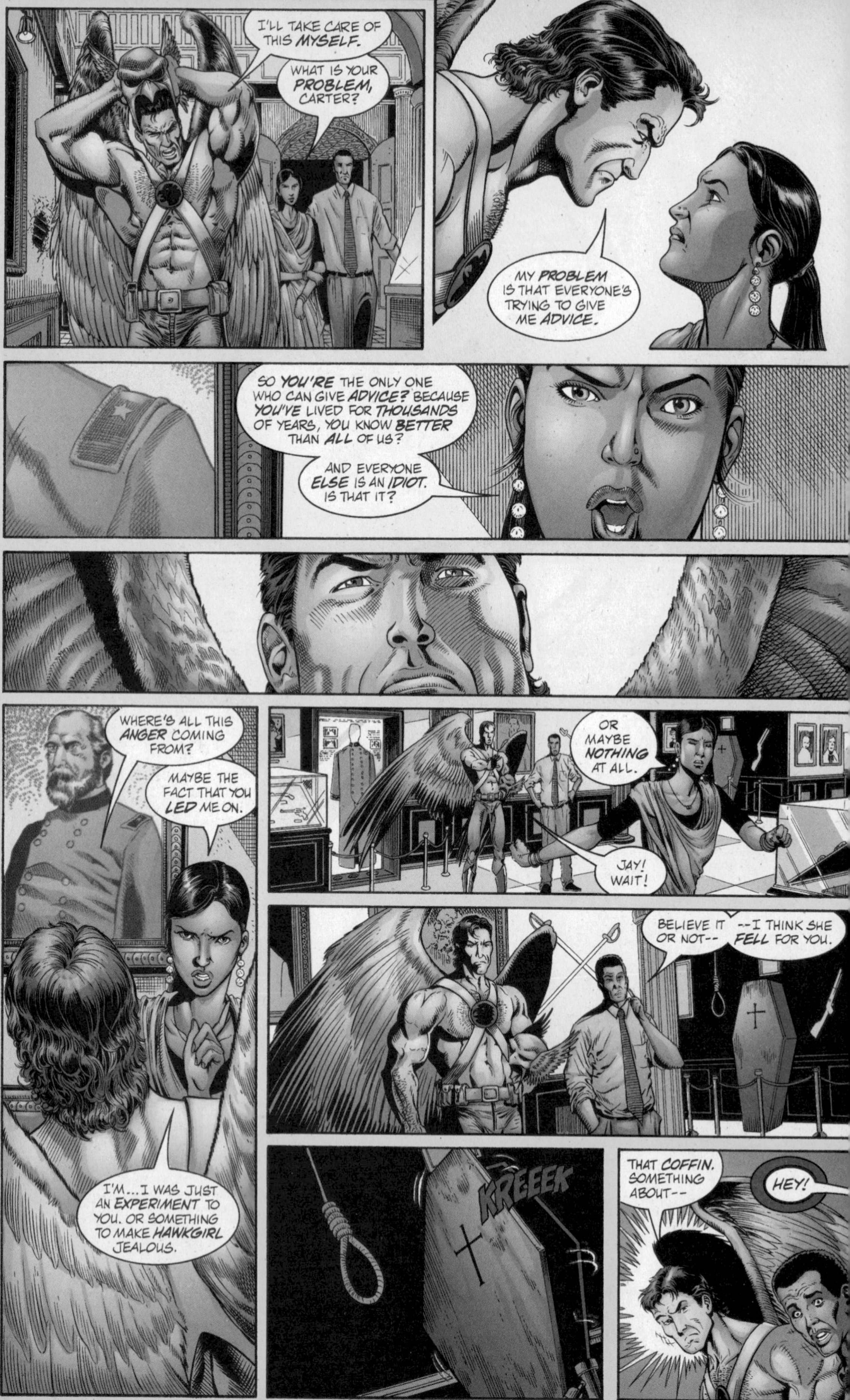
I'LL TAKE CARE OF THIS MYSELF.
WHAT IS YOUR PROBLEM, CARTER?
MY PROBLEM IS THAT EVERYONE'S TRYING TO GIVE ME ADVICE.
SO YOU'RE THE ONLY ONE WHO CAN GIVE ADVICE? BECAUSE YOU'VE LIVED FOR THOUSANDS OF YEARS, YOU KNOW BETTER THAN ALL OF US?
AND EVERYONE ELSE IS AN IDIOT. IS THAT IT?
WHERE'S ALL THIS ANGER COMING FROM?
MAYBE THE FACT THAT YOU LED ME ON.
I'M... I WAS JUST AN EXPERIMENT TO YOU. OR SOMETHING TO MAKE HAWKGIRL JEALOUS.
OR MAYBE NOTHING AT ALL.
JAY! WAIT!
BELIEVE IT OR NOT--
--I THINK SHE FELL FOR YOU.
KREEEK
THAT COFFIN. SOMETHING ABOUT--
HEY!

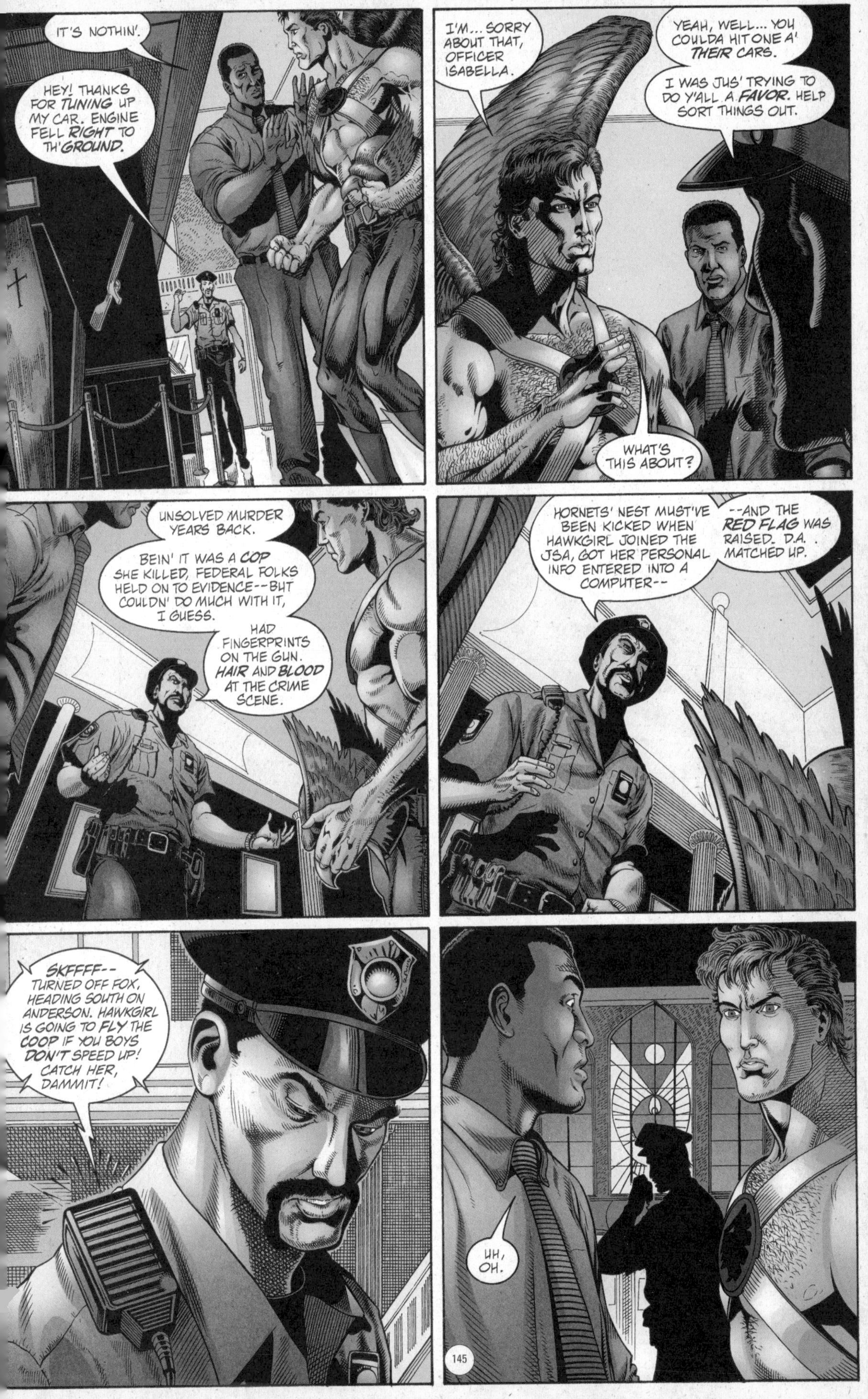
IT'S NOTHIN'.
HEY! THANKS FOR TUNING UP MY CAR. ENGINE FELL RIGHT TO TH'GROUND.
I'M... SORRY ABOUT THAT, OFFICER ISABELLA.
YEAH, WELL... YOU COULDA HIT ONE A' THEIR CARS.
I WAS JUS' TRYING TO DO Y'ALL A FAVOR. HELP SORT THINGS OUT.
WHAT'S THIS ABOUT?
UNSOLVED MURDER YEARS BACK.
BEIN' IT WAS A COP SHE KILLED, FEDERAL FOLKS HELD ON TO EVIDENCE--BUT COULDN' DO MUCH WITH IT, I GUESS.
HAD FINGERPRINTS ON THE GUN. HAIR AND BLOOD AT THE CRIME SCENE.
HORNETS' NEST MUST'VE BEEN KICKED WHEN HAWKGIRL JOINED THE JSA, GOT HER PERSONAL INFO ENTERED INTO A COMPUTER--
--AND THE RED FLAG WAS RAISED. D.A. MATCHED UP.
SKFFFF-- TURNED OFF FOX, HEADING SOUTH ON ANDERSON. HAWKGIRL IS GOING TO FLY THE COOP IF YOU BOYS DON'T SPEED UP! CATCH HER, DAMMIT!
UH, OH.

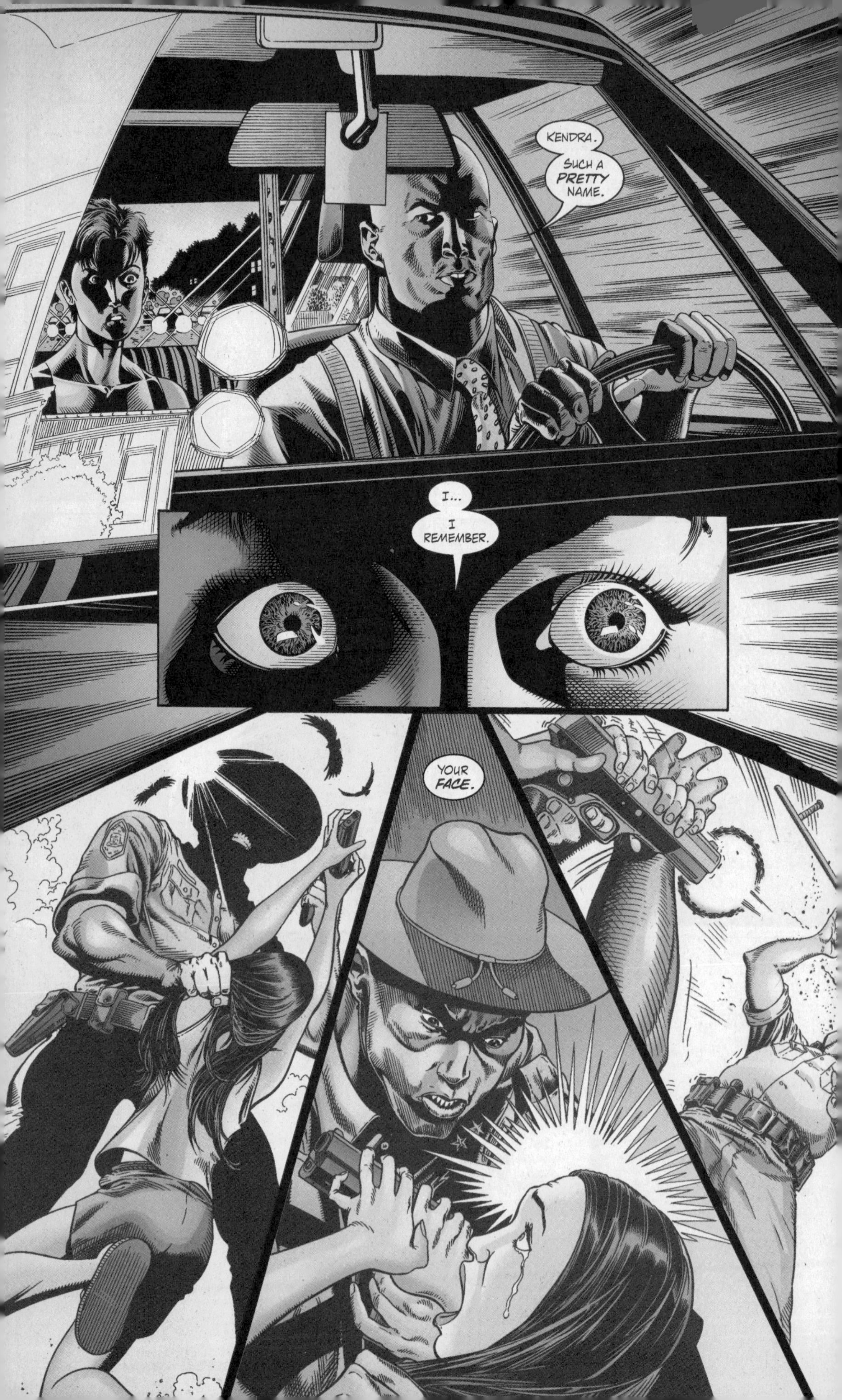
KENDRA.
SUCH A PRETTY NAME.
I... I REMEMBER.
YOUR FACE.

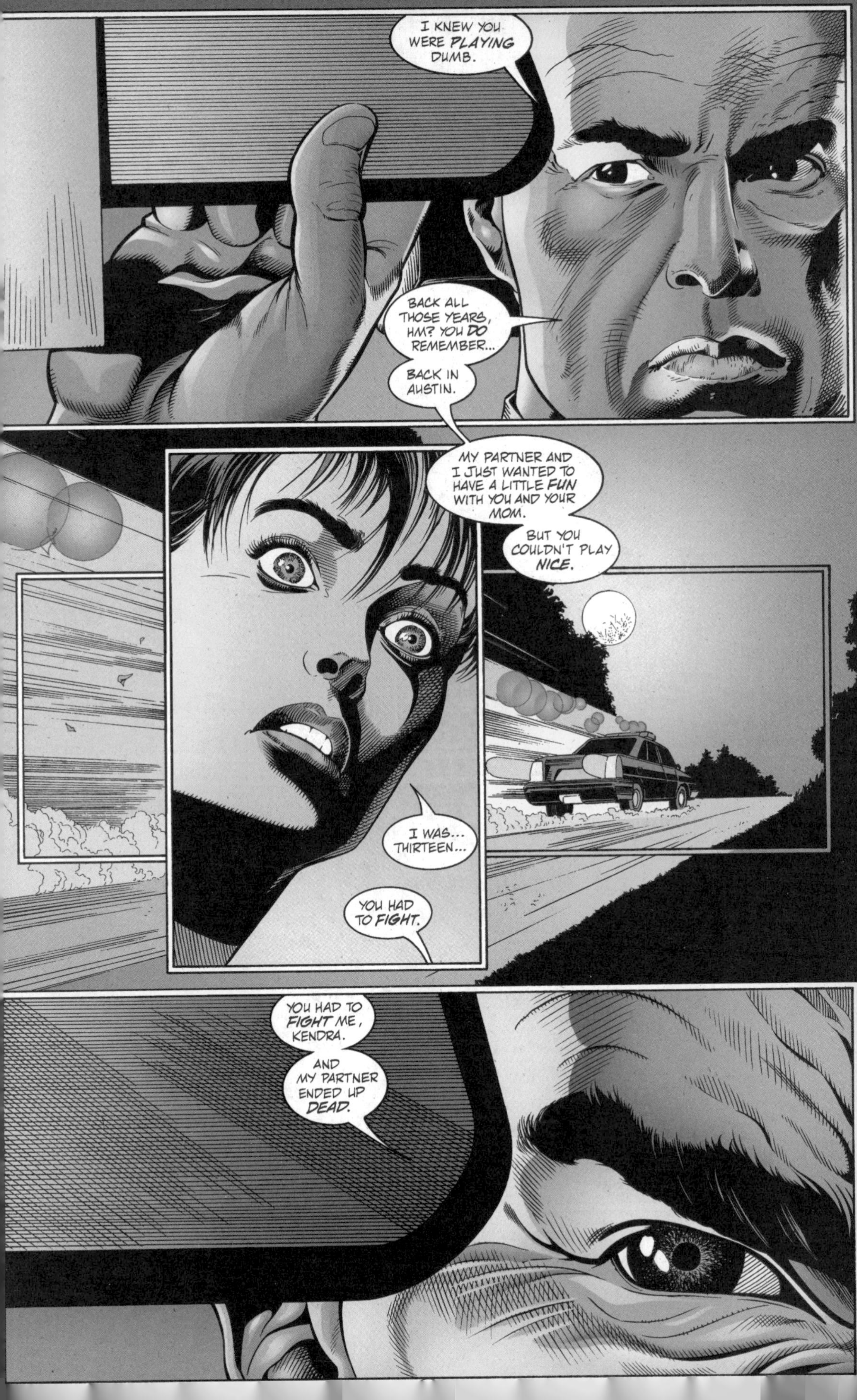
I KNEW YOU WERE PLAYING DUMB.
BACK ALL THOSE YEARS, HM? YOU DO REMEMBER...
BACK IN AUSTIN.
MY PARTNER AND I JUST WANTED TO HAVE A LITTLE FUN WITH YOU AND YOUR MOM.
BUT YOU COULDN'T PLAY NICE.
I WAS... THIRTEEN...
YOU HAD TO FIGHT.
YOU HAD TO FIGHT ME, KENDRA.
AND MY PARTNER ENDED UP DEAD.

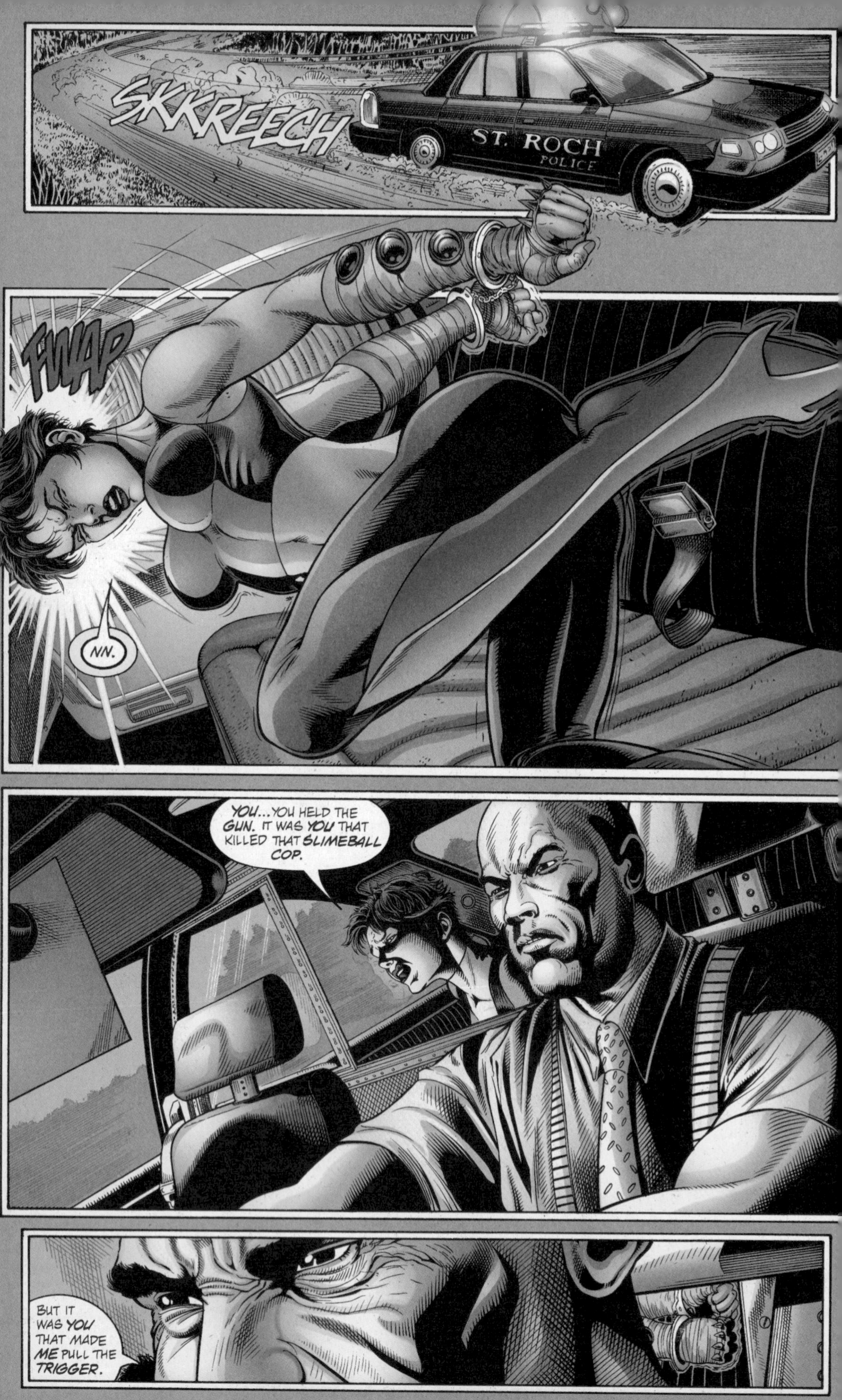
SKKREECH
ST. ROCH POLICE
FWAP
NN.
YOU...YOU HELD THE GUN. IT WAS YOU THAT KILLED THAT SLIMEBALL COP.
BUT IT WAS YOU THAT MADE ME PULL THE TRIGGER.

I WAS YOUNG AND STUPID... SO I RAN.

CHANGED MY NAME. GOT A JOB ON THE ST. ROCH POLICE FORCE. MANAGED TO WORK MY WAY *WAY* UP THE LADDER.

WOMEN IN *THIS* CITY ARE MUCH EASIER TO... *SUBDUE* THAN IN TEXAS.

BUT MY PAST WOULDN'T LET ME GO. I SUPPOSE TH' PAST *NEVER* LETS US GO.

IT ALWAYS FOLLOWS US.

YOUR MOTHER DIDN'T TELL THE POLICE. PROBABLY TRYING TO *PROTECT* YOU. ... BUT SHE *DID* TELL YOUR FATHER.

THEY STARTED NOSING AROUND. CAME TO ST. ROCH A FEW TIMES. SO I LED THEM BACK HERE.

WITH THE TELEGRAM. THAT GUY *WARWHIP*. THAT'S WHY YOU *SHOT* HIM. YOU *HIRED* HIM.

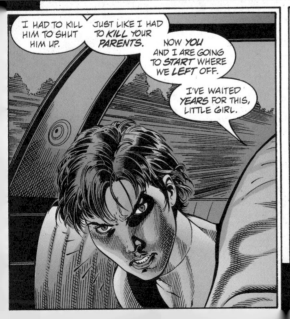

I HAD TO KILL HIM TO SHUT HIM UP.

JUST LIKE I HAD TO *KILL* YOUR *PARENTS*.

NOW *YOU* AND I ARE GOING TO *START* WHERE WE *LEFT* OFF.

I'VE WAITED *YEARS* FOR THIS, LITTLE GIRL.

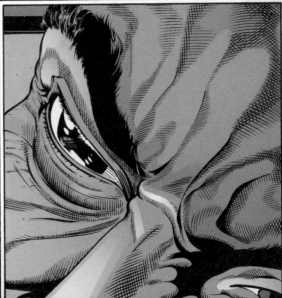

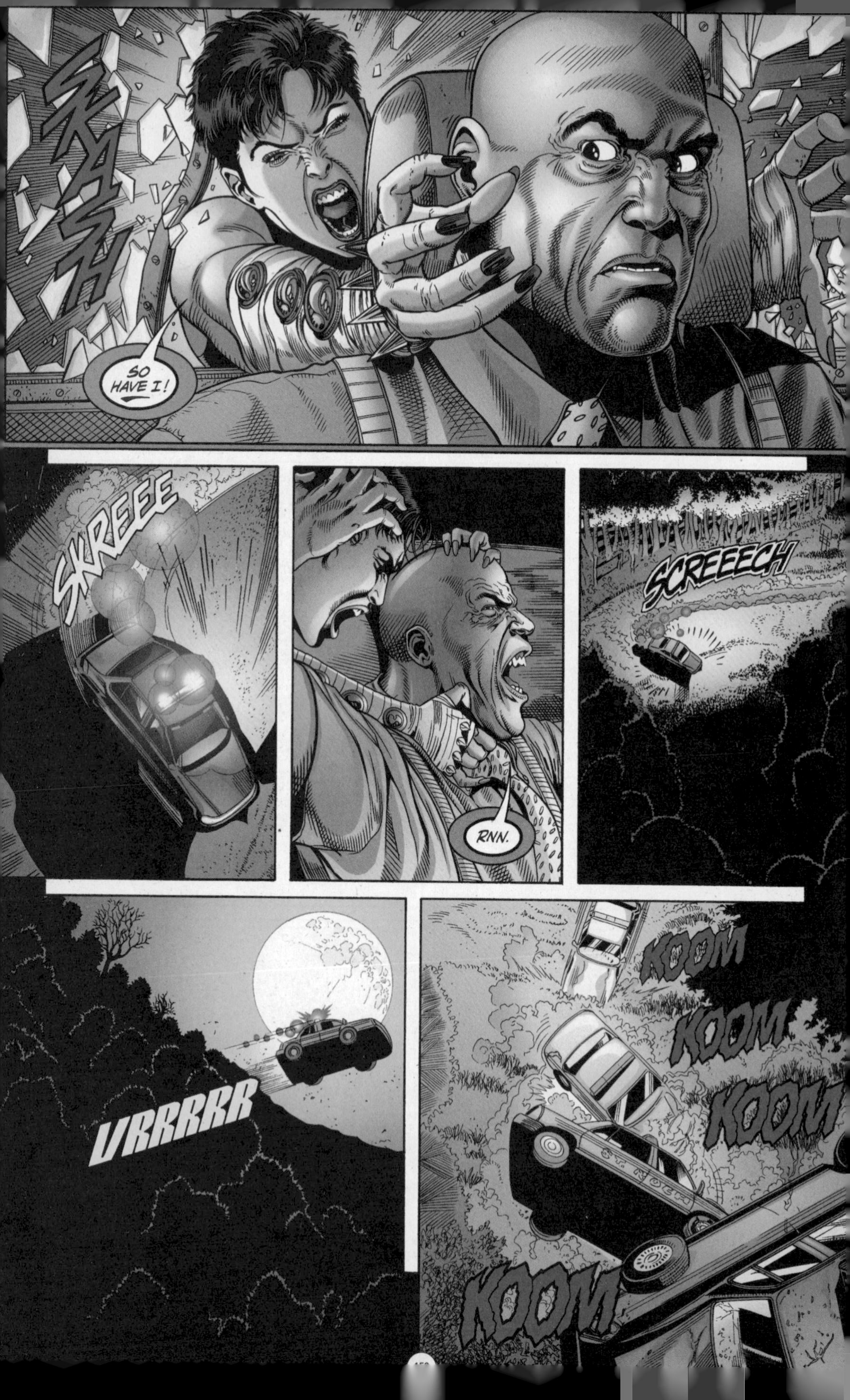
SKASH
SO HAVE I!
SKREEE
RNN.
SCREEECH
VRRRRRR
KOOM
KOOM
KOOM
KOOM

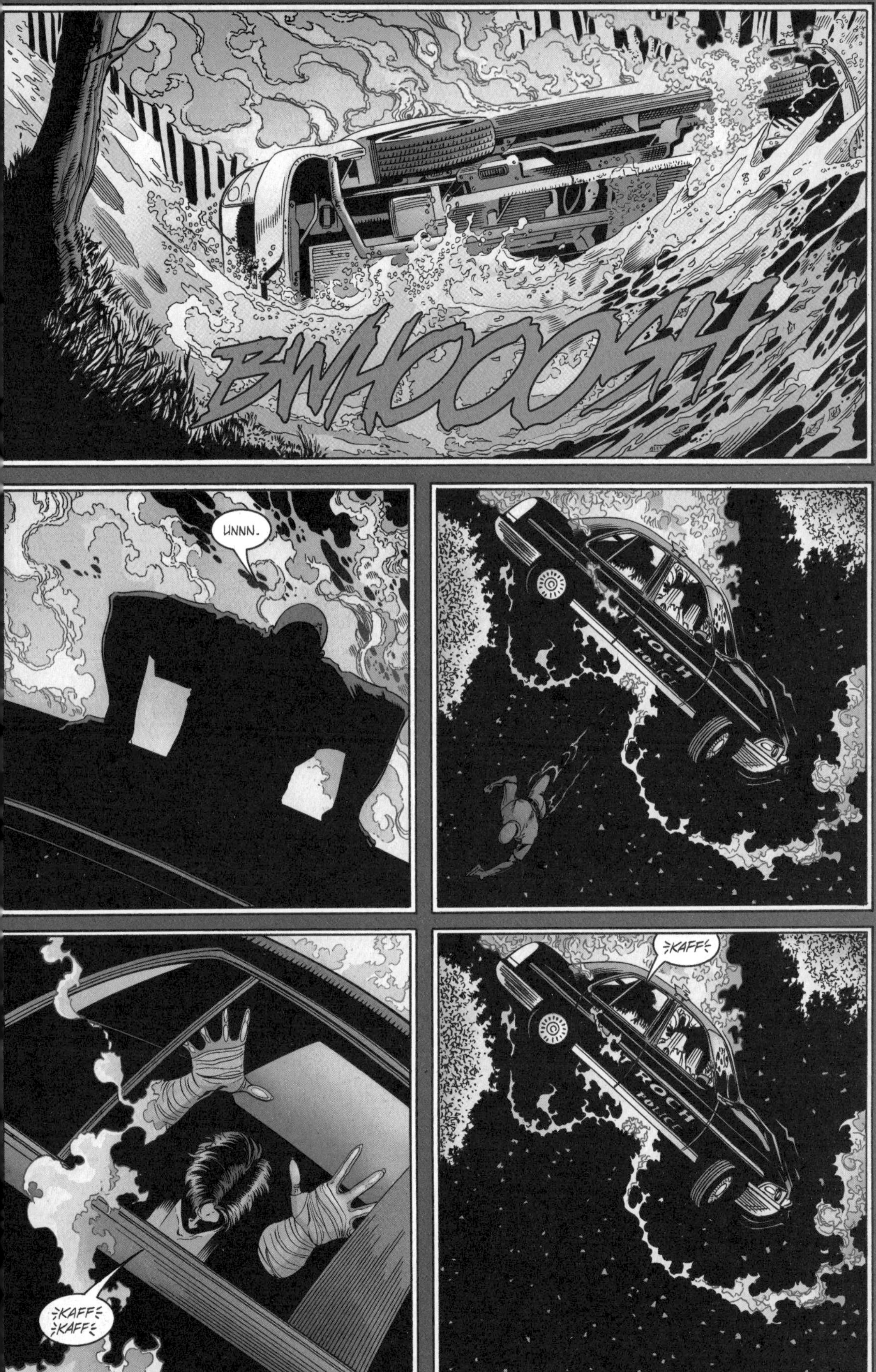
BWHOOOSH
UNNN.
ROCH
POLICE
KAFF
KAFF
KAFF

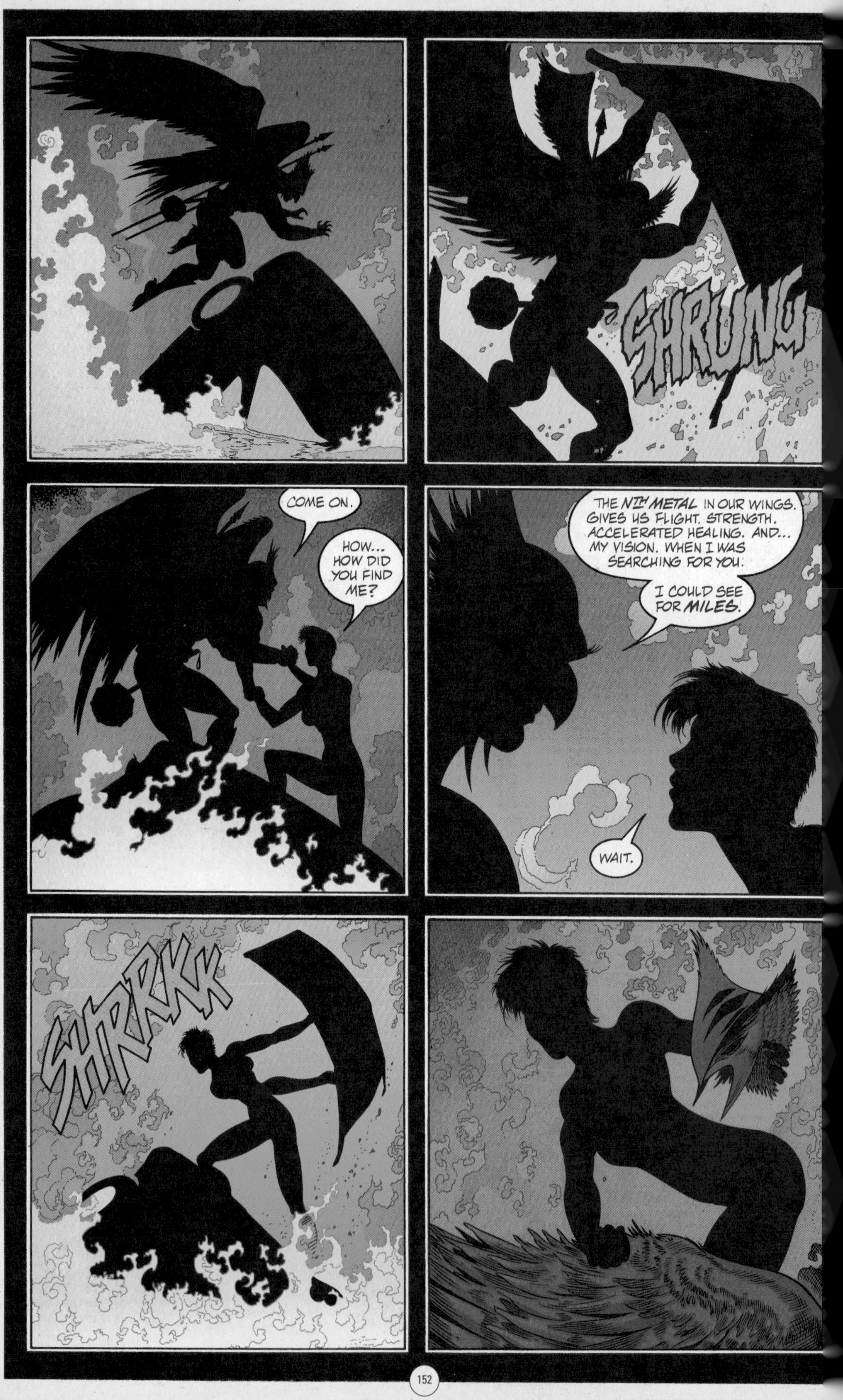

SHRUNG
COME ON.
HOW... HOW DID YOU FIND ME?
THE NTH METAL IN OUR WINGS. GIVES US FLIGHT. STRENGTH. ACCELERATED HEALING. AND... MY VISION. WHEN I WAS SEARCHING FOR YOU:
I COULD SEE FOR MILES.
WAIT.
SHRRKK

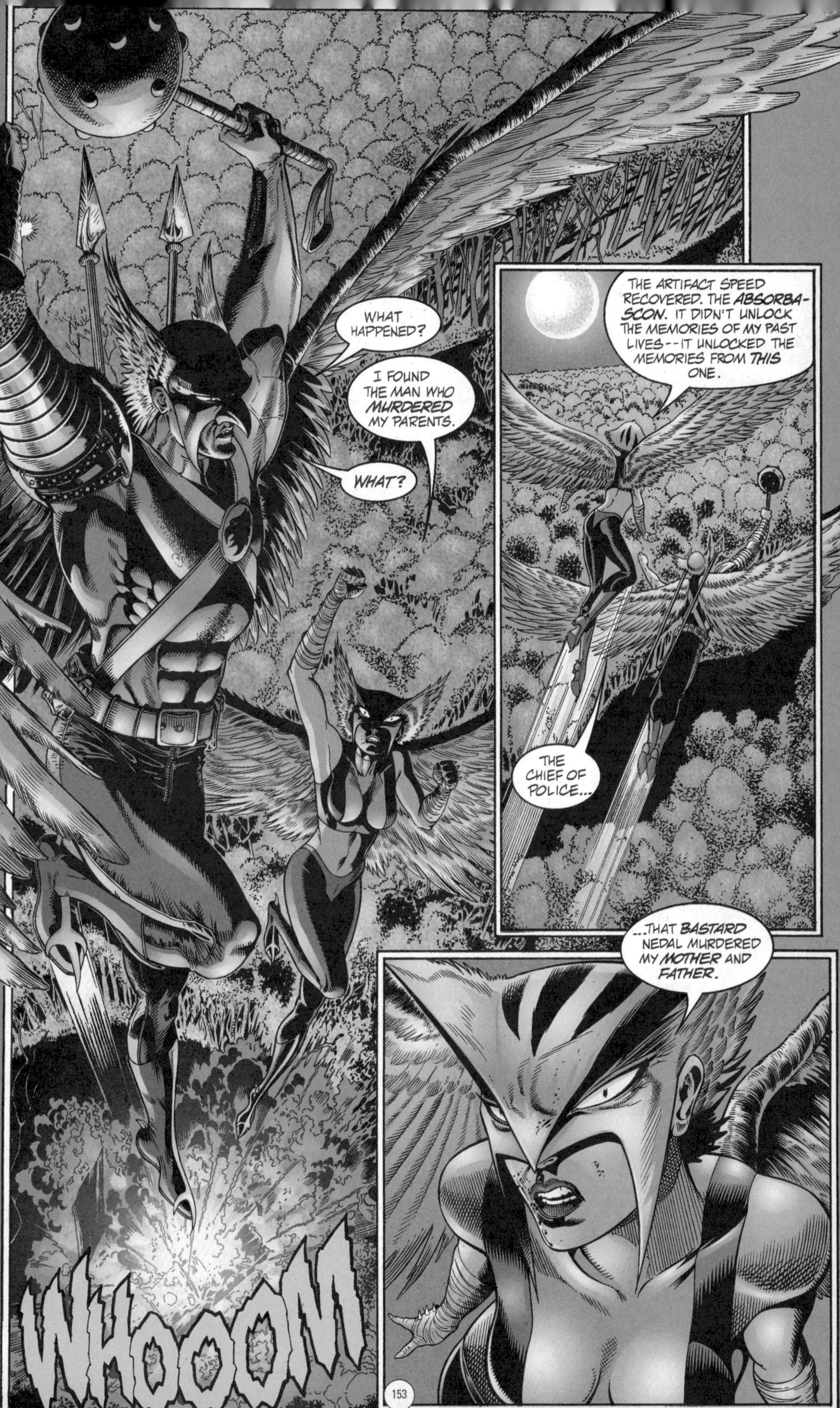
WHAT HAPPENED?
I FOUND THE MAN WHO MURDERED MY PARENTS.
WHAT?
THE ARTIFACT SPEED RECOVERED. THE ABSORBA-SCON. IT DIDN'T UNLOCK THE MEMORIES OF MY PAST LIVES--IT UNLOCKED THE MEMORIES FROM THIS ONE.
THE CHIEF OF POLICE...
...THAT BASTARD NEDAL MURDERED MY MOTHER AND FATHER.
WHOOOM

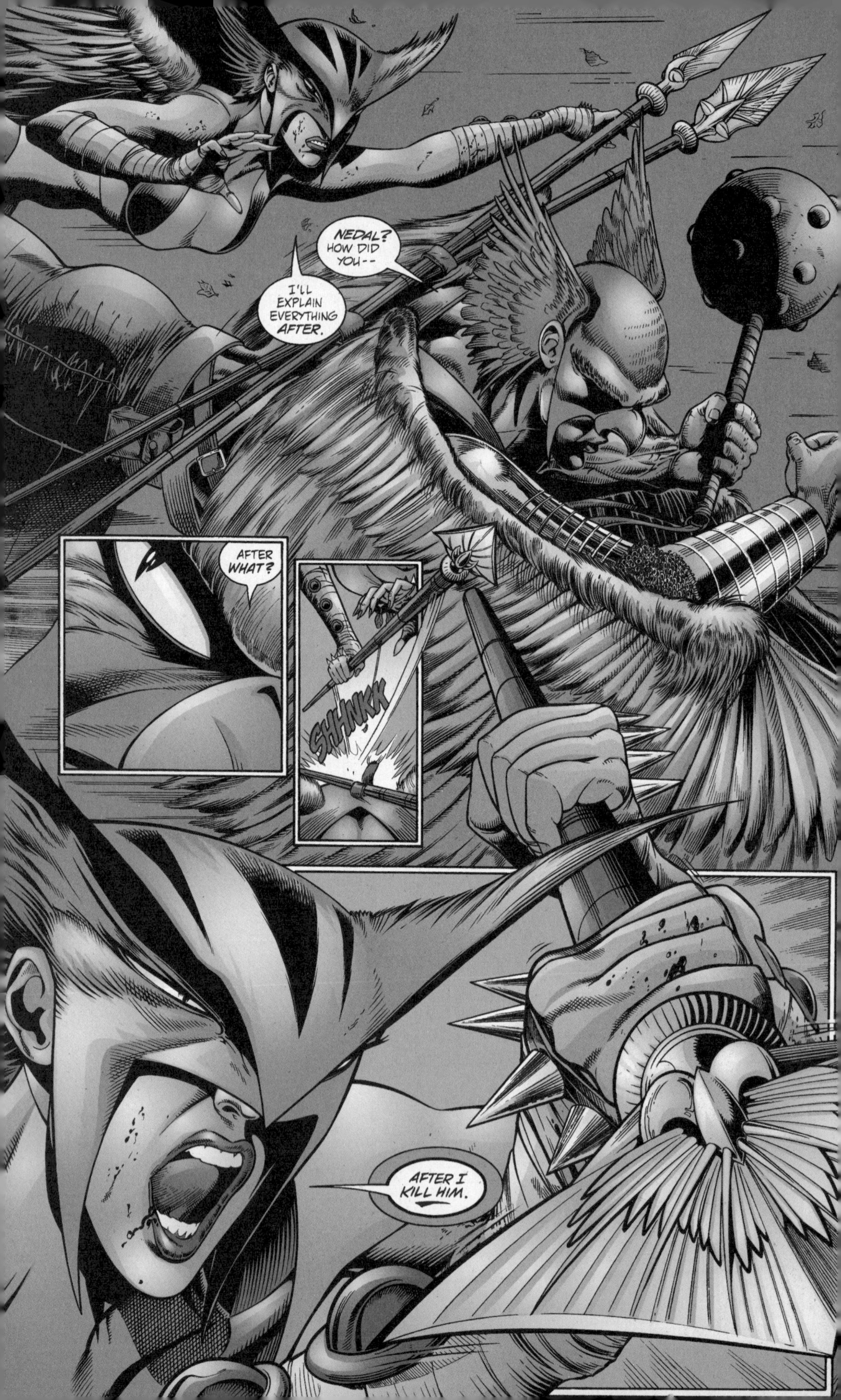
NEDAL? HOW DID YOU--
I'LL EXPLAIN EVERYTHING AFTER.
AFTER WHAT?
SHHNKK
AFTER I KILL HIM.

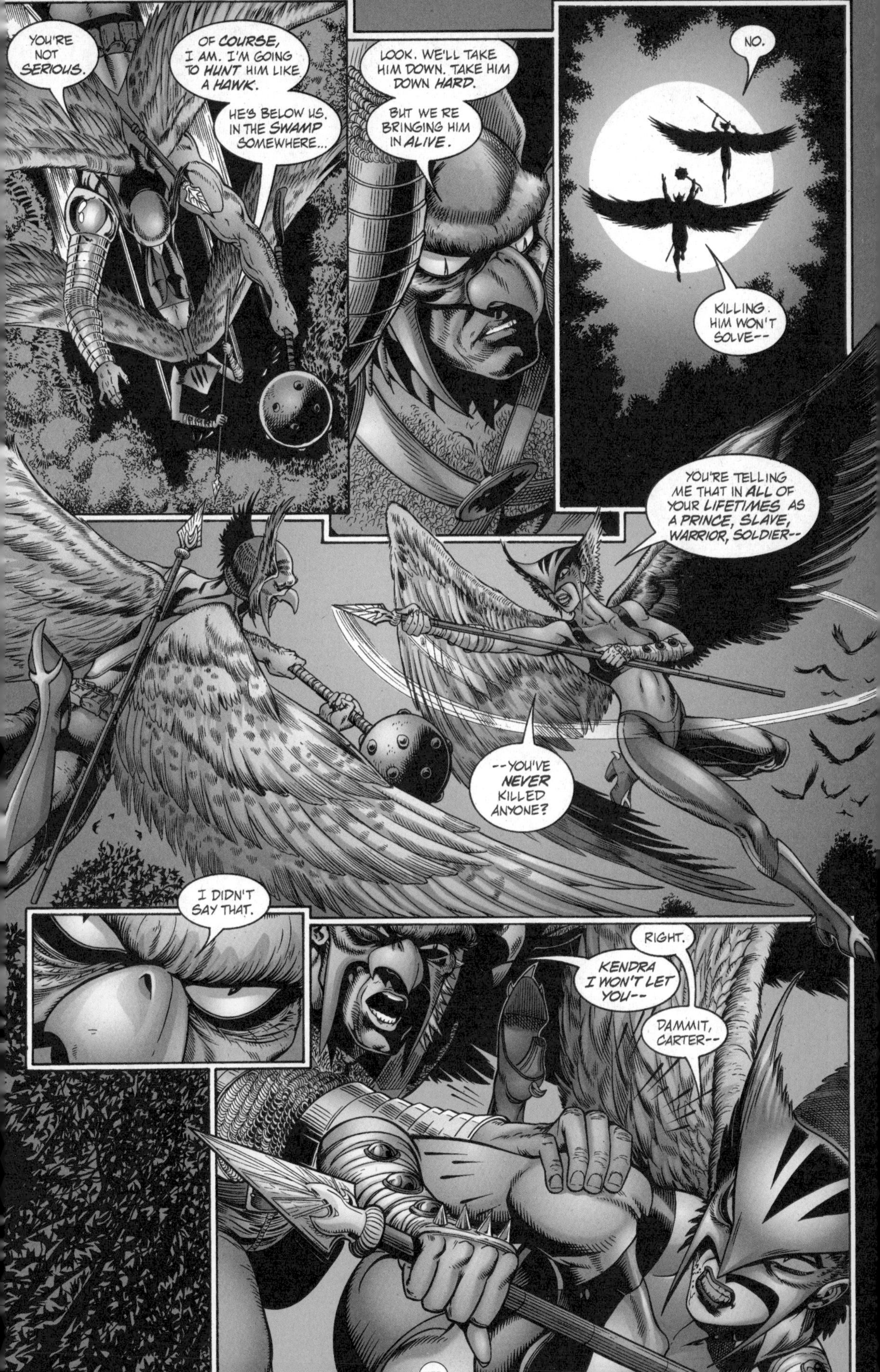

YOU'RE NOT SERIOUS.
OF COURSE, I AM. I'M GOING TO HUNT HIM LIKE A HAWK.
HE'S BELOW US. IN THE SWAMP SOMEWHERE...
LOOK. WE'LL TAKE HIM DOWN. TAKE HIM DOWN HARD.
BUT WE RE BRINGING HIM IN ALIVE.
NO.
KILLING. HIM WON'T SOLVE--
YOU'RE TELLING ME THAT IN ALL OF YOUR LIFETIMES AS A PRINCE, SLAVE, WARRIOR, SOLDIER--
--YOU'VE NEVER KILLED ANYONE?
I DIDN'T SAY THAT.
RIGHT.
KENDRA I WON'T LET YOU--
DAMMIT, CARTER--

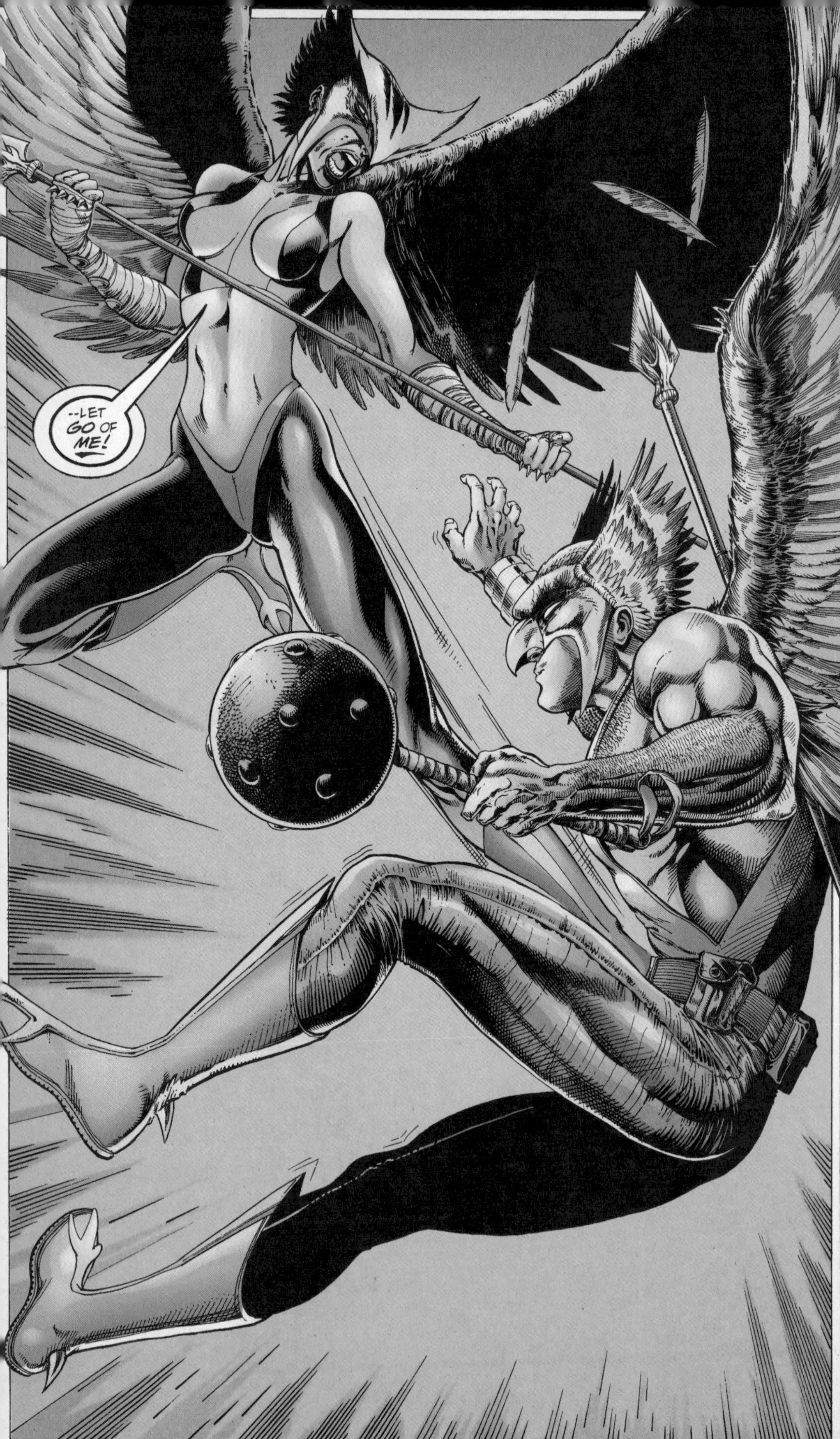
--LET GO OF ME!

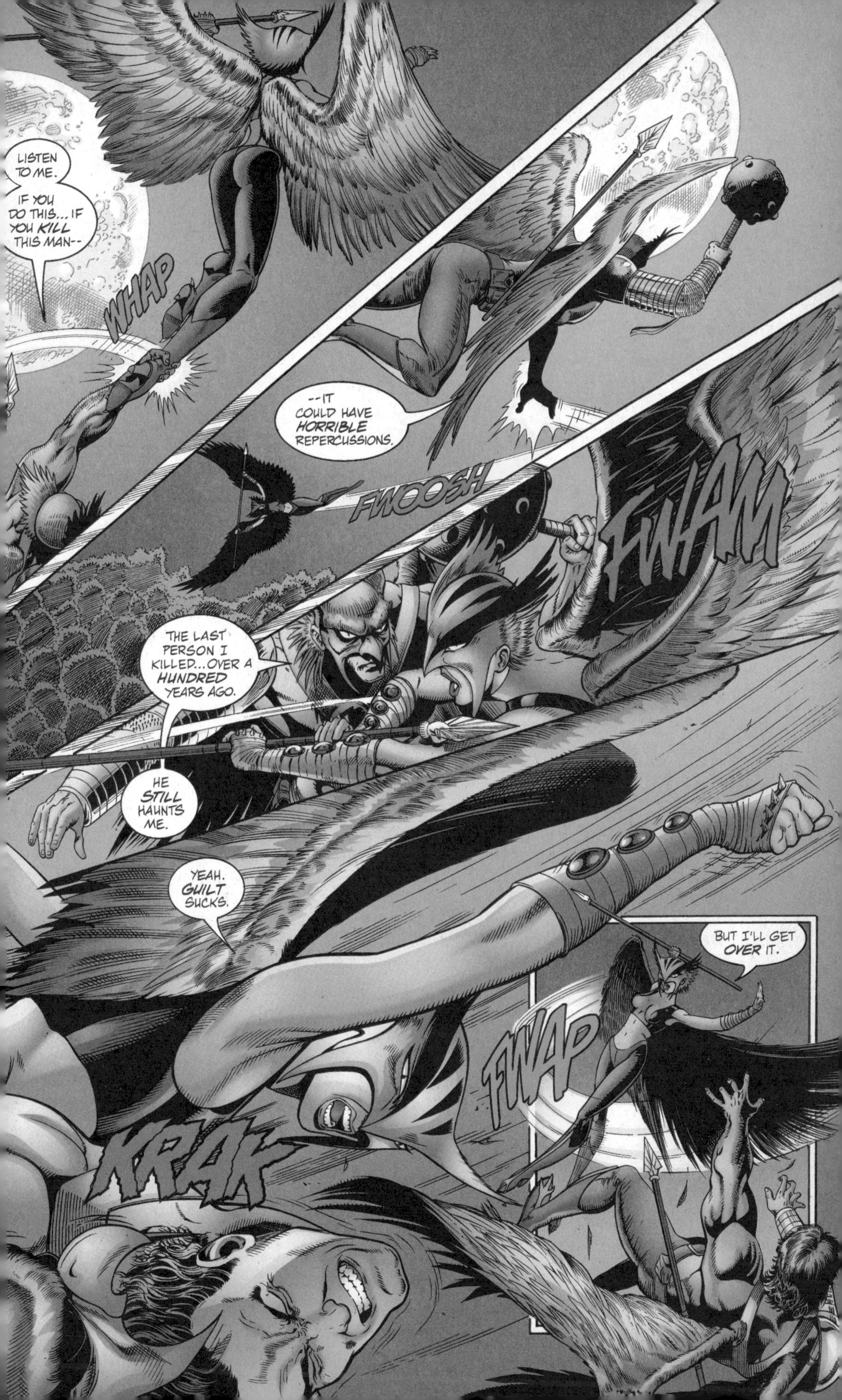
LISTEN TO ME.
IF YOU DO THIS... IF YOU KILL THIS MAN--
WHAP
--IT COULD HAVE HORRIBLE REPERCUSSIONS.
FWOOSH
FWAM
THE LAST PERSON I KILLED...OVER A HUNDRED YEARS AGO.
HE STILL HAUNTS ME.
YEAH. GUILT SUCKS.
BUT I'LL GET OVER IT.
FWAP
KRAK

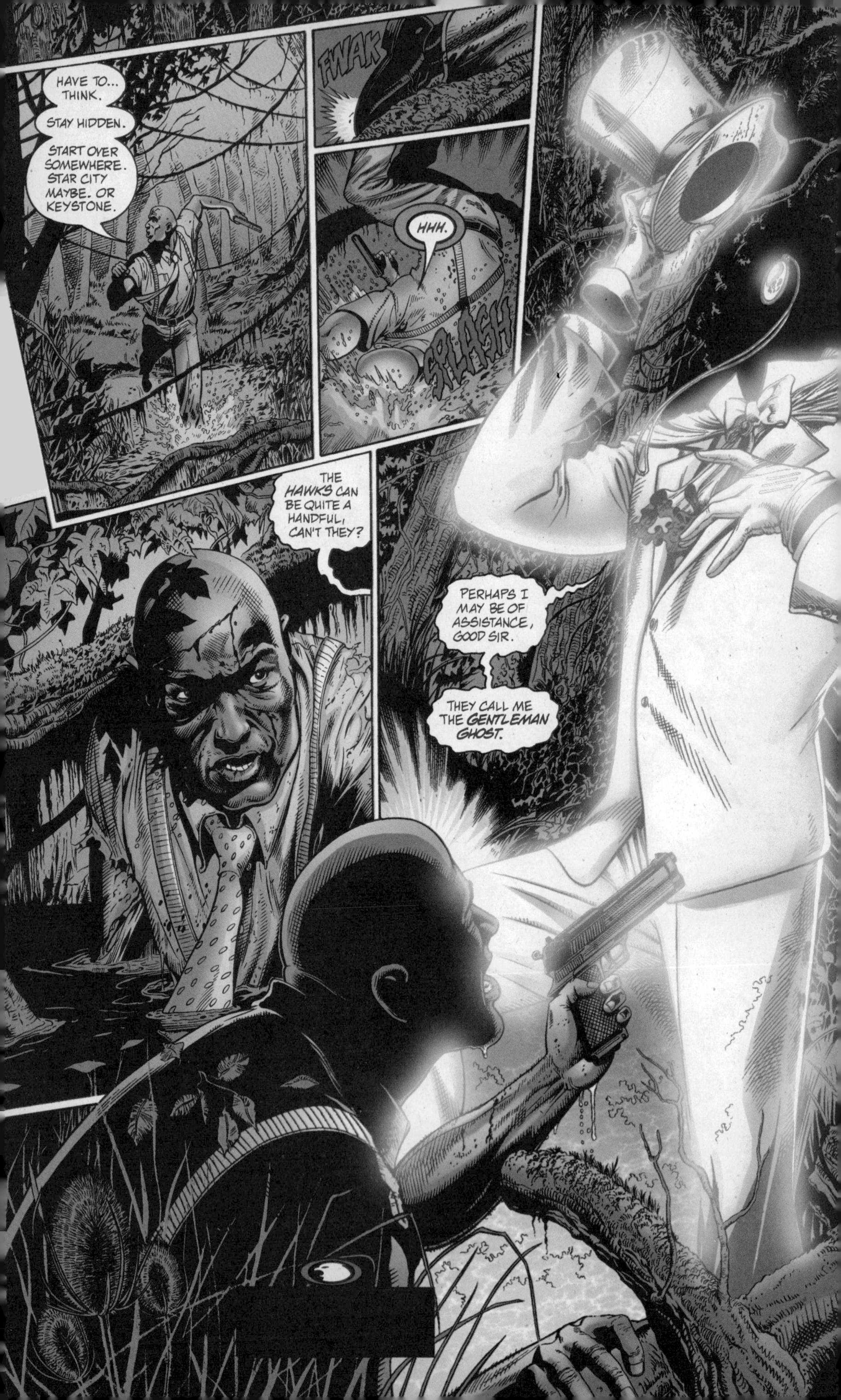
HAVE TO... THINK.
STAY HIDDEN.
START OVER SOMEWHERE. STAR CITY MAYBE. OR KEYSTONE.
FWAK
HHH.
SPLASH
THE *HAWKS* CAN BE QUITE A HANDFUL, CAN'T THEY?
PERHAPS I MAY BE OF ASSISTANCE, GOOD SIR.
THEY CALL ME THE *GENTLEMAN GHOST*.

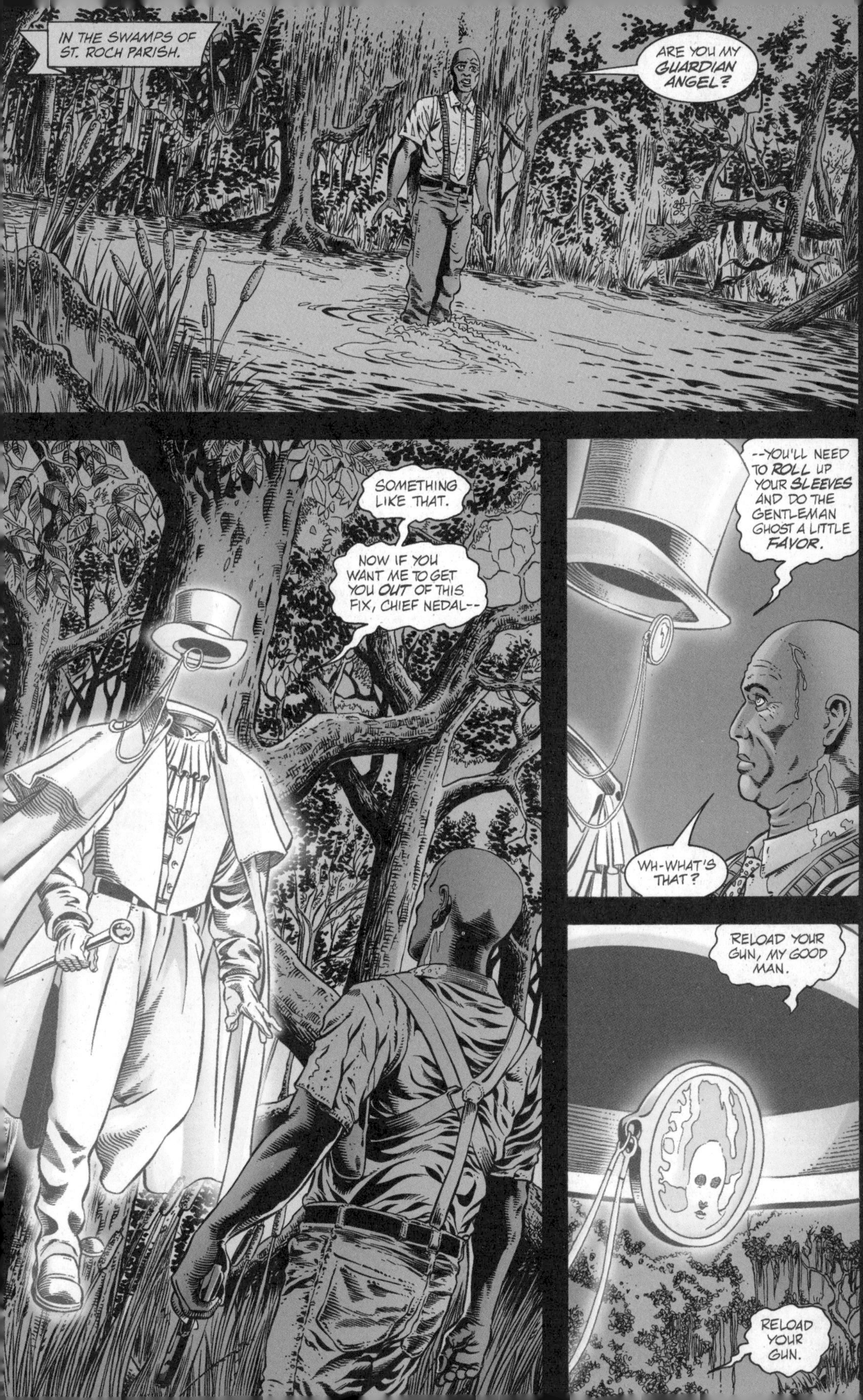
IN THE SWAMPS OF ST. ROCH PARISH.
ARE YOU MY GUARDIAN ANGEL?
SOMETHING LIKE THAT.
NOW IF YOU WANT ME TO GET YOU OUT OF THIS FIX, CHIEF NEDAL--
--YOU'LL NEED TO ROLL UP YOUR SLEEVES AND DO THE GENTLEMAN GHOST A LITTLE FAVOR.
WH-WHAT'S THAT?
RELOAD YOUR GUN, MY GOOD MAN.
RELOAD YOUR GUN.

Thousands of years ago, an Egyptian Prince and his Princess discovered an alien spacecraft from the planet Thanagar. The ship was powered by a mysterious antigravity element they called Nth metal. The unearthly energies of the Nth metal, enhanced by the strength of their love, transformed the souls of the Prince and Princess. For centuries, they were reincarnated, life after life, destined to meet one another and rekindle their love...until today...Today they are Carter Hall and Kendra Saunders, archaeologists and adventurers. The winged warriors known as HAWKMAN and HAWKGIRL!

YEARS LATER, KENDRA'S PARENTS TRACKED THE SURVIVING ATTACKER TO ST. ROCH, WHERE HE AMBUSHED AND MURDERED THEM. TODAY, KENDRA HAS HUNTED FOR HER PARENTS' KILLER, LEARNING THAT HE IS ST. ROCH'S CHIEF OF POLICE, ALBERT NEDAL.

KENDRA SAUNDERS HAS BEEN HAUNTED BY NIGHTMARES OF HER PAST, WHEN SHE AND HER MOTHER WERE ASSAULTED BY TWO POLICE OFFICERS. THOUGH ONLY A CHILD, KENDRA FOUGHT BACK AND DURING THE CHAOS, ONE OF THE ATTACKERS ACCIDENTALLY SHOT AND KILLED THE OTHER AND FLED.

MEANWHILE, A STRANGE SPECTER STANDS IN THE MIDDLE OF ALL THIS. A BEING KNOWN AS THE GENTLEMAN GHOST.

KILLERS PART TWO

GEOFF JOHNS	DON KRAMER	PRENTIS ROLLINS	JOHN KALISZ	HEROIC AGE	KEN LOPEZ	VALERIE D'ORAZIO	PETER TOMASI
WRITER	GUEST PENCILLER	GUEST INKER	COLORIST	SEPARATOR	LETTERER	ASSISTANT EDITOR	EDITOR

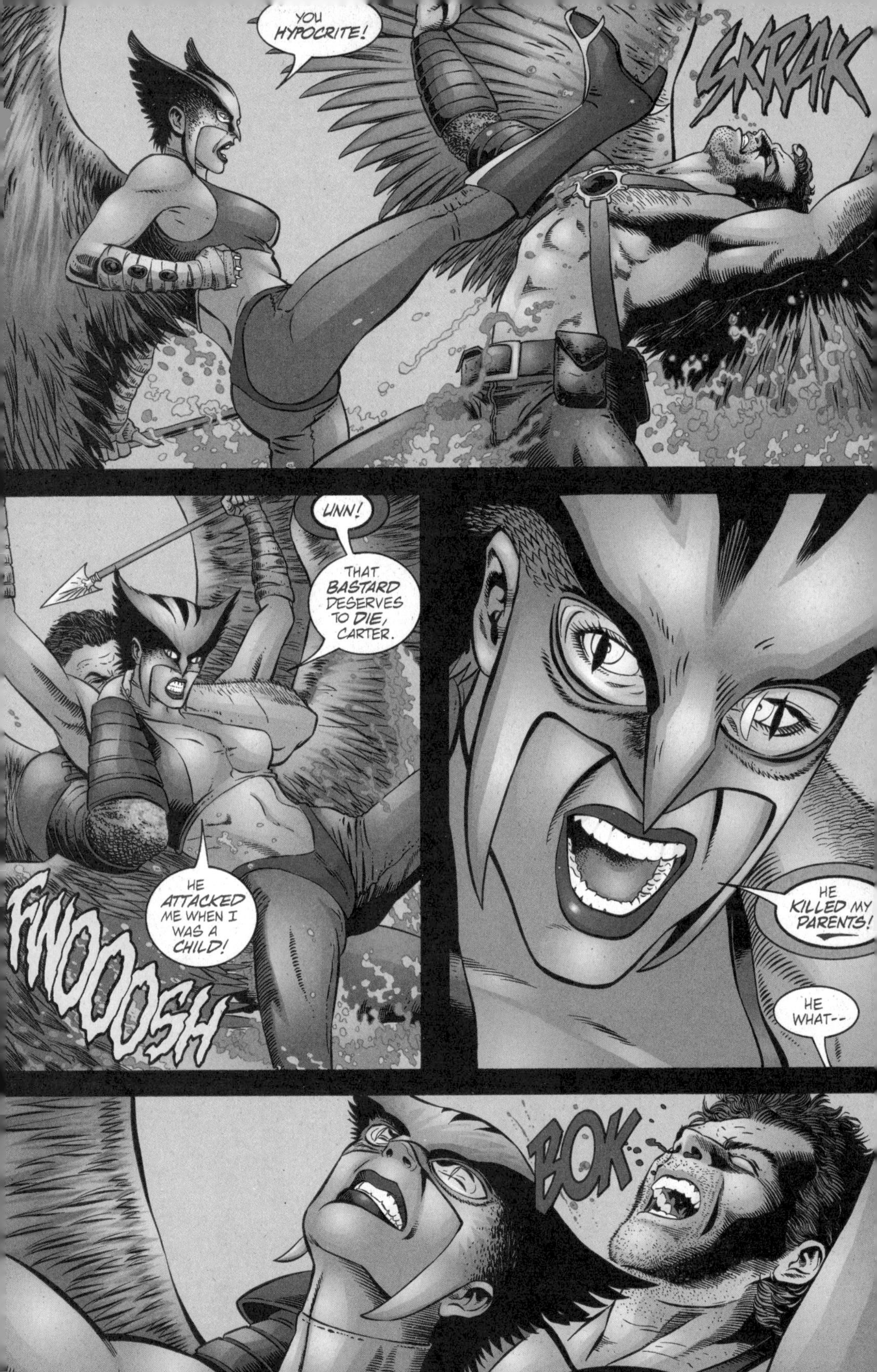

YOU HYPOCRITE!
SKRAK
UNN!
THAT BASTARD DESERVES TO DIE, CARTER.
HE ATTACKED ME WHEN I WAS A CHILD!
FWOOOSH
HE KILLED MY PARENTS!
HE WHAT--
BOK

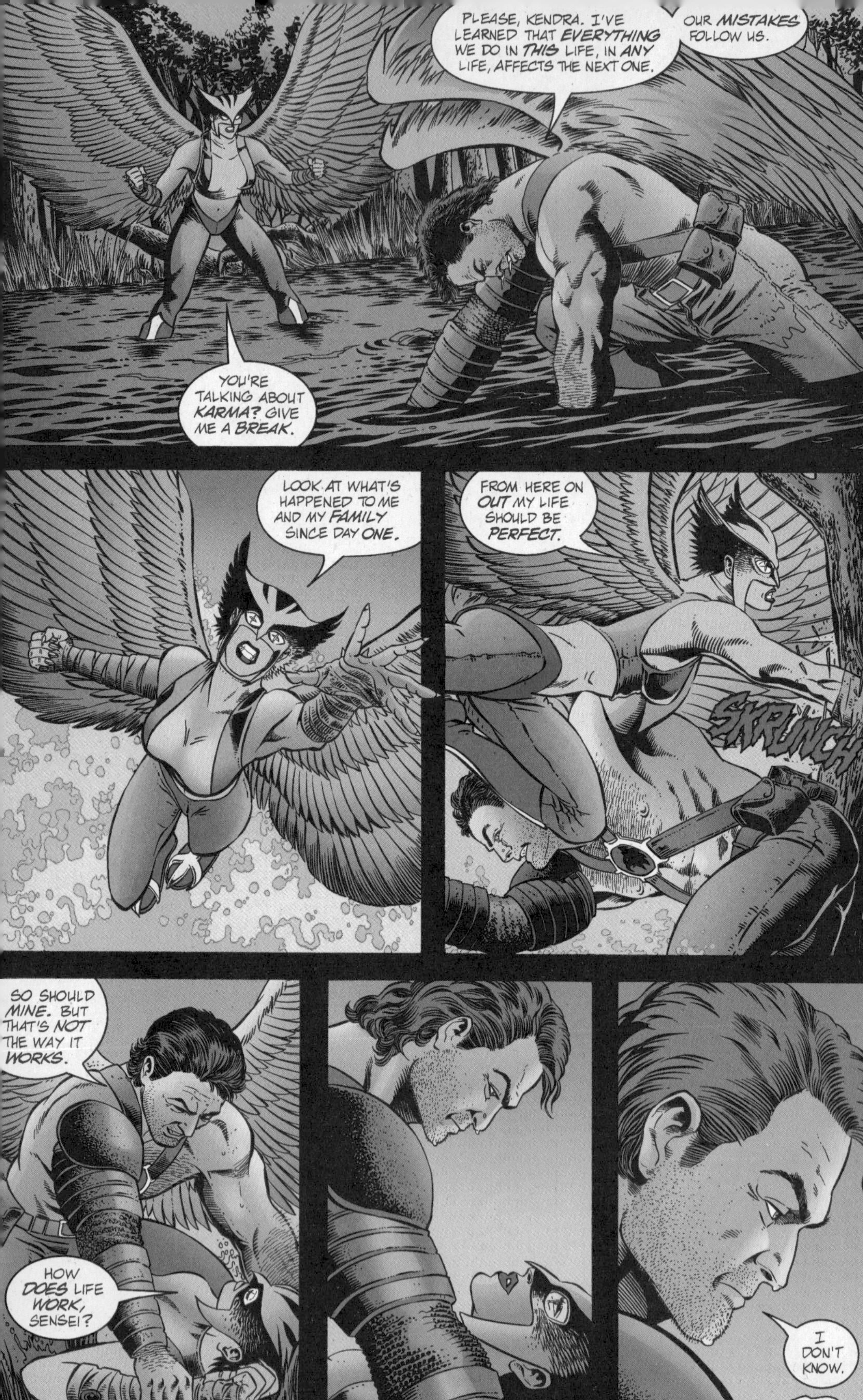
PLEASE, KENDRA. I'VE LEARNED THAT EVERYTHING WE DO IN THIS LIFE, IN ANY LIFE, AFFECTS THE NEXT ONE.
OUR MISTAKES FOLLOW US.
YOU'RE TALKING ABOUT KARMA? GIVE ME A BREAK.
LOOK AT WHAT'S HAPPENED TO ME AND MY FAMILY SINCE DAY ONE.
FROM HERE ON OUT MY LIFE SHOULD BE PERFECT.
SKRUNCH
SO SHOULD MINE. BUT THAT'S NOT THE WAY IT WORKS.
HOW DOES LIFE WORK, SENSEI?
I DON'T KNOW.
OH MY.

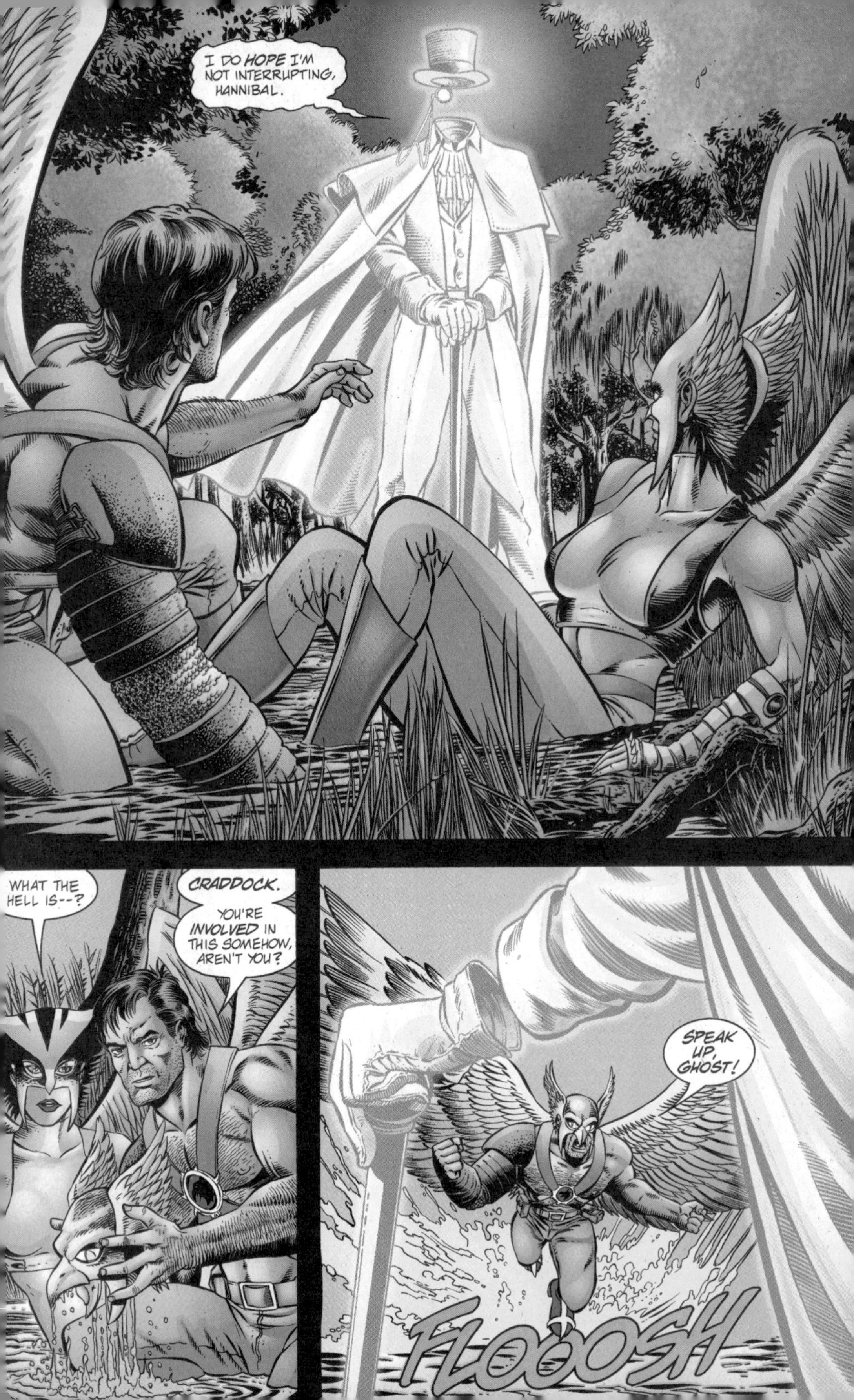

I DO HOPE I'M NOT INTERRUPTING, HANNIBAL.
WHAT THE HELL IS--?
CRADDOCK.
YOU'RE INVOLVED IN THIS SOMEHOW, AREN'T YOU?
SPEAK UP, GHOST!
FLOOOSH

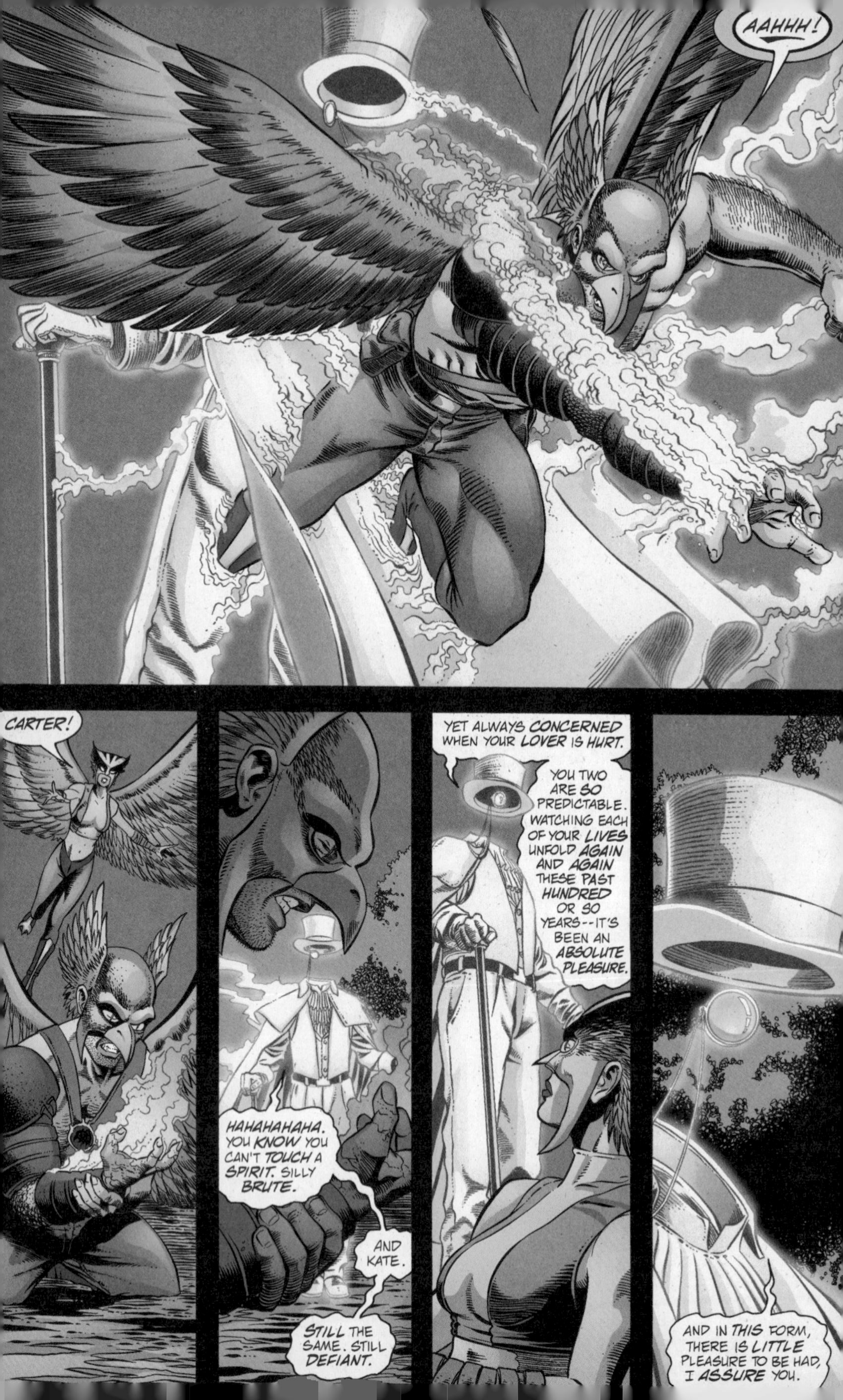
AAHHH!
CARTER!
HAHAHAHAHA. YOU KNOW YOU CAN'T TOUCH A SPIRIT. SILLY BRUTE.
AND KATE.
STILL THE SAME. STILL DEFIANT.
YET ALWAYS CONCERNED WHEN YOUR LOVER IS HURT.
YOU TWO ARE SO PREDICTABLE. WATCHING EACH OF YOUR LIVES UNFOLD AGAIN AND AGAIN THESE PAST HUNDRED OR SO YEARS--IT'S BEEN AN ABSOLUTE PLEASURE.
AND IN THIS FORM, THERE IS LITTLE PLEASURE TO BE HAD, I ASSURE YOU.

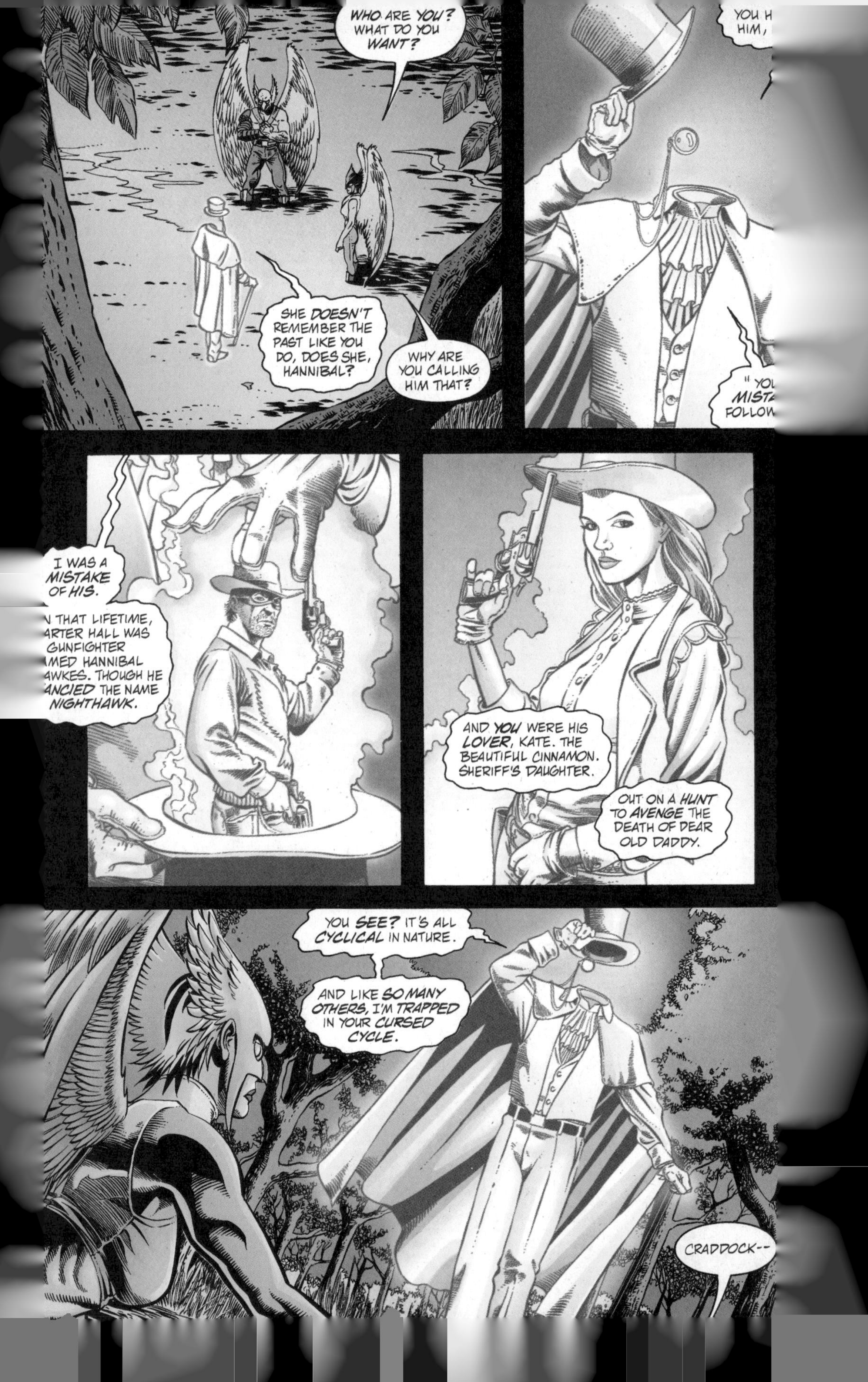

WHO ARE YOU? WHAT DO YOU WANT?
SHE DOESN'T REMEMBER THE PAST LIKE YOU DO, DOES SHE, HANNIBAL?
WHY ARE YOU CALLING HIM THAT?
YOU H HIM,
" YOU MISTA FOLLOW
I WAS A MISTAKE OF HIS.
N THAT LIFETIME, ARTER HALL WAS GUNFIGHTER AMED HANNIBAL AWKES. THOUGH HE ANCIED THE NAME NIGHTHAWK.
AND YOU WERE HIS LOVER, KATE. THE BEAUTIFUL CINNAMON. SHERIFF'S DAUGHTER.
OUT ON A HUNT TO AVENGE THE DEATH OF DEAR OLD DADDY.
YOU SEE? IT'S ALL CYCLICAL IN NATURE.
AND LIKE SO MANY OTHERS, I'M TRAPPED IN YOUR CURSED CYCLE.
CRADDOCK--

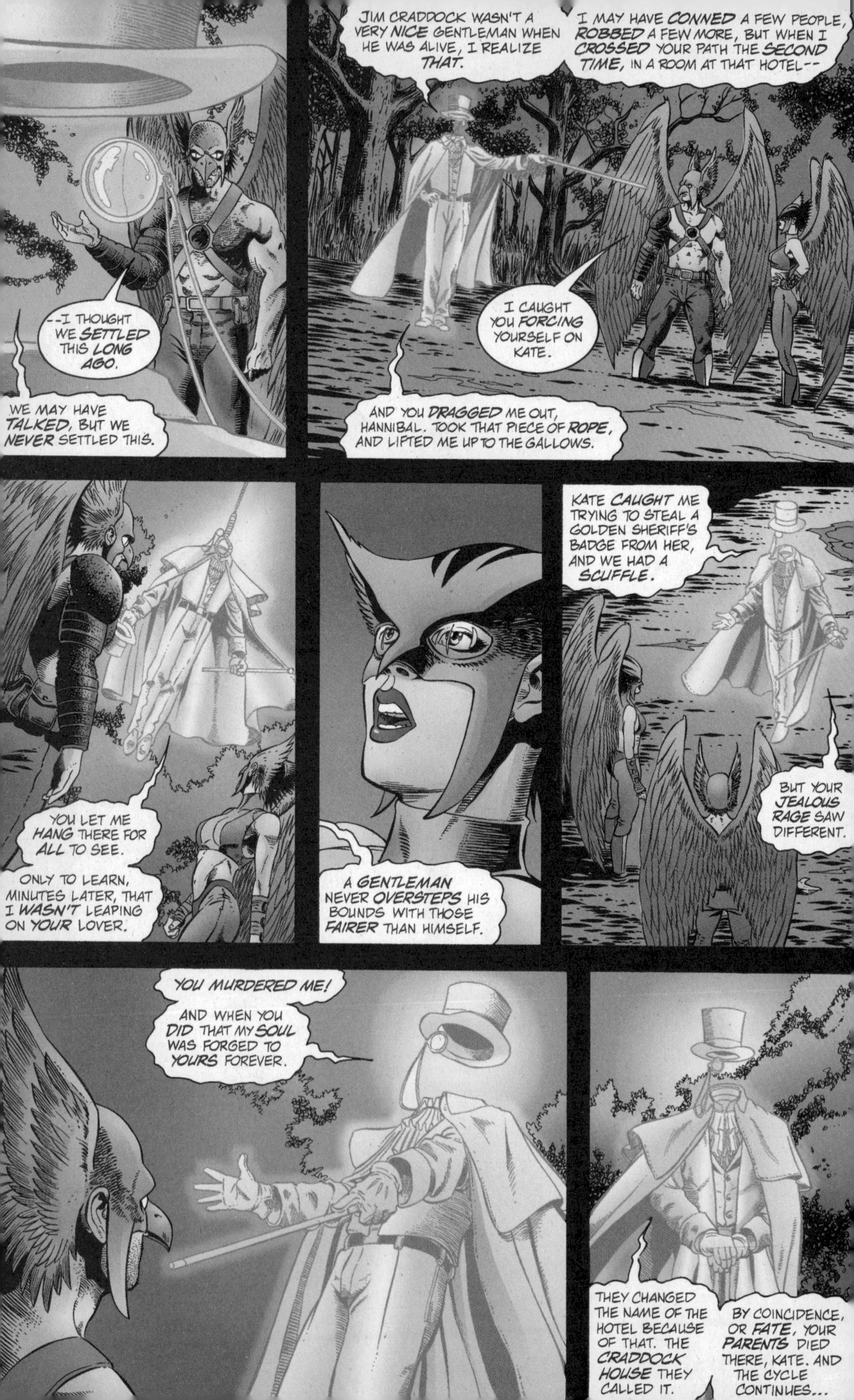

--I THOUGHT WE SETTLED THIS LONG AGO.
WE MAY HAVE TALKED, BUT WE NEVER SETTLED THIS.
JIM CRADDOCK WASN'T A VERY NICE GENTLEMAN WHEN HE WAS ALIVE, I REALIZE THAT.
I MAY HAVE CONNED A FEW PEOPLE, ROBBED A FEW MORE, BUT WHEN I CROSSED YOUR PATH THE SECOND TIME, IN A ROOM AT THAT HOTEL--
I CAUGHT YOU FORCING YOURSELF ON KATE.
AND YOU DRAGGED ME OUT, HANNIBAL. TOOK THAT PIECE OF ROPE, AND LIFTED ME UP TO THE GALLOWS.
YOU LET ME HANG THERE FOR ALL TO SEE.
ONLY TO LEARN, MINUTES LATER, THAT I WASN'T LEAPING ON YOUR LOVER.
A GENTLEMAN NEVER OVERSTEPS HIS BOUNDS WITH THOSE FAIRER THAN HIMSELF.
KATE CAUGHT ME TRYING TO STEAL A GOLDEN SHERIFF'S BADGE FROM HER, AND WE HAD A SCUFFLE.
BUT YOUR JEALOUS RAGE SAW DIFFERENT.
YOU MURDERED ME!
AND WHEN YOU DID THAT MY SOUL WAS FORGED TO YOURS FOREVER.
THEY CHANGED THE NAME OF THE HOTEL BECAUSE OF THAT. THE CRADDOCK HOUSE THEY CALLED IT.
BY COINCIDENCE, OR FATE, YOUR PARENTS DIED THERE, KATE. AND THE CYCLE CONTINUES...

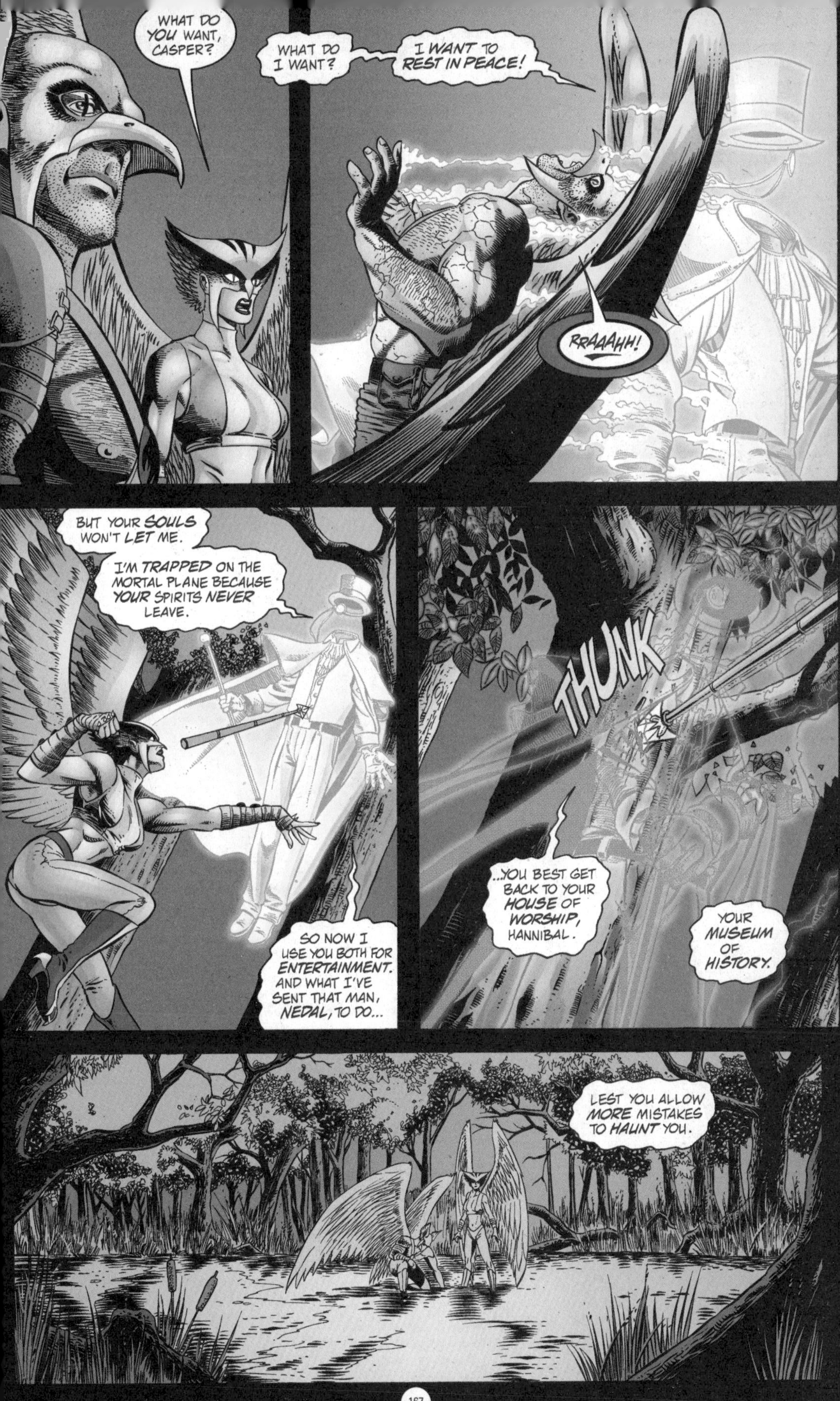

WHAT DO YOU WANT, CASPER?
WHAT DO I WANT?
I WANT TO REST IN PEACE!
RRAAAHH!
BUT YOUR SOULS WON'T LET ME.
I'M TRAPPED ON THE MORTAL PLANE BECAUSE YOUR SPIRITS NEVER LEAVE.
SO NOW I USE YOU BOTH FOR ENTERTAINMENT. AND WHAT I'VE SENT THAT MAN, NEDAL, TO DO...
THUNK
...YOU BEST GET BACK TO YOUR HOUSE OF WORSHIP, HANNIBAL.
YOUR MUSEUM OF HISTORY.
LEST YOU ALLOW MORE MISTAKES TO HAUNT YOU.

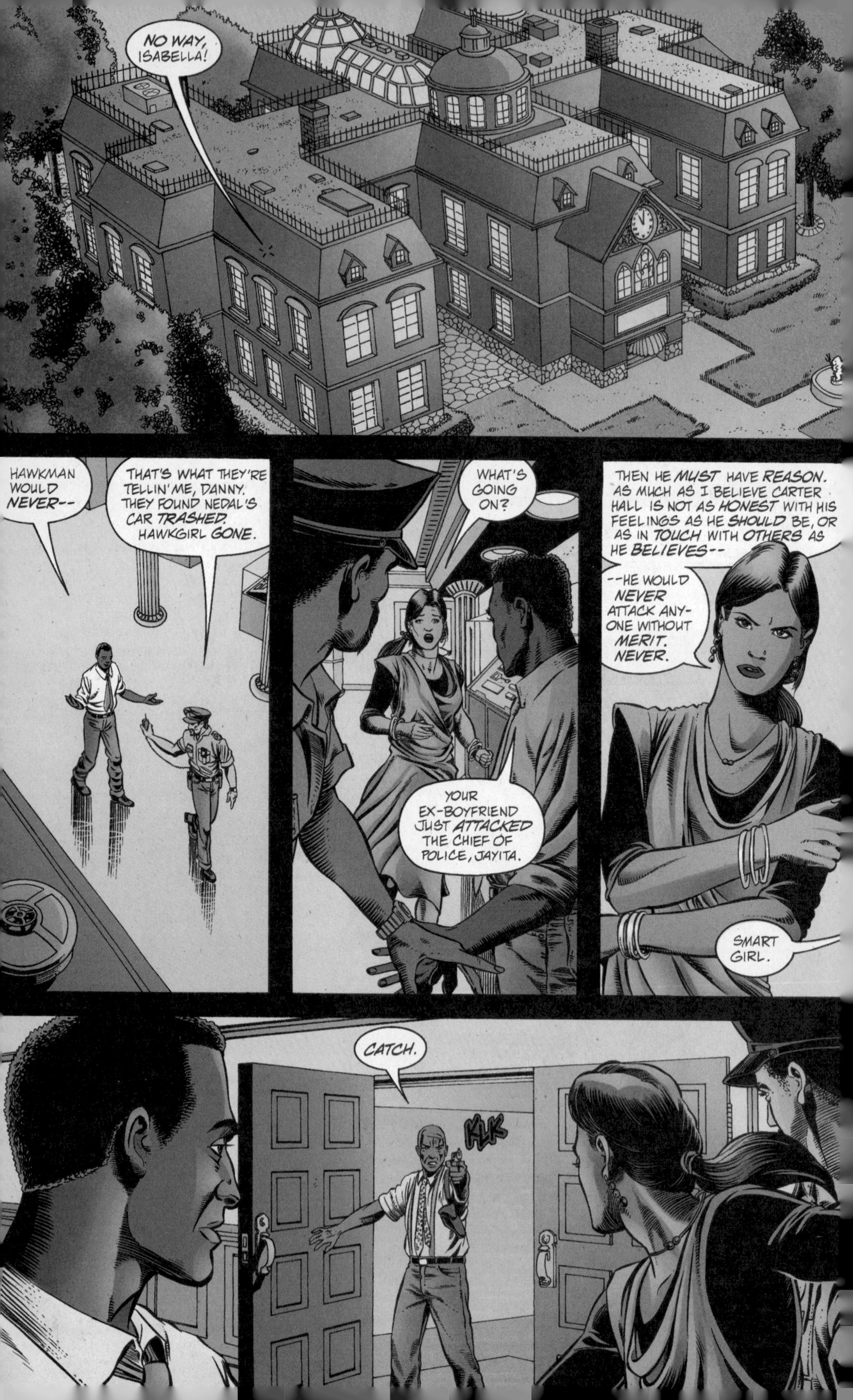

NO WAY, ISABELLA!
HAWKMAN WOULD NEVER--
THAT'S WHAT THEY'RE TELLIN' ME, DANNY. THEY FOUND NEDAL'S CAR TRASHED. HAWKGIRL GONE.
WHAT'S GOING ON?
YOUR EX-BOYFRIEND JUST ATTACKED THE CHIEF OF POLICE, JAYITA.
THEN HE MUST HAVE REASON. AS MUCH AS I BELIEVE CARTER HALL IS NOT AS HONEST WITH HIS FEELINGS AS HE SHOULD BE, OR AS IN TOUCH WITH OTHERS AS HE BELIEVES--
--HE WOULD NEVER ATTACK ANYONE WITHOUT MERIT. NEVER.
SMART GIRL.
CATCH.
KLIK

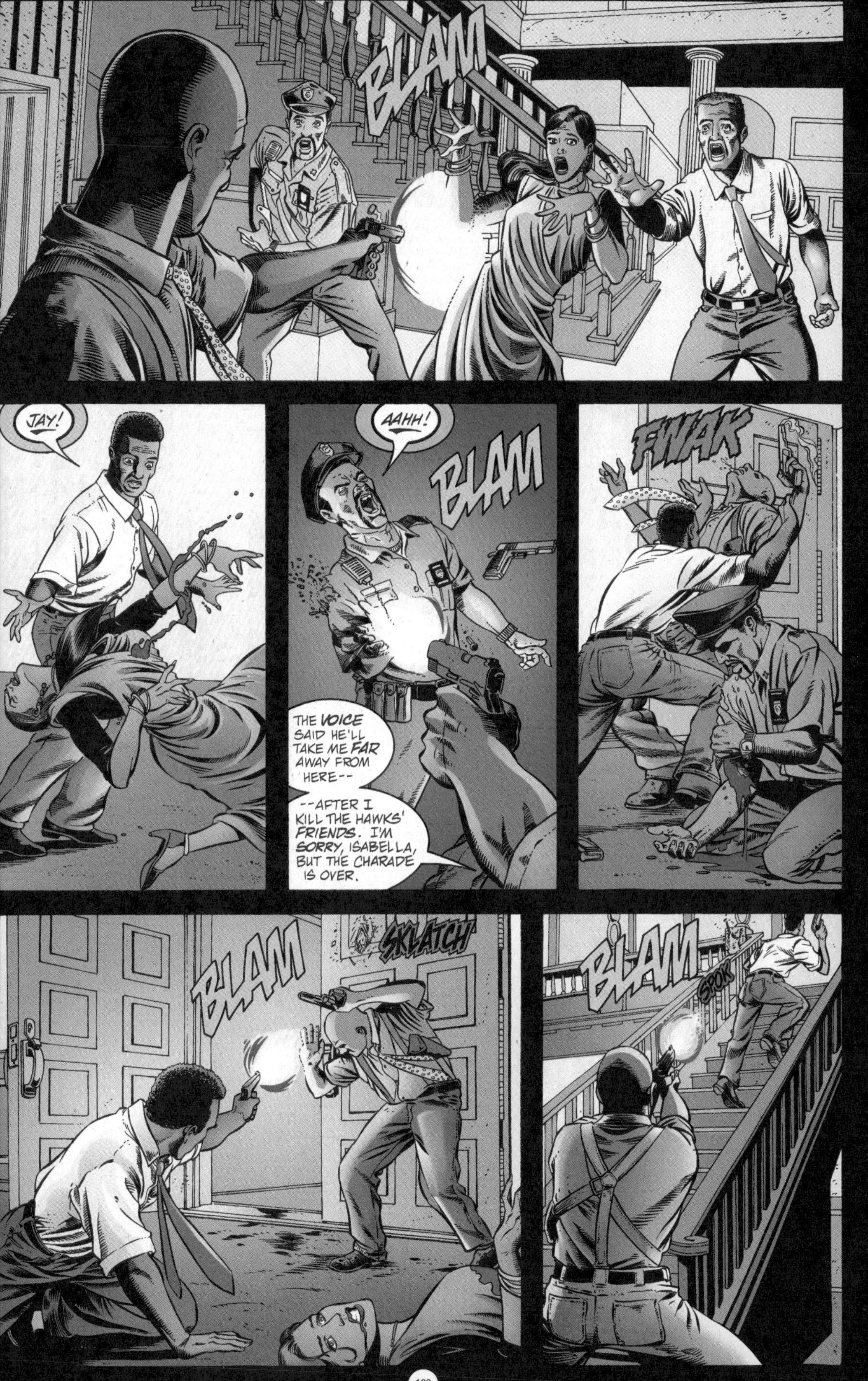
BLAM
JAY!
AAHH!
BLAM
THE VOICE SAID HE'LL TAKE ME FAR AWAY FROM HERE--
--AFTER I KILL THE HAWKS' FRIENDS. I'M SORRY, ISABELLA, BUT THE CHARADE IS OVER.
FWAK
BLAM
SKLATCH
BLAM
SPOK

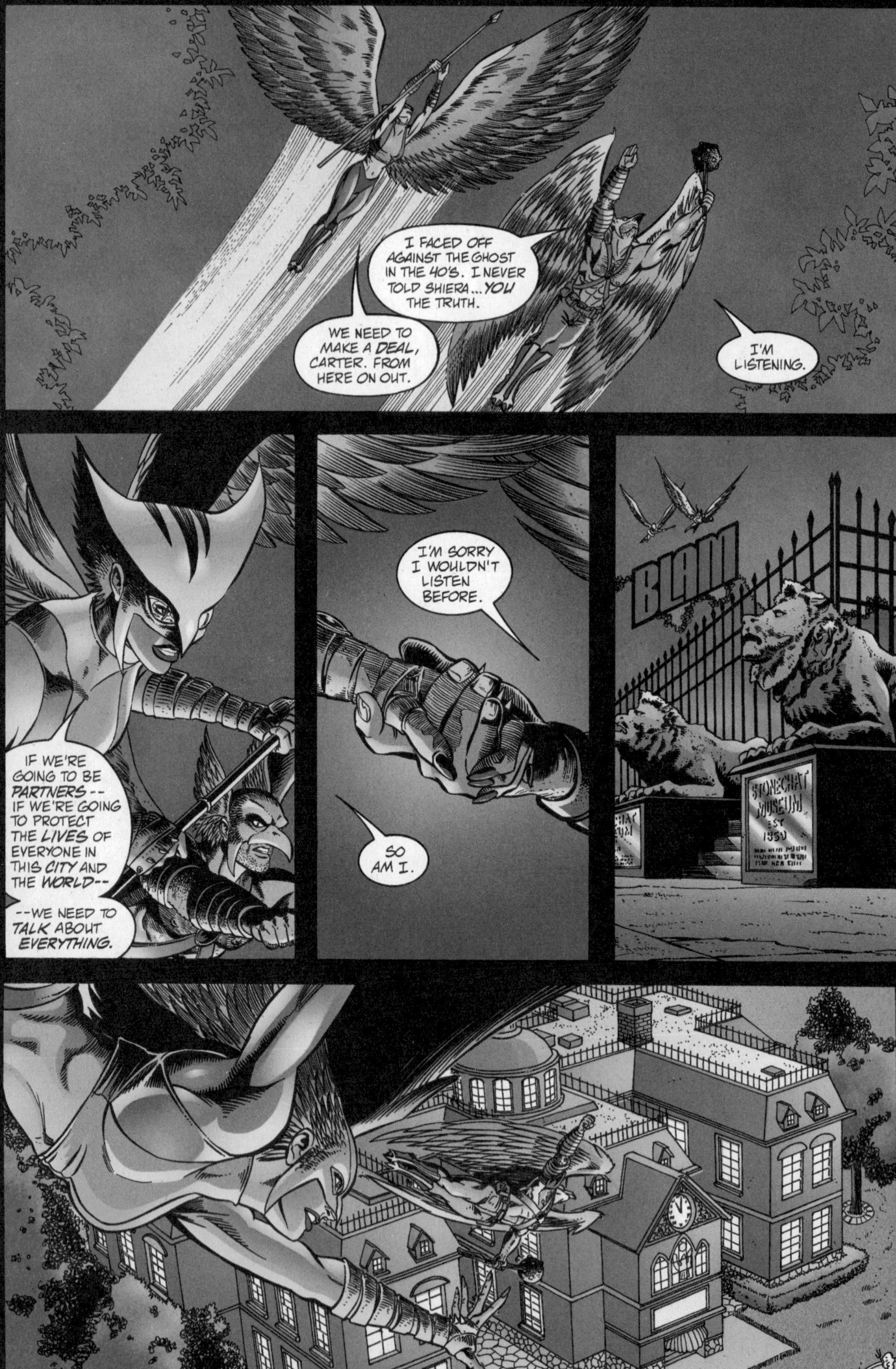
I FACED OFF AGAINST THE GHOST IN THE 40'S. I NEVER TOLD SHIERA... YOU THE TRUTH.
WE NEED TO MAKE A DEAL, CARTER. FROM HERE ON OUT.
I'M LISTENING.
IF WE'RE GOING TO BE PARTNERS -- IF WE'RE GOING TO PROTECT THE LIVES OF EVERYONE IN THIS CITY AND THE WORLD--
--WE NEED TO TALK ABOUT EVERYTHING.
I'M SORRY I WOULDN'T LISTEN BEFORE.
SO AM I.
BLAM
STONECHAT MUSEUM EST 1959

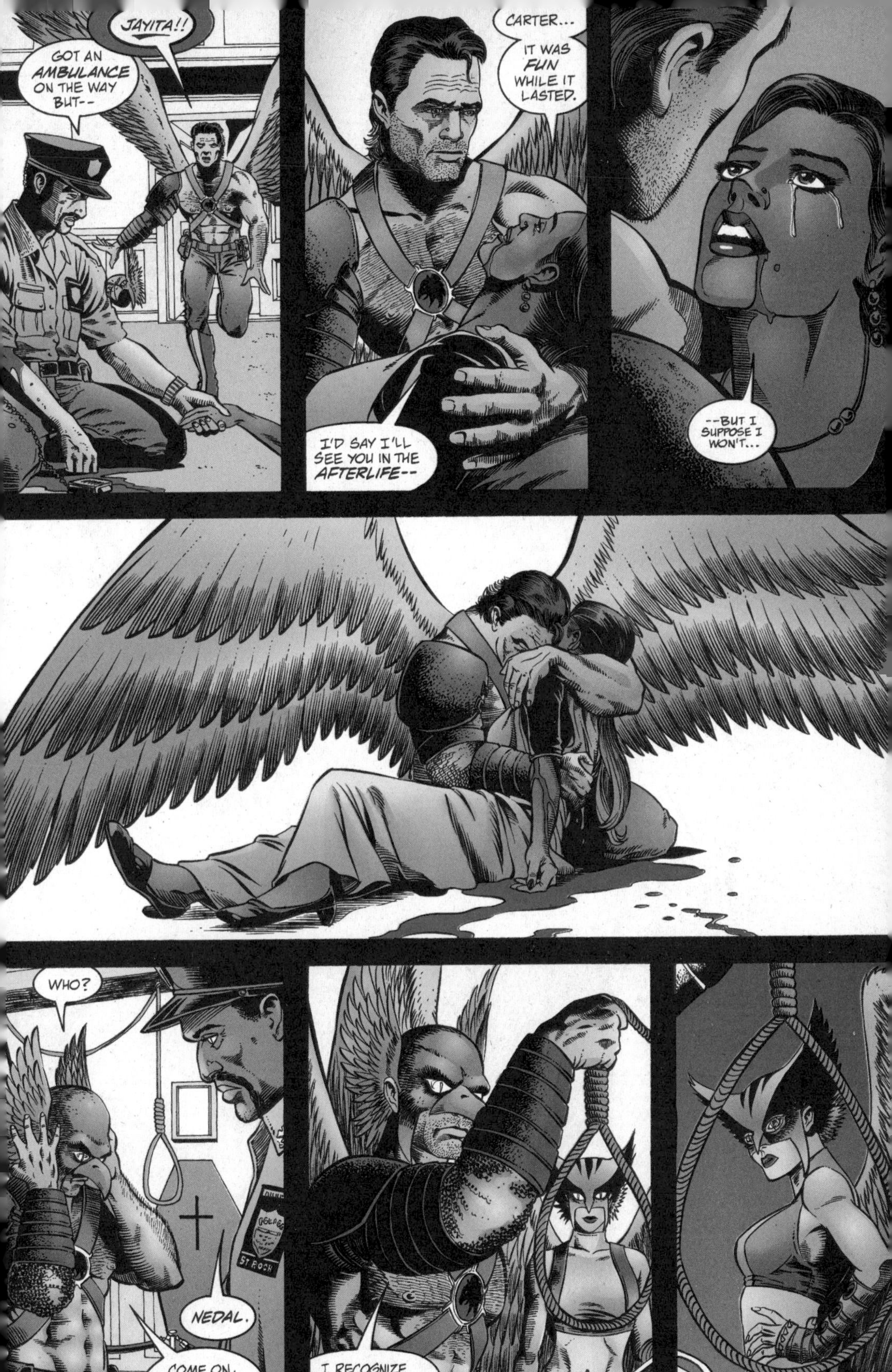
GOT AN AMBULANCE ON THE WAY BUT--
JAYITA!!
CARTER... IT WAS FUN WHILE IT LASTED.
I'D SAY I'LL SEE YOU IN THE AFTERLIFE--
--BUT I SUPPOSE I WON'T...
WHO?
NEDAL.
COME ON, KENDRA. WE DO THIS YOUR WAY.
I RECOGNIZE THIS COFFIN NOW. CRADDOCK'S.
DESTINY WINS AGAIN.
TIME FOR ANOTHER MAN TO HANG.

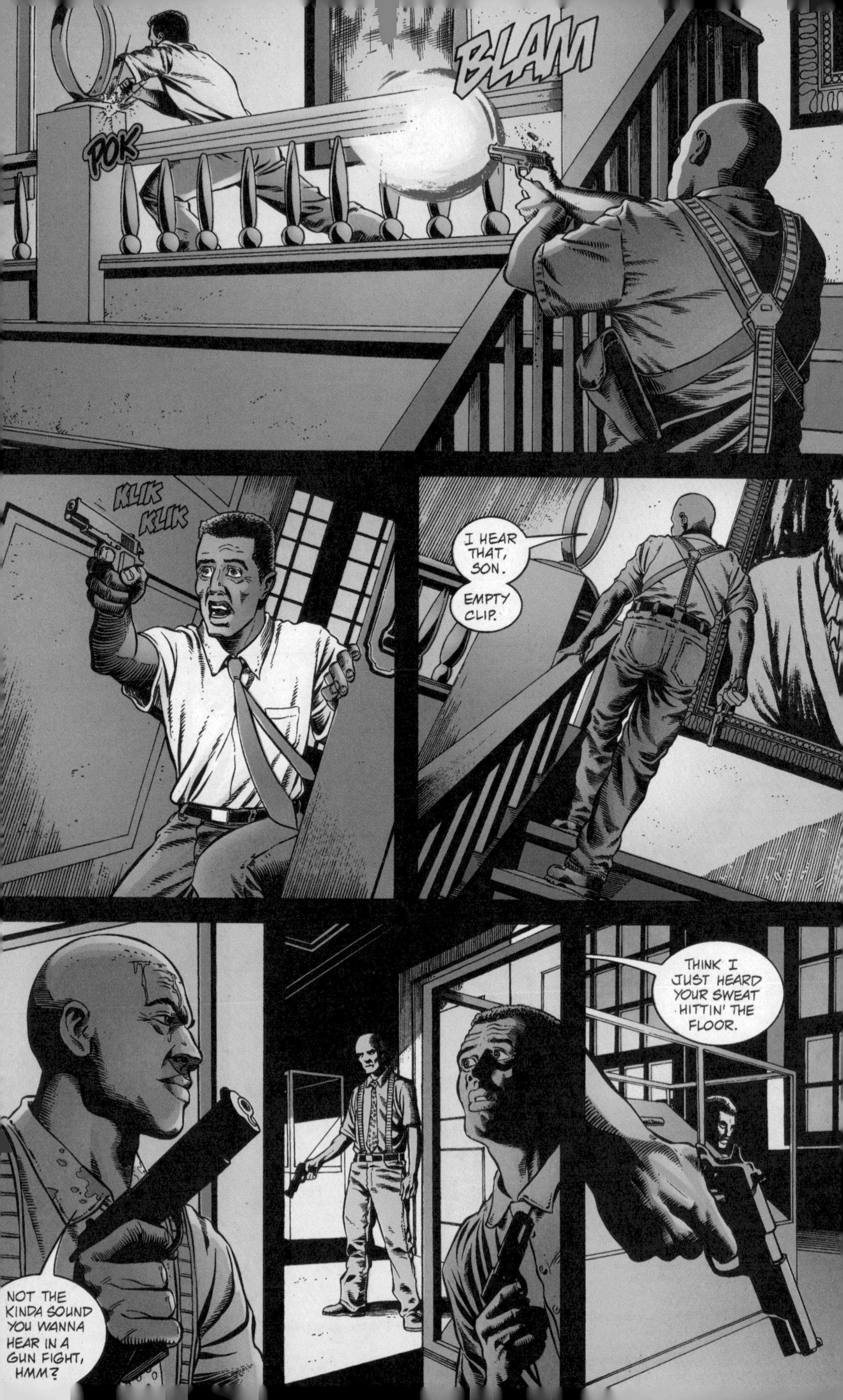
BLAM
POK
KLIK KLIK
I HEAR THAT, SON.
EMPTY CLIP.
NOT THE KINDA SOUND YOU WANNA HEAR IN A GUN FIGHT, HMM?
THINK I JUST HEARD YOUR SWEAT HITTIN' THE FLOOR.

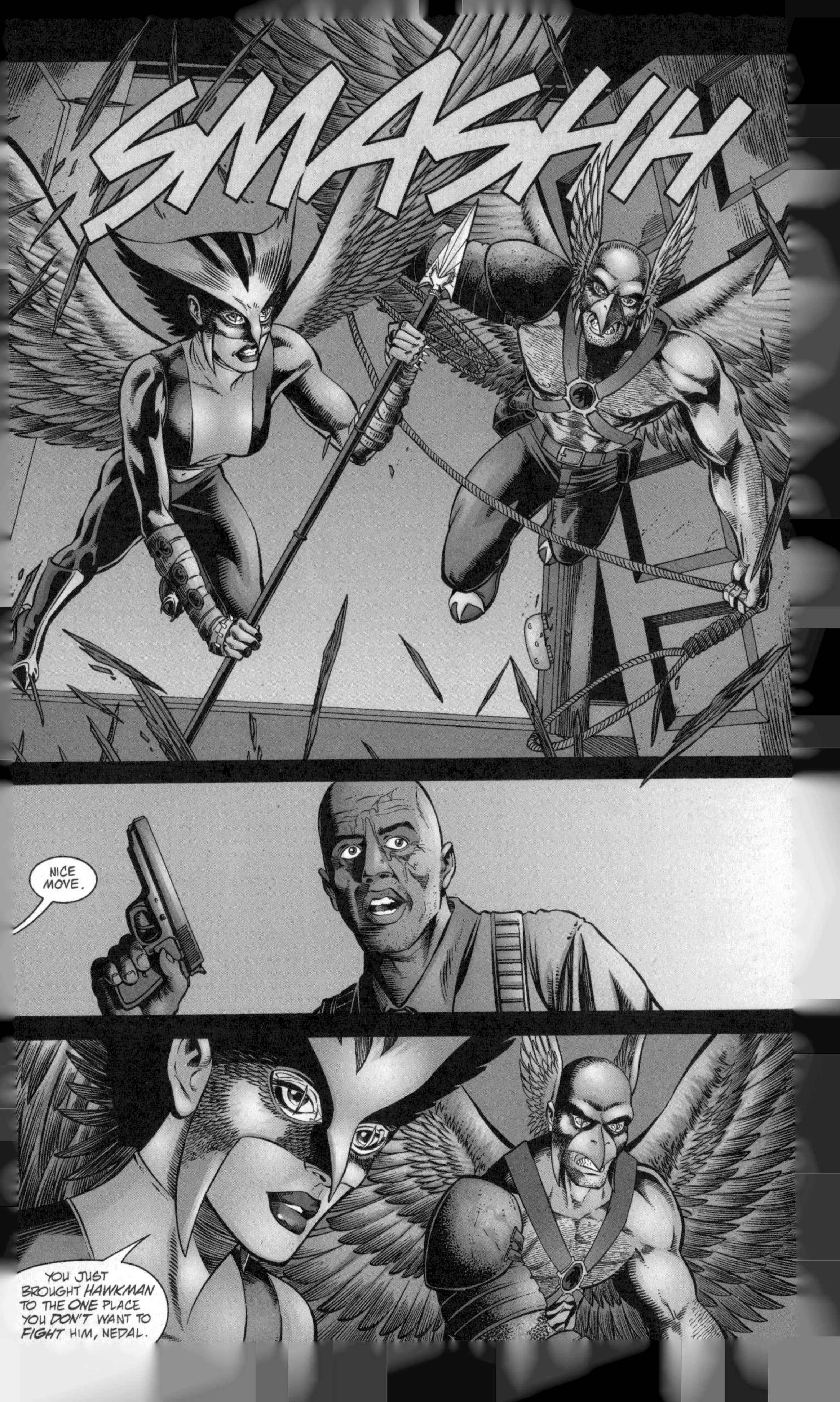
SMASHH
NICE MOVE.
YOU JUST BROUGHT HAWKMAN TO THE ONE PLACE YOU DON'T WANT TO FIGHT HIM, NEDAL.

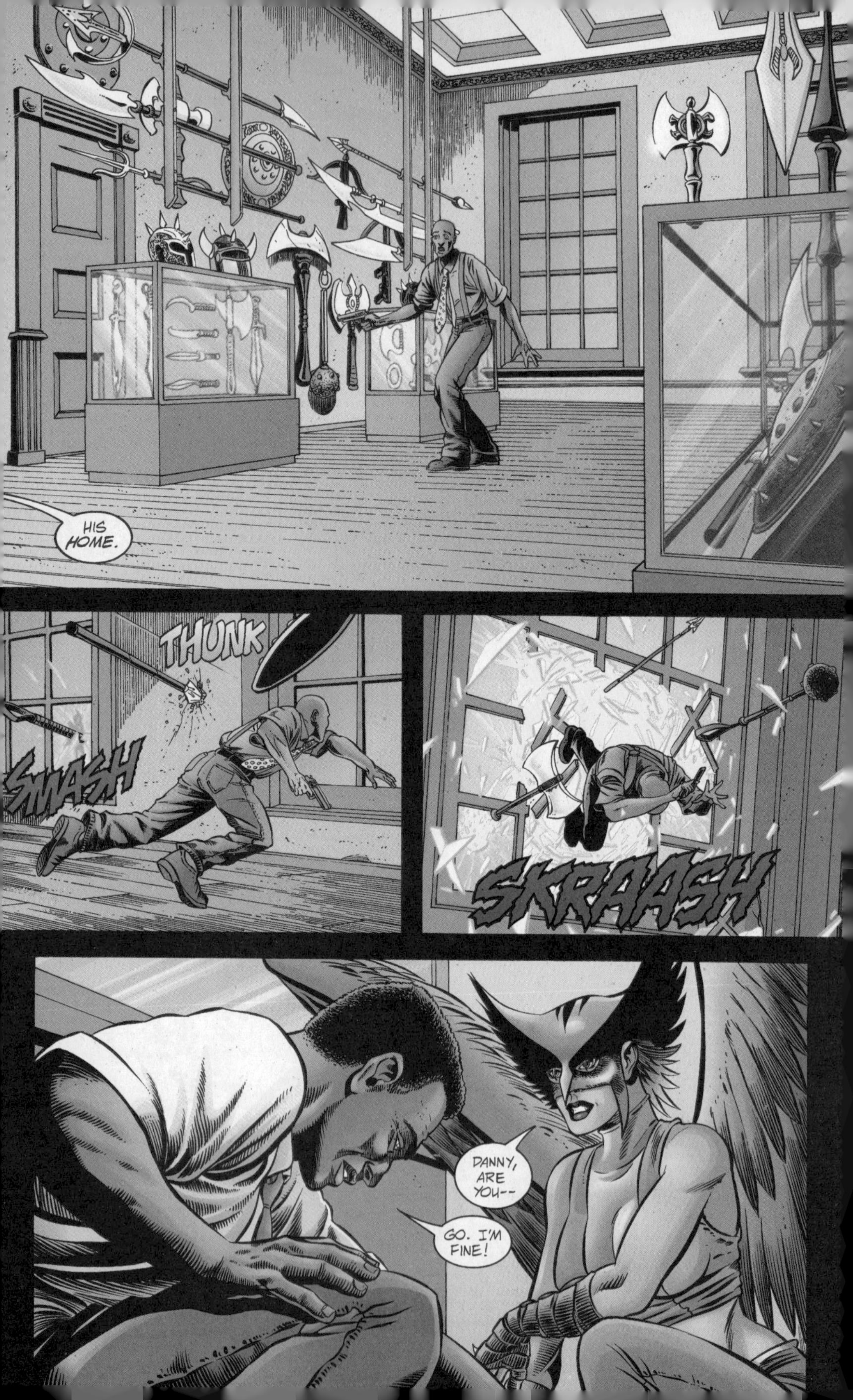
HIS HOME.
THUNK
SMASH
SKRAASH
DANNY, ARE YOU--
GO. I'M FINE!

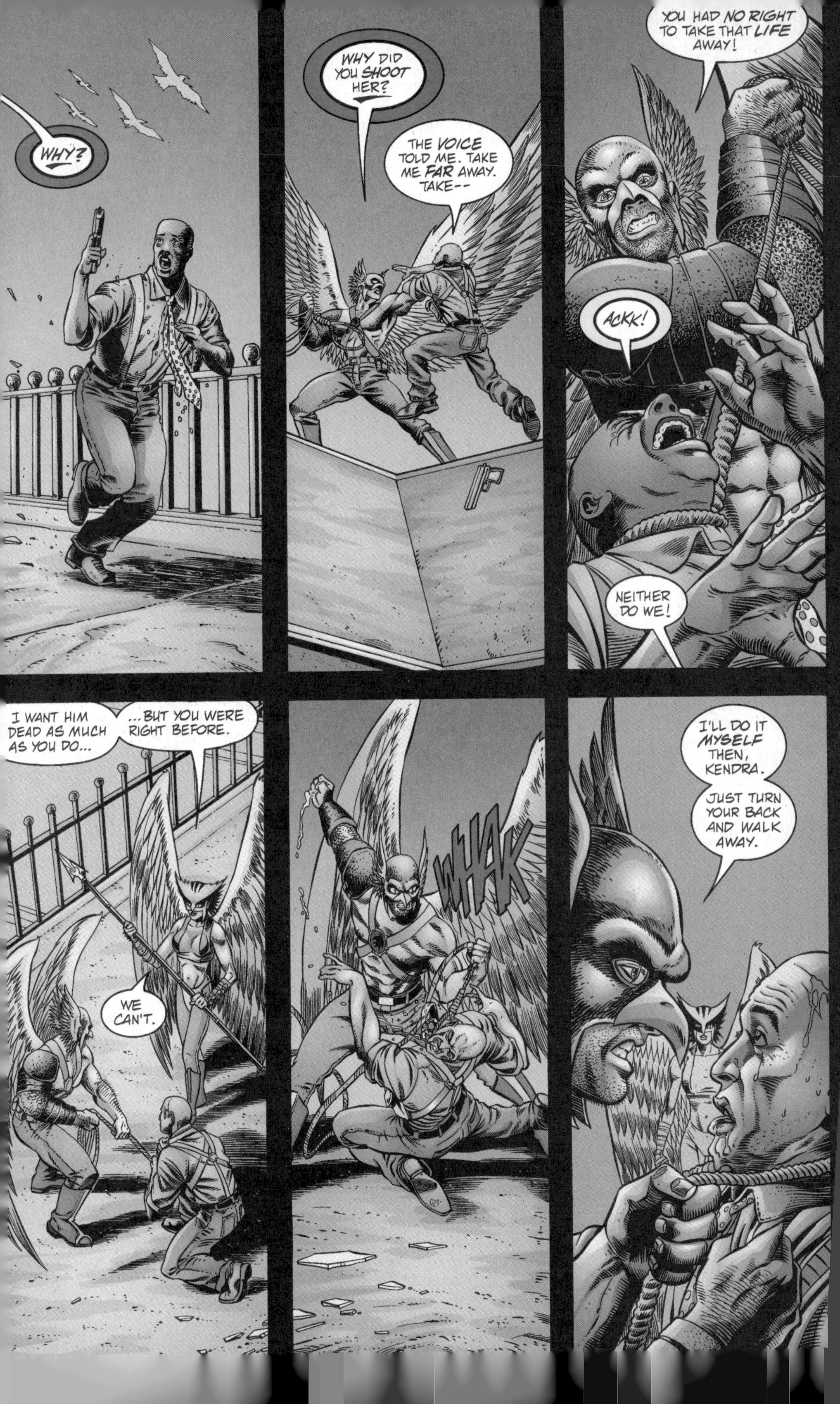

WHY?
WHY DID YOU SHOOT HER?
THE VOICE TOLD ME. TAKE ME FAR AWAY. TAKE--
YOU HAD NO RIGHT TO TAKE THAT LIFE AWAY!
ACKK!
NEITHER DO WE!
I WANT HIM DEAD AS MUCH AS YOU DO...
...BUT YOU WERE RIGHT BEFORE.
WE CAN'T.
WHAK
I'LL DO IT MYSELF THEN, KENDRA.
JUST TURN YOUR BACK AND WALK AWAY.

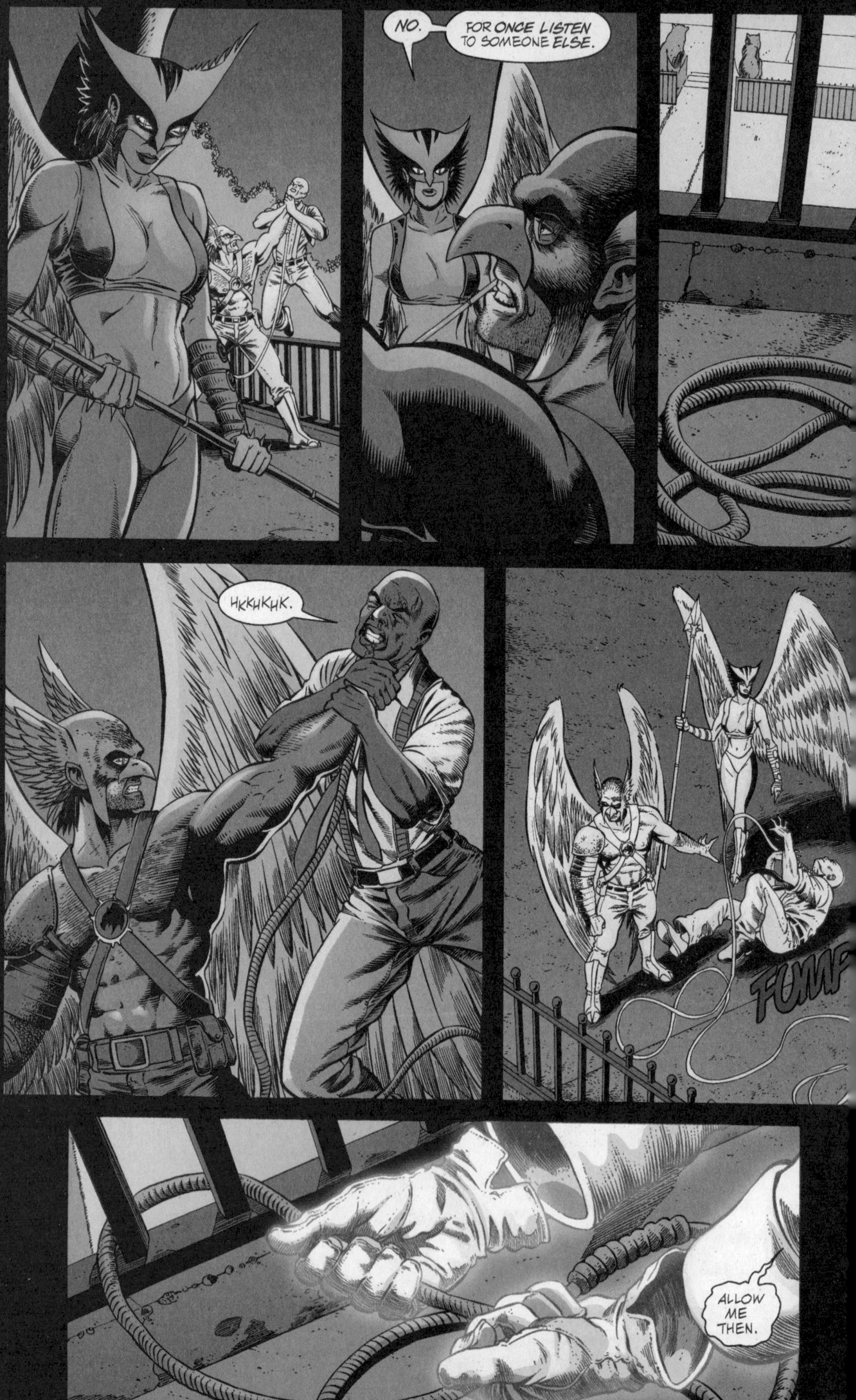

NO.
FOR ONCE LISTEN TO SOMEONE ELSE.
HKKHKHK.
FUMF
ALLOW ME THEN.

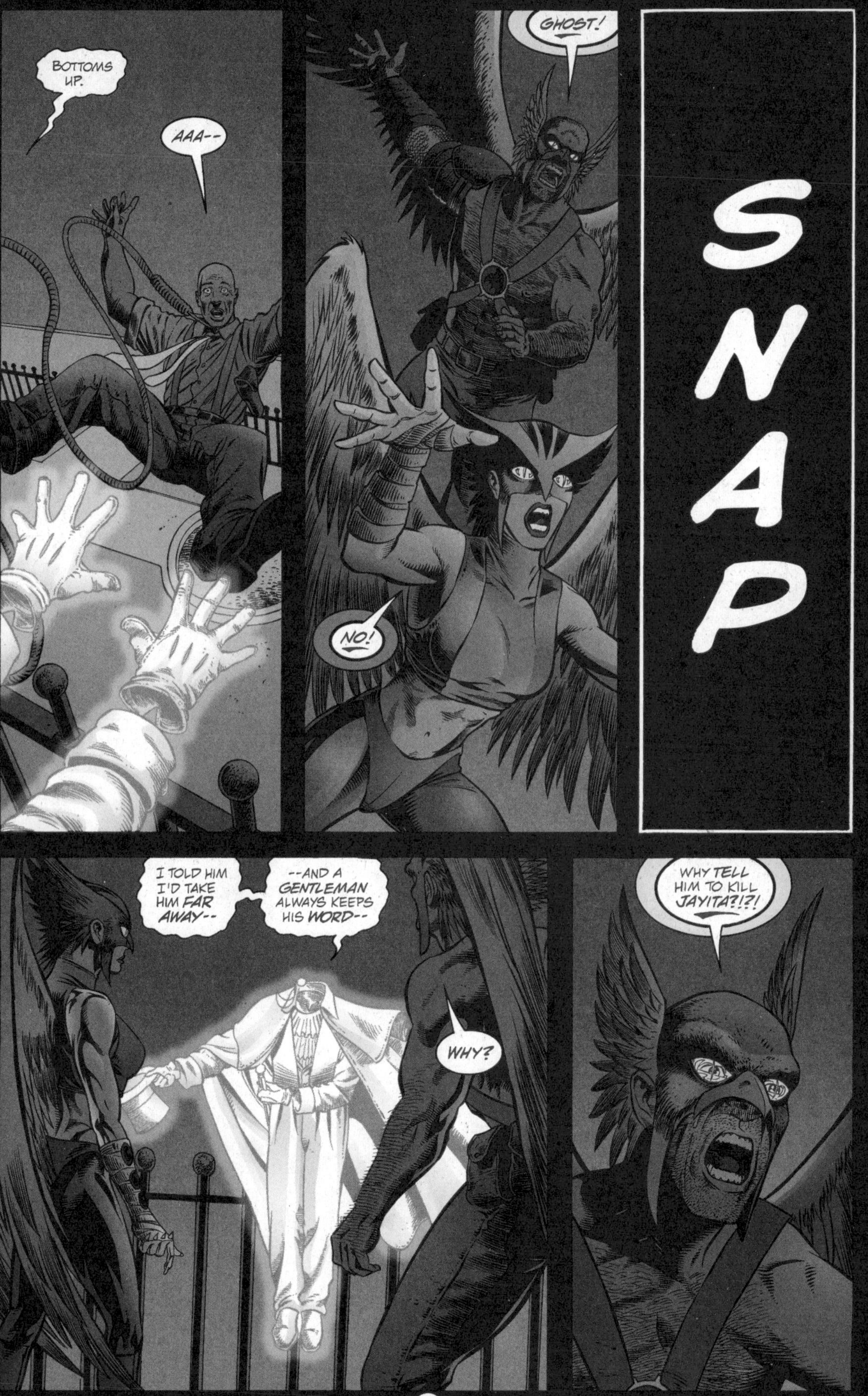

BOTTOMS UP.
AAA--
GHOST!
NO!
SNAP
I TOLD HIM I'D TAKE HIM FAR AWAY--
--AND A GENTLEMAN ALWAYS KEEPS HIS WORD--
WHY?
WHY TELL HIM TO KILL JAYITA?!?!

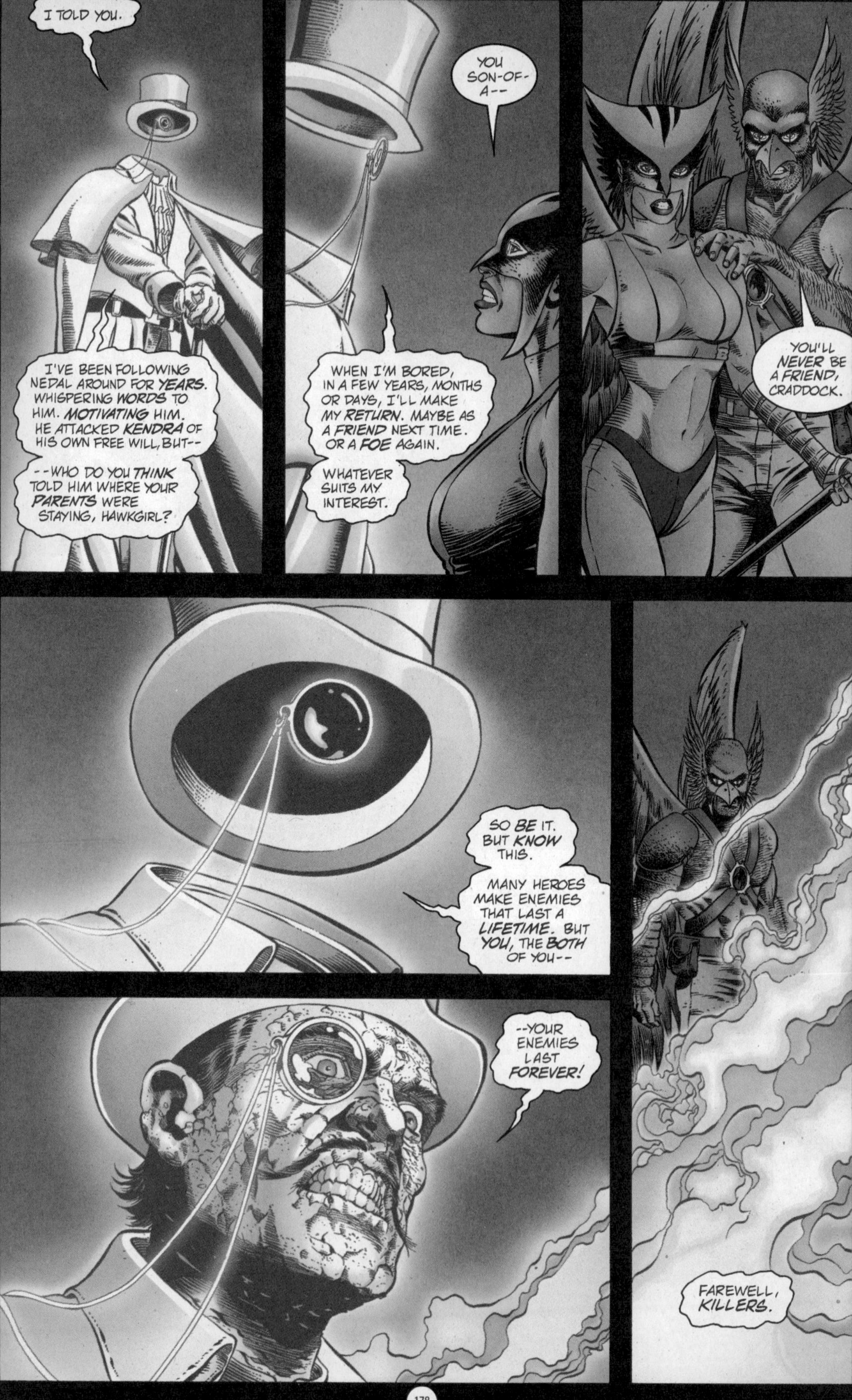
I TOLD YOU.
I'VE BEEN FOLLOWING NEDAL AROUND FOR YEARS. WHISPERING WORDS TO HIM. MOTIVATING HIM. HE ATTACKED KENDRA OF HIS OWN FREE WILL, BUT--
--WHO DO YOU THINK TOLD HIM WHERE YOUR PARENTS WERE STAYING, HAWKGIRL?
YOU SON-OF-A--
WHEN I'M BORED, IN A FEW YEARS, MONTHS OR DAYS, I'LL MAKE MY RETURN. MAYBE AS A FRIEND NEXT TIME. OR A FOE AGAIN.
WHATEVER SUITS MY INTEREST.
YOU'LL NEVER BE A FRIEND, CRADDOCK.
SO BE IT. BUT KNOW THIS.
MANY HEROES MAKE ENEMIES THAT LAST A LIFETIME. BUT YOU, THE BOTH OF YOU--
--YOUR ENEMIES LAST FOREVER!
FAREWELL, KILLERS.

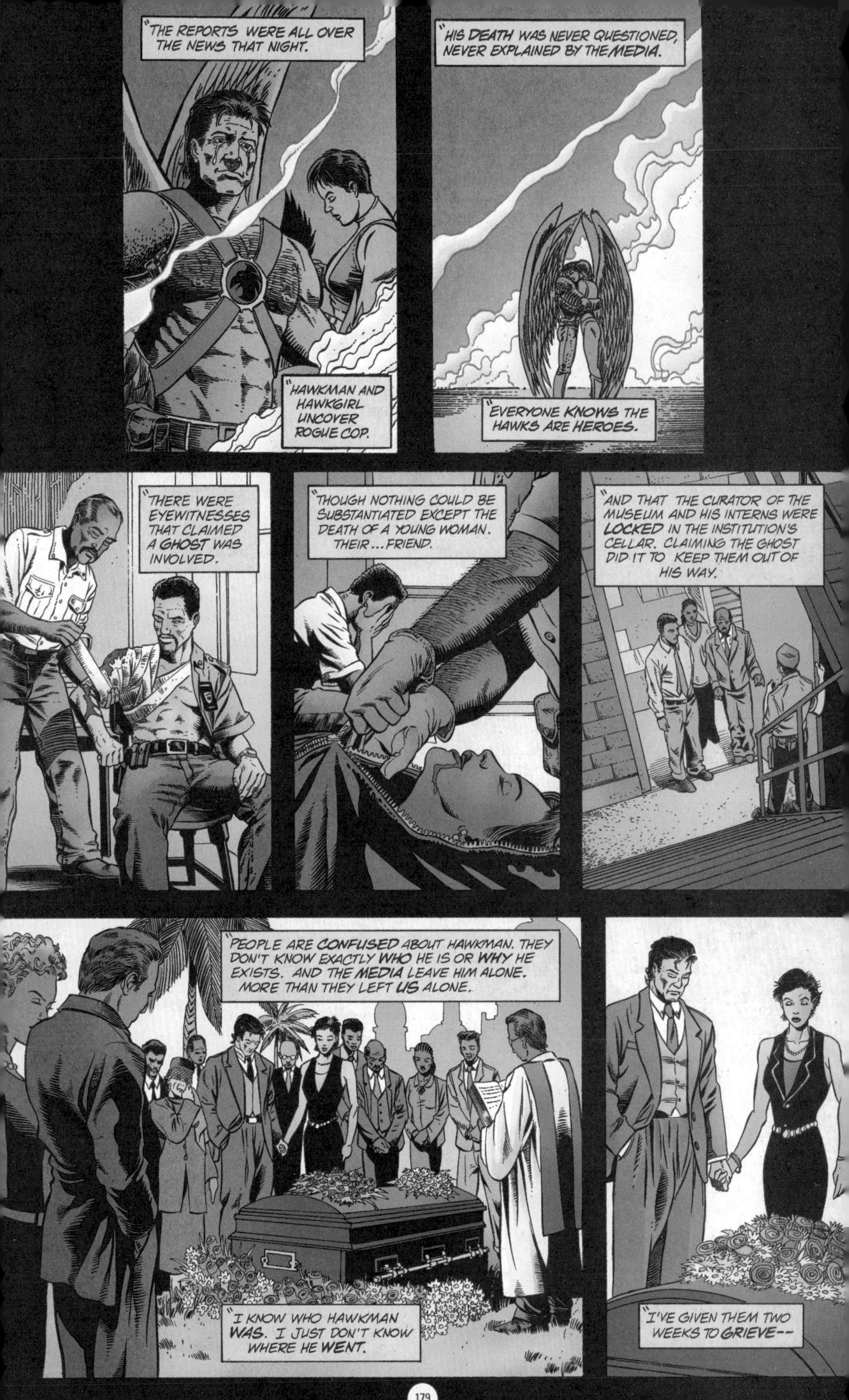
"THE REPORTS WERE ALL OVER THE NEWS THAT NIGHT.
"HAWKMAN AND HAWKGIRL UNCOVER ROGUE COP.
"HIS DEATH WAS NEVER QUESTIONED, NEVER EXPLAINED BY THE MEDIA.
"EVERYONE KNOWS THE HAWKS ARE HEROES.
"THERE WERE EYEWITNESSES THAT CLAIMED A GHOST WAS INVOLVED.
"THOUGH NOTHING COULD BE SUBSTANTIATED EXCEPT THE DEATH OF A YOUNG WOMAN. THEIR...FRIEND.
"AND THAT THE CURATOR OF THE MUSEUM AND HIS INTERNS WERE LOCKED IN THE INSTITUTION'S CELLAR. CLAIMING THE GHOST DID IT TO KEEP THEM OUT OF HIS WAY.
"PEOPLE ARE CONFUSED ABOUT HAWKMAN. THEY DON'T KNOW EXACTLY WHO HE IS OR WHY HE EXISTS. AND THE MEDIA LEAVE HIM ALONE. MORE THAN THEY LEFT US ALONE.
"I KNOW WHO HAWKMAN WAS. I JUST DON'T KNOW WHERE HE WENT.
"I'VE GIVEN THEM TWO WEEKS TO GRIEVE--

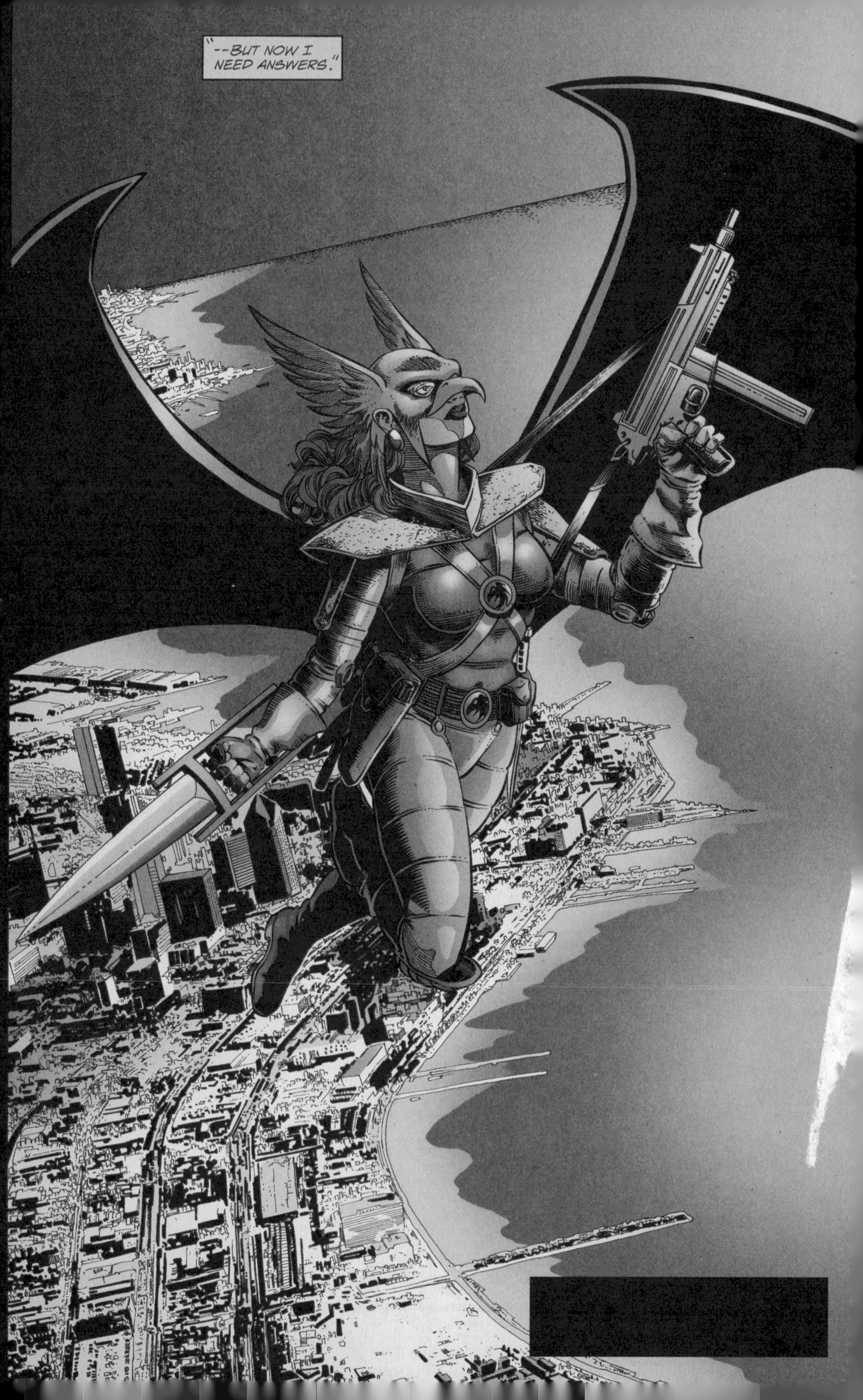
"--BUT NOW I NEED ANSWERS."
[redacted]

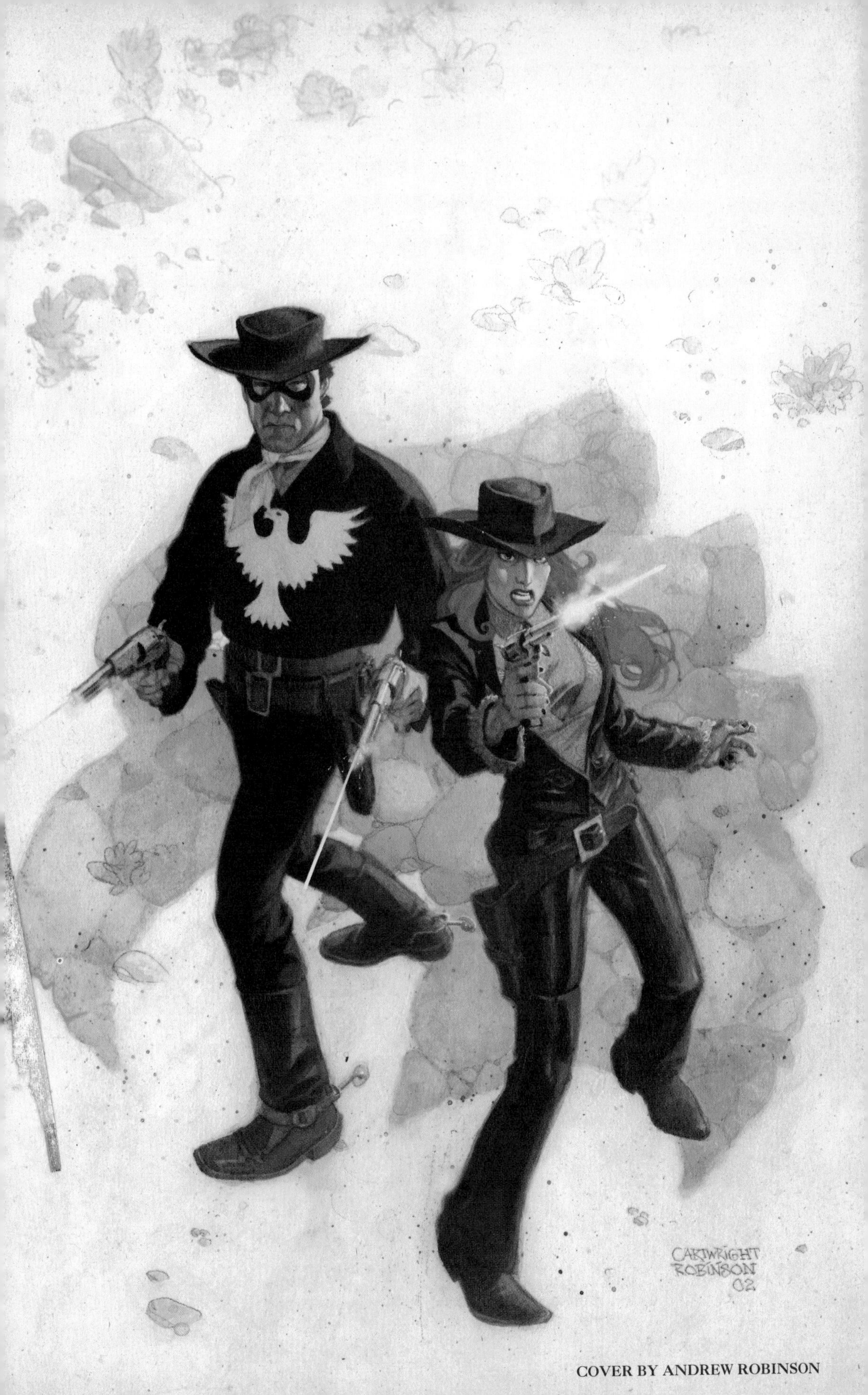
CARTWRIGHT
ROBINSON
02

COVER BY ANDREW ROBINSON

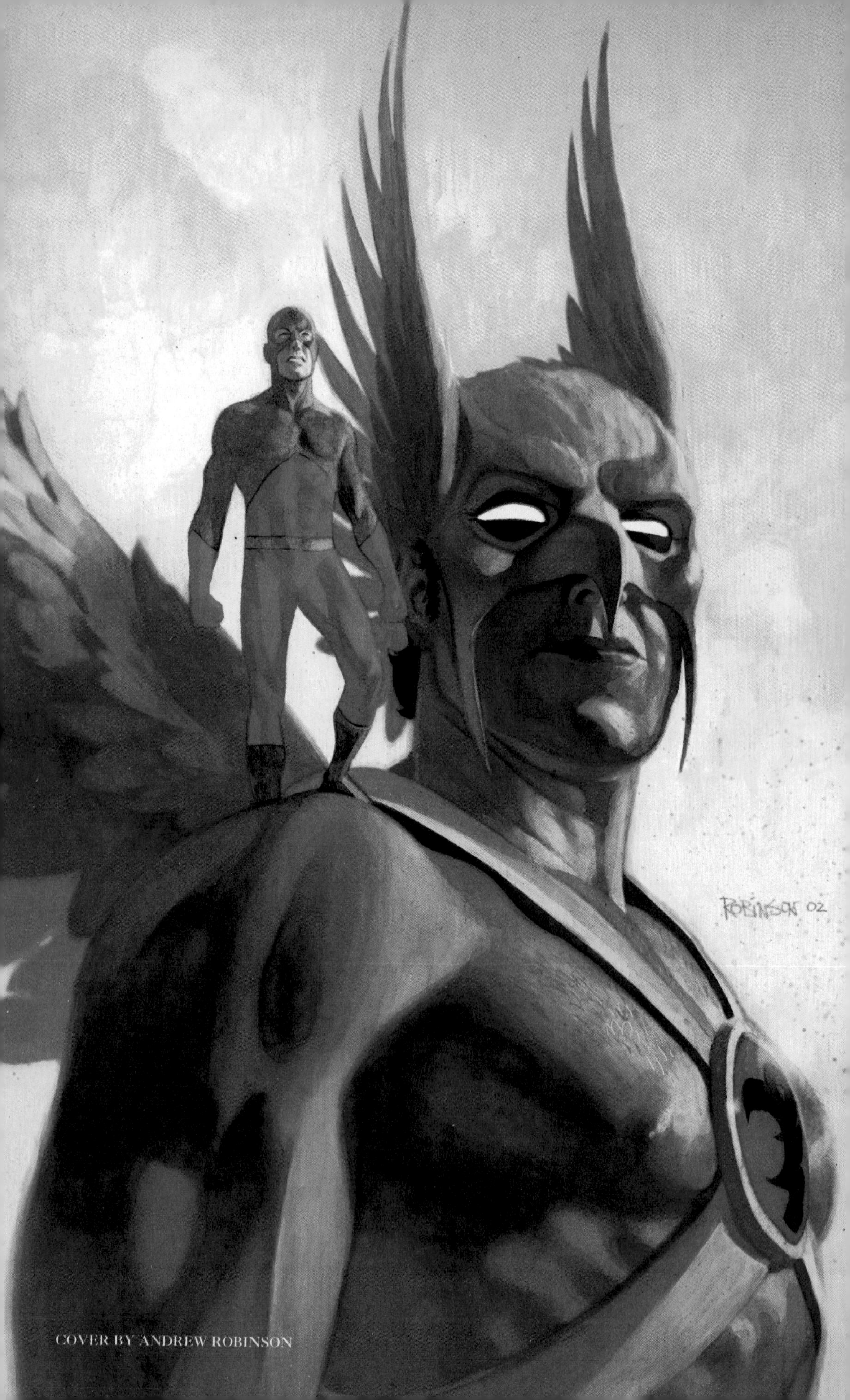
ROBINSON 02

COVER BY ANDREW ROBINSON

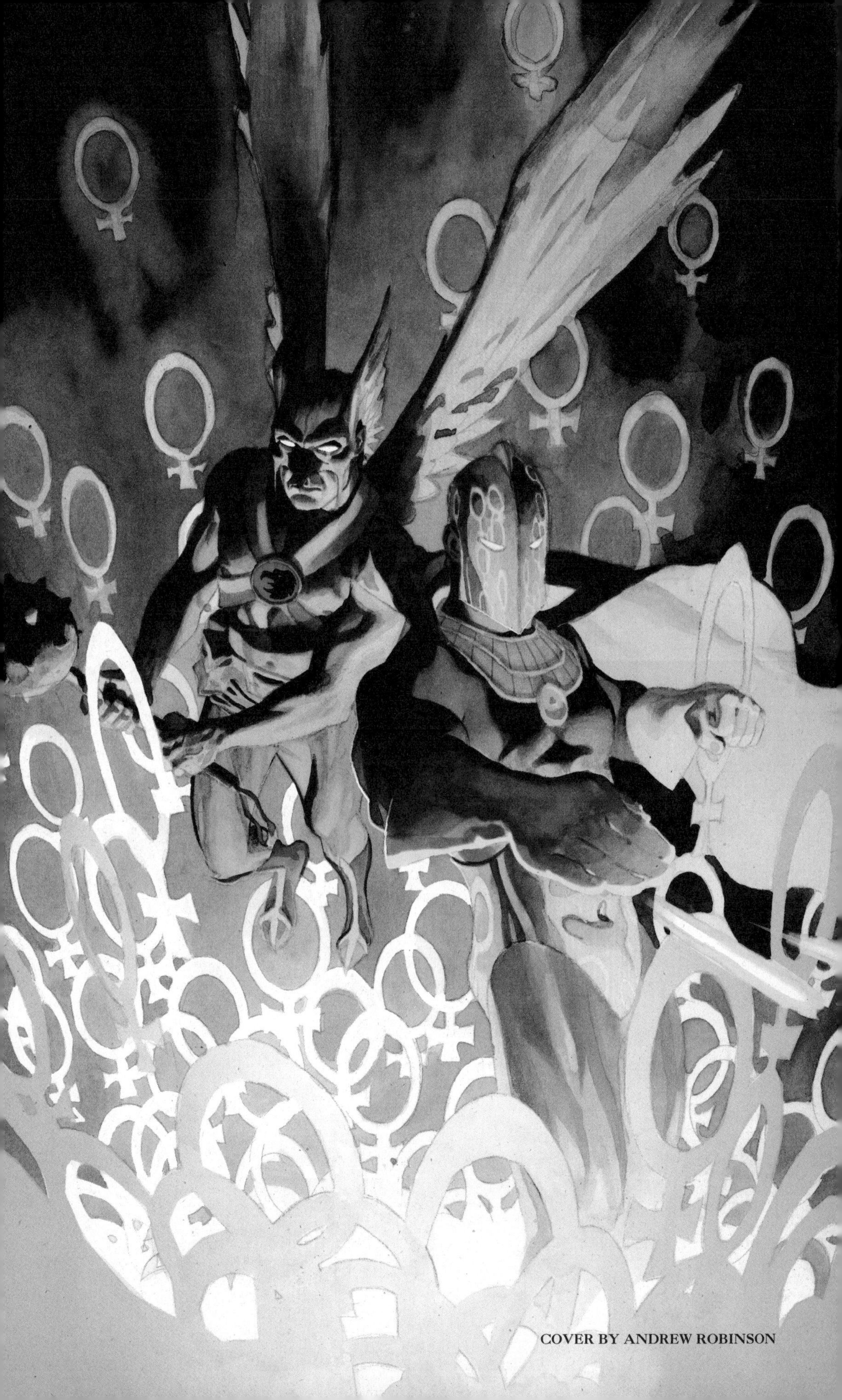

COVER BY ANDREW ROBINSON

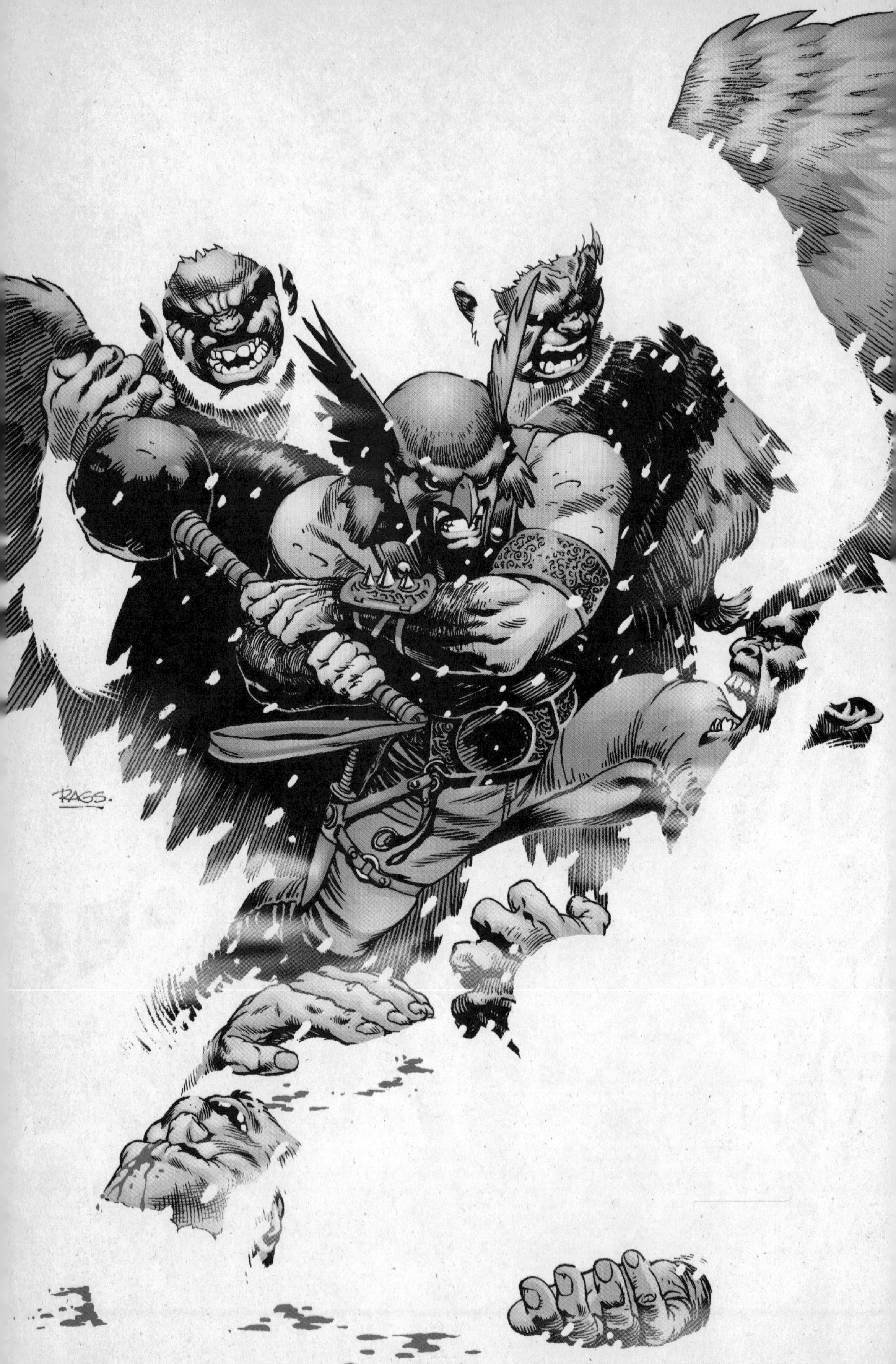
RAGS.

COVER BY RAGS MORALES

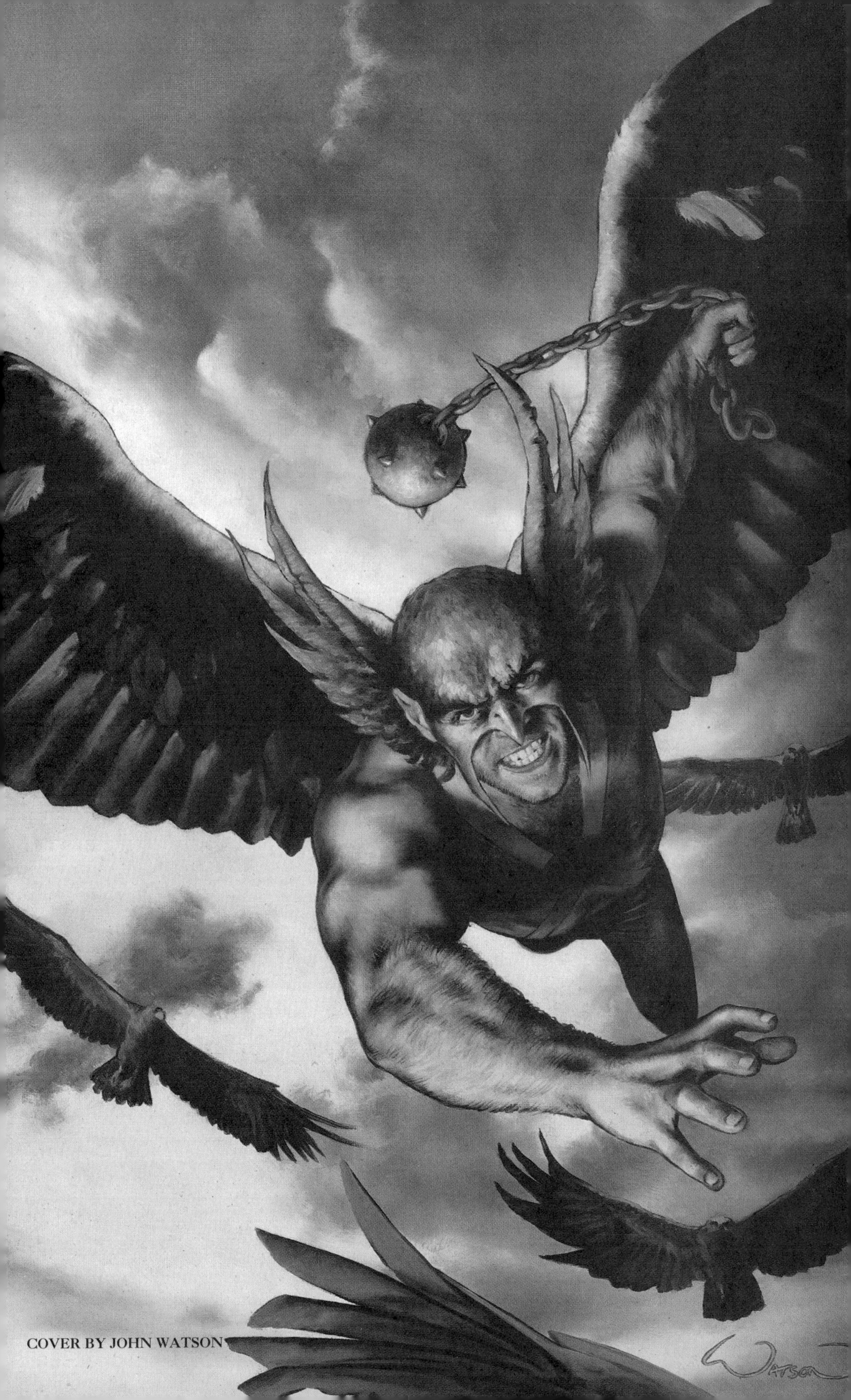

COVER BY JOHN WATSON

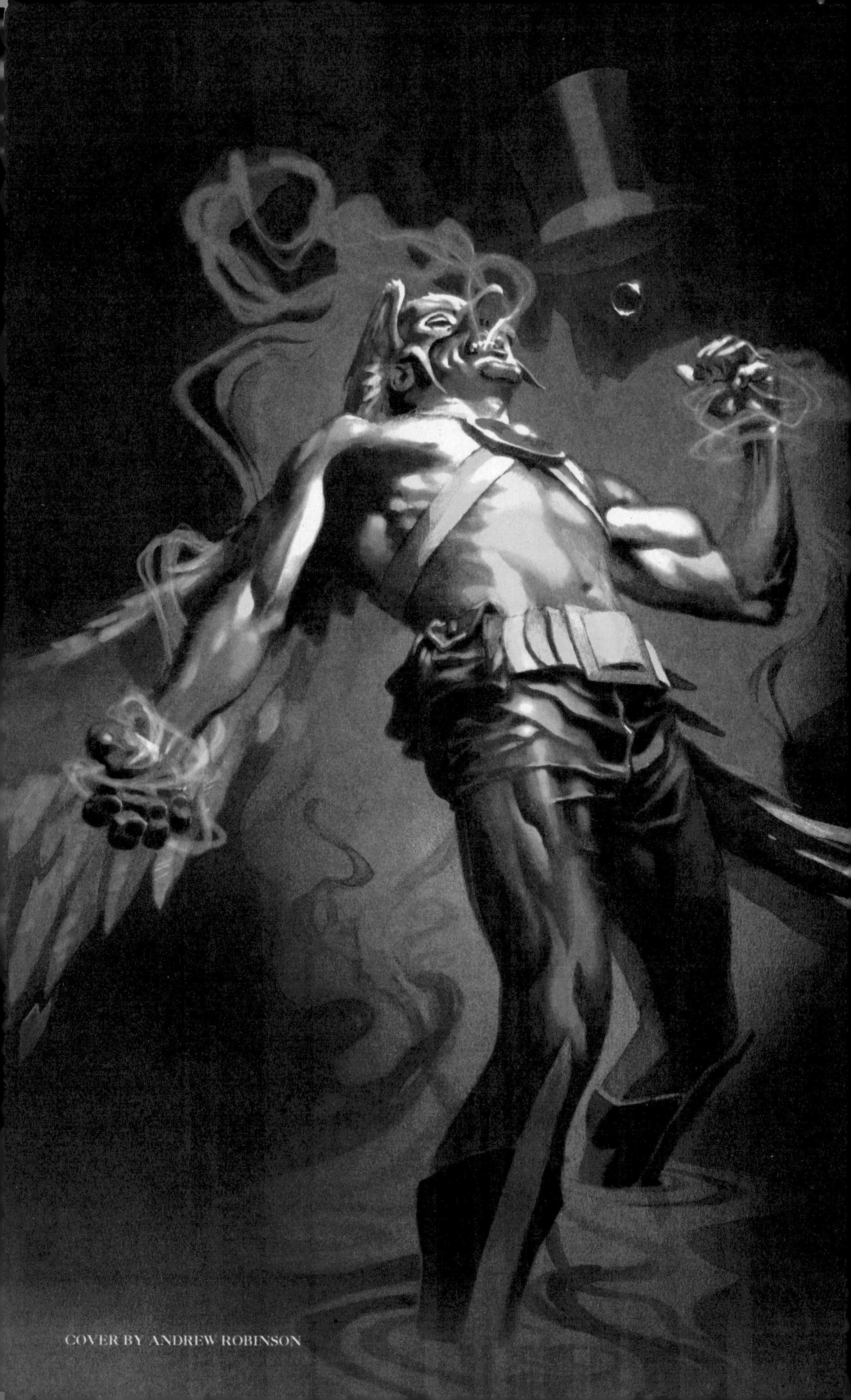

COVER BY ANDREW ROBINSON

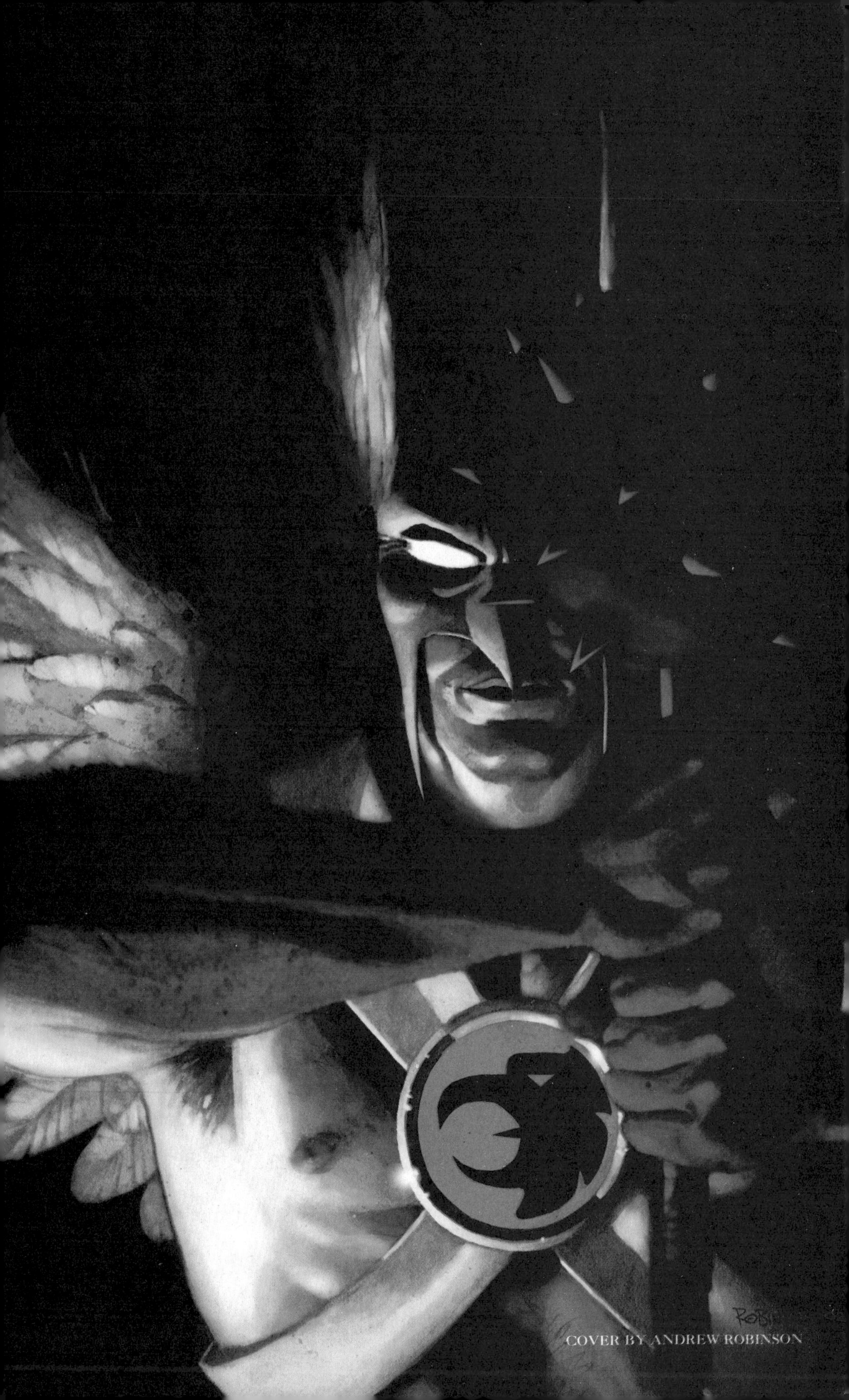

COVER BY ANDREW ROBINSON

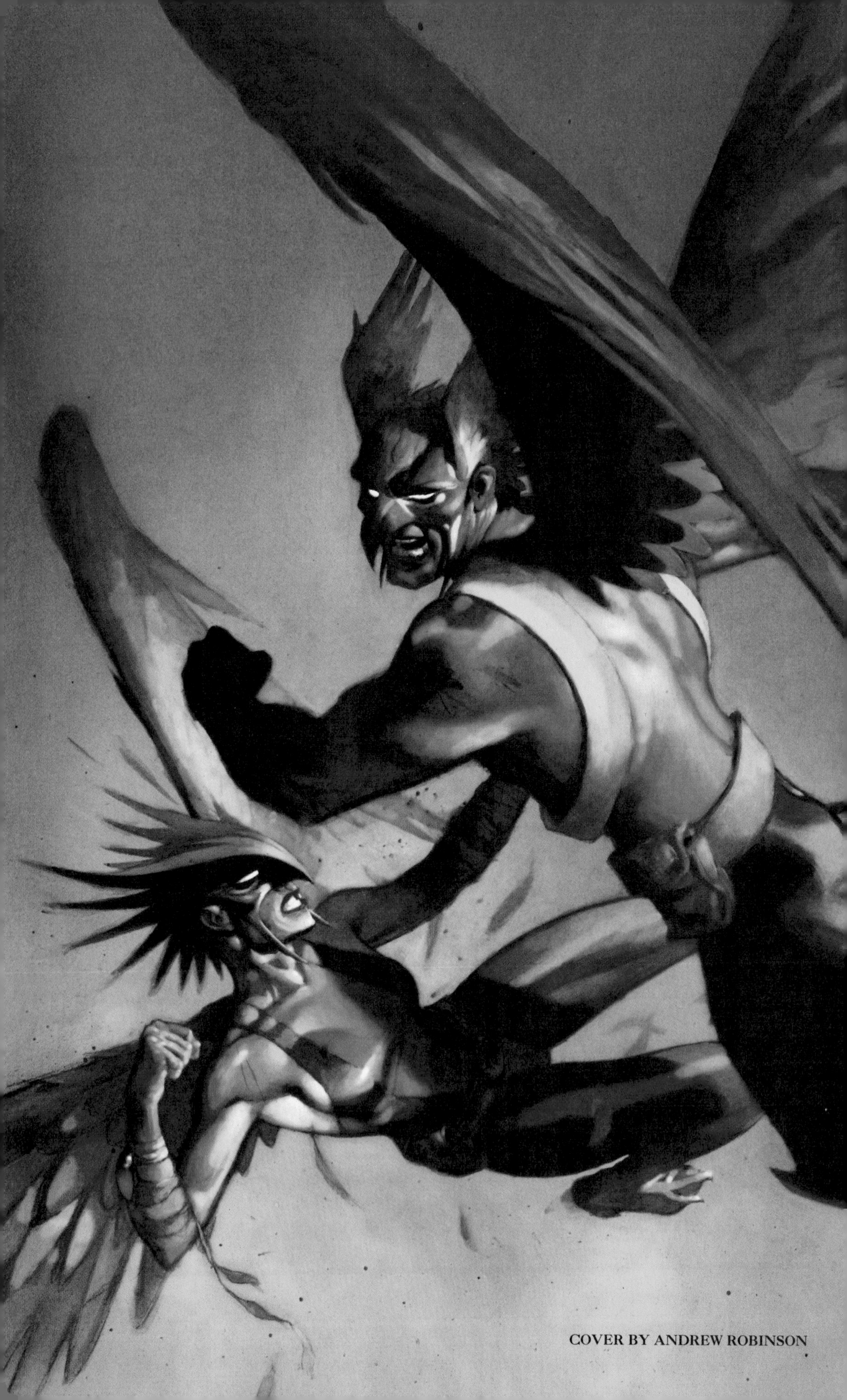
COVER BY ANDREW ROBINSON

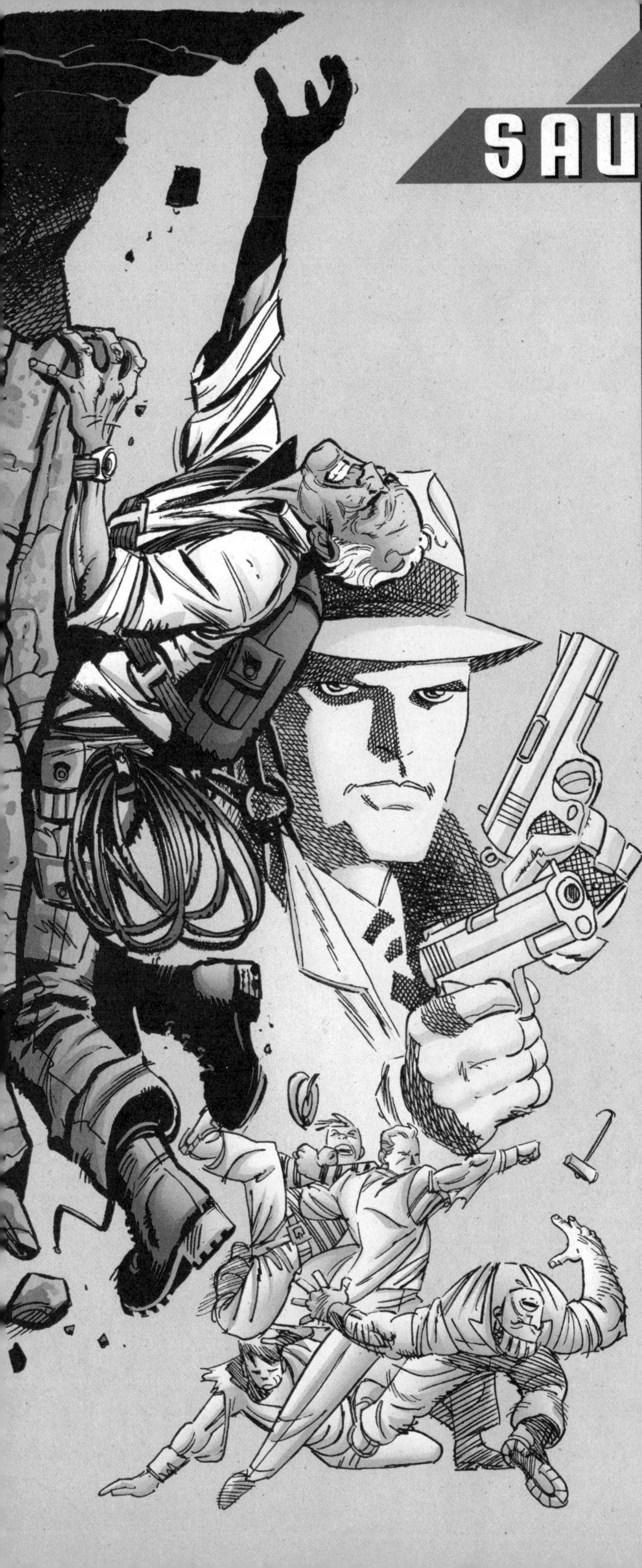

SPEED SAUNDERS

Real Name: Cyril Saunders
Occupation: Retired
Base of Operations: Various
Marital Status: Divorced
Ht: 5' 11" Wt: 160 lbs.
Eyes: Hazel Hair: Grey
First Appearance: DETECTIVE COMICS #1 (March, 1937)

Little is known about the childhood and early life of Cyril "Speed" Saunders, save that he was born in Columbus, Ohio, and raised abroad by parents who paid little attention to him. At an early age, he was said to have traveled across the world on mysterious missions against injustice. It has been speculated that Speed was a founding member of the OSS (a precursor of the CIA).

Speed's adventures brought him into occasional contact with the Justice Society of America during the 1940s, during which time he formed a lifelong friendship with Wesley Dodds, the original Sandman.

Decades later, Speed took charge of his granddaughter Kendra after the untimely and mysterious deaths of her parents. Once she reached the age of eighteen, Speed began to train Kendra, against her wishes, to fill the role of Hawkgirl. This plan came to fruition after the death of Wesley Dodds, which precipitated the creation of a new JSA. Only Speed knew that Kendra was the reincarnated soul of the original Hawkgirl.

Allegedly retired from his adventurous career, Speed travels the globe with an insatiable wanderlust. Well into his golden years, he retains a remarkable youthful vigor and has lost none of his keen deductive abilities.

Speed now searches for a mysterious relic that he hopes will help Kendra with her troubling situation.

Written by Geoff Johns & Jim Beard.
Art by Rich Burchett.
Color by Tom McCraw.

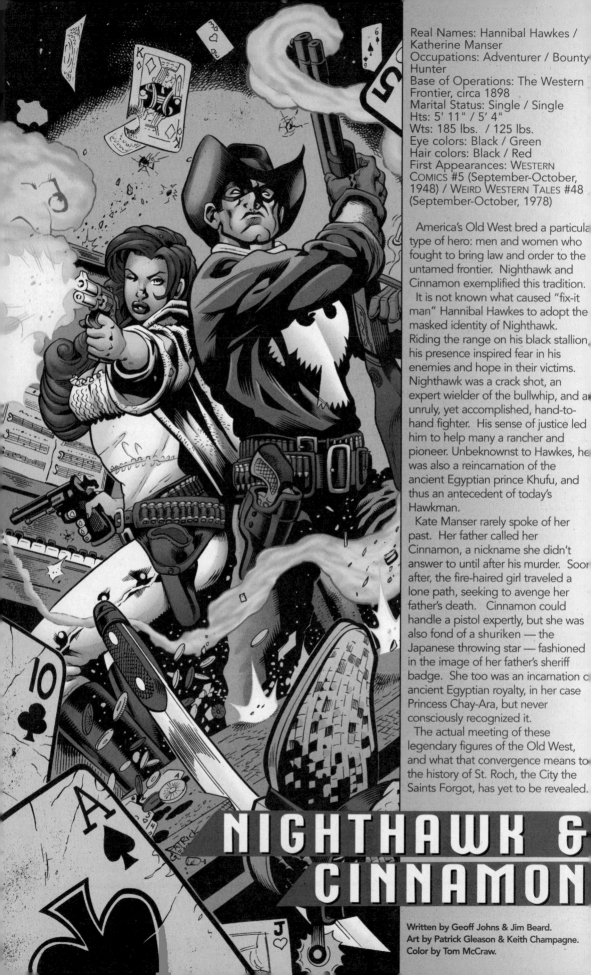

Real Names: Hannibal Hawkes /
Katherine Manser
Occupations: Adventurer / Bounty
Hunter
Base of Operations: The Western
Frontier, circa 1898
Marital Status: Single / Single
Hts: 5' 11" / 5' 4"
Wts: 185 lbs. / 125 lbs.
Eye colors: Black / Green
Hair colors: Black / Red
First Appearances: WESTERN
COMICS #5 (September-October,
1948) / WEIRD WESTERN TALES #48
(September-October, 1978)

America's Old West bred a particula[r]
type of hero: men and women who
fought to bring law and order to the
untamed frontier. Nighthawk and
Cinnamon exemplified this tradition.

It is not known what caused "fix-it
man" Hannibal Hawkes to adopt the
masked identity of Nighthawk.
Riding the range on his black stallion,
his presence inspired fear in his
enemies and hope in their victims.
Nighthawk was a crack shot, an
expert wielder of the bullwhip, and a[n]
unruly, yet accomplished, hand-to-
hand fighter. His sense of justice led
him to help many a rancher and
pioneer. Unbeknownst to Hawkes, he
was also a reincarnation of the
ancient Egyptian prince Khufu, and
thus an antecedent of today's
Hawkman.

Kate Manser rarely spoke of her
past. Her father called her
Cinnamon, a nickname she didn't
answer to until after his murder. Soon
after, the fire-haired girl traveled a
lone path, seeking to avenge her
father's death. Cinnamon could
handle a pistol expertly, but she was
also fond of a shuriken — the
Japanese throwing star — fashioned
in the image of her father's sheriff
badge. She too was an incarnation o[f]
ancient Egyptian royalty, in her case
Princess Chay-Ara, but never
consciously recognized it.

The actual meeting of these
legendary figures of the Old West,
and what that convergence means to
the history of St. Roch, the City the
Saints Forgot, has yet to be revealed.

NIGHTHAWK &
CINNAMON

Written by Geoff Johns & Jim Beard.
Art by Patrick Gleason & Keith Champagne.
Color by Tom McCraw.

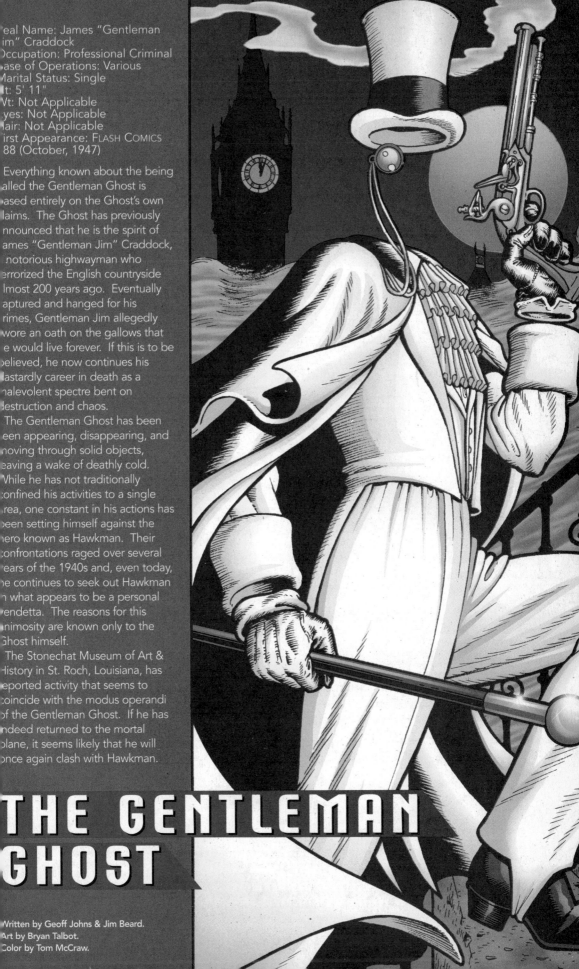

Real Name: James "Gentleman
Jim" Craddock
Occupation: Professional Criminal
Base of Operations: Various
Marital Status: Single
Ht: 5' 11"
Wt: Not Applicable
Eyes: Not Applicable
Hair: Not Applicable
First Appearance: FLASH COMICS
#88 (October, 1947)

Everything known about the being
called the Gentleman Ghost is
based entirely on the Ghost's own
claims. The Ghost has previously
announced that he is the spirit of
James "Gentleman Jim" Craddock,
a notorious highwayman who
terrorized the English countryside
almost 200 years ago. Eventually
captured and hanged for his
crimes, Gentleman Jim allegedly
swore an oath on the gallows that
he would live forever. If this is to be
believed, he now continues his
dastardly career in death as a
malevolent spectre bent on
destruction and chaos.

The Gentleman Ghost has been
seen appearing, disappearing, and
moving through solid objects,
leaving a wake of deathly cold.
While he has not traditionally
confined his activities to a single
area, one constant in his actions has
been setting himself against the
hero known as Hawkman. Their
confrontations raged over several
years of the 1940s and, even today,
he continues to seek out Hawkman
in what appears to be a personal
vendetta. The reasons for this
animosity are known only to the
Ghost himself.

The Stonechat Museum of Art &
History in St. Roch, Louisiana, has
reported activity that seems to
coincide with the modus operandi
of the Gentleman Ghost. If he has
indeed returned to the mortal
plane, it seems likely that he will
once again clash with Hawkman.

THE GENTLEMAN
GHOST

Written by Geoff Johns & Jim Beard.
Art by Bryan Talbot.
Color by Tom McCraw.

THE STARS OF THE
DC UNIVERSE
CAN ALSO BE FOUND IN THESE BOOKS: